Sixth Grade Math with Confidence

Student Workbook

Part A

Sixth Grade Math with Confidence

Student Workbook Part A

KATE SNOW

WELL-TRAINED MIND PRESS

Names: Snow, Kate (Teacher), author.
Title: Sixth grade math with confidence. Student workbook part A / Kate Snow.
Other titles: Student workbook part A
Description: [Charles City, Virginia] : Well-Trained Mind Press, [2026] | Series: Snow, Kate (Teacher). Math with confidence. | Interest grade level: 6. | Summary: Learn Sixth Grade Math with confidence! Use Workbooks Part A and Part B to teach and reinforce the lessons in the Sixth Grade Math with Confidence Instructor Guide. These colorful pages offer clear, step-by-step examples, varied practice with new concepts, and systematic review of previously-learned skills. Lesson activity pages include visual aids, real-world applications, and game boards to simplify your teaching. Practice pages provide written practice with new concepts. Review pages ensure students retain what what they've learned and master essential skills. Unit Wrap-Ups at the end of each unit provide review and assessment. You'll use Workbook Part A for Units 1-8, and Workbook Part B for Units 9-16.-- Publisher.
Identifiers: ISBN: 9781944481933 (paperback)
Subjects: LCSH: Mathematics--Study and teaching (Elementary) | CYAC: Mathematics. | LCGFT: Problems and exercises. | BISAC: JUVENILE NONFICTION / Mathematics / Algebra. | JUVENILE NONFICTION / Mathematics / Fractions.
Classification: LCC: QA107.2 .S666 2026 | DDC: 372.7--dc23

1 2 3 4 5 6 7 8 9   Versa   30 29 28 27 26

Table of Contents

Author's Note

You'll need three books to teach *Sixth Grade Math with Confidence*. All three books are essential for the program.

- The Instructor Guide contains the scripted lesson plans for the entire year.
- Student Workbook Part A contains the workbook pages for the first half of the year (Units 1–8).
- Student Workbook Part B contains the workbook pages for the second half of the year (Units 9–16).

The Student Workbooks are not meant to be used as stand-alone workbooks. The hands-on teaching activities in the Instructor Guide are an essential part of the program. You'll need the directions in the Instructor Guide to guide your child through the Lesson Activities pages. The icon with two heads means that your child should complete these pages with you, and that she is not expected to complete these pages on her own.

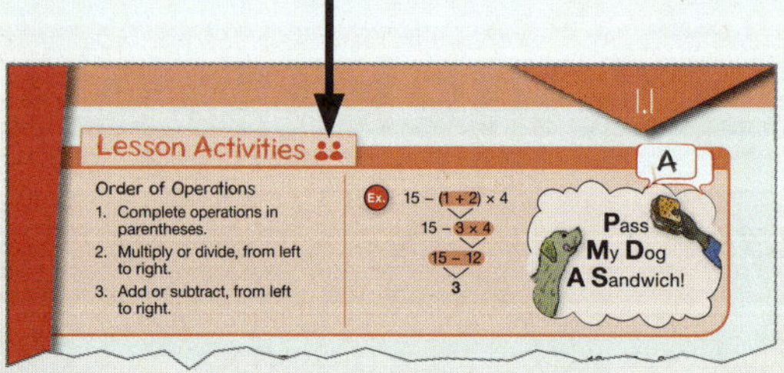

The Practice and Review pages give your child practice with new concepts and review previously-learned skills. The icon with one head means that your child may complete these pages on his own. Most sixth-graders will be able to complete these pages independently, and it's fine if your child sometimes needs a little extra support or coaching.

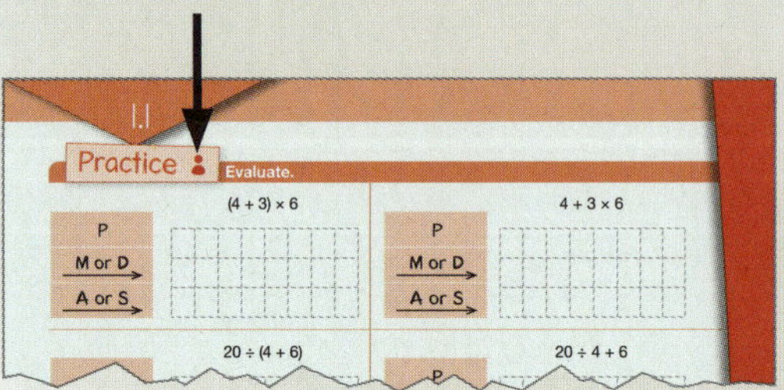

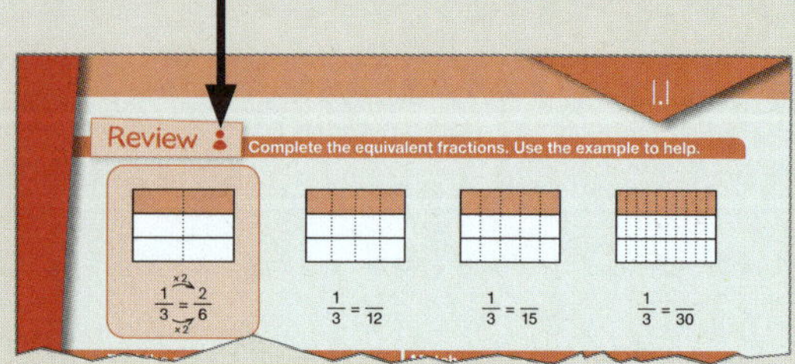

Lesson Activities

Order of Operations

1. Complete operations in parentheses.
2. Multiply or divide, from left to right.
3. Add or subtract, from left to right.

Ex.

$$15 - (1 + 2) \times 4$$
$$15 - 3 \times 4$$
$$15 - 12$$
$$3$$

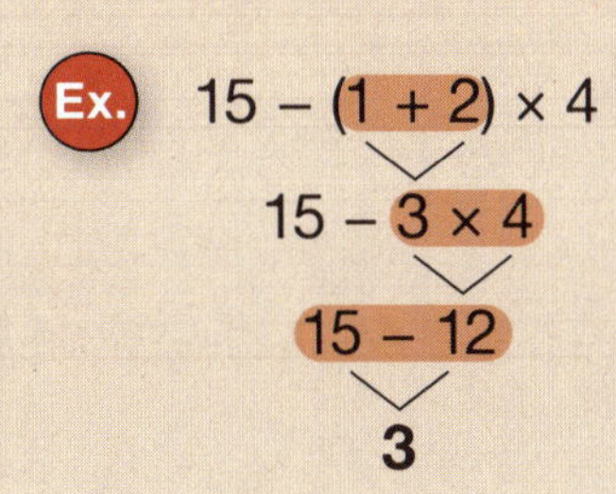

$$6 + (7 + 3) \times 4$$

P

M or D →

A or S →

$$18 - 15 \div 3$$

P

M or D →

A or S →

B

Order of Operations War (2-Player Game)

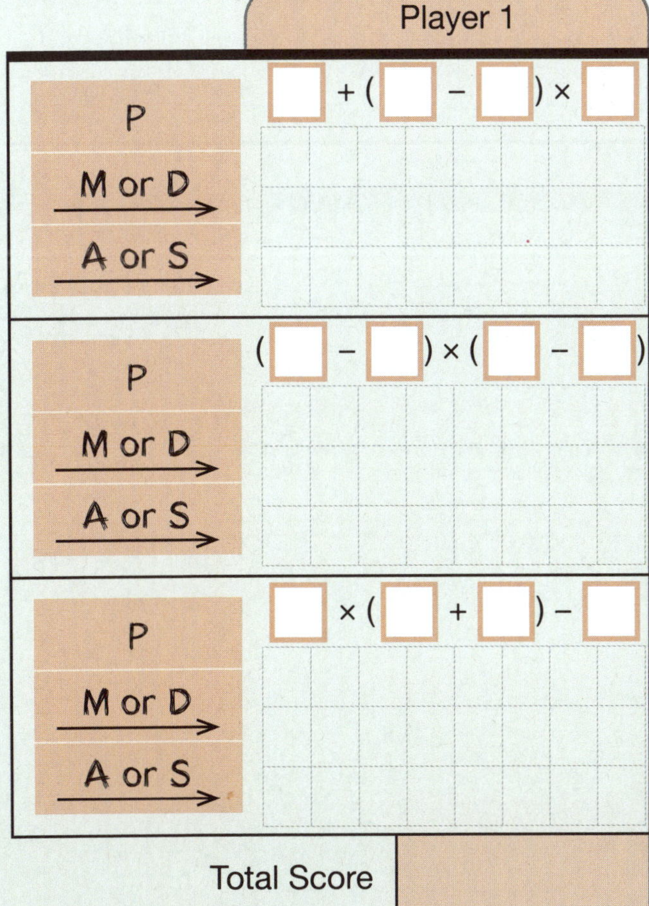

Player 1

$$\square + (\square - \square) \times \square$$

P

M or D →

A or S →

$$(\square - \square) \times (\square - \square)$$

P

M or D →

A or S →

$$\square \times (\square + \square) - \square$$

P

M or D →

A or S →

Total Score

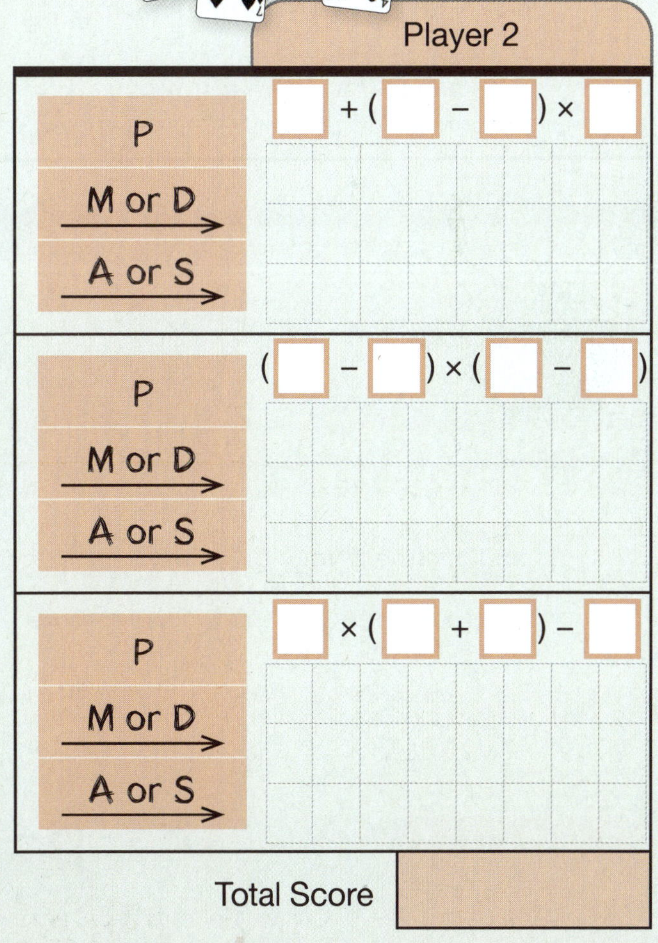

Player 2

$$\square + (\square - \square) \times \square$$

P

M or D →

A or S →

$$(\square - \square) \times (\square - \square)$$

P

M or D →

A or S →

$$\square \times (\square + \square) - \square$$

P

M or D →

A or S →

Total Score

Practice 

Evaluate.

$(4 + 3) \times 6$

P
M or D →
A or S →

$4 + 3 \times 6$

P
M or D →
A or S →

$20 \div (4 + 6)$

P
M or D →
A or S →

$20 \div 4 + 6$

P
M or D →
A or S →

$(15 - 5) \div 5 + 4$

P
M or D →
A or S →

$15 - 5 \div 5 + 4$

P
M or D →
A or S →

$7 \times (5 - 5) \times 3$

P
M or D →
A or S →

$7 \times 5 - 5 \times 3$

P
M or D →
A or S →

**Circle the expression that best matches the word problem.
Then, evaluate the expression to find the answer to the word problem.**

Levi had $100. Then, he bought a pair of socks for $12 and a pair of hiking boots for $80. How much money does he have now?

$100 - 12 + 80$

$100 - (12 + 80)$

Sophie had $17. She bought 3 packs of markers for $4 each. Then, she earned $20. How much money does she have now?

$17 - 3 \times 4 + 20$

$17 - 3 \times (4 + 20)$

Review

Complete the equivalent fractions. Use the example to help.

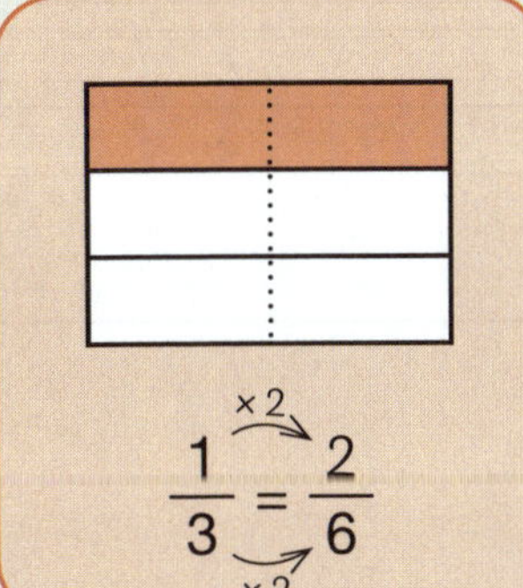

$$\frac{1}{3} \xrightarrow{\times 2} = \frac{2}{6} \xleftarrow{\times 2}$$

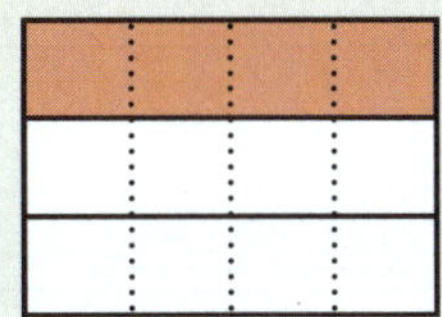

$$\frac{1}{3} = \frac{}{12}$$

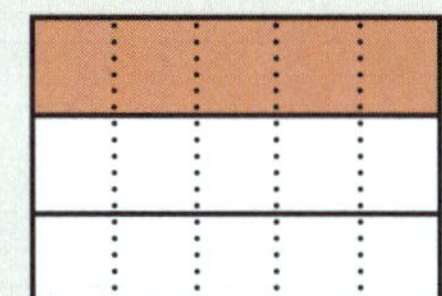

$$\frac{1}{3} = \frac{}{15}$$

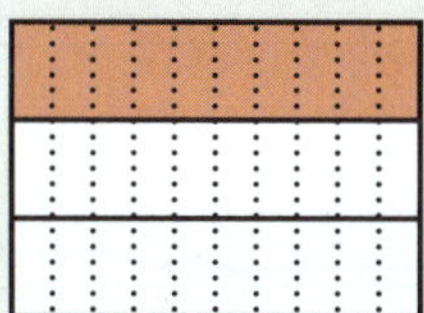

$$\frac{1}{3} = \frac{}{30}$$

Find the product.

		3	8	2			
	×			4			

		1 , 2	8	0			
	×			7			

	9	0	6
×			8

8 , 8	8	8
×		8

Match.

The sum of 8 and 4	8 − 4
The product of 8 and 4	8 ÷ 4
The difference between 8 and 4	8 + 4
The quotient of 8 and 4	8 × 4

Complete the chart.

Number of bags of rice	1	3	10	8		4		
Total weight (lb.)	5				35		50	100

Find the area and perimeter of the yard. Write the equations you use.

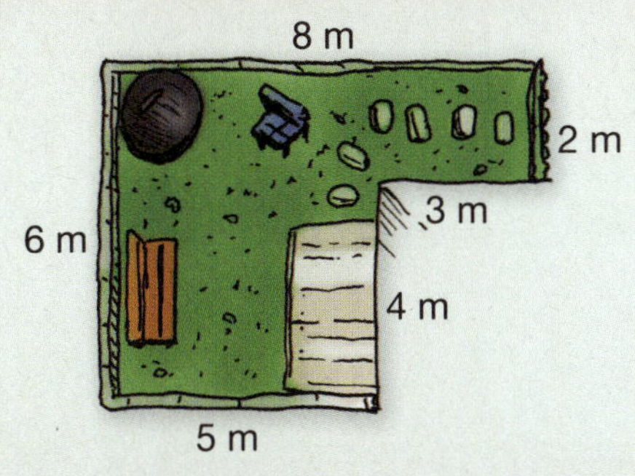

Perimeter: _______________

Area: _______________

Lesson Activities

$1 \times 1 \times 1 \times 1 \times 1 =$ _________ $2 \times 2 \times 2 \times 2 =$ _________ $3 \times 3 \times 3 =$ _________

Exponents

Exponents are a shortcut for writing repeated multiplication. The base is the number you multiply. The exponent tells how many times the base is multiplied.

base   exponent

$$4^3 = 4 \times 4 \times 4 = 64$$

We read 4^3 as "4 to the third power" or "4 to the power of 3."

Ex. $2^5 = 2 \times 2 \times 2 \times 2 \times 2 = \mathbf{32}$

Ex. $7^2 = 7 \times 7 = \mathbf{49}$

Ex. $3^0 = \mathbf{1}$
Any number to the power of 0 is 1.

$3^4 =$ _________ $10^3 =$ _________ $36^0 =$ _________

Exponent Three in a Row (2-Player Game)

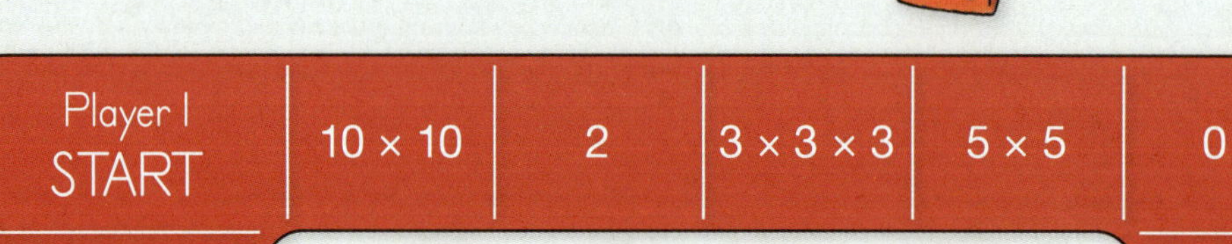

Player 1 START	10×10	2	$3 \times 3 \times 3$	5×5	$0 \times 0 \times 0$
$2 \times 2 \times 2 \times 2$	6^2	10^3	2^2	5^3	4×4
3×3	4^1	5^2	10^2	7^2	$1 \times 1 \times 1 \times 1$
$10 \times 10 \times 10$	2^3	2^1	4^2	1^4	2×2
	2^4	3^2	0^3	3^3	
$5 \times 5 \times 5$	7×7	4	$2 \times 2 \times 2$	6×6	Player 2 START

Practice 👤 Match.

5 × 5	6^3	2 to the fifth power
6 × 6 × 6	10^3	5 to the power of 2
10 × 10 × 10	5^2	10 to the third power
3 × 3 × 3 × 3 × 3 × 3	2^5	6 to the power of 3
2 × 2 × 2 × 2 × 2	3^6	3 to the sixth power

Complete the chart.

	Base	Exponent	Repeated Multiplication	Value
2^6	2	6	2 × 2 × 2 × 2 × 2 × 2	64
4^3				
			8 × 8	
			10 × 10 × 10 × 10	
	1	7		
	7	1		
⭐	3			27
⭐		2		81

Review

Complete the equivalent fractions.

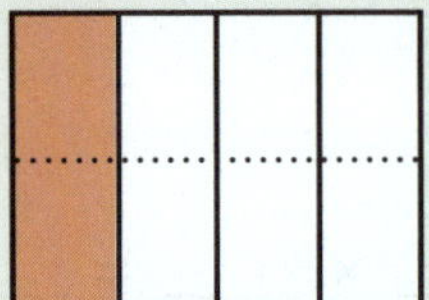 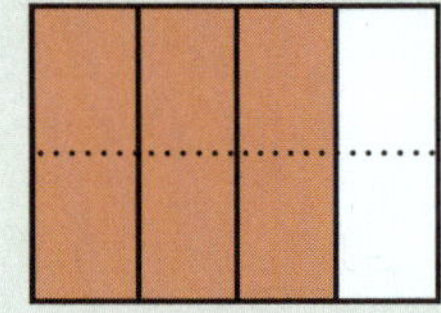 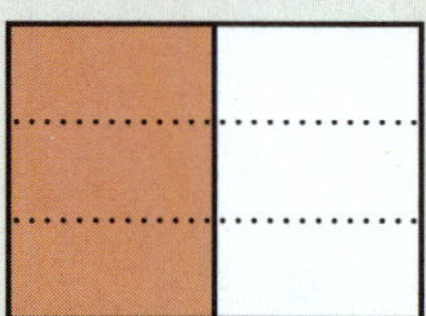 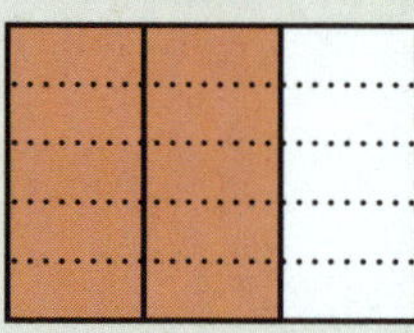

$$\frac{1}{4} = \frac{}{8} \qquad \frac{3}{4} = \frac{}{8} \qquad \frac{1}{2} = \frac{3}{} \qquad \frac{2}{3} = \frac{}{15}$$

Use logical reasoning to complete with <, >, or =.
You do not need to find the exact value of the expressions.

$26 \times (5 + 2)$ ◯ $27 \times (5 + 2)$	$38 \times 5 + 19 \times 3$ ◯ $38 \times 5 - 19 \times 3$
$8 \times (7 + 3)$ ◯ $8 \times 7 + 8 \times 3$	$27 \times 15 \times 1$ ◯ $27 \times 15 \times 0$
$16 \times 24 \times 73$ ◯ $73 \times 24 \times 16$	$97 + 38 + 72$ ◯ $72 + 38 + 97$

Complete.

$3{,}289 + 10 =$ _______	$456 \times 10 =$ _______	$20{,}000 \div 10 =$ _______
$3{,}289 + 100 =$ _______	$456 \times 100 =$ _______	$20{,}000 \div 100 =$ _______
$3{,}289 + 1{,}000 =$ _______	$456 \times 1{,}000 =$ _______	$20{,}000 \div 1{,}000 =$ _______

Match.

3 times the sum of 6 and 2	$(3 \times 6) + 2$
The product of 3 and 6, increased by 2	$3 \times (6 + 2)$
The difference between 6 and 3, multiplied by 2	$(6 \div 3) - 2$
The quotient of 6 and 3, decreased by 2	$(6 - 3) \times 2$

Lesson Activities

$1^2 =$ _____ $\times$ _____ $=$ _____ $5^2 =$ _____ $\times$ _____ $=$ _____ $9^2 =$ _____ $\times$ _____ $=$ _____

$2^2 =$ _____ $\times$ _____ $=$ _____ $6^2 =$ _____ $\times$ _____ $=$ _____ $10^2 =$ _____ $\times$ _____ $=$ _____

$3^2 =$ _____ $\times$ _____ $=$ _____ $7^2 =$ _____ $\times$ _____ $=$ _____ $11^2 =$ _____ $\times$ _____ $=$ _____

$4^2 =$ _____ $\times$ _____ $=$ _____ $8^2 =$ _____ $\times$ _____ $=$ _____ $12^2 =$ _____ $\times$ _____ $=$ _____

Square and Cube Numbers

When we square a number, we raise it to the second power. The result is called a square number.

Ex. What is 5 squared?

$$5^2 = 5 \times 5 = 25$$

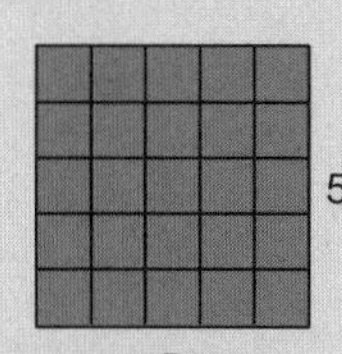

When we cube a number, we raise it to the third power. The result is called a cube number.

Ex. What is 5 cubed?

$$5^3 = 5 \times 5 \times 5 = 125$$

Four in a Row (2-Player Game)

36	10^2	25	7^2	9	2^3
8^2	1	4^2	64	9^2	121
49	6^2	4	1^3	100	12^2
5^2	81	1^2	144	3^2	16
8	11^2	27	2^2	1	3^3

Practice

Draw a line from Start to End so that each problem is followed by the correct answer.
You do not have to solve every problem.

START

7^2	14	8^2	24	0^3	1	2^4
49		16		3		8
5^2	25	2^3	8	10^2	18	9^2
10		4		100		92
3^3	9	10^2	6	3^2	12	7^2
6		20		9		28
4^2	1	1^2	36	6^2	20	10^2
16		2		12		40
12^2	144	8^2	64	2^2	4	11^2
24		16		8		121
3^4	12	2^3	14	7^2	27	3^3
27		28		49		9
5^3	15	4^3	32	END	100	5^3

Review 👤 Complete the equivalent fractions.

$\dfrac{1}{5} = \dfrac{3}{15}$ (×3)

$\dfrac{2}{5} = \dfrac{}{15}$

$\dfrac{3}{5} = \dfrac{}{15}$

$\dfrac{4}{5} = \dfrac{}{15}$

$\dfrac{1}{4} = \dfrac{}{12}$

$\dfrac{2}{4} = \dfrac{}{12}$

$\dfrac{3}{4} = \dfrac{}{12}$

$\dfrac{4}{4} = \dfrac{}{12}$

Evaluate.

$5 \times 9 - 5 \times 3$

$(5 \times 9) - (5 \times 3)$

$5 \times (9 - 5) \times 3$

Complete the chart.

	40	50	60	70	80	90	100	110
÷ 2	20							

Solve. Write the equations you use.

Marisa's family buys 9 bushes at the garden center. Each bush costs $39. What is the total cost of the bushes?

Marisa's family also buys 3 trees. Each tree costs $235. What is the total cost of the trees?

Lesson Activities 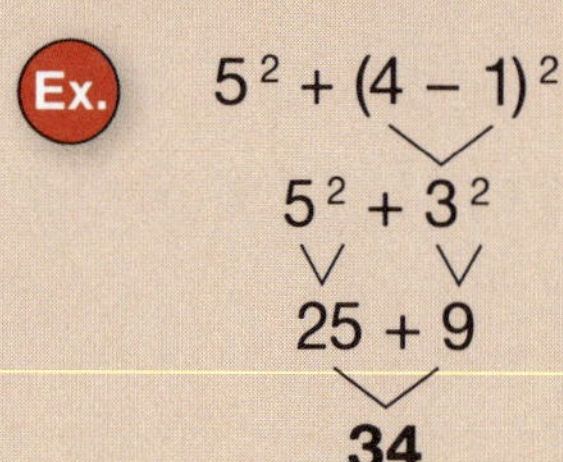

Order of Operations

1. Complete operations in parentheses.
2. Evaluate exponents.
3. Multiply or divide, from left to right.
4. Add or subtract, from left to right.

Ex.
$$5^2 + (4 - 1)^2$$
$$5^2 + 3^2$$
$$25 + 9$$
$$\mathbf{34}$$

	$(4 + 2)^2 - 1^3$
P	
E	
M or D $\longrightarrow$	
A or S $\longrightarrow$	

	$20 \div 2^2$
P	
E	
M or D $\longrightarrow$	
A or S $\longrightarrow$	

Order of Operations Dice War (2-Player Game)

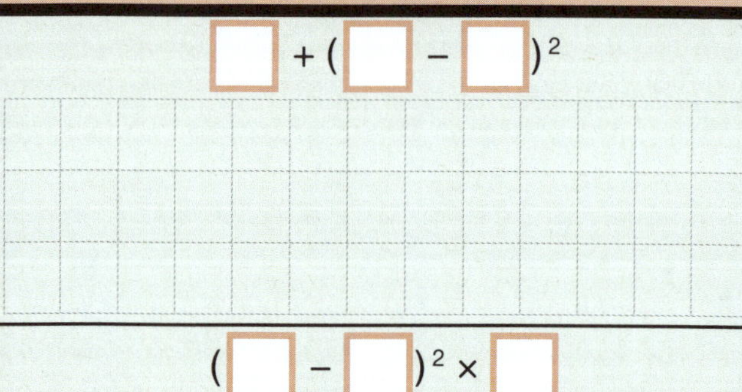

Player 1	Player 2
$\square + (\square - \square)^2$	$\square + (\square - \square)^2$
$(\square - \square)^2 \times \square$	$(\square - \square)^2 \times \square$
$\square^2 + \square \times \square$	$\square^2 + \square \times \square$

Practice

Evaluate. Then, find the blanks that match the answer. Write the matching letter in the blanks to solve the riddle.

Q $5^2 - 4^2$

A $(5 - 4)^2$

E $10 - 3^2 + 1$

U $(10 - 3)^2 + 1$

S $2^3 \times 8 - 6^2$

L $2^3 \times (8 - 6)^2$

M $(6^2 + 4) \div 10$

R $(6 + 4)^2 \div 10$

What do hungry math students like to eat after they study exponents?

| 1 | | 28 | 9 | 50 | 1 | 10 | 2 |

| 4 | 2 | 1 | 32 |

Review

Write each fraction in simplest form.
Use the example to help.

$$\frac{6}{12} \overset{\div 6}{\underset{\div 6}{=}} \frac{1}{2}$$

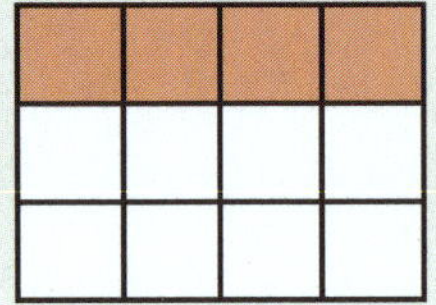

$$\frac{4}{12} =$$

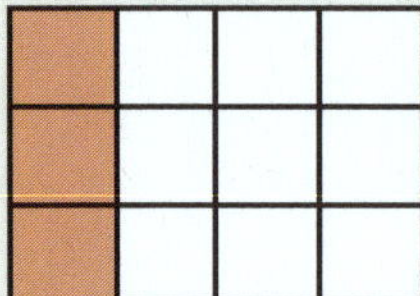

$$\frac{3}{12} =$$

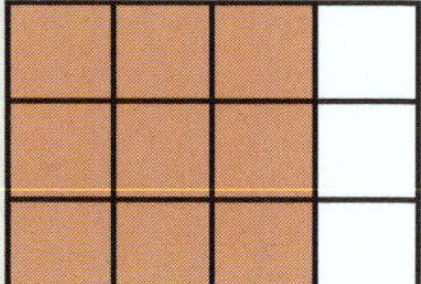

$$\frac{9}{12} =$$

Find the products. Use the example to help.

```
    1
   42          42          42          42
 × 38        × 38        × 38        × 38
 ────        ────        ────        ────
  336    →    336    →    336    →     336
               0        + 1,260     + 1,260
                                    ───────
                                      1,596
```

```
      2 3          4 1          3 8          7 5
    × 1 3        × 2 5        × 1 4        × 3 4
    ─────        ─────        ─────        ─────
```

Use the clues to complete the chart.

- There are 15 children on the cross-country team.
- There are twice as many children on the football team as on the cross-country team.
- There are 5 more children on the soccer team than on the cross-country team.
- There are half as many children on the swimming team as there are on the soccer team.

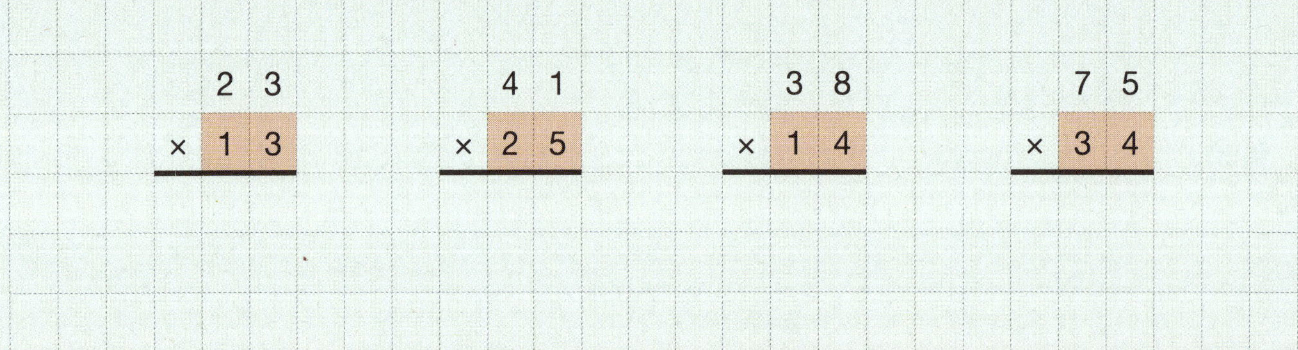

Sport	Number of Children	
Football		
Soccer		
Cross-country		
Swimming		

Lesson Activities 

A

$10^1 = 10 = $ _______________ $10^4 = 10 \times 10 \times 10 \times 10 = $ _______________

$10^2 = 10 \times 10 = $ _______________ $10^5 = 10 \times 10 \times 10 \times 10 \times 10 = $ _______________

$10^3 = 10 \times 10 \times 10 = $ _______________ $10^6 = 10 \times 10 \times 10 \times 10 \times 10 \times 10 = $ _______________

B

Powers of 10

The powers of 10 are numbers that can be expressed with a base of 10 and an exponent. The exponent tells the number of zeros in the original number.

Ex.  Write 100,000,000 as a power of 10.

100,000,000 has 8 zeros.
So, 8 is the exponent.

$100,000,000 = \mathbf{10^8}$

To multiply a number by a power of 10, tack on the matching number of zeros. Then, write commas as needed.

Ex. 372×10^5

$372 \times 10^5 = \mathbf{37,200,000}$

OCEAN FACTS

Volume of the world's oceans	14×10^8 cu. km	
Volume of the Pacific Ocean	7×10^8 cu. km	
Area of the world's oceans	36×10^7 sq. km	
Area of the Pacific Ocean	17×10^7 sq. km	
Average depth of the world's oceans	37×10^2 m	
Depth of the lowest point in the oceans	11×10^3 m	

Practice — Write the missing exponents.

$10^{\boxed{0}} = 1$ $10^{\boxed{}} = 100$ $10^{\boxed{}} = 10,000$

$10^{\boxed{}} = 1,000$ $10^{\boxed{}} = 10$ $10^{\boxed{}} = 100,000$

$10^{\boxed{}} = 1,000,000$ $10^{\boxed{}} = 100,000,000$ $10^{\boxed{}} = 1,000,000,000$

Find the products.

$75 \times 10^3 = \underline{\hspace{3cm}}$ $39 \times 10^1 = \underline{\hspace{3cm}}$

$879 \times 10^2 = \underline{\hspace{3cm}}$ $756 \times 10^0 = \underline{\hspace{3cm}}$

$104 \times 10^4 = \underline{\hspace{3cm}}$ $577 \times 10^5 = \underline{\hspace{3cm}}$

Write the missing exponents.

$6 = 6 \times 10^{\boxed{}}$ $90 = 9 \times 10^{\boxed{}}$ $4,000,000 = 4 \times 10^{\boxed{}}$

$500 = 5 \times 10^{\boxed{}}$ $8,000 = 8 \times 10^{\boxed{}}$ $20,000 = 2 \times 10^{\boxed{}}$

Complete the circles with <, >, or =.

$10^3 \bigcirc 10^5$	$10^7 \bigcirc 10^9$	$10^4 \bigcirc 10,000$
$10^1 \bigcirc 10$	$10^0 \bigcirc 10$	$10^0 \bigcirc 1$
$7 \times 10^5 \bigcirc 7 \times 10^4$	$7 \times 10^4 \bigcirc 7 \times 10^4$	$7 \times 10^3 \bigcirc 7 \times 10^4$
$4 \times 10^6 \bigcirc 5 \times 10^6$	$4 \times 10^6 \bigcirc 5 \times 10^7$	$4 \times 10^7 \bigcirc 5 \times 10^6$

Review 👤 Use mental math to complete.

$3 \times 70 =$ _____________ $30 \times 70 =$ _____________ $300 \times 70 =$ ___________

$3 \times 700 =$ _____________ $30 \times 700 =$ _____________ $300 \times 700 =$ ___________

$3 \times 7,000 =$ _____________ $30 \times 7,000 =$ ___________ $300 \times 7,000 =$ _________

Circle the numbers in the triangle that evenly divide the number in the box.

Divisibility Rules

All even numbers are divisible by 2.

A number is divisible by 5 if it has 0 or 5 in its ones-place.

A number is divisible by 10 if it has 0 in its ones-place.

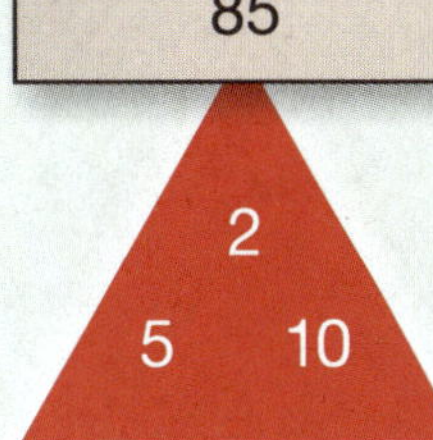

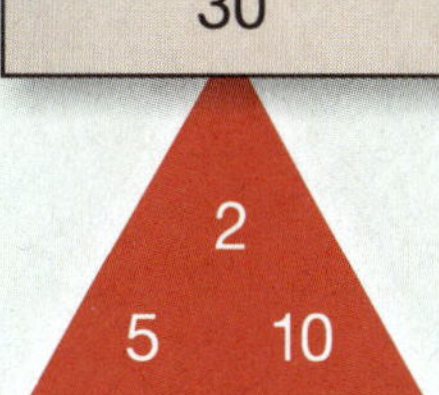

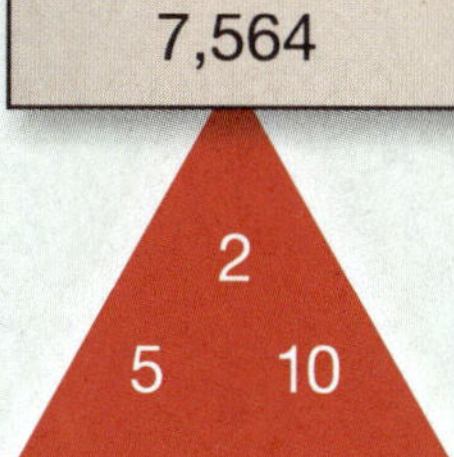

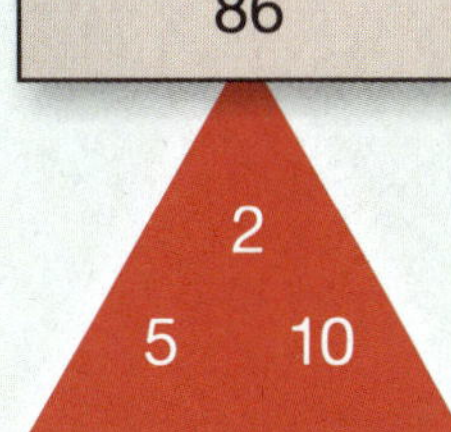

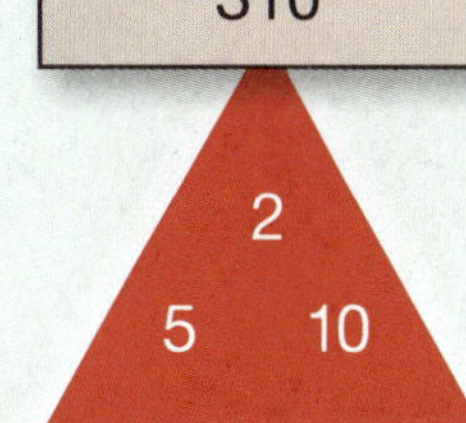

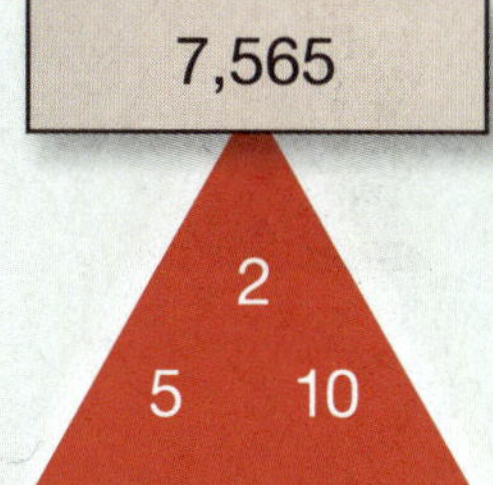

Complete.

$\dfrac{1}{3}$ of 15 = _____________

$\dfrac{1}{5}$ of 15 = _____________

$\dfrac{1}{15}$ of 15 = _____________

Solve. Write the equations you use.

There are 20 children in the choir. 13 of the children are 11 years old, and the rest are 12 years old. What fraction of the children are 11 years old?

What fraction of the children are 12 years old?

A soccer coach spends $260 on T-shirts. Each T-shirt costs $10. How many T-shirts does she buy?

Lesson Activities 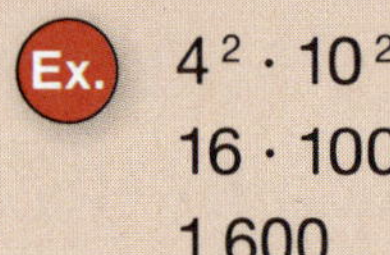

Multiplication Dot
Another symbol for multiplication is a dot.

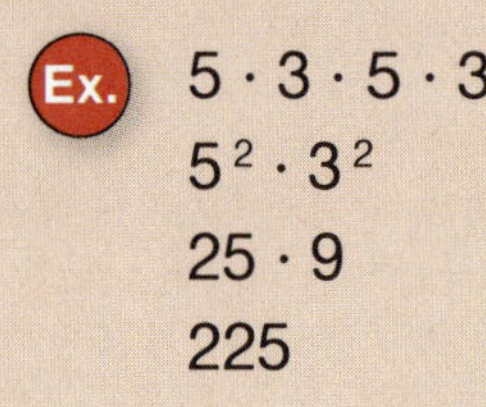

Ex. $4^2 \cdot 10^2$
16 · 100
1,600

Associative Property
The associative property of multiplication says that we can group numbers in any order when multiplying. We can use this property to simplify and evaluate long multiplication expressions.

Ex. $5 \cdot 3 \cdot 5 \cdot 3$
$5^2 \cdot 3^2$
25 · 9
225

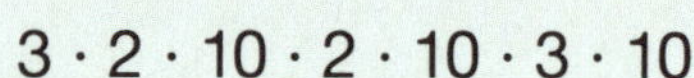

$3 \cdot 2 \cdot 3 \cdot 2 \cdot 2$

$10 \cdot 10 \cdot 5 \cdot 5 \cdot 10 \cdot 10$

$3 \cdot 2 \cdot 10 \cdot 2 \cdot 10 \cdot 3 \cdot 10$

Exponent Roll (2-Player Game)

Expression	Points
Player 1 Total:	

Expression	Points
Player 2 Total:	

Scoring Guide

One Pair = 100
Two Pairs = 200
Three of a Kind = 300

Three of a Kind and One Pair = 500
Four of a Kind = 600
Five of a Kind = 1,000

Practice

Evaluate.

$6 \cdot 9$	$7 \cdot 70$	$90 \cdot 80$
$7 \cdot 2^3$	$5^2 \cdot 3$	$0 \cdot 6^3$
$3^2 \cdot 2^2$	$4^2 \cdot 1^5$	$7^2 \cdot 6^0$
$8^2 \cdot 10^3$	$5^3 \cdot 10^2$	$9^2 \cdot 10^4$

Match the equivalent expressions.

$6 \cdot 6 \cdot 6 \cdot 7 \cdot 7 \cdot 7$	$6^4 \cdot 7^2$	$6 \cdot 7 \cdot 6 \cdot 6 \cdot 6 \cdot 6$
$6 \cdot 6 \cdot 7 \cdot 7 \cdot 7 \cdot 7$	$6^3 \cdot 7^3$	$7 \cdot 6 \cdot 7 \cdot 7 \cdot 6 \cdot 7$
$6 \cdot 6 \cdot 6 \cdot 6 \cdot 7 \cdot 7$	$6^5 \cdot 7$	$6 \cdot 7 \cdot 6 \cdot 6 \cdot 7 \cdot 6$
$6 \cdot 6 \cdot 6 \cdot 6 \cdot 6 \cdot 7$	$6^2 \cdot 7^4$	$7 \cdot 7 \cdot 7 \cdot 6 \cdot 7 \cdot 7$
$6 \cdot 7 \cdot 7 \cdot 7 \cdot 7 \cdot 7$	$6 \cdot 7^5$	$6 \cdot 7 \cdot 6 \cdot 7 \cdot 6 \cdot 7$

Review

Find the products.

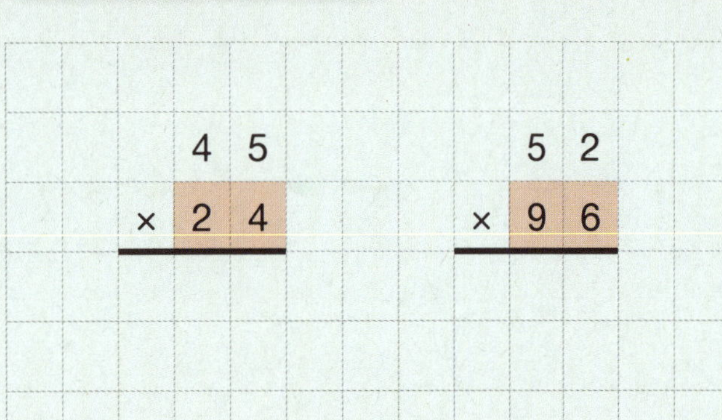

$$\begin{array}{r} 4\ 5 \\ \times\ 2\ 4 \\ \hline \end{array} \qquad \begin{array}{r} 5\ 2 \\ \times\ 9\ 6 \\ \hline \end{array}$$

Evaluate.

$$(3 - 1)^4$$

$$3 - 1^4$$

Complete.

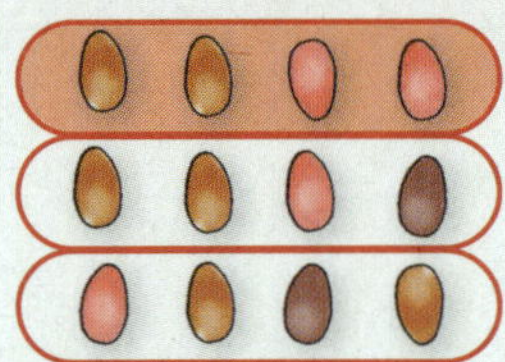

$\dfrac{1}{3}$ of 12 = _________

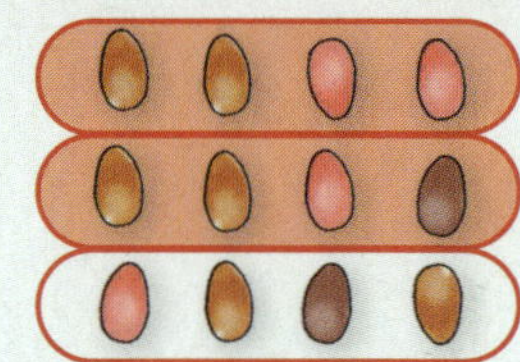

$\dfrac{2}{3}$ of 12 = _________

$\dfrac{3}{3}$ of 12 = _________

Find the volume of each solid. Each solid is made of centimeter cubes.

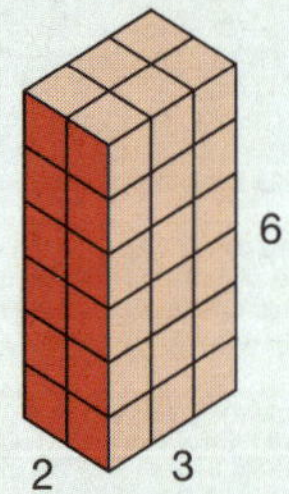

Volume: _________ cubic cm

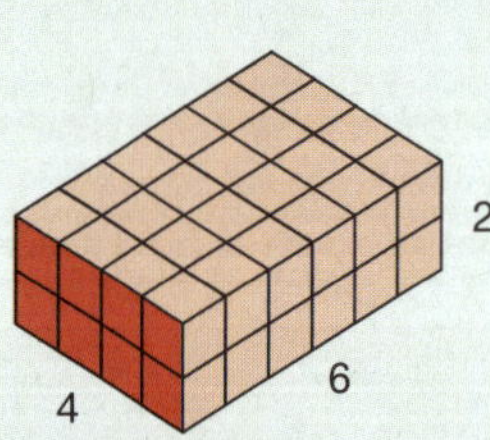

Volume: _________ cubic cm

Volume: _________ cubic cm

Solve. Write the equations you use.

Angelica buys a pencil case for $6.49 and a pack of drawing pencils for $10.89. How much does she spend in all?

Gilbert has $40. Then, he buys a backpack for $34.59. How much money does he have left?

Lesson Activities 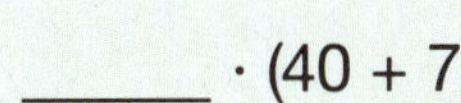

$3 \cdot (20 + 4)$

$3 \cdot 20 + 3 \cdot 4$

Distributive Property

When we multiply a number by a sum in parentheses, we can evaluate the expression two different ways. Either way, we get the same answer.

Option 1:

Find the sum in parentheses, then multiply.

Option 2:

Multiply in parts, then add. This is called "distributing" the factor.

 **Ex.** Evaluate $9 \cdot (30 + 8)$ two different ways.

Option 1:

Add, then multiply.

$$9 \cdot (30 + 8)$$
$$9 \cdot 38$$
342

Option 2:

Distribute the factor.

$$9 \cdot (30 + 8)$$
$$9 \cdot 30 + 9 \cdot 8$$
$$270 + 72$$
342

Roll and Distribute (2-Player Game) 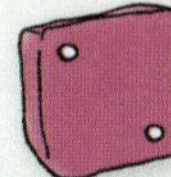

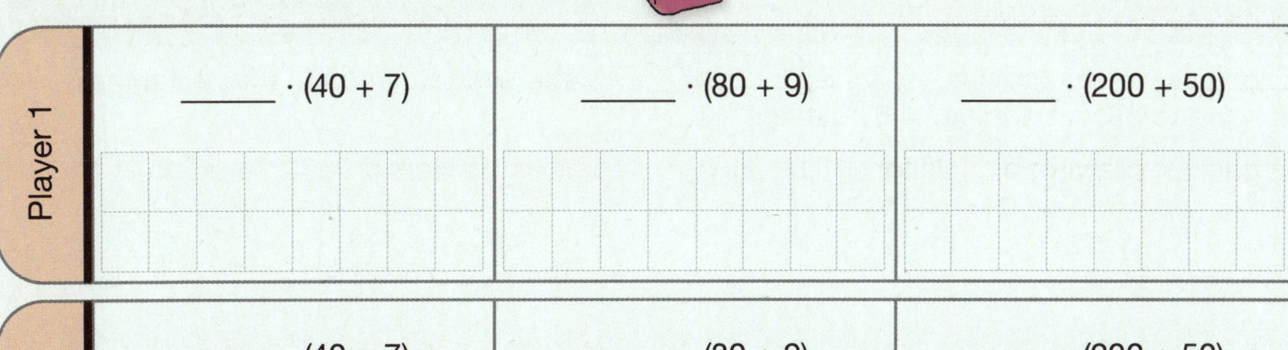

Player 1	____ · (40 + 7)	____ · (80 + 9)	____ · (200 + 50)
Player 2	____ · (40 + 7)	____ · (80 + 9)	____ · (200 + 50)

Practice  Match.

6 · (20 + 3)	3 · 20 + 3 · 6	126
2 · (60 + 3)	6 · 20 + 6 · 3	192
3 · (20 + 6)	6 · 30 + 6 · 2	78
6 · (30 + 2)	2 · 60 + 2 · 3	138

Complete the blanks. You do not need to evaluate.

$5 \cdot (10 + 3) = \underline{\qquad} \cdot 10 + \underline{\qquad} \cdot 3$

$30 \cdot 57 + 30 \cdot 3 = 30 \cdot (57 + \underline{\qquad})$

$15 \cdot (6 + 30) = 15 \cdot 6 + 15 \cdot \underline{\qquad}$

$36 \cdot 99 + 36 \cdot 1 = 36 \cdot (\underline{\qquad} + 1)$

$9 \cdot (100 + 4) = 9 \cdot \underline{\qquad} + 9 \cdot 4$

$7 \cdot 44 + 7 \cdot 6 = \underline{\qquad} \cdot (44 + 6)$

★ $12 \cdot (45 + 8) = 12 \cdot \underline{\qquad} + \underline{\qquad} \cdot 8$

★ $18 \cdot 20 + 18 \cdot 4 = \underline{\qquad} \cdot (20 + \underline{\qquad})$

Circle the expression that best matches the problem. Then, evaluate the expression to find the answer to the word problem.

Each ticket to the concert costs $40. Each ticket also has an additional $2 service fee. How much do 6 tickets cost?

6 · 40 + 2

6 · (40 + 2)

What is the total area of the rectangle?

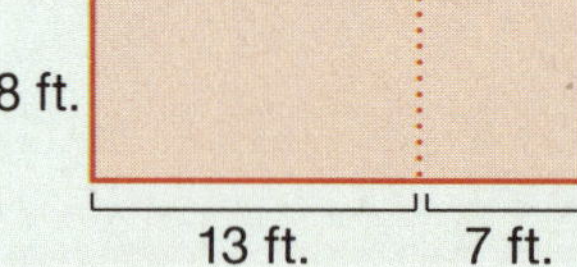

8 · 13 + 8 · 7

8 · 13 + 7

Review
Use mental math to complete.

1,500 ÷ 5 = _______________   1,500 ÷ 50 = _____________   1,500 ÷ 500 = ____________

15,000 ÷ 5 = _____________   15,000 ÷ 50 = ____________   15,000 ÷ 500 = __________

Circle the numbers in the triangle that evenly divide the number in the box.

Divisibility Rules

All even numbers are divisible by 2.

A number is divisible by 3 if the sum of its digits is divisible by 3.

A number is divisible by 6 if it is divisible by both 2 and 3.

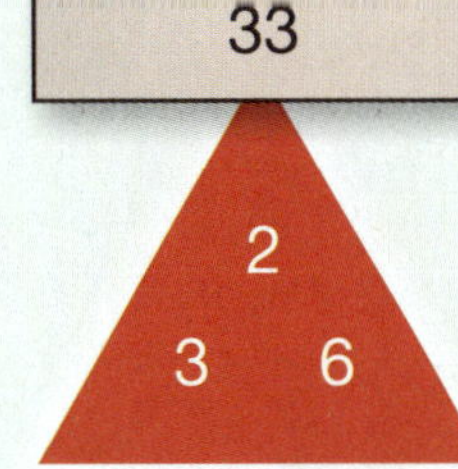

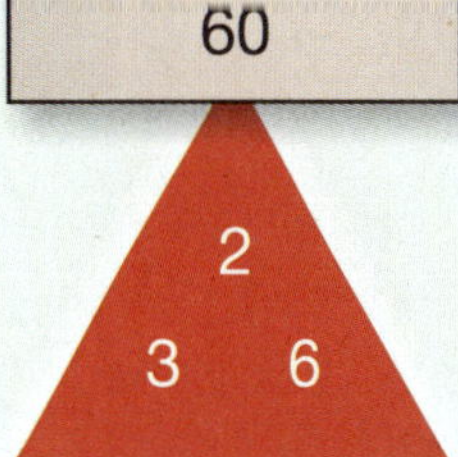

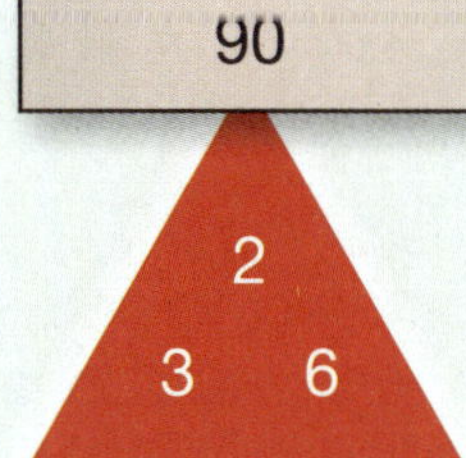

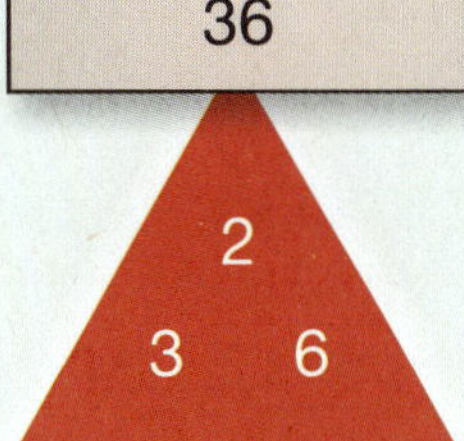

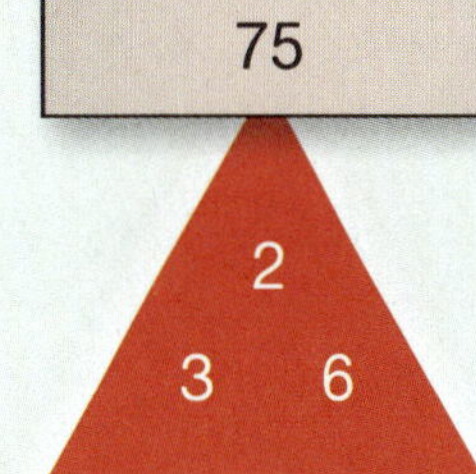

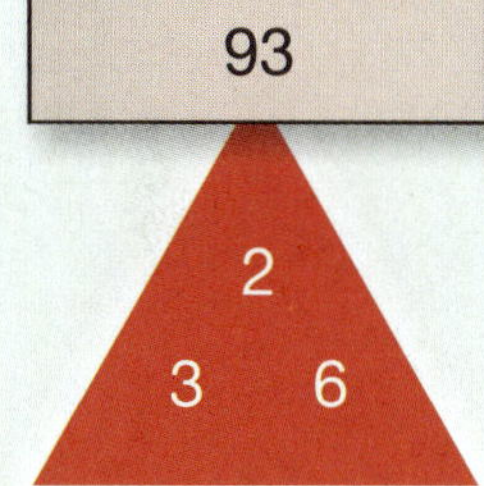

Complete.

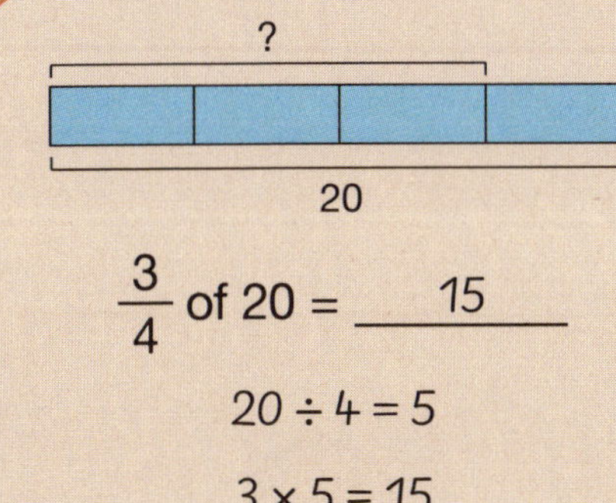

$\frac{3}{4}$ of 20 = ___15___

20 ÷ 4 = 5

3 × 5 = 15

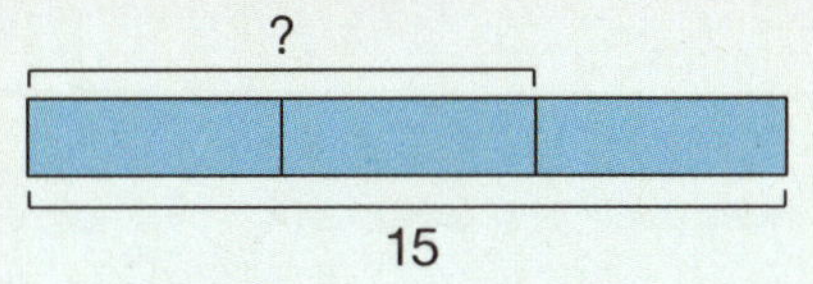

$\frac{2}{3}$ of 15 = _________

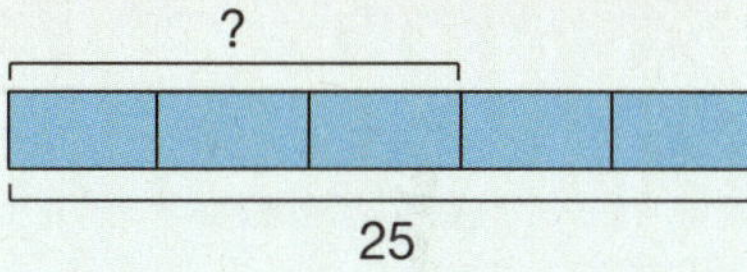

$\frac{3}{5}$ of 25 = _________

Find the products.

8×10^{3} = ___________________________ $32 \cdot 10^{2}$ = ___________________________

$9 \cdot 10^{6}$ = ___________________________ 297×10^{4} = _______________________

5×10^{1} = ___________________________ $109 \cdot 10^{6}$ = _______________________

Lesson Activities

A

$12 \div 4 =$ _______ $\dfrac{12}{4} =$ _______ $18 \div 3 =$ _______ $\dfrac{18}{3} =$ _______

B

Use a Fraction Bar to Show Division

We can use a fraction bar to show division.

Ex. $\dfrac{20}{5}$

$\dfrac{20}{5} = \mathbf{4}$

$20 \div 5 = 4$

The fraction bar is a grouping symbol, just like parentheses. If there are expressions above or below the fraction bar, evaluate the expressions first. Then, follow the order of operations like usual.

Ex. $\dfrac{2 \times 7}{3 + 4}$

$\dfrac{14}{7} = \mathbf{2}$

$(2 \times 7) \div (3 + 4)$

$14 \div 7$

2

$\dfrac{3 \times 10}{8 - 2}$

$\dfrac{5 \times 8}{2 \times 2}$

$\dfrac{3 \cdot 8}{4} + 5$

C

Hit the Target (1-Player Game)

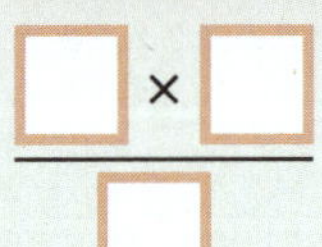

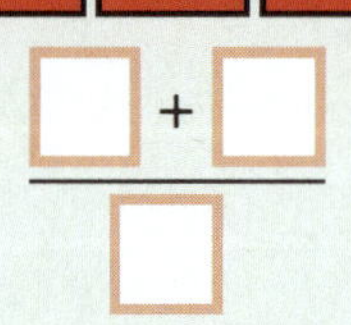

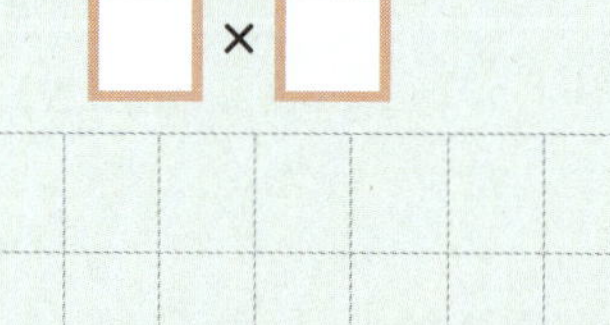

Practice 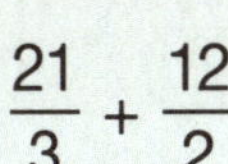 Write the quotients.

$\dfrac{15}{1} =$ _________

$\dfrac{16}{2} =$ _________

$\dfrac{0}{4} =$ _________

$\dfrac{42}{6} =$ _________

$\dfrac{81}{9} =$ _________

$\dfrac{64}{8} =$ _________

$\dfrac{49}{7} =$ _________

$\dfrac{54}{6} =$ _________

$\dfrac{72}{9} =$ _________

$\dfrac{63}{7} =$ _________

$\dfrac{90}{10} =$ _________

$\dfrac{56}{8} =$ _________

Evaluate.

$\dfrac{28}{4} + 10$

$\dfrac{21}{3} + \dfrac{12}{2}$

$\dfrac{8 + 7}{5 - 2}$

$\dfrac{5 \cdot 6}{2 \cdot 3}$

Circle the expression that best matches the word problem. Then, evaluate the expression to find the answer to the word problem.

Avery buys 4 packs of gum. Each pack holds 5 sticks of gum. Then, she splits the gum evenly with her sister. How many sticks of gum does each person get?

$\dfrac{4 \times 5}{2}$

$\dfrac{4 + 5}{2}$

Jackson's mom has 1 son and 3 daughters. She buys 8 cookies and wants to share them equally among her children. How many cookies should she give each child?

$\dfrac{1 + 3}{8}$

$\dfrac{8}{1 + 3}$

Review

Find the sum or difference. Use the examples to help.

$$\frac{3}{5} + \frac{1}{5} = \frac{4}{5}$$

$$\frac{5}{8} + \frac{2}{8} = \underline{\hspace{2cm}}$$

$$\frac{1}{6} + \frac{4}{6} = \underline{\hspace{2cm}}$$

$$\frac{3}{5} - \frac{1}{5} = \frac{2}{5}$$

$$\frac{5}{8} - \frac{2}{8} = \underline{\hspace{2cm}}$$

$$\frac{3}{6} - \frac{2}{6} = \underline{\hspace{2cm}}$$

Use long division to solve.

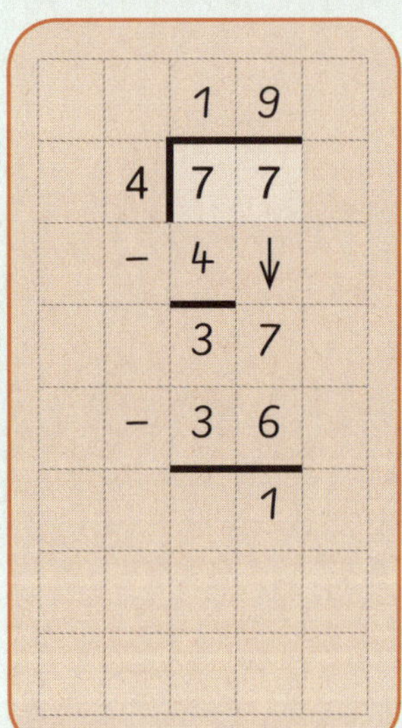

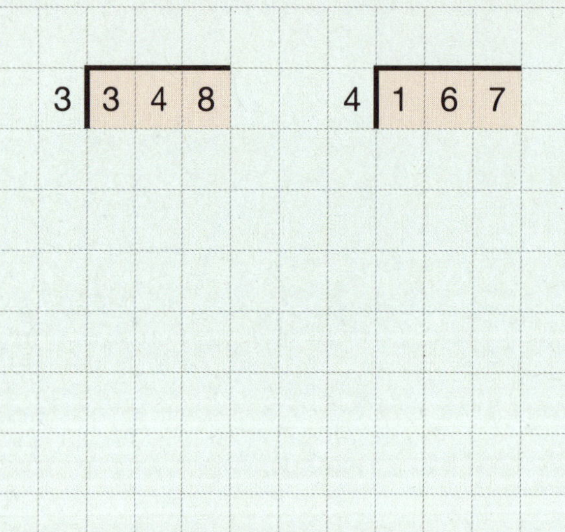

Evaluate.

$$3^2 \cdot (5 + 2)$$

$$(9 - 3)^2 \div 4$$

Write the ordered pair that describes the location of each point.

Point	Ordered Pair
A	(2,5)
B	
C	
D	
E	

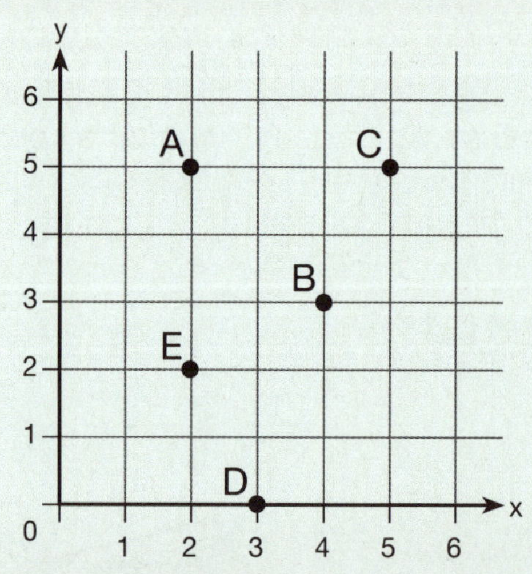

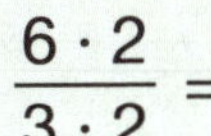

Lesson Activities

A

$$\frac{6 \cdot 2}{3 \cdot 2} =$$

$$\frac{8 \cdot 3}{3 \cdot 4} =$$

$$\frac{10 \cdot 2 \cdot 3}{2 \cdot 3} =$$

B

Cancel Common Factors

If there are multiplication expressions above and below the division bar, we can simplify the expression before solving. Crossing out (or "cancelling") the common factors is a quick way to divide both expressions by the same number.

1. Look for common factors above and below the division bar.

2. Cross out the common factors in pairs. One factor must be above the bar and one factor must be below the bar.

3. Complete the problem.

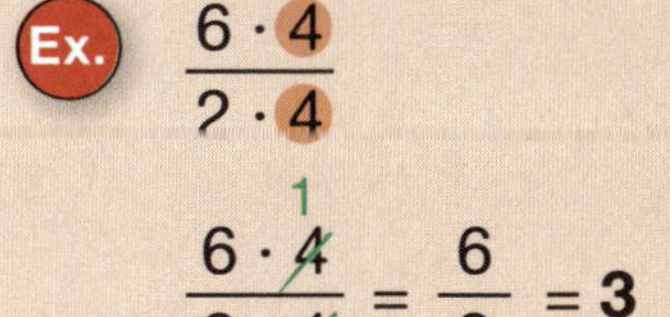

Ex. $\dfrac{6 \cdot 4}{2 \cdot 4}$

$$\frac{6 \cdot \cancel{4}}{2 \cdot \cancel{4}} = \frac{6}{2} = 3$$

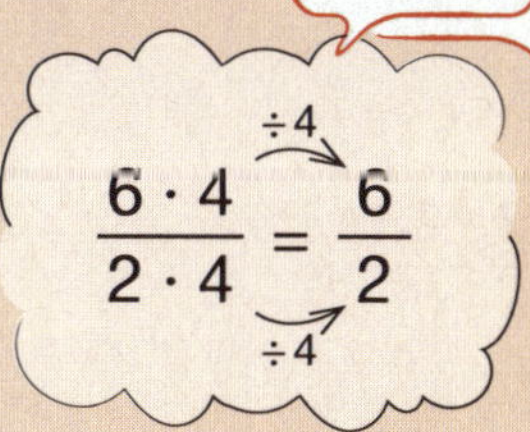

$$\frac{6 \cdot 4}{2 \cdot 4} \xrightarrow{\div 4} = \frac{6}{2} \xrightarrow{\div 4}$$

Ex. $\dfrac{9 \cdot 7 \cdot 11}{11 \cdot 7 \cdot 3}$

$$\frac{9 \cdot \cancel{7} \cdot \cancel{11}}{\cancel{11} \cdot \cancel{7} \cdot 3} = \frac{9}{3} = 3$$

Ex. $\dfrac{5 \cdot 4 \cdot 5}{5}$

$$\frac{\cancel{5} \cdot 4 \cdot 5}{\cancel{5}} = \frac{4 \cdot 5}{1} = \frac{20}{1} = 20$$

C

Slash It! (2-Player Game)

$\dfrac{7 \cdot 15}{3 \cdot 7} =$	$\dfrac{15 \cdot 16}{8 \cdot 15} =$	$\dfrac{6 \cdot 6}{2 \cdot 6} =$
$\dfrac{3 \cdot 12 \cdot 3}{3 \cdot 3 \cdot 4} =$	$\dfrac{8 \cdot 24}{8 \cdot 8} =$	$\dfrac{2 \cdot 10 \cdot 2}{2 \cdot 2 \cdot 2} =$
$\dfrac{7 \cdot 9 \cdot 5}{9 \cdot 7} =$	$\dfrac{6 \cdot 8 \cdot 7}{8 \cdot 6 \cdot 7} =$	$\dfrac{0 \cdot 8}{8 \cdot 17} =$

Practice

**Evaluate. Use cancelling where possible.
(Not all problems have numbers that can be cancelled.)**

$$\frac{20 \cdot 6}{6} =$$

$$\frac{7 \cdot 10}{2 \cdot 7} =$$

$$\frac{13 \cdot 18}{3 \cdot 13} =$$

$$\frac{25 \cdot 14}{7 \cdot 25} =$$

$$\frac{4 \cdot 8 \cdot 3}{3 \cdot 4 \cdot 4} =$$

$$\frac{9 \cdot 45}{9 \cdot 9} =$$

$$\frac{8 \cdot 4}{8 \cdot 4} =$$

$$\frac{3 \cdot 12 \cdot 3}{3 \cdot 3 \cdot 3} =$$

$$\frac{8 \cdot 11 \cdot 5}{11 \cdot 8} =$$

$$\frac{11 \cdot 13 \cdot 17}{17 \cdot 11 \cdot 13} =$$

$$\frac{14 \cdot 0}{2 \cdot 5} =$$

★ $$\frac{14 + 0}{2 + 5} =$$

Arrange the numbers in the blanks so that the expression equals the target number.

| 7 | 7 | 8 |

$$\frac{\Box \times \Box}{\Box} = \;\; 8$$

| 5 | 9 | 9 | 10 |

$$\frac{\Box \times \Box}{\Box \times \Box} = \;\; 2$$

| 2 | 3 | 4 | 4 | 6 |

$$\frac{\Box \times \Box \times \Box}{\Box \times \Box} = \;\; 1$$

Review

Color the diagrams to match each mixed number.
Then, convert to a fraction.

$2\dfrac{1}{3} = \dfrac{}{3}$

$2\dfrac{1}{4} = \dfrac{}{4}$

$2\dfrac{1}{5} = \dfrac{}{5}$

Use long division to solve.

$6\overline{)7\ 4}$ $5\overline{)6\ 0\ 7}$ $8\overline{)4\ 3\ 2}$

Complete.

$10^3 = $ _______________

$10^5 = $ _______________

$10^6 = $ _______________

$8 \cdot 10^2 = $ _______________

$7 \cdot 10^4 = $ _______________

$32 \cdot 10^4 = $ _______________

Follow the directions to find the mean and median for the data set. Write the equations you use.

How to Find the Mean (Average)

1. Add up all the numbers in the data set.
2. Divide by the number of numbers in the data set.

How to Find the Median

1. Write the numbers in order from least to greatest.
2. Choose the number in the middle.
3. If there are an even number of numbers, find the mean of the two numbers in the middle.

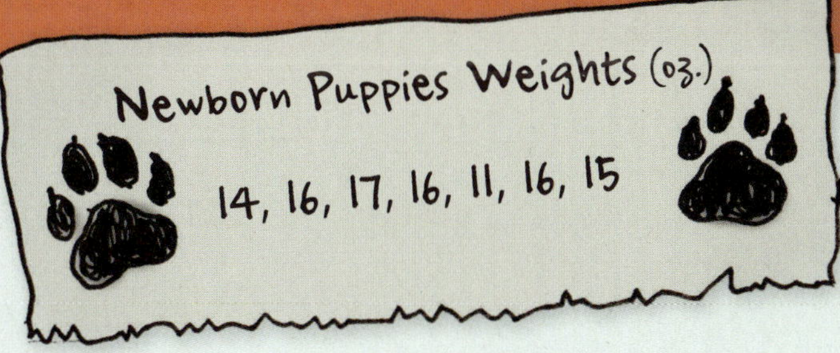

Mean: _____________   Median: _____________

Lesson Activities 👥

Factor Pairs of 14	Factor Pairs of 16	Factor Pairs of 19

Prime and Composite Numbers

Prime numbers have exactly two factors: 1 and the number itself.

Composite numbers have more than two factors.

1 has only one factor. So, it is neither a composite number nor a prime number.

Ex. Is 18 prime or composite?
Factors of 18: 1, 2, 3, 6, 9, 18
18 has more than two factors, so it is **composite.**

Ex. Is 17 prime or composite?
Factors of 17: 1, 17
17 has exactly two factors, so it is **prime.**

How to Find All Prime Numbers to 100

1. Cross out 1 (since 1 is not a prime number).
2. Circle 2 (since 2 is a prime number). Cross out all other multiples of 2.
3. Circle 3. Cross out all other multiples of 3.
4. Circle 5. Cross out all other multiples of 5.
5. Circle 7. Cross out all other multiples of 7.
6. Circle the remaining numbers.

1	2	3	4	5	6	7	8	9	10
11	12	13	14	15	16	17	18	19	20
21	22	23	24	25	26	27	28	29	30
31	32	33	34	35	36	37	38	39	40
41	42	43	44	45	46	47	48	49	50
51	52	53	54	55	56	57	58	59	60
61	62	63	64	65	66	67	68	69	70
71	72	73	74	75	76	77	78	79	80
81	82	83	84	85	86	87	88	89	90
91	92	93	94	95	96	97	98	99	100

Practice 👤 Circle the prime numbers. X the numbers that are not prime.

1	2	3	4	5	6	7	8	9	10
11	12	13	14	15	16	17	18	19	20
21	22	23	24	25	26	27	28	29	30

Complete each blank with a prime number to make the equation true.

$4 = 2 \cdot \underline{\ \ 2\ \ }$

$6 = 2 \cdot \underline{\hspace{1cm}}$

$8 = 2 \cdot 2 \cdot \underline{\hspace{1cm}}$

$9 = \underline{\hspace{1cm}} \cdot 3$

$10 = 2 \cdot \underline{\hspace{1cm}}$

$12 = 2 \cdot 2 \cdot \underline{\hspace{1cm}}$

$14 = \underline{\hspace{1cm}} \cdot 7$

$15 = \underline{\hspace{1cm}} \cdot 5$

$16 = 2 \cdot 2 \cdot 2 \cdot \underline{\hspace{1cm}}$

$18 = 2 \cdot \underline{\hspace{1cm}} \cdot 3$

$20 = \underline{\hspace{1cm}} \cdot 2 \cdot 5$

$21 = 3 \cdot \underline{\hspace{1cm}}$

$22 = \underline{\hspace{1cm}} \cdot 11$

$24 = 2 \cdot 2 \cdot \underline{\hspace{1cm}} \cdot 3$

$25 = \underline{\hspace{1cm}} \cdot 5$

$26 = 2 \cdot \underline{\hspace{1cm}}$

$27 = 3 \cdot 3 \cdot \underline{\hspace{1cm}}$

$28 = 2 \cdot \underline{\hspace{1cm}} \cdot 7$

$30 = \underline{\hspace{1cm}} \cdot 3 \cdot 5$

$32 = 2 \cdot 2 \cdot 2 \cdot 2 \cdot \underline{\hspace{1cm}}$

$33 = \underline{\hspace{1cm}} \cdot 11$

$34 = \underline{\hspace{1cm}} \cdot 17$

$35 = 5 \cdot \underline{\hspace{1cm}}$

$36 = 2 \cdot 2 \cdot 3 \cdot \underline{\hspace{1cm}}$

> *Every* whole number greater than 1 is either a prime number
> or can be expressed as the product of prime numbers!

Review

Convert each fraction to a mixed number.

$$\frac{11}{4} = 2\,\frac{3}{4}$$

$$\frac{13}{4} = \underline{\hspace{3cm}}$$

$$\frac{15}{4} = \underline{\hspace{3cm}}$$

Use the lists of multiples to answer the questions.

Multiples of 3:
3, 6, 9, 12, 15, 18

Multiples of 4:
4, 8, 12, 16, 20, 24

Multiples of 5:
5, 10, 15, 20, 25, 30

What is the least common multiple of 3 and 4?

What is the least common multiple of 4 and 5?

What is the least common multiple of 3 and 5?

Complete the chart.

Number of tacos	1	6	9					20	21
Total cost ($)	3			12	24	36			

Use long division to solve.
Use the example and multiplication table to help.

```
          2  4  3
  2  0 | 4, 8  6  0
      - 4  0 ↓
         8  6
       -  8  0 ↓
            6  0
          -  6  0
               0
```

```
  2  0 | 5, 7  4  0
```

× 20	
1	20
2	40
3	60
4	80
5	100
6	120
7	140
8	160
9	180

Complete.

$$2^2 = \underline{\hspace{2cm}}$$

$$2^3 = \underline{\hspace{2cm}}$$

$$3^2 = \underline{\hspace{2cm}}$$

$$3^3 = \underline{\hspace{2cm}}$$

$$4^2 = \underline{\hspace{2cm}}$$

$$4^3 = \underline{\hspace{2cm}}$$

Lesson Activities

Factor Trees and Prime Factorization

Factor trees help us find all prime factors of a number. To make a factor tree:

1. Write the target number at the top.

2. Draw two branches below the target number. Label the branches with a factor pair for the number above the branches.

3. Continue until each branch ends in a prime number.

Every whole number greater than 1 is prime or can be expressed as the product of prime numbers. This product is called the prime factorization of the number.

 **Ex.** Draw a factor tree for 28.

There are often many different ways to make a factor tree. Here are two ways to make a factor tree for 28.

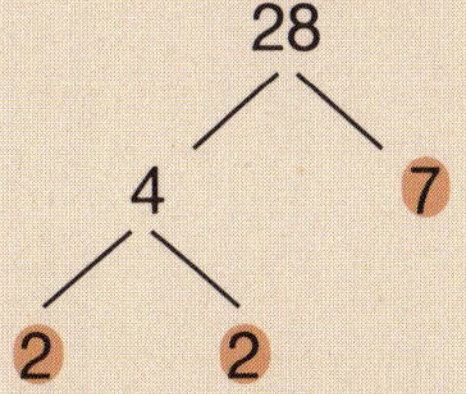 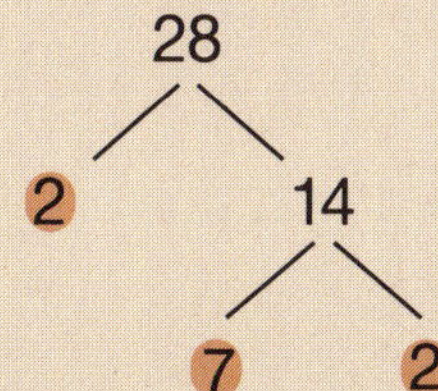

 **Ex.** What is the prime factorization of 28?

$28 = 2 \cdot 2 \cdot 7$

36

40

Prime factorization: _______________

Prime factorization: _______________

Practice 

Use a factor tree to find the prime factorization for each number. Write the prime factors in order from least to greatest.

25

Prime factorization: _______________

35

Prime factorization: _______________

27

Prime factorization: _______________

45

Prime factorization: _______________

49

Prime factorization: _______________

50

Prime factorization: _______________

60

Prime factorization: _______________

90

Prime factorization: _______________

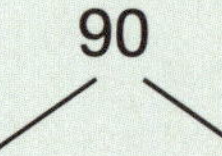

Review

Find the sum. Use the example to help.

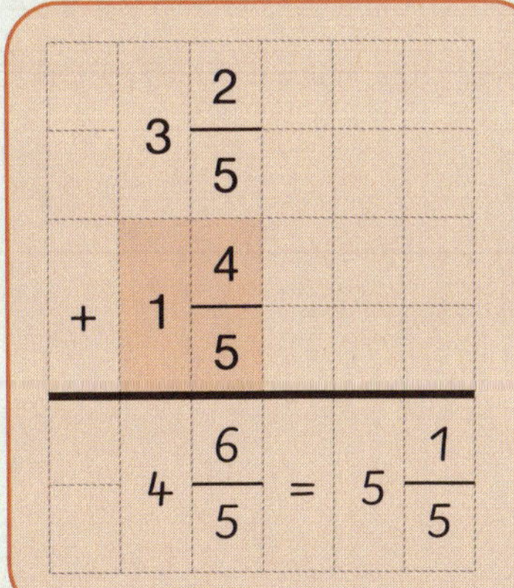

$$3\frac{2}{5} + 1\frac{4}{5} = 4\frac{6}{5} = 5\frac{1}{5}$$

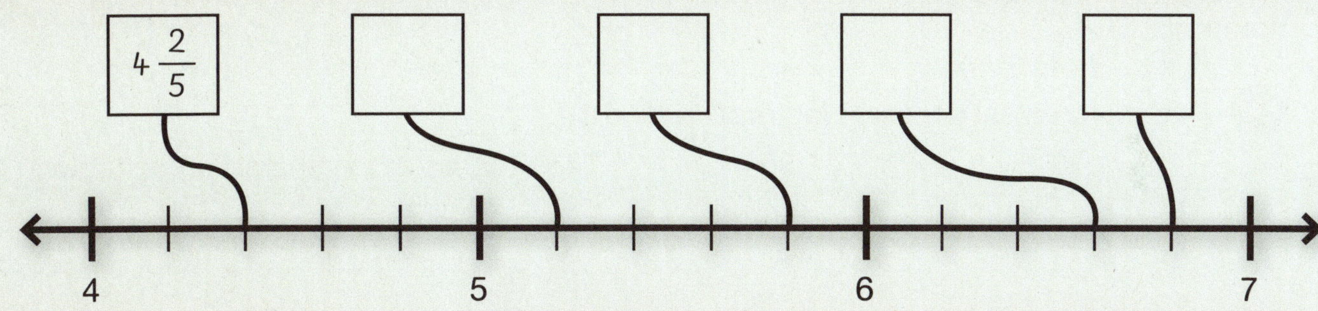

$$2\frac{2}{3} + 3\frac{2}{3} =$$

$$1\frac{7}{8} + 2\frac{1}{8} =$$

Write a mixed number to label each number on the number line.

$4\frac{2}{5}$

4   5   6   7

Use mental math to complete.

	25	50	75	100	125	150	175	200
÷ 25	1							

Complete the missing factors in the factor pairs. Then, answer the questions.

Factor Pairs of 40	Factor Pairs of 45	Factor Pairs of 50
1 × __40__	1 × ______	1 × ______
2 × ______	3 × ______	2 × ______
4 × ______	5 × ______	5 × ______
5 × ______		

What is the greatest common factor of 40 and 45?

What is the greatest common factor of 45 and 50?

What is the greatest common factor of 40 and 50?

Lesson Activities

Factor Pairs of 18	Factor Pairs of 30

A

What factors do 18 and 30 have in common?

What is the greatest common factor (GCF) of 18 and 30?

B

Greatest Common Factor

The greatest common factor (GCF) of two numbers is the highest factor they have in common.

Ex. Find the greatest common factor of 18 and 30.

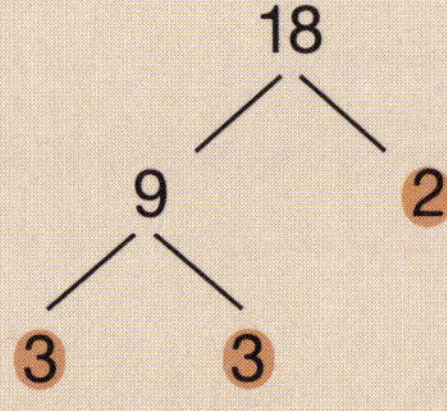

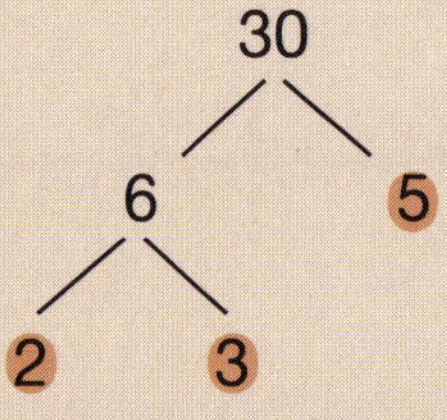

The product of the shared prime factors is the greatest common factor.

$18 = 2 \cdot 3 \cdot 3$ $30 = 2 \cdot 3 \cdot 5$

$18 = 2 \cdot 3 \cdot 3$ $30 = 2 \cdot 3 \cdot 5$ $2 \cdot 3 = 6$, so the GCF of 18 and 30 is **6**.

24

60

24 = ______________________

60 = ______________________

GCF: ______________________

20

45

20 = ______________________

45 = ______________________

GCF: ______________________

Practice

Create a factor tree to find the prime factorization for each number. (Write the prime factors in order from least to greatest.) Then, find the GCF for each pair of numbers.

56

72

Prime Factorizations

56 =

72 = _________________________

GCF: _________________________

32

48

Prime Factorizations

32 = _________________________

48 = _________________________

GCF: _________________________

35

36

Prime Factorizations

35 = _________________________

36 = _________________________

GCF: _________________________

Hint: If two numbers do not have any prime factors in common, their GCF is 1.

Review

Find the sum. Write the answer in simplest form.

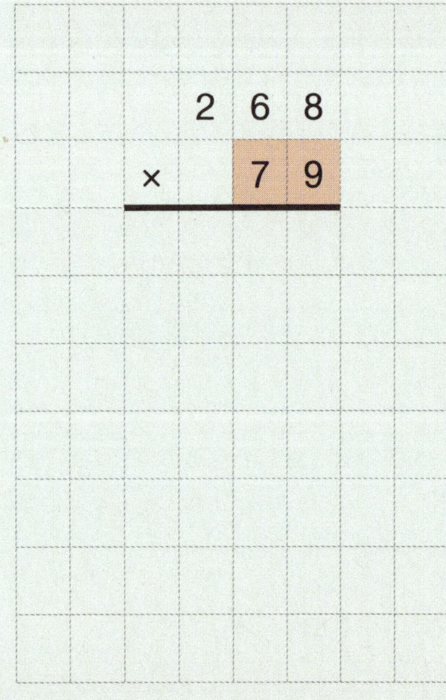

$$2\tfrac{5}{6}$$
$$+\ 1\tfrac{2}{6}$$
$$3\tfrac{7}{6} = 4\tfrac{1}{6}$$

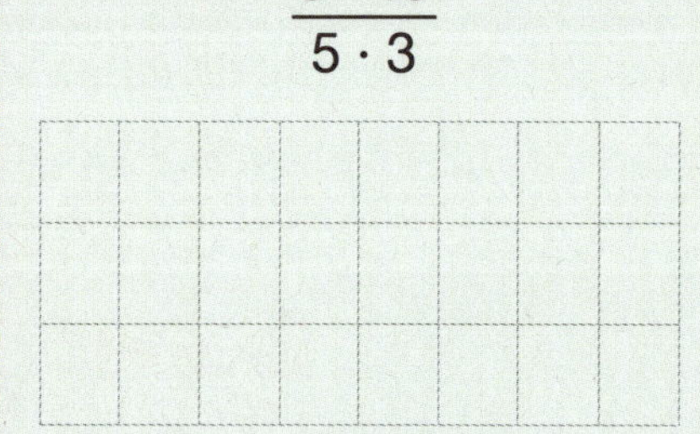

$$2\tfrac{3}{4}$$
$$+\ 5\tfrac{3}{4}$$

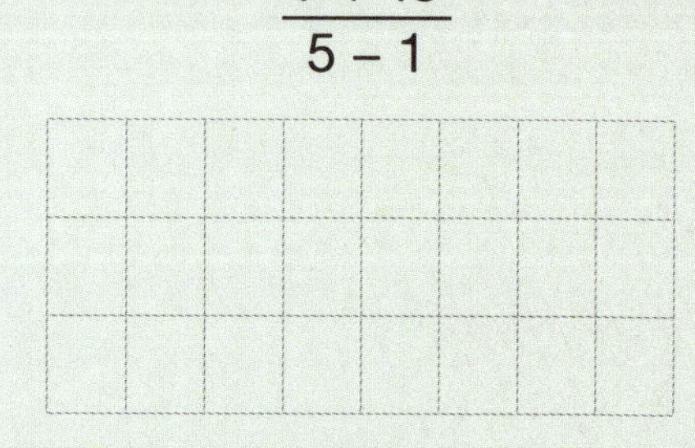

$$1\tfrac{7}{8}$$
$$+\ 4\tfrac{3}{8}$$

Match the equivalent expressions. (Equivalent expressions have the same value. You do not need to evaluate the expressions.)

$43 \cdot (18 + 29)$	$29 \cdot 43 \cdot 18$
$43 \cdot 18 \cdot 29$	$(43 \cdot 18) + 29$
$29 \cdot 18 + 29 \cdot 43$	$43 \cdot 18 + 43 \cdot 29$
$43 \cdot 18 + 29$	$29 \cdot (18 + 43)$

Find the product.

$$\begin{array}{r} 2\ 6\ 8 \\ \times\quad 7\ 9 \\ \hline \end{array}$$

Evaluate. Use cancelling where possible.

$$\frac{3 \cdot 10}{5 \cdot 3}$$

$$\frac{7 + 13}{5 - 1}$$

$$\frac{5^{2}}{5}$$

$$\frac{7 \cdot 19}{19 \cdot 7}$$

Unit Wrap-Up

Match.

4 cubed	4^5
4 squared	4^1
4 to the power of 5	4^2
4 to the first power	4^3

Use the distributive property to evaluate.

$$8 \cdot (20 + 6)$$

Complete the chart.

	Base	Exponent	Repeated Multiplication	Value
5^3				
			$2 \times 2 \times 2 \times 2$	
	10			100,000
	1	5		

Match.

9	1^2	4	10^2
49	12^2	100	8^2
36	3^2	64	4^2
1	7^2	81	11^2
144	5^2	121	9^2
25	6^2	16	2^2

Unit Wrap-Up

Evaluate.

$10 - 9 + 3 \times 4$

$\dfrac{7 \cdot 9}{3 \cdot 7}$

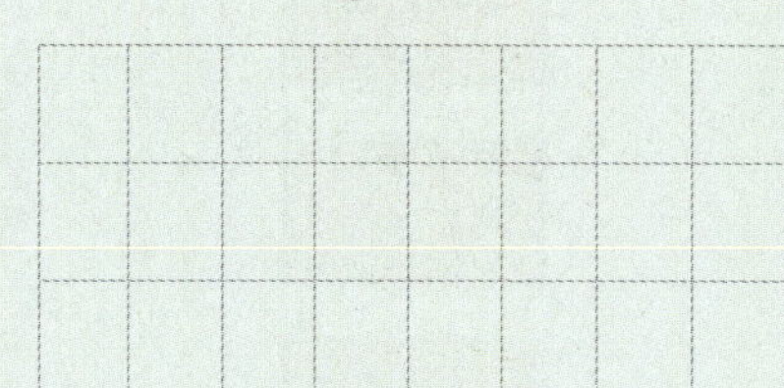

$\dfrac{8 \cdot 8 \cdot 8}{8 \cdot 8}$

$3 + 10^6$

$4^2 + 1^5$

$\dfrac{2^3 - 3}{5}$

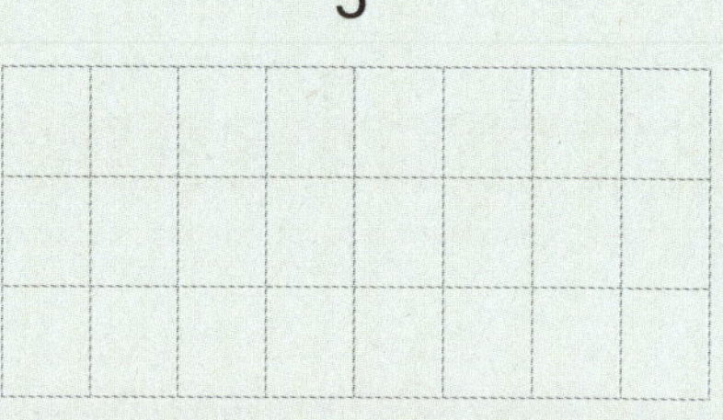

Circle the prime numbers. X the numbers that are not prime.

1	2	3	4	5	6	7	8	9	10
11	12	13	14	15	16	17	18	19	20
21	22	23	24	25	26	27	28	29	30

Use a factor tree to find the prime factorization for each number. (Write the prime factors in order from least to greatest.) Then, find the GCF.

100

64

Prime Factorizations

100 = _______________________

64 = _______________________

GCF: _______________________

Fractions

Fractions
- numerator: top number, tells number of parts

- denominator: bottom number, tells how many parts the whole was split into

$$\frac{2}{3}$$

Mixed Numbers
- combination of whole number and fraction

- multiply denominator by the whole number and add numerator

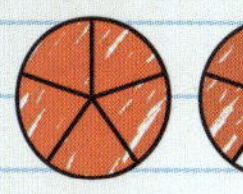

$$1\frac{2}{5} = \boxed{}$$

Improper Fractions
- numerator greater than or equal to denominator

- divide numerator by denominator

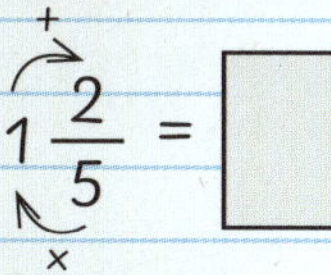

$$\frac{7}{4} = \boxed{}$$

Equivalent Fractions
- different numerator and denominator, but same value

- multiply (or divide) numerator and denominator by the same number

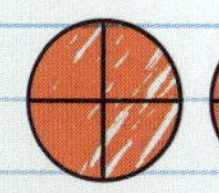 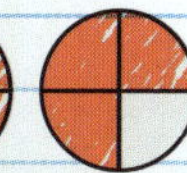

$$\frac{1}{2} \overset{\times 5}{\underset{\times 5}{=}} \boxed{}$$

Simplest Form
- equivalent fraction with the smallest numerator and denominator possible

- divide numerator and denominator by common factors (or GCF) until you can't divide anymore

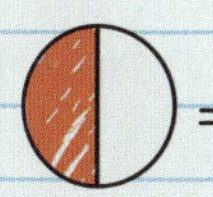 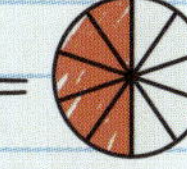

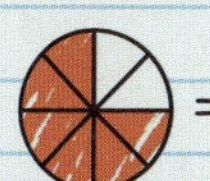 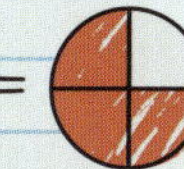

$$\frac{6}{8} \overset{\div 2}{\underset{\div 2}{=}} \boxed{}$$

Practice 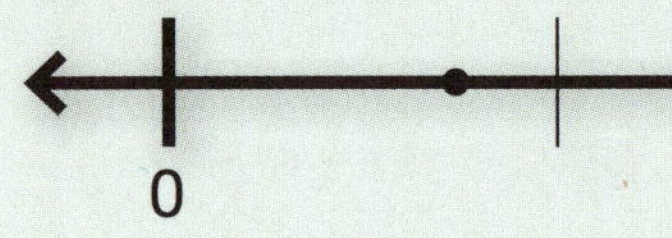

Match each number to its location on the number line. Then, compare the numbers with <, >, or =.

$\frac{7}{8}$	$1\frac{1}{10}$	$\frac{3}{8}$	$2\frac{5}{6}$	$1\frac{2}{3}$	$2\frac{1}{4}$

$$\overset{}{\longleftarrow\!\!\!\!|\!\!\!\!\underset{0}{}\!\!\!\!\underset{}{\bullet}\!\!\!\!|\!\!\!\!\underset{1}{}\!\!\!\!\underset{}{\bullet}\!\!\!\!|\!\!\!\!\underset{2}{}\!\!\!\!\underset{}{\bullet}\!\!\!\!|\!\!\!\!\underset{3}{}\!\!\!\!\longrightarrow}$$

$\frac{3}{8}\ \bigcirc\ \frac{7}{8}$	$1\frac{2}{3}\ \bigcirc\ 1\frac{1}{10}$	$1\frac{2}{3}\ \bigcirc\ 2\frac{1}{4}$	$2\frac{1}{4}\ \bigcirc\ 2$
$1\frac{1}{10}\ \bigcirc\ \frac{3}{8}$	$1\frac{2}{3}\ \bigcirc\ 2$	$2\frac{5}{6}\ \bigcirc\ 2\frac{1}{4}$	$2\frac{1}{4}\ \bigcirc\ \frac{9}{4}$

Write each mixed number as a fraction.
Write each fraction as a whole or mixed number.

$3\frac{5}{8} =$ ________ $1\frac{7}{10} =$ ________ $\frac{19}{6} =$ ________ $\frac{12}{2} =$ ________

Complete the missing number in each pair of equivalent fractions.

$\frac{4}{5} = \frac{\ \ }{15}$	$\frac{5}{7} = \frac{10}{\ \ }$	$\frac{5}{8} = \frac{\ \ }{24}$
$\frac{12}{20} = \frac{\ \ }{5}$	$\frac{4}{16} = \frac{1}{\ \ }$	$\frac{25}{30} = \frac{5}{\ \ }$

Solve.

The track is $\frac{1}{4}$ mi. long. Noah runs 11 laps.
- How far does he run? Write your answer as a fraction.

 Alexa has $2\frac{1}{2}$ L of lemonade. She pours $\frac{1}{2}$ L into each glass. How many glasses does she fill?

- How far does he run? Write your answer as a mixed number.

Review   **Find the difference. Use the example to help.**

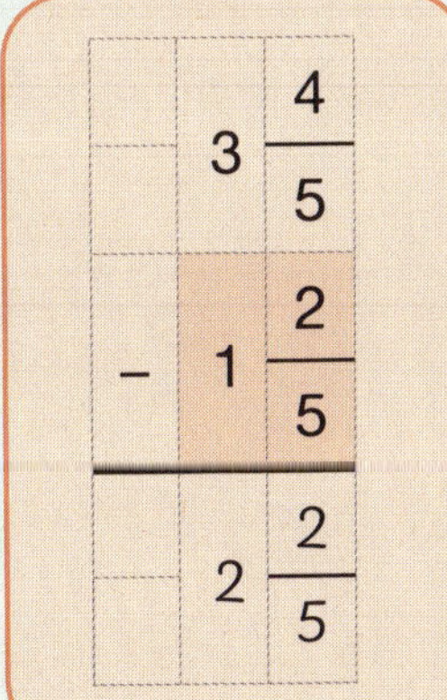

$$3\frac{4}{5}$$
$$-\ 1\frac{2}{5}$$
$$2\frac{2}{5}$$

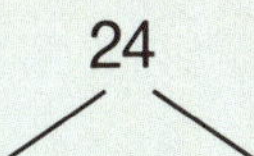

$$2\frac{2}{3}$$
$$-\ 1\frac{1}{3}$$

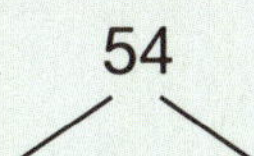

$$4\frac{7}{8}$$
$$-\ 2\frac{4}{8}$$

$$5\frac{5}{6}$$
$$-\ 3\frac{4}{6}$$

Use a factor tree to find the prime factorization for each number. (Write the prime factors in order from least to greatest.) Then, find the GCF.

24

54

Prime Factorizations

24 = ________________________

54 = ________________________

GCF: ________________________

Write whether each angle is acute, right, obtuse, or straight.

Right angles measure 90°.

Straight angles measure 180°.

Acute angles measure less than 90°.

Obtuse angles measure more than 90° and less than 180°.

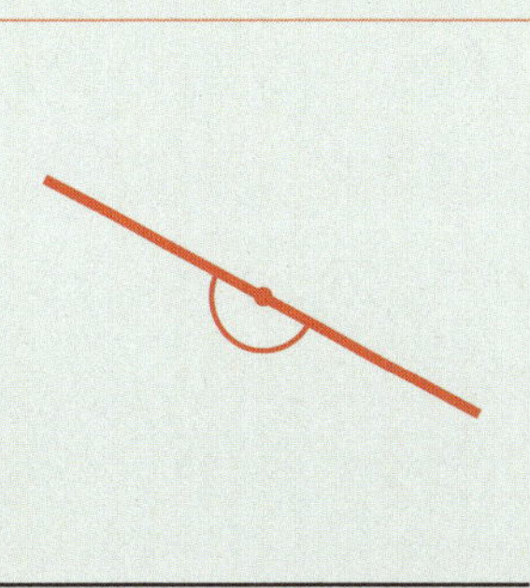

____

____

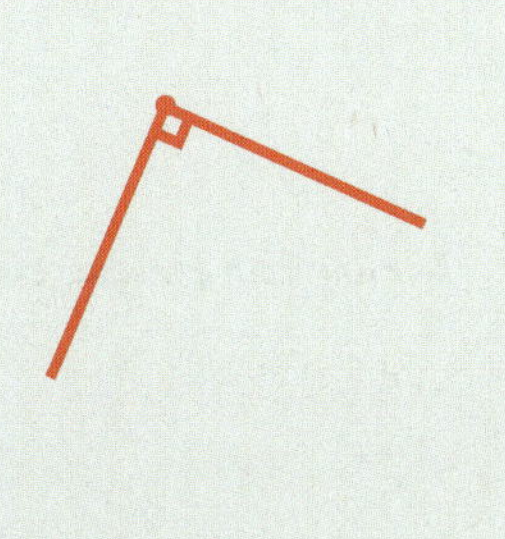

____

____

Lesson Activities 

A

$$\frac{20}{24} =$$

$$\frac{36}{60} =$$

$$\frac{35}{100} =$$

B

Use Cancelling to Simplify Fractions

The simplest form of a fraction is the equivalent fraction with the smallest numerator and denominator possible.

To find the simplest form of a fraction, divide the numerator and denominator by common factors until they have no common factors (other than 1).

Ex. Express $\frac{12}{15}$ in simplest form.

$$\frac{12}{15} = \frac{4}{5}$$

$$\frac{12}{15} \overset{\div 3}{\underset{\div 3}{=}} \frac{4}{5}$$

Ex. Express $\frac{28}{42}$ in simplest form.

$$\frac{28}{42} \rightarrow \frac{28}{42} = \frac{2}{3}$$

$$\frac{28}{42} \overset{\div 7}{\underset{\div 7}{=}} \frac{4}{6} \overset{\div 2}{\underset{\div 2}{=}} \frac{2}{3}$$

To simplify the fraction in one step, divide both the numerator and the denominator by their greatest common factor (GCF).

Ex. The GCF of 28 and 42 is 14. So, you can divide both by 14 to simplify the fraction in one step.

$$\frac{28}{42} = \frac{2}{3}$$

$$\frac{28}{42} \overset{\div 14}{\underset{\div 14}{=}} \frac{2}{3}$$

$$\frac{28}{32} =$$

$$\frac{60}{80} =$$

$$\frac{48}{100} =$$

C

Flip and Simplify (2-Player Game)

$$\frac{36}{40} =$$

$$\frac{40}{60} =$$

$$\frac{25}{50} =$$

$$\frac{24}{36} =$$

$$\frac{14}{42} =$$

$$\frac{35}{63} =$$

$$\frac{15}{45} =$$

$$\frac{28}{70} =$$

Practice

Write each fraction in simplest form.
If the fraction is already in simplest form, circle the fraction.

$\dfrac{32}{64} =$	$\dfrac{50}{60} =$	$\dfrac{35}{55} =$	$\dfrac{17}{36} =$
$\dfrac{21}{70} =$	$\dfrac{6}{19} =$	$\dfrac{80}{100} =$	$\dfrac{12}{60} =$

Create a factor tree to find the prime factorization for each number.
Then, answer the questions.

48 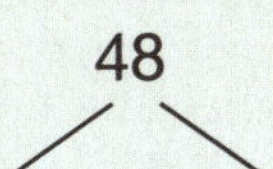

84 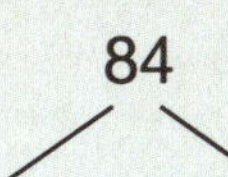

What is the GCF of 48 and 84?

Use the GCF to write $\dfrac{48}{84}$ in simplest form.

$$\dfrac{48}{84} =$$

Prime factorization of 48: ______________________

Prime factorization of 84: ______________________

Use the chart to answer the questions. Write your answers in simplest form.

What fraction of people chose strawberry?

What fraction of people chose mint chip?

What fraction of people chose cookie dough?

What fraction of people chose other?

Favorite Ice Cream Flavor
Survey Results

Flavor	Number of People
Strawberry	25
Mint Chip	17
Cookie Dough	35
Other	23
Total	100

Review

Find the difference. Use the example to help.

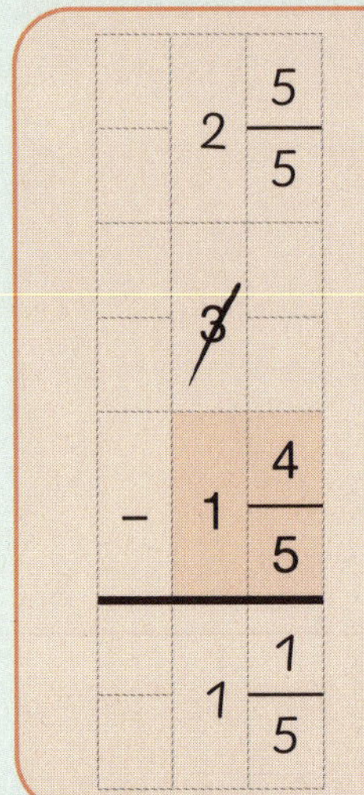

$$2\ \frac{5}{5}$$
$$\cancel{3}$$
$$-\ 1\ \frac{4}{5}$$
$$\overline{\qquad}$$
$$1\ \frac{1}{5}$$

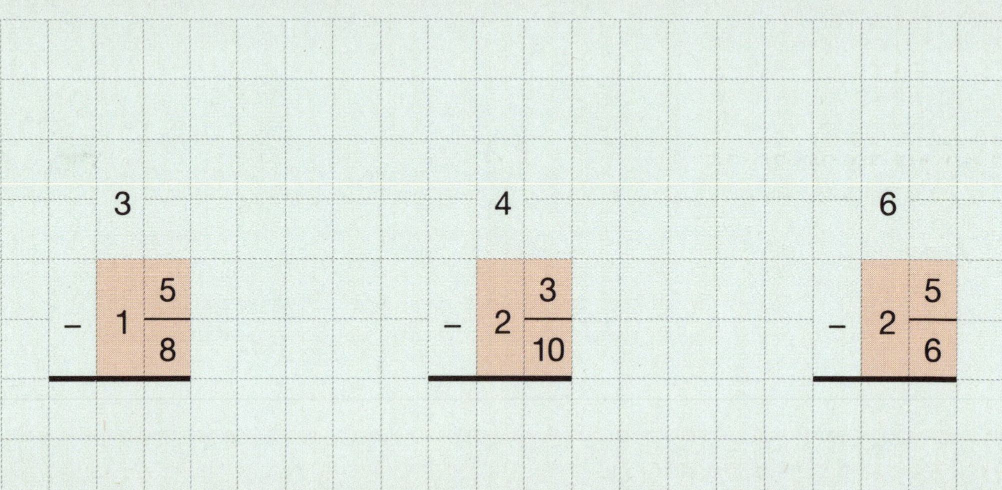

3

$$-\ 1\ \frac{5}{8}$$

4

$$-\ 2\ \frac{3}{10}$$

6

$$-\ 2\ \frac{5}{6}$$

Use the lists of multiples to answer the questions.

Multiples of 2:
2, 4, 6, 8, 10, 12

Multiples of 4:
4, 8, 12, 16, 20, 24

Multiples of 6:
6, 12, 18, 24, 30, 36

What is the least common multiple of 2 and 4?

What is the least common multiple of 4 and 6?

What is the least common multiple of 2 and 6?

Evaluate.

$$8^2 + 1 \times 6$$

$$\frac{10 \cdot 4}{5}$$

$$\frac{7 \cdot 5}{5 \cdot 7}$$

$$8 \cdot (40 + 6)$$

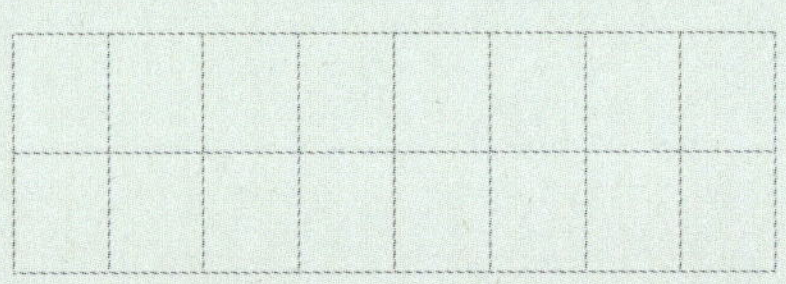

$$3^0 + 4^0 + 5^0$$

$$7^2 \cdot 10^5$$

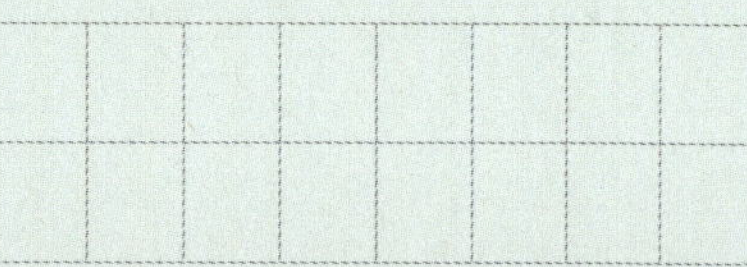

Lesson Activities 👥

LCM of 5 and 7: __________

Multiples of 5:
5, 10, 15, 20, 25, 30, 35

Multiples of 7:
7, 14, 21, 28, 35, 42, 49

Which bar of soap weighs more?

$$\frac{2}{7} =$$

$$\frac{1}{5} =$$

Find the Least Common Multiple of 3 Numbers

The least common multiple (LCM) of a set of numbers is the lowest multiple they have in common.

Make a list of the first few multiples of each number. Look for the lowest multiple they have in common.

Ex. Find the least common multiple of 4, 5, and 10.

Multiples of 4: 4, 8, 12, 16, 20, 24...

Multiples of 5: 5, 10, 15, 20, 25, 30...

Multiples of 10: 10, 20, 30, 40, 50, 60...

LCM of 4, 5, and 10: **20**

Or, make a list of the first few multiples of the greatest number. Check whether each multiple is also a multiple of the smaller numbers.

Ex. Find the least common multiple of 4, 5, and 10.

Multiples of 10: 10, 20, 30, 40, 50, 60...

20 is also a multiple of 4 and 5, so it's the least common multiple of 4, 5, and 10.

Compare 3 or More Fractions

Use the LCM as the denominator to write equivalent fractions for all the fractions you are comparing. Then, compare the equivalent fractions.

Ex. Write these fractions in order from least to greatest: $\frac{1}{4}, \frac{2}{5}, \frac{3}{10}$

$$\frac{1}{4} = \frac{5}{20} \qquad \frac{2}{5} = \frac{8}{20} \qquad \frac{3}{10} = \frac{6}{20}$$

$$\frac{5}{20} < \frac{6}{20} < \frac{8}{20}$$

$$\frac{1}{4} < \frac{3}{10} < \frac{2}{5}$$

C

Fraction Battle (2-Player Game)

Fraction to Beat	Player 1	Player 2	LCM and Equivalent Fractions
$\frac{5}{12}$	Score:	Score:	
$\frac{1}{6}$	Score:	Score:	
$\frac{3}{4}$	Score:	Score:	

Scoring Guide

If your fraction is greater than the fraction to beat: 5 points
If your fraction is greater than your opponent's fraction: 3 points
If your fraction is greater than both: 8 points

Practice

Find the LCM. Use the LCM to write equivalent fractions with a common denominator.
Then, write the fractions in order from least to greatest.

LCM of 10, 5, and 3: __________

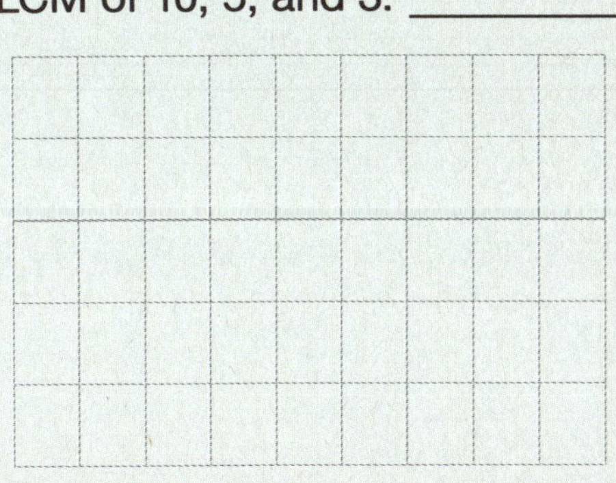

$$\frac{7}{10} =$$

__________ ← least

$$\frac{3}{5} =$$

____

$$\frac{2}{3} =$$

__________ ← greatest

Review

Find the sum or difference. Write your answers in simplest form. If the answer is an improper fraction, convert it to a whole number or mixed number.

$$\frac{4}{3} + \frac{1}{3} =$$

$$\frac{5}{8} + \frac{7}{8} =$$

$$\frac{7}{6} + \frac{5}{6} =$$

$$\frac{5}{3} - \frac{2}{3} =$$

$$\frac{11}{10} - \frac{6}{10} =$$

$$\frac{15}{4} - \frac{7}{4} =$$

Match.

4 squared	3^1	16
3 cubed	3^4	1
3 to the power of 1	4^3	3
3 to the fourth power	4^2	81
3 to the power of 0	3^3	27
4 to the third power	3^0	64

Lesson Activities

LCM of 4, 8, and 2: _______   LCM of 3, 2, and 4: _______   LCM of 6, 8, and 4: _______

How to Use Common Denominators to Add or Subtract Fractions

1. Find the least common multiple (LCM) of all denominators. You will use this number for the common denominator.

2. Rewrite each fraction as an equivalent fraction with the common denominator.

3. Add or subtract the fractions.

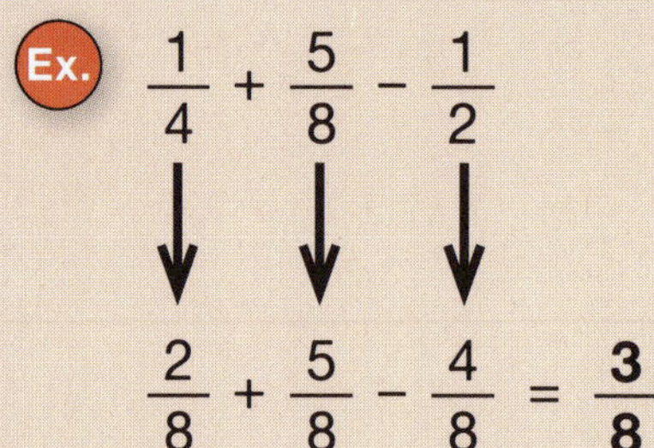

Ex. $\dfrac{1}{4} + \dfrac{5}{8} - \dfrac{1}{2}$

$\dfrac{2}{8} + \dfrac{5}{8} - \dfrac{4}{8} = \dfrac{3}{8}$

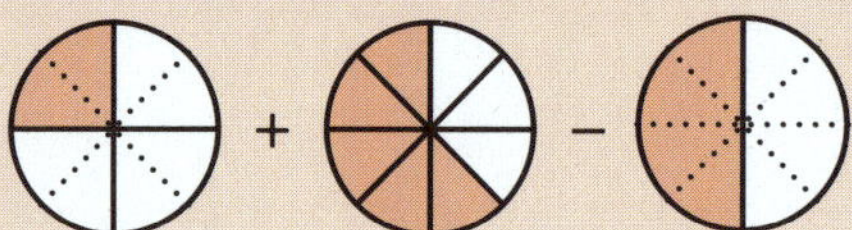

$\dfrac{1}{2} + \dfrac{1}{4} - \dfrac{3}{8}$

$\dfrac{3}{4} + \dfrac{1}{3} - \dfrac{1}{2}$

$\dfrac{5}{6} - \dfrac{3}{8} - \dfrac{1}{4}$

Leaf Fight (2-Player Game)

Player 1

Player 2

Practice

Evaluate.

LCM of 2, 4, and 6: _______   LCM of 2, 3, and 6: _______   LCM of 3, 4, and 8: _______

Evaluate. Use the LCMs (above) to help find the common denominators. Write your answers in simplest form. If your answer is an improper fraction, convert the improper fraction to a mixed number.

$\dfrac{5}{6} - \dfrac{1}{2} + \dfrac{1}{4}$

$\dfrac{1}{2} + \dfrac{2}{3} - \dfrac{1}{6}$

$\dfrac{2}{3} - \dfrac{1}{4} - \dfrac{3}{8}$

$\dfrac{7}{6} + \dfrac{2}{3} - \dfrac{3}{2}$

$\dfrac{1}{4} + \dfrac{4}{3} + \dfrac{3}{8}$

$\dfrac{3}{2} - \dfrac{5}{6} + \dfrac{5}{4}$

Solve. Write the equations you use. Write your answers in simplest form. If your answer is an improper fraction, convert the improper fraction to a mixed number.

Conan makes trail mix with $\dfrac{2}{3}$ c. of raisins, $\dfrac{1}{2}$ c. of dried cherries, and $\dfrac{3}{4}$ c. of dried apples. How much dried fruit is there in all?

Sarah has $\dfrac{9}{10}$ m of ribbon. She uses $\dfrac{1}{2}$ m to make a craft project and $\dfrac{1}{5}$ m to make a bookmark. How much ribbon does she have left?

Review

Find the difference. Use the example to help.

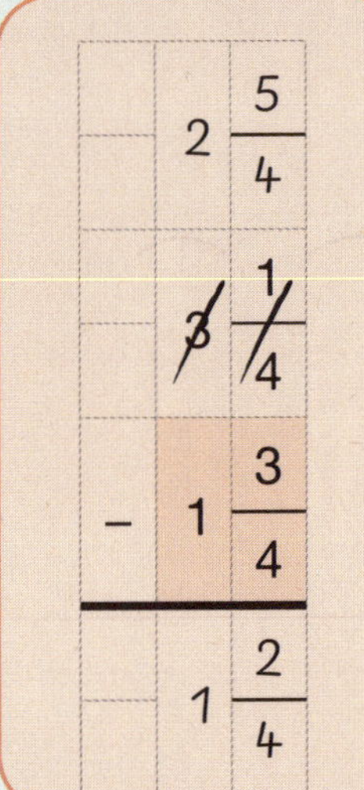

Example:
$$2\frac{5}{4}$$
$$\cancel{3}\frac{1}{4}$$
$$- 1\frac{3}{4}$$
$$1\frac{2}{4}$$

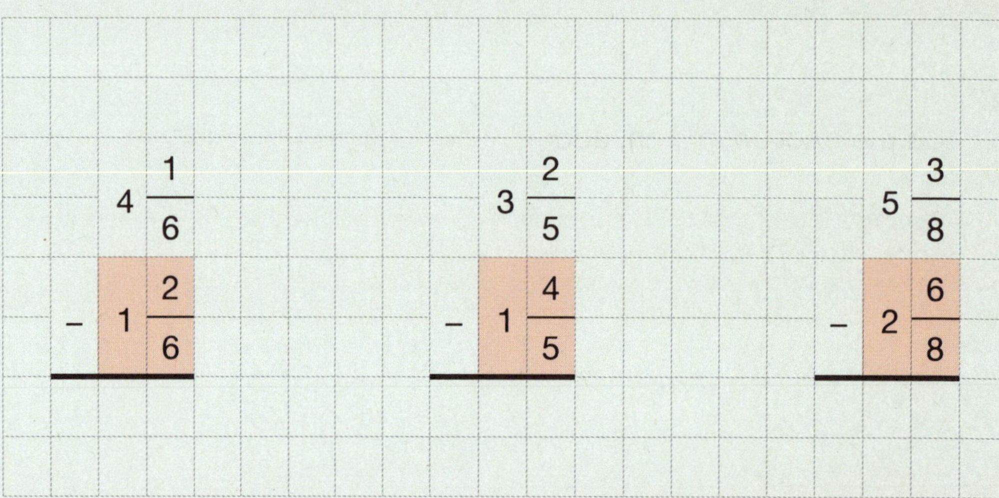

$$4\frac{1}{6}$$
$$- 1\frac{2}{6}$$

$$3\frac{2}{5}$$
$$- 1\frac{4}{5}$$

$$5\frac{3}{8}$$
$$- 2\frac{6}{8}$$

Circle the prime numbers. X the numbers that are not prime.

1	2	3	4	5	6	7	8	9	10
11	12	13	14	15	16	17	18	19	20

Use mental math to complete the chart.

Weeks	1	6		10	12	20	21	23
Days	7		56					

Solve.

Simon's closet is 6 ft. long, 3 ft. wide, and 8 ft. high. What is the volume of his closet?

Annabel has 60 books on her shelves. 36 of the books are fiction. What fraction of the books are fiction? Write your answer in simplest form.

What fraction of the books are not fiction? Write your answer in simplest form.

Lesson Activities

Add Mixed Numbers

1. Rewrite the fractions with common denominators.

2. Add the fractions. Then, add the whole numbers.

3. If you have an improper fraction in the sum, convert the improper fraction to a mixed number. Add it to the whole number.

4. Simplify if needed.

$$4\frac{4}{5} = 4\frac{8}{10}$$
$$+ 1\frac{3}{10} = 1\frac{3}{10}$$

$$2\frac{1}{3}$$
$$+ 1\frac{5}{6}$$

$$3\frac{7}{8}$$
$$+ 2\frac{1}{4}$$

Subtract Mixed Numbers

1. Rewrite the fractions with common denominators.

2. If the top fraction is less than the bottom fraction, trade 1 whole for fractional parts.

3. Subtract the fractions. Then, subtract the whole numbers.

4. Simplify if needed.

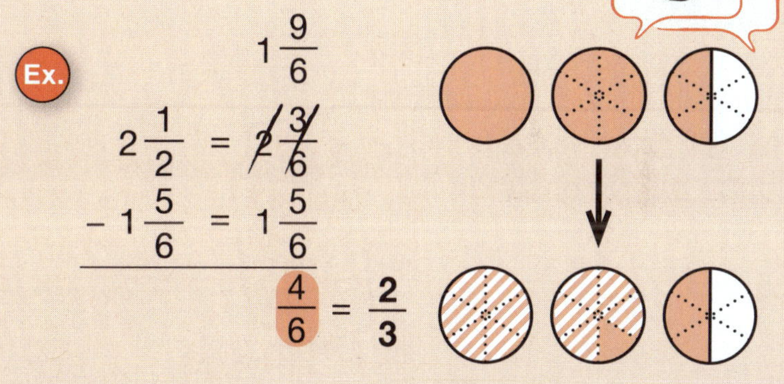

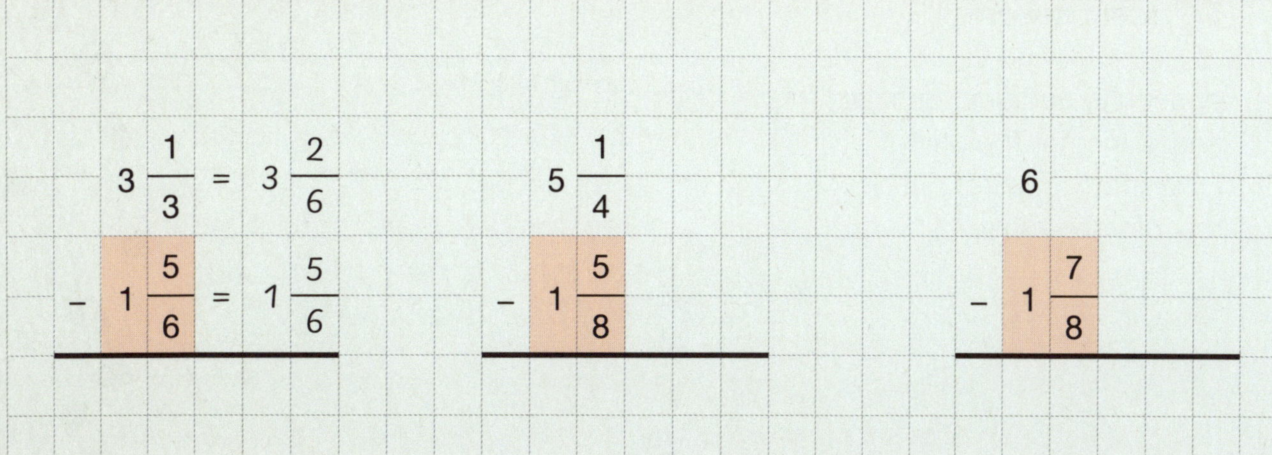

$$3\frac{1}{3} = 3\frac{2}{6}$$
$$- 1\frac{5}{6} = 1\frac{5}{6}$$

$$5\frac{1}{4}$$
$$- 1\frac{5}{8}$$

$$6$$
$$- 1\frac{7}{8}$$

Practice

Solve. Write the equations you use.
Write your answers in simplest form.

Thomas has a board $6\frac{1}{2}$ ft. long. He cuts off a piece from the board that is $2\frac{3}{4}$ ft. long. How much of the original board is left?

Maddie mixed $3\frac{1}{4}$ L of lemon-lime soda and $1\frac{5}{8}$ L of orange juice to make punch for a party. How much punch did she make?

After the party, $1\frac{1}{2}$ L of punch was left. How much punch did the party guests drink?

Maddie mixed together $5\frac{1}{2}$ c. of popcorn, $1\frac{2}{3}$ c. of peanuts, and $2\frac{1}{4}$ c. of chocolate candies to make snack mix for the party. How many cups of snack mix did she make?

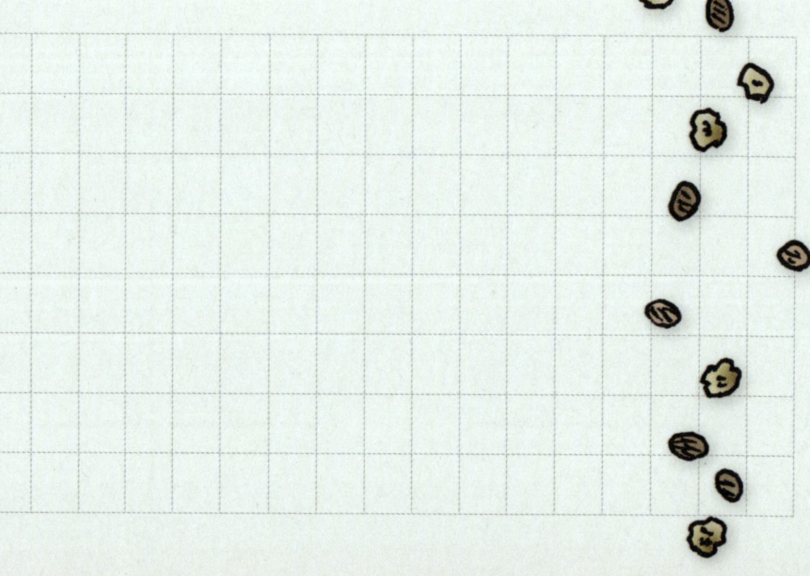

Review   **Evaluate.**

$10^2 =$ _______	$3^2 =$ _______	$9^2 =$ _______
$2^2 =$ _______	$8^2 =$ _______	$12^2 =$ _______
$7^2 =$ _______	$11^2 =$ _______	$6^2 =$ _______
$5^2 =$ _______	$1^2 =$ _______	$4^2 =$ _______

Complete.

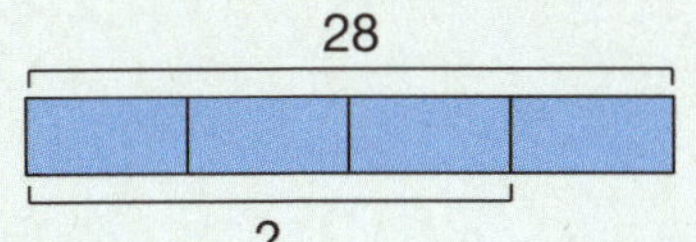

$\dfrac{3}{4}$ of 28 = _______

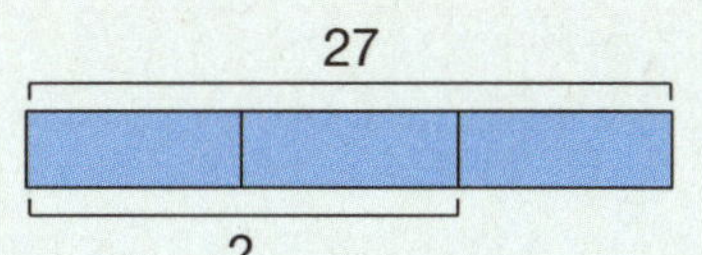

$\dfrac{2}{3}$ of 27 = _______

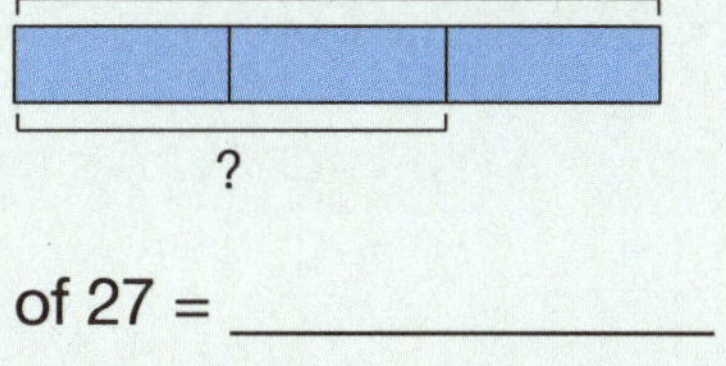

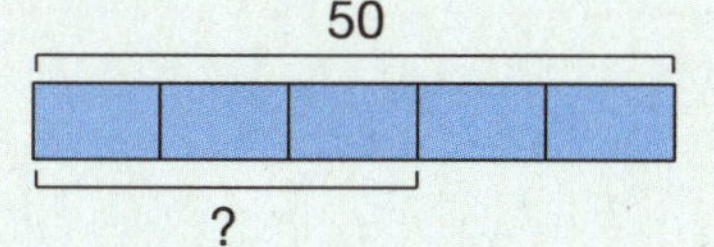

$\dfrac{3}{5}$ of 50 = _______

Draw and label each point in the correct location on the coordinate plane.

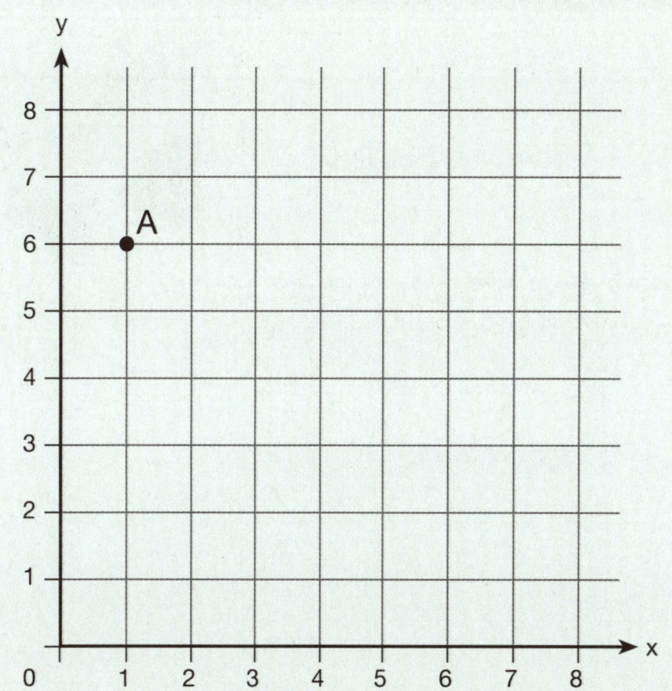

Point	Ordered Pair
A	(1,6)
B	(4,6)
C	(7,7)
D	(0,2)
E	(7,0)
F	(5,3)
G	(5,8)

2.6

Lesson Activities

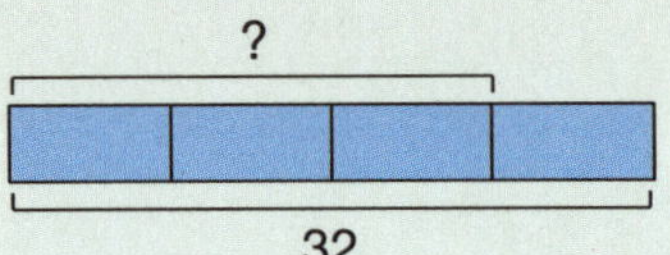

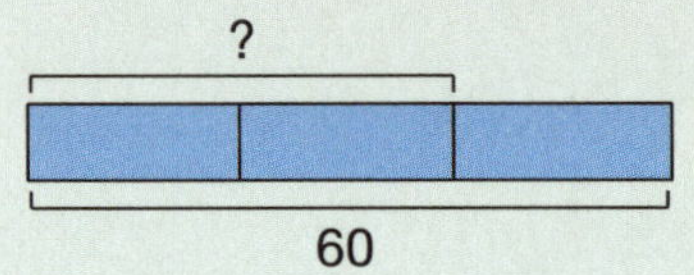

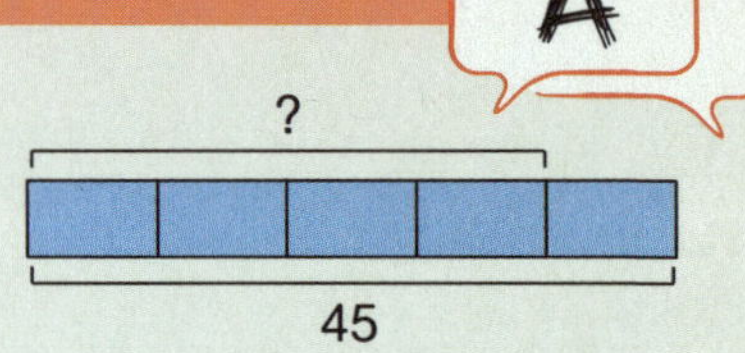

$\frac{3}{4}$ of 32 = _______________

$\frac{2}{3}$ of 60 = _______________

$\frac{4}{5}$ of 45 = _______________

Two Ways to Solve Fraction Word Problems

Ex. Aurora has \$80. She uses $\frac{3}{4}$ of her money to buy roller skates. How much money does she have left?

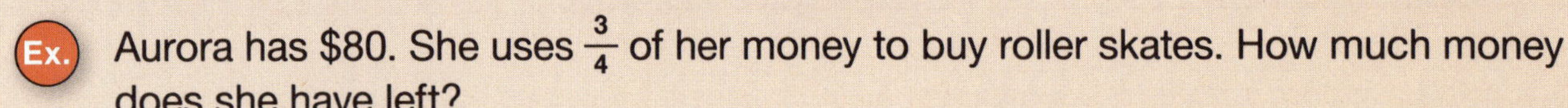

Find a Part, Then Subtract

$80 \div 4 = 20$

$3 \times 20 = 60$

$\frac{3}{4}$ of 80 is 60.

The roller skates cost \$60.

$80 - 60 = 20$

Aurora has **\$20** left.

Subtract, Then Find a Part

$1 - \frac{3}{4} = \frac{1}{4}$

If Aurora spends $\frac{3}{4}$ of her money on roller skates, she has $\frac{1}{4}$ of her money left.

$80 \div 4 = 20$

$\frac{1}{4}$ of 80 is 20.

Aurora has **\$20** left.

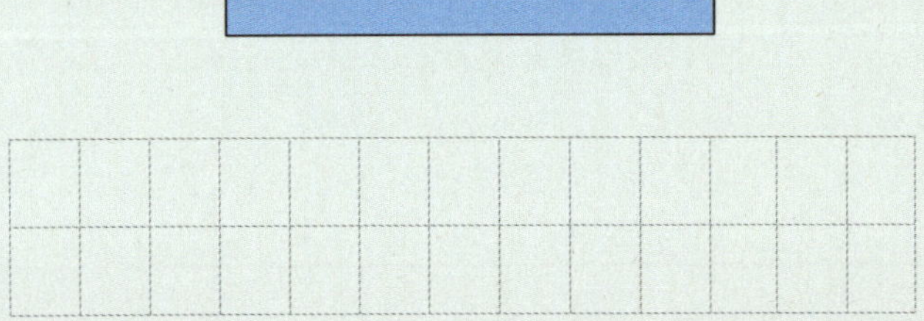

Andrew earns \$100. He decides to save $\frac{3}{5}$ of his money and spend the rest. How much money does he have to spend?

Andrew then uses $\frac{5}{8}$ of his spending money to buy a board game. How much does the board game cost?

Practice    Complete.

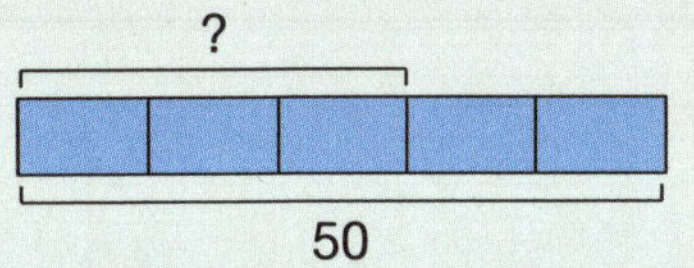

$$\frac{3}{5} \text{ of } 50 = \underline{\hspace{3cm}}$$

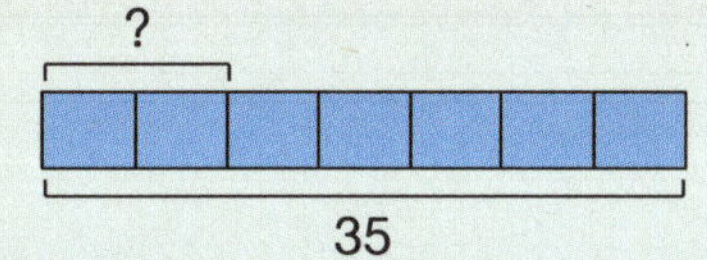

$$\frac{2}{7} \text{ of } 35 = \underline{\hspace{3cm}}$$

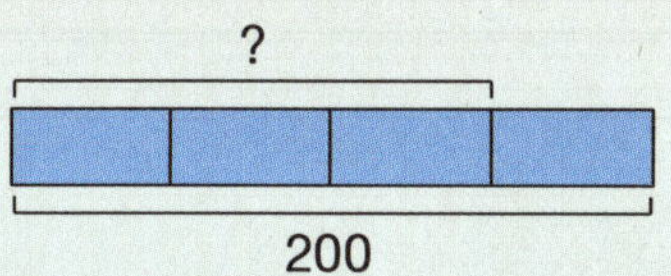

$$\frac{3}{4} \text{ of } 200 = \underline{\hspace{3cm}}$$

Use bar models to solve. Write the equations you use.

Elsie scores $\frac{1}{4}$ of her team's points at the basketball game. Her team scores 36 points. How many points do her teammates score?

Kristian has 250 baseball cards in his collection. He keeps $\frac{3}{10}$ of his cards in a binder, and the rest in boxes. How many of his baseball cards are in boxes?

Ahren buys a set of 900 interlocking plastic blocks. He uses $\frac{7}{9}$ of the set to build a plane. How many blocks does he use?

How many blocks does he have left?

★ Ahren uses $\frac{7}{10}$ of the remaining blocks to build a robot. How many blocks does he use to build the robot?

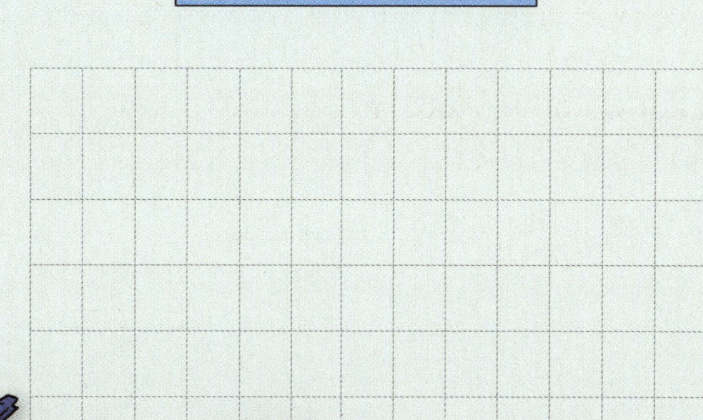

Review

Circle the fractions whose simplest form is the fraction in the star.

$\frac{1}{2}$ $\frac{4}{8}$ $\frac{6}{11}$ $\frac{7}{14}$ $\frac{5}{9}$ $\frac{40}{80}$ $\frac{100}{200}$

$\frac{1}{4}$ $\frac{2}{10}$ $\frac{3}{12}$ $\frac{4}{16}$ $\frac{7}{28}$ $\frac{30}{80}$ $\frac{25}{100}$

$\frac{1}{3}$ $\frac{4}{12}$ $\frac{4}{9}$ $\frac{8}{12}$ $\frac{7}{10}$ $\frac{5}{15}$ $\frac{10}{30}$

$\frac{2}{3}$ $\frac{6}{9}$ $\frac{9}{15}$ $\frac{14}{21}$ $\frac{3}{6}$ $\frac{40}{60}$ $\frac{15}{30}$

Use long division to complete. | Complete the missing base in each equation.

$3 \overline{)\ 5\ 7\ 8}$

$3^2 = 9$	$\square^2 = 16$
$\square^2 = 25$	$\square^2 = 100$
$\square^2 = 1$	$\square^2 = 4$
$\square^2 = 49$	$\square^2 = 144$
$\square^2 = 121$	$\square^2 = 36$
$\square^2 = 64$	$\square^2 = 81$

Find the LCM, and use the LCM to write equivalent fractions with a common denominator. Then, write the fractions in order from least to greatest.

LCM of 5, 10, and 3: __________

$\frac{4}{5} =$

$\frac{7}{10} =$

$\frac{2}{3} =$

__________ ← least

____

__________ ← greatest

Lesson Activities 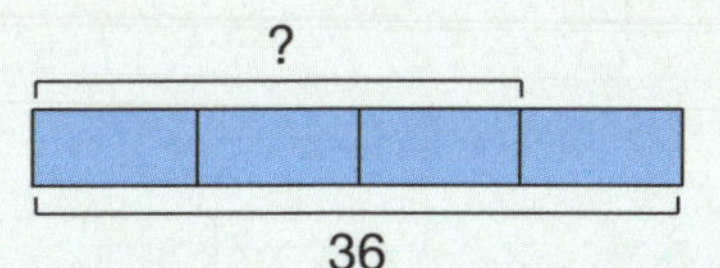

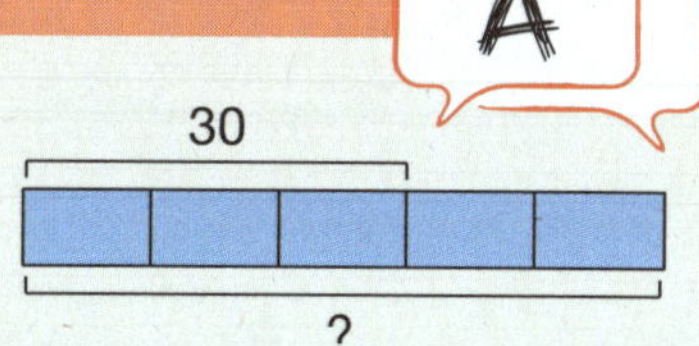

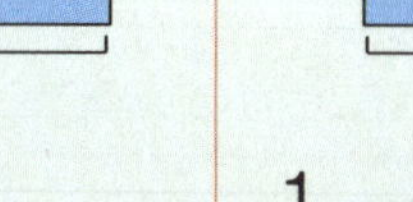

? / 36

$\frac{3}{4}$ of 36 = ______________

25 / ?

$\frac{1}{4}$ of ______________ = 25

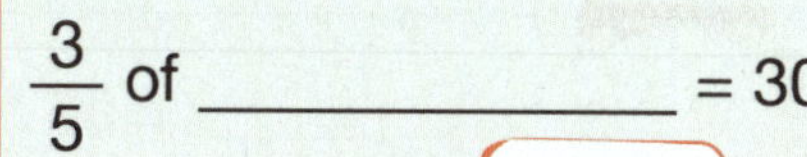

30 / ?

$\frac{3}{5}$ of ______________ = 30

Find the Whole Amount

Ex. Gideon spends $\frac{3}{4}$ of his money on a bag of marbles. The marbles cost \$18. How much money did he start with?

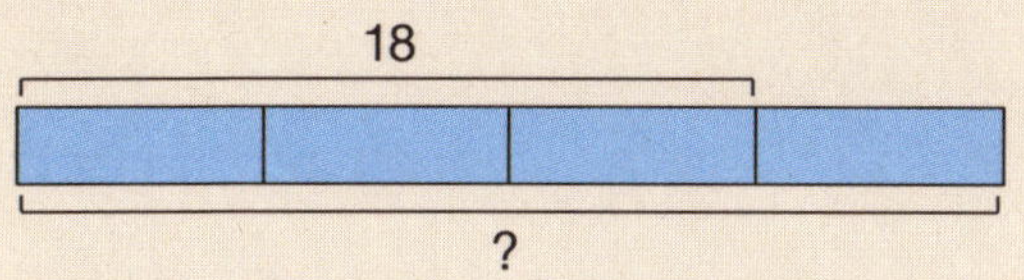

18 / ?

$18 \div 3 = 6$
Each unit bar stands for \$6.

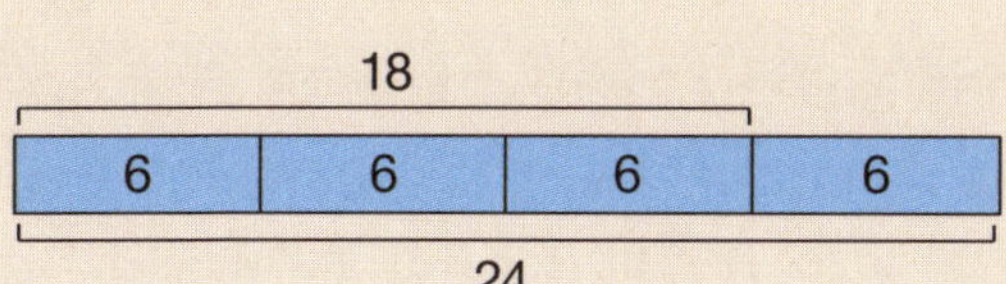

18
| 6 | 6 | 6 | 6 |
24

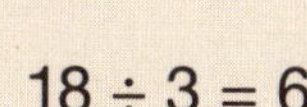

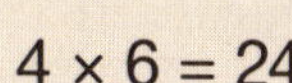

$4 \times 6 = 24$
Gideon started with **\$24**.

In a survey, 12 people said cereal is their favorite breakfast food. These 12 people were $\frac{3}{8}$ of all the people surveyed. How many people answered the survey?

Edith has completed $\frac{7}{10}$ of the pages in her scrapbook. She has completed 42 pages. How many pages are in the scrapbook?

Zipporah has a collection of porcelain dolls. $\frac{2}{5}$ of her dolls have black hair. If she has 6 dolls with black hair, how many dolls are in her whole collection?

Liam ran 32 laps around the indoor track. He sprinted for $\frac{5}{8}$ of the laps and jogged for the rest. How many laps did he sprint?

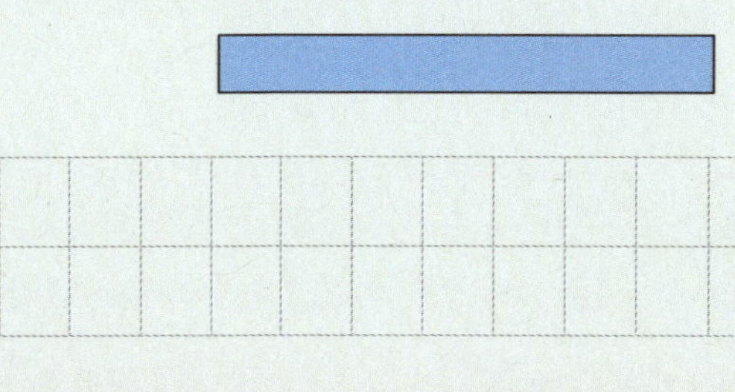

Practice

Evaluate.

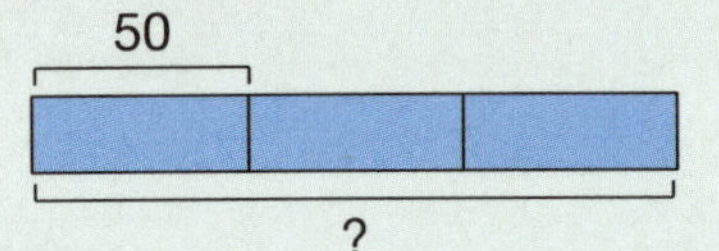

$\dfrac{1}{3}$ of _____________ = 50

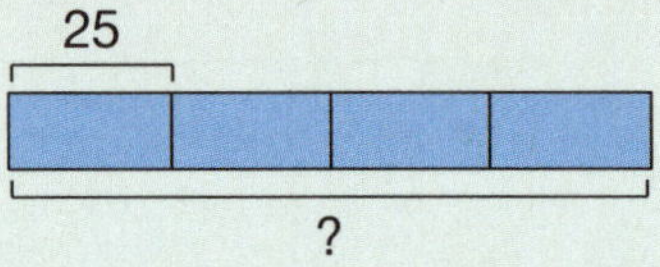

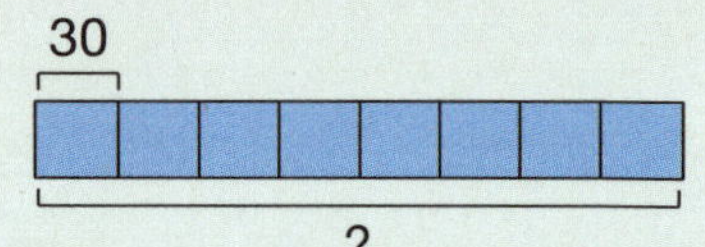

$\dfrac{1}{4}$ of _____________ = 25

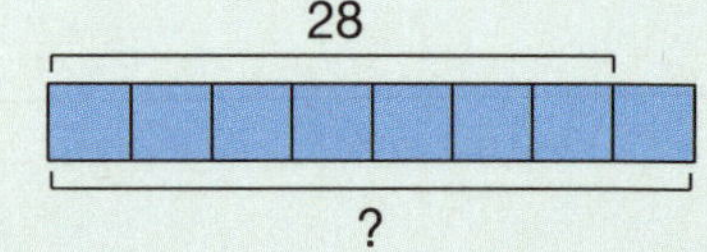

$\dfrac{1}{8}$ of _____________ = 30

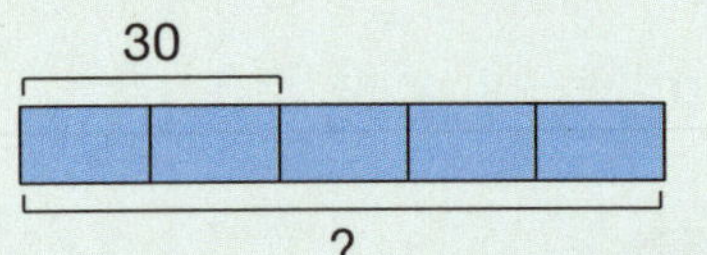

$\dfrac{2}{5}$ of _____________ = 30

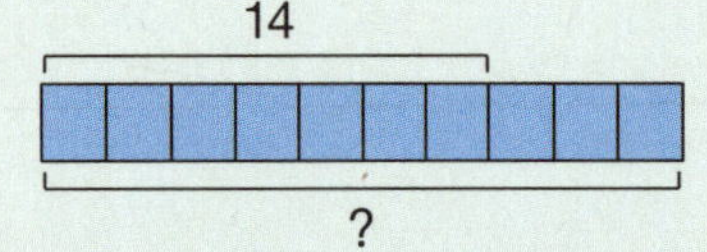

$\dfrac{7}{10}$ of _____________ = 14

$\dfrac{7}{8}$ of _____________ = 28

Use bar models to solve. Write the equations you use.

Zephaniah has visited $\dfrac{3}{10}$ of the Major League Baseball stadiums. He has visited 9 stadiums. How many stadiums are there in all?

Vivian knitted for 45 minutes. She spent $\dfrac{2}{3}$ of the time knitting a scarf and the rest of the time knitting a hat. How much time did she spend knitting the scarf?

Jacob helped his parents plant fall flowers in the garden. He planted $\dfrac{1}{3}$ of the flowers, and his parents planted the rest. Jacob planted 12 flowers. How many flowers did his family plant in all?

⭐ Cora collects horse figurines. She keeps $\dfrac{1}{5}$ of her collection on her dresser and the rest on her bookshelf. She has 16 horses on her bookshelf. How many horses does she have in all?

Review

Evaluate. Write your answers in simplest form. If your answer is an improper fraction, convert the improper fraction to a mixed number.

$$\frac{5}{6} - \frac{1}{3} + \frac{1}{2}$$

$$\frac{1}{2} + \frac{7}{10} - \frac{4}{5}$$

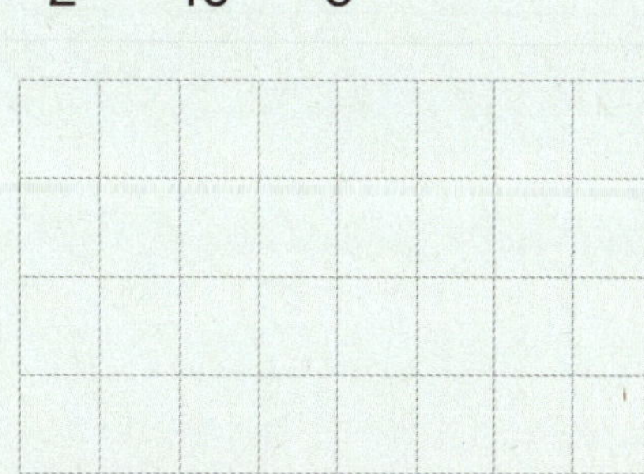

$$\frac{3}{2} + \frac{3}{4} + \frac{3}{8}$$

Match.

5 times the difference between 17 and 3	$5 \times (17 + 3)$
The product of 5 and 17, increased by 3	$5 \times (17 - 3)$
5 times the quantity 17 plus 3	$(5 \times 17) + 3$
The product of 5 and 17, decreased by 3	$(5 \times 17) - 3$

Follow the directions to find the mean and median for the data set. Write the equations you use.

How to Find the Mean (Average)

1. Add up all the numbers in the data set.
2. Divide by the number of numbers in the data set.

How to Find the Median

1. Write the numbers in order from least to greatest.
2. Choose the number in the middle.
3. If there are an even number of numbers, find the mean of the two numbers in the middle.

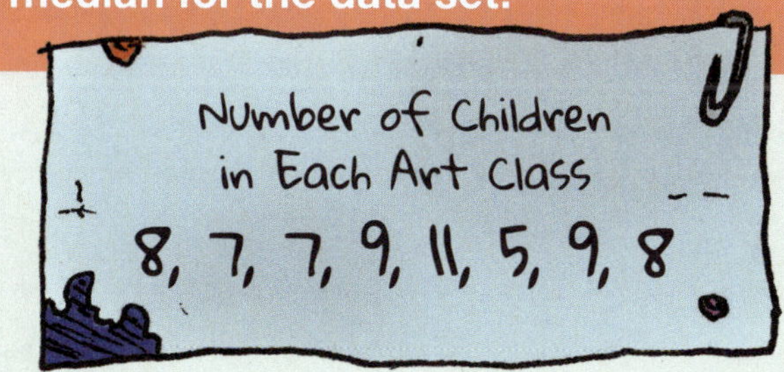

Mean: ______________   Median: ______________

Lesson Activities

Ex. Austin spends $50 on a hockey jersey. He spends $\frac{2}{5}$ as much on a pack of hockey pucks as he spends on the jersey. How much does he spend in all? How much more does the jersey cost than the hockey pucks?

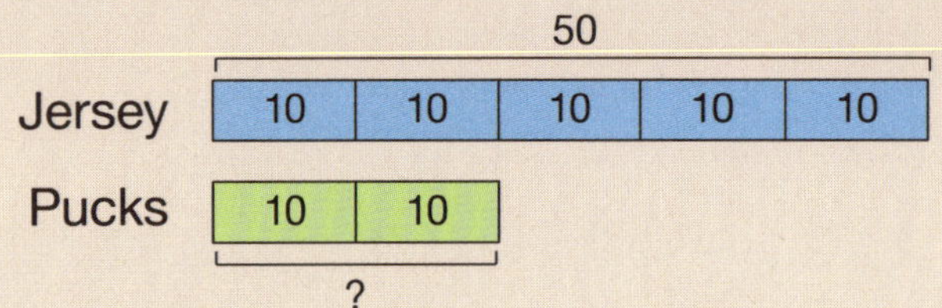

First, find the cost of the hockey pucks.

$50 \div 5 = 10$

$2 \times 10 = 20$

$\frac{2}{5}$ of $50 = 20$, so the pucks cost $20.

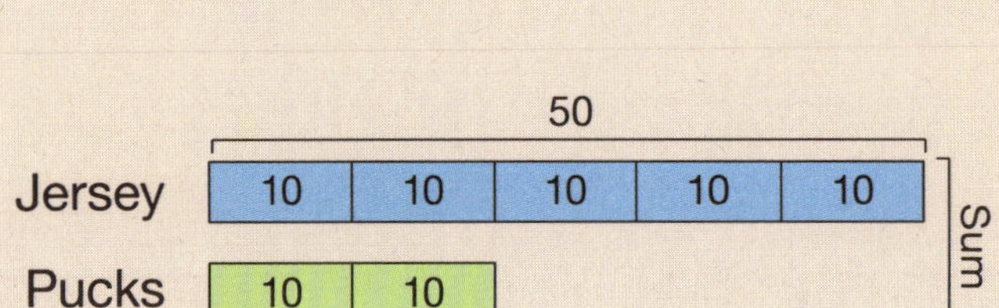

Add to find the total amount he spends.

$50 + $20 = **$70**

Subtract to find the difference between the prices.

$50 - $20 = **$30**

Bryce bakes 24 oatmeal raisin cookies for the bake sale. He bakes $\frac{3}{4}$ as many chocolate chip cookies as oatmeal raisin cookies. How many cookies does he bake in all?

How many more oatmeal raisin cookies than chocolate chip cookies does he bake?

Oatmeal raisin

Chocolate chip

Coralie bakes 90 vanilla cupcakes for the bake sale. She bakes $\frac{2}{3}$ as many chocolate cupcakes as vanilla cupcakes. How many fewer chocolate cupcakes than vanilla cupcakes does she bake?

How many cupcakes does Coralie bake in all?

Vanilla

Chocolate

Practice

Use bar models to solve.

Madelyn has 36 small rubber ducks. She has $\frac{1}{4}$ as many large rubber ducks as small rubber ducks. How many rubber ducks does she have in all?

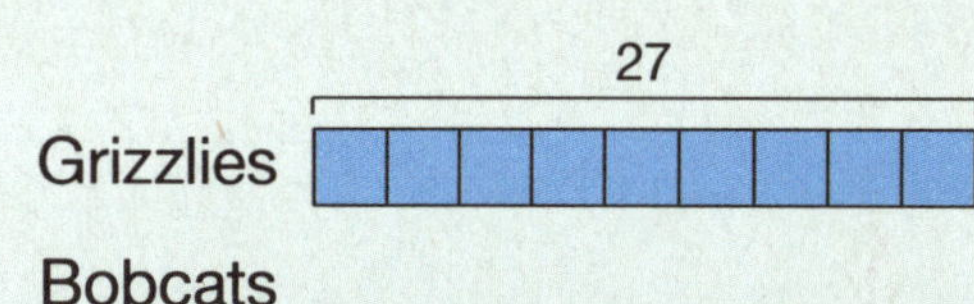

The Grizzlies scored 27 points in the football game. The Bobcats scored $\frac{7}{9}$ as many points as the Grizzlies. By how many points did the Grizzlies win?

 Latte, Parker, and Emma helped raise money for the new playground.

- Latte raised \$60.

- Parker raised $\frac{3}{5}$ as much as Latte.

- Emma raised $\frac{2}{3}$ as much as Parker.

How much money did they raise in all?

Review

Find the product.

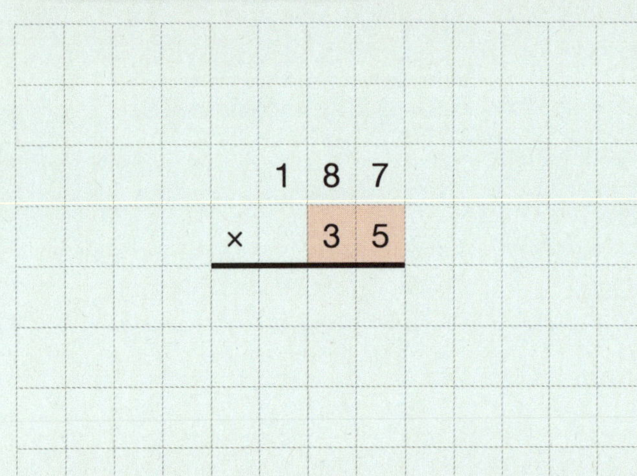

$$\begin{array}{r} 1\ 8\ 7 \\ \times\quad 3\ 5 \\ \hline \end{array}$$

Complete.

$2^4 =$ _____________ $9 \times 10^2 =$ _____________

$4^2 =$ _____________ $7 \times 10^6 =$ _____________

$1^3 =$ _____________ $42 \times 10^1 =$ _____________

$3^1 =$ _____________ $86 \times 10^3 =$ _____________

$5^0 =$ _____________ $35 \times 10^0 =$ _____________

Find the sum or difference. Write your answers in simplest form.

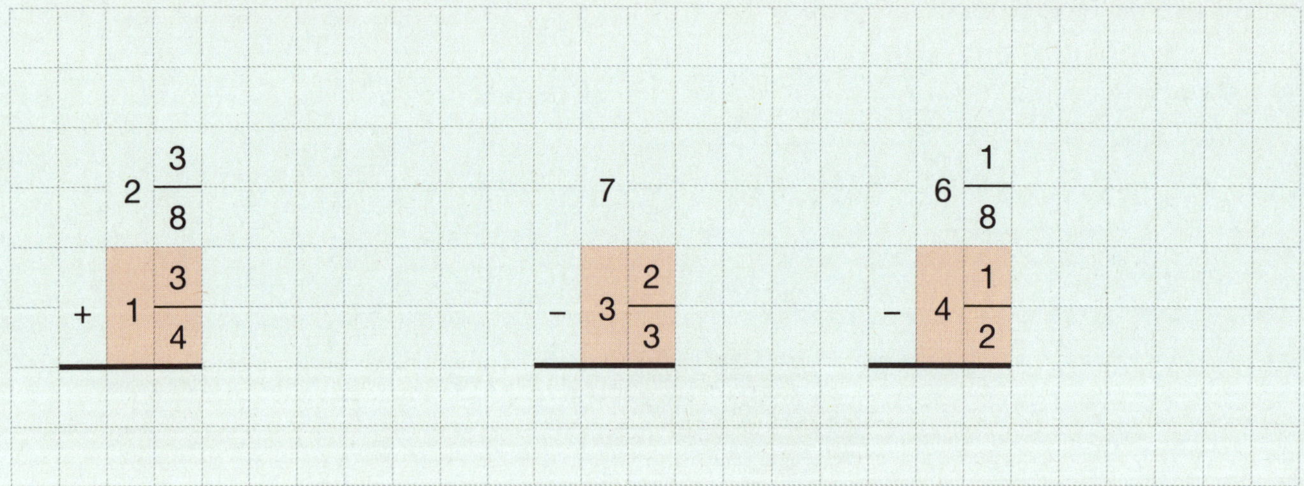

$$\begin{array}{r} 2\dfrac{3}{8} \\[2mm] +\ 1\dfrac{3}{4} \\ \hline \end{array} \qquad\qquad \begin{array}{r} 7 \\[2mm] -\ 3\dfrac{2}{3} \\ \hline \end{array} \qquad\qquad \begin{array}{r} 6\dfrac{1}{8} \\[2mm] -\ 4\dfrac{1}{2} \\ \hline \end{array}$$

Find the perimeter and area of each shape. Make sure to use the correct units.

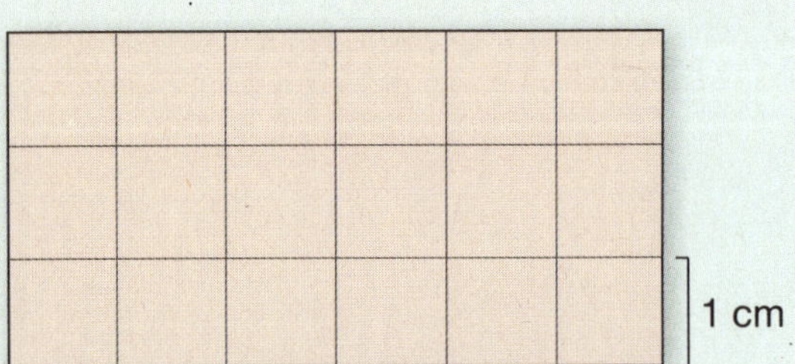

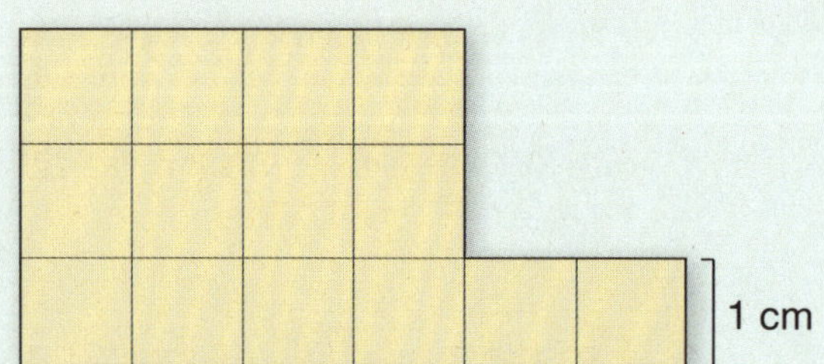

Perimeter: _________________________

Perimeter: _________________________

Area: _________________________

Area: _________________________

Unit Wrap-Up

Write each fraction in simplest form. If the fraction is already in simplest form, circle the fraction.

$\dfrac{15}{20} =$	$\dfrac{6}{14} =$	$\dfrac{9}{21} =$	$\dfrac{8}{15} =$
$\dfrac{16}{64} =$	$\dfrac{75}{100} =$	$\dfrac{19}{20} =$	$\dfrac{20}{36} =$

Find the LCM. Then, use the LCM to evaluate the expressions. Write your answers in simplest form.

LCM of 6, 5, and 3: __________

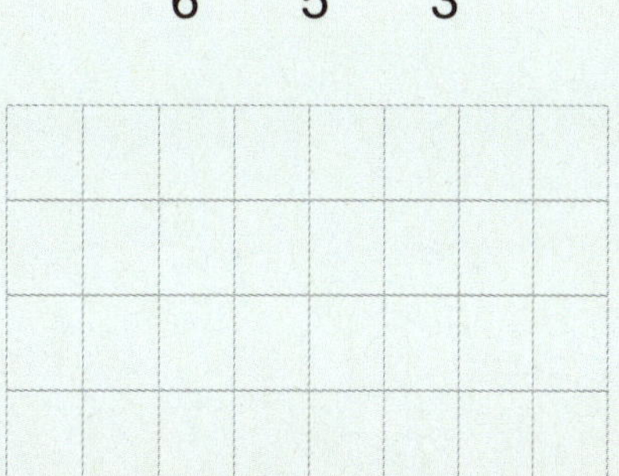

$$\frac{5}{6} + \frac{2}{5} - \frac{1}{3}$$

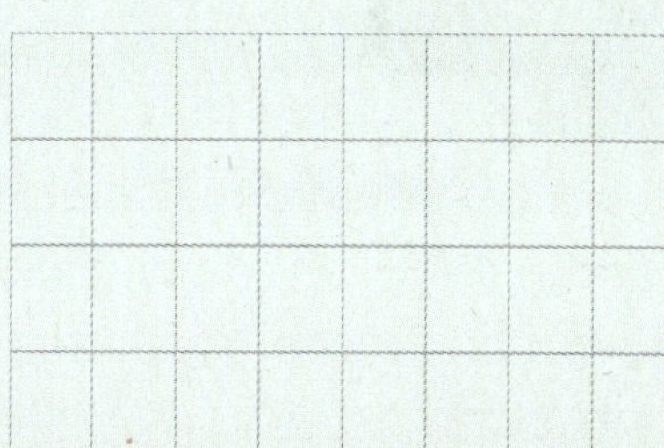

$$\frac{4}{3} - \frac{3}{5} - \frac{1}{6}$$

Solve. Write the equations you use. Write your answers as a mixed number in simplest form.

Moira is making a queen costume. She uses $3\frac{1}{4}$ yd. of blue fabric and $1\frac{2}{3}$ yd. of green fabric. How many yards of fabric does she use in all?

How many more yards of blue fabric than green fabric does she use?

Unit Wrap-Up  **Use bar models to solve.**

Emery has $40. She spends $\frac{3}{5}$ of her money at the movie theater. How much money does she have left?

Judah collects shells. $\frac{3}{10}$ of his shells are snail shells, and the rest are from other creatures. He has 12 snail shells. How many shells does he have in all?

At soccer practice, Daniel kicks 30 goals. Eliza kicks $\frac{5}{6}$ as many goals as Daniel. How many more goals does Daniel kick than Eliza?

Daniel

Eliza

Abby read 36 fiction books last year. She read $\frac{1}{3}$ as many non-fiction books as fiction books. How many fiction and non-fiction books did Abby read in all?

Fiction

Non-Fiction

 $\frac{2}{3}$ of the non-fiction books were about horses. How many books about horses did Abby read?

Lesson Activities 

Formulas for the Perimeter and Area of a Rectangle

A formula is an equation that describes a mathematical rule. We can use words or letters to write formulas.

Perimeter = length + width + length + width
$$P = l + w + l + w$$

Area = length · width
$$A = l \cdot w$$

Ex. Find the area and perimeter of the rectangle.

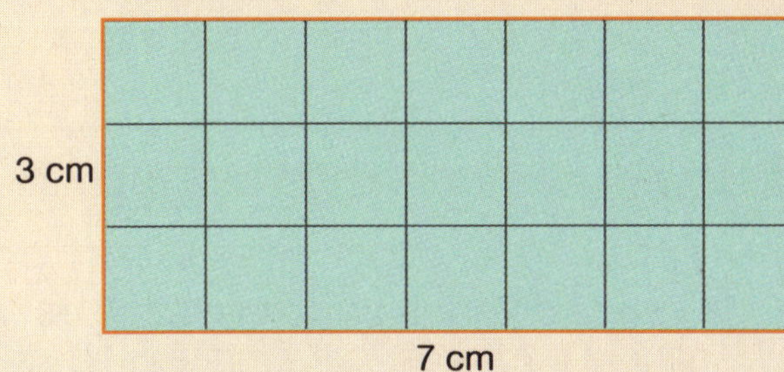

$P = l + w + l + w$
$P = 7 \text{ cm} + 3 \text{ cm} + 7 \text{ cm} + 3 \text{ cm}$
$P = \mathbf{20 \text{ cm}}$

$A = l \cdot w$
$A = 7 \text{ cm} \cdot 3 \text{ cm}$
$A = \mathbf{21 \text{ sq. cm}}$

	Length (l)	Width (w)	Perimeter ($l + w + l + w$)	Area ($l \cdot w$)
A	7	5		
B		2		18
C	5		18	
D			14	6
E			22	24

Practice

Complete the charts.

Length (l)	Width (w)	Perimeter (l + w + l + w)
9	1	
5	5	
7	3	
10	10	
25	4	

Length (l)	Width (w)	Area (l · w)
9	1	
5	5	
7	3	
10	10	
25	4	

Complete the drawing challenges.

Draw 3 different rectangles that each have an area of 12 square units.

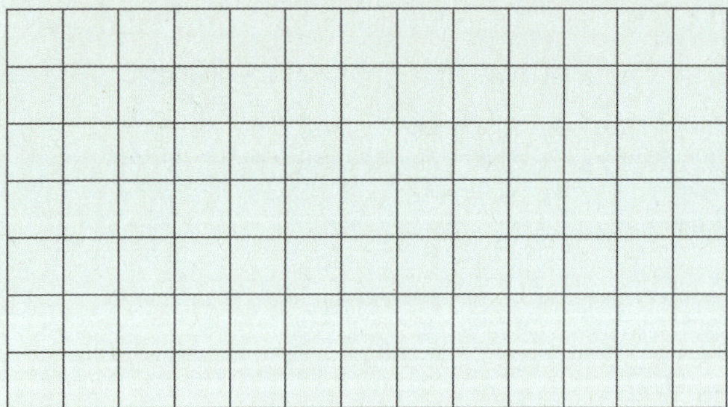

Draw 3 different rectangles that each have a perimeter of 12 units.

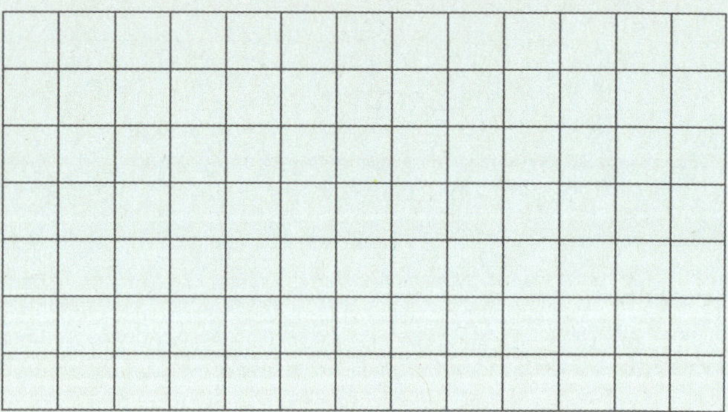

Solve. Write the equations you use.

The rectangular rug is $8\frac{1}{2}$ ft. long and $3\frac{1}{2}$ ft. wide. What is the perimeter of the rug?

★ The bedroom is shaped like a rectangle. It is 18 ft. long. Its width is $\frac{2}{3}$ as long as its length. What is the area of the bedroom floor?

Review

Write whether each angle is acute, right, or obtuse.

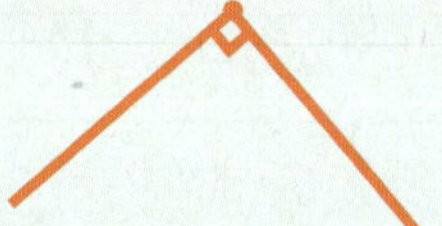

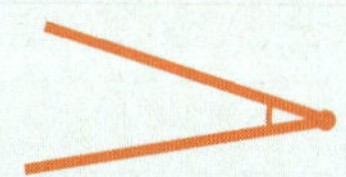

____

____

____

Evaluate. Write your answer in simplest form.

Write each fraction as a decimal. Use the decimal squares to help.

$$\frac{4}{5} - \frac{3}{10} + \frac{7}{20}$$

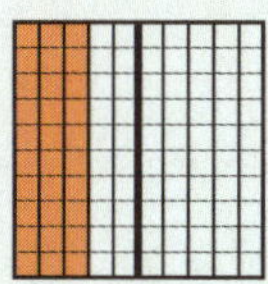

$$\frac{3}{10} = \underline{\quad 0.3 \quad}$$

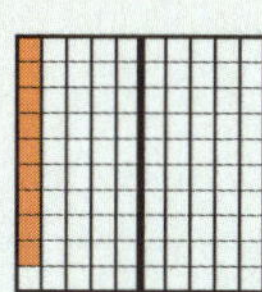

$$\frac{9}{100} = \underline{\qquad}$$

$$\frac{3}{4} + \frac{3}{16} - \frac{7}{8}$$

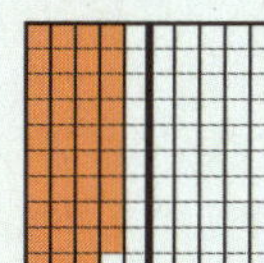

$$\frac{39}{100} = \underline{\qquad}$$

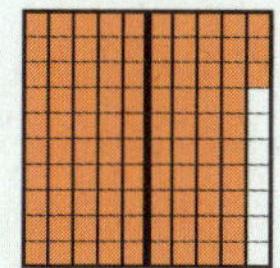

$$\frac{93}{100} = \underline{\qquad}$$

Solve. Write the equations you use.

Marleigh spent 90 minutes at the barn. She spent $\frac{1}{6}$ of the time grooming her horse and the rest of the time riding her horse. How many minutes did she spend riding her horse?

Jordyn's mom buys a 5 lb. bag of dried beans. She uses $2\frac{1}{3}$ lb. of the beans to make soup. How many pounds of beans does she have left?

Lesson Activities

$$\frac{17 \cdot 17}{17} =$$

$$\frac{19 \cdot 23}{23 \cdot 19} =$$

$$\frac{9 \cdot 8 \cdot 9}{8 \cdot 9} =$$

$$\frac{9 \cdot 4}{4 \cdot 3} =$$

Multiply and Divide Units

When we multiply or divide measurements, we multiply or divide the measurement units, too. The units follow the same rules as numbers.

Ex. The garden is 7 ft. by 4 ft. What is the area of the garden?

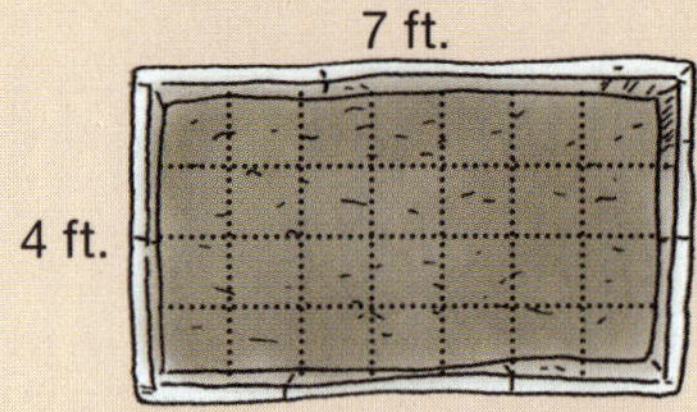

$$7 \text{ ft.} \times 4 \text{ ft.} = 28 \text{ ft.}^2$$

We can use exponents to show the product of the same unit. An exponent of 2 means square units.

Ex. The photo has an area of 96 cm^2 and a width of 8 cm. What is the length of the photo?

$$\frac{96 \text{ cm}^2}{8 \text{ cm}} = \frac{96 \text{ cm} \cdot \text{cm}}{8 \text{ cm}} = 12 \text{ cm}$$

If the same unit is above and below the fraction bar, we can cancel.

Ex. Everly has 20 ft. of ribbon. She cuts the ribbon into 4 equal pieces. How long is each piece?

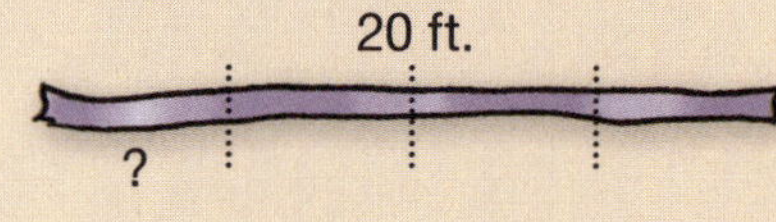

$$\frac{20 \text{ ft.}}{4} = 5 \text{ ft.}$$

Numbers that tell the number of groups or parts do not have a unit.

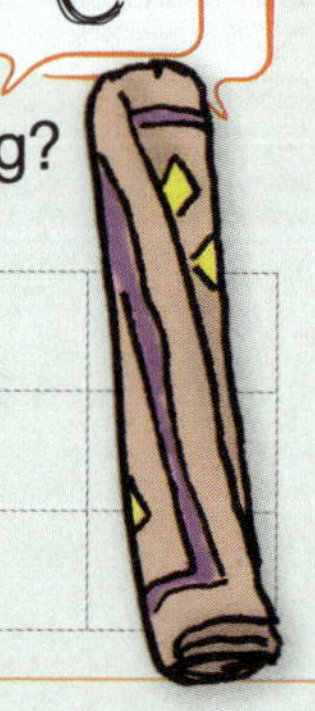

The garden is 9 m long and 6 m wide. What is the area of the garden?

The rug is 8 ft. long. It has an area of 40 ft.^{2}. How wide is the rug?

Millie has 9 rolls of tape. Each roll has 6 m of tape. How much tape does Millie have?

Walker has a piece of cloth with an area of 40 ft.^{2}. He cuts the cloth into 8 equal pieces. What is the area of each piece?

Practice

Complete the missing units to answer the questions. Leave the blank empty if the number tells the number of groups or parts. Use exponents for square units.

The rectangle is 8 cm by 6 cm. What is its area?	Each side of the hexagon is 8 in. long. What is the hexagon's perimeter?	Each side of the octagon is 6 in. long. What is the octagon's perimeter?

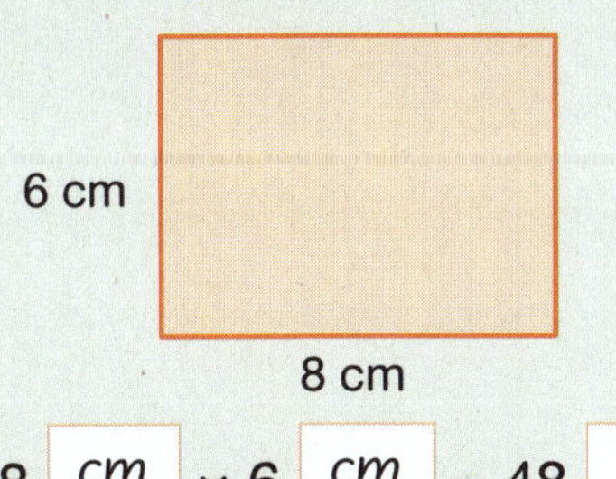

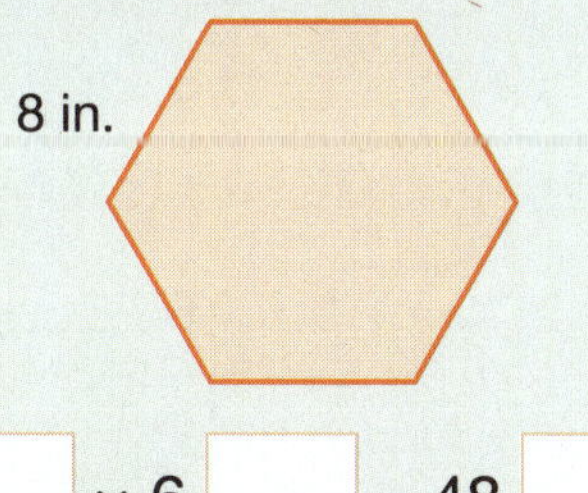

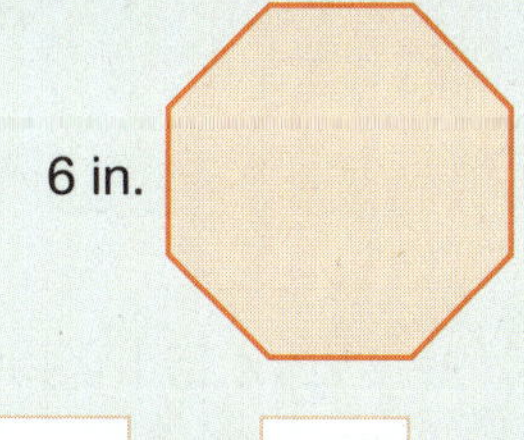

8 [cm] × 6 [cm] = 48 [ ]   8 [ ] × 6 [ ] = 48 [ ]   8 [ ] × 6 [ ] = 48 [ ]

The rectangle has an area of 40 ft.^{2}. It is 4 ft. wide. What is its length?	The rectangle has an area of 40 ft.^{2}. If you split it into 4 equal pieces, what is the area of each piece?	The rectangle has an area of 40 ft.^{2}. If you cut it into pieces that each have an area of 4 ft.^{2}, how many pieces do you make?

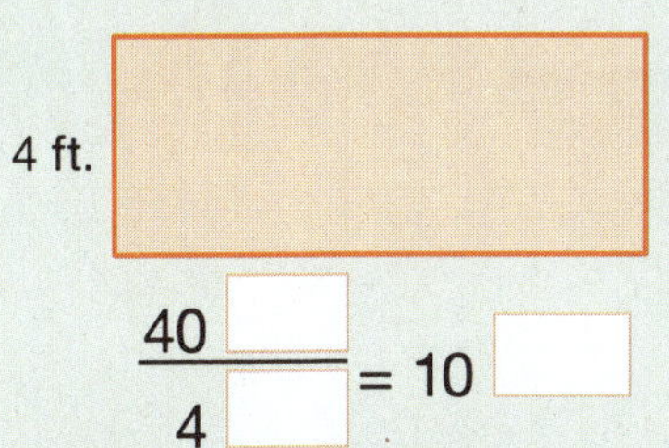

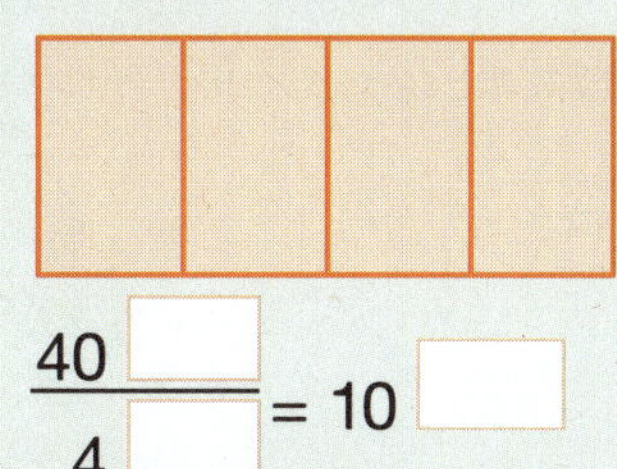

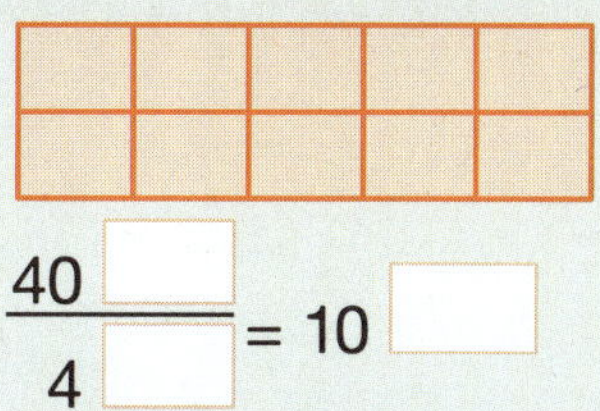

$$\frac{40\ [\ ]}{4\ [\ ]} = 10\ [\ ] \qquad \frac{40\ [\ ]}{4\ [\ ]} = 10\ [\ ] \qquad \frac{40\ [\ ]}{4\ [\ ]} = 10\ [\ ]$$

The rope is 30 m long. If you split it into 5 equal parts, how long is each part?	The rope is 30 m long. If you cut it into pieces that are each 5 meters, how many pieces do you get?	The pentagon has a perimeter of 30 m. All sides of the pentagon are equal. How long is each side?

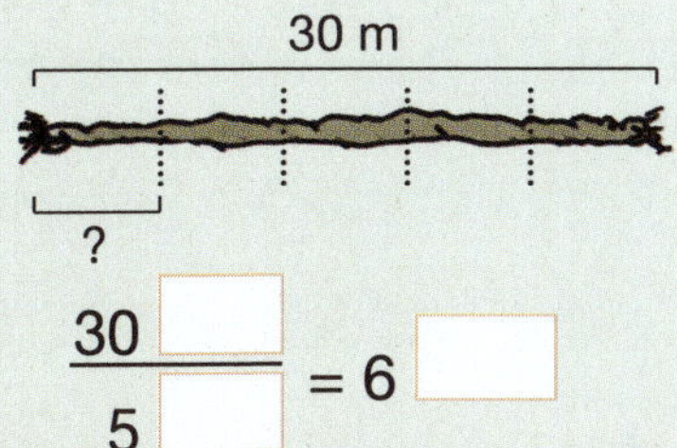

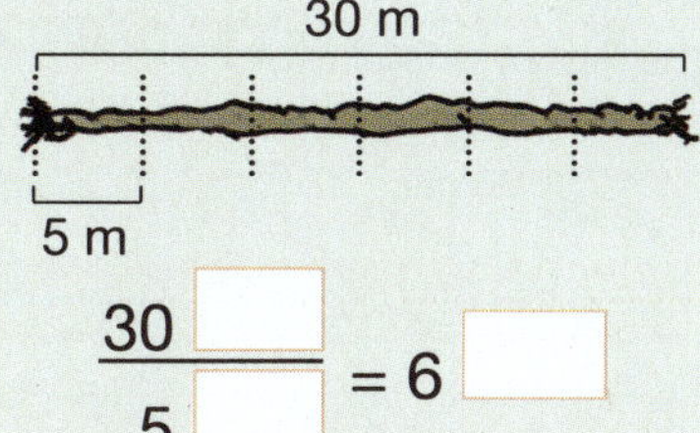

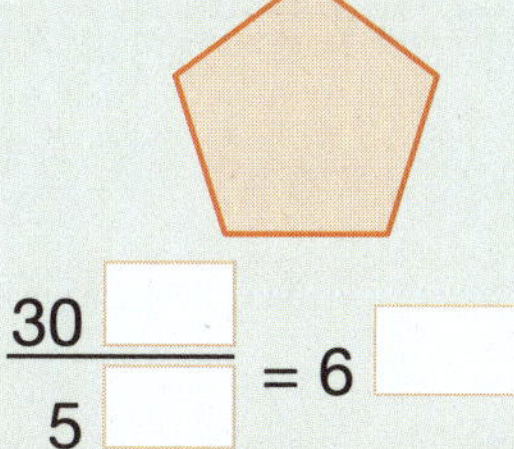

$$\frac{30\ [\ ]}{5\ [\ ]} = 6\ [\ ] \qquad \frac{30\ [\ ]}{5\ [\ ]} = 6\ [\ ] \qquad \frac{30\ [\ ]}{5\ [\ ]} = 6\ [\ ]$$

Complete. Make sure to include the correct units.

15 × 20 ft. = __________	15 ft. × 20 = __________	15 ft. × 20 ft. = __________

$$\frac{180\text{ m}^2}{30\text{ m}^2} = \underline{\qquad} \qquad \frac{180\text{ m}^2}{30\text{ m}} = \underline{\qquad} \qquad \frac{180\text{ m}^2}{30} = \underline{\qquad}$$

Review

Color the decimal squares to match.
Then, complete the circles with <, >, or =.

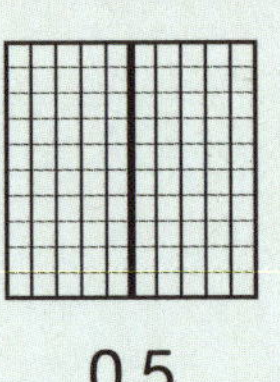 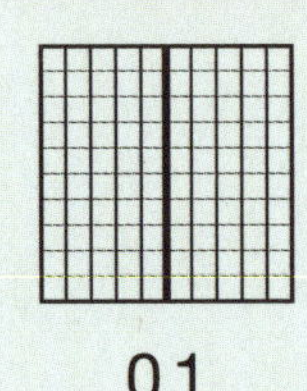 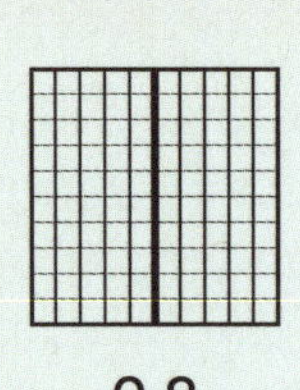

0.5   0.1   0.8

0.5 ◯ 0.1

0.1 ◯ 0.8

0.5 ◯ 0.8

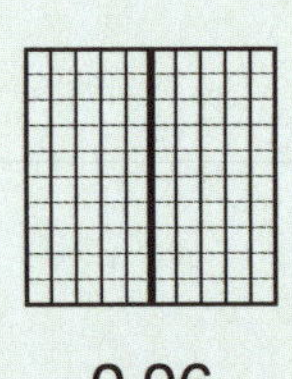 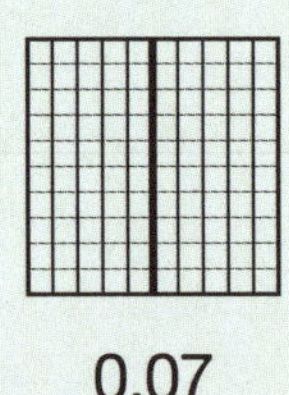 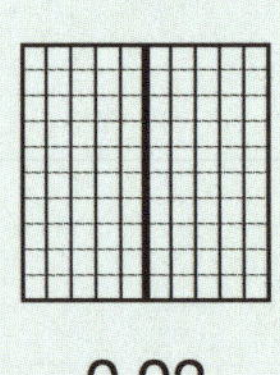

0.06   0.07   0.02

0.06 ◯ 0.07

0.07 ◯ 0.02

0.06 ◯ 0.02

Match each shape to the name and definition that most specifically describe it.

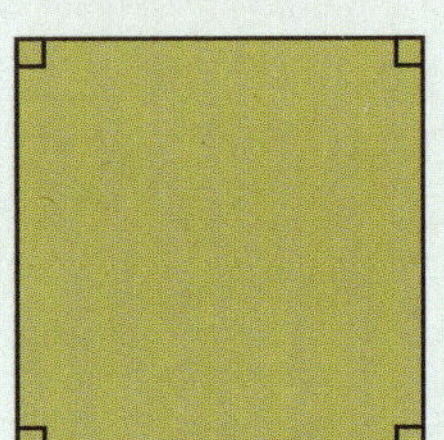  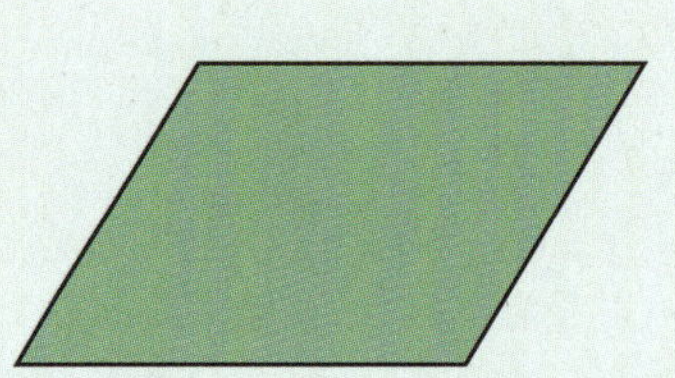 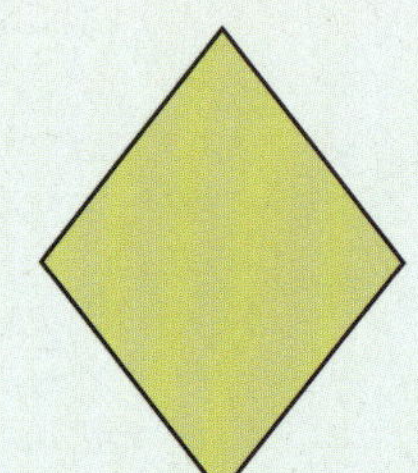

Rectangle
(4 right angles)

Parallelogram
(2 pairs of
parallel sides)

Rhombus
(2 pairs of
parallel sides and
4 equal sides)

Square
(4 equal sides
and 4 right
angles)

Label the missing sides. Then, find the perimeter and area.

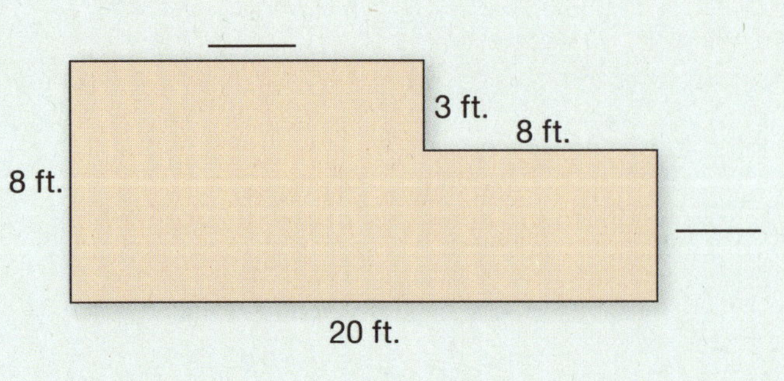

Perimeter: ___________   Area: ___________

Lesson Activities

Area of a Parallelogram

Any parallelogram can be transformed into a rectangle. Just cut off the right triangle at one end and move it to the other end! You create a rectangle with the same base and height as the parallelogram.

To find the area of a parallelogram, multiply the base by the height.

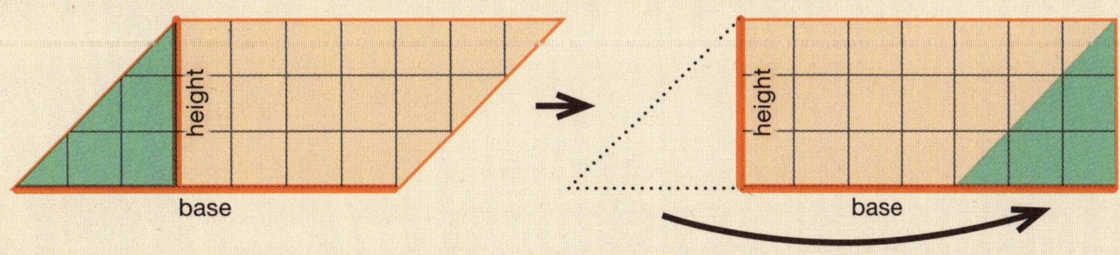

Area = base · height
$$A = b \cdot h$$

Ex. What is the area of this parallelogram?

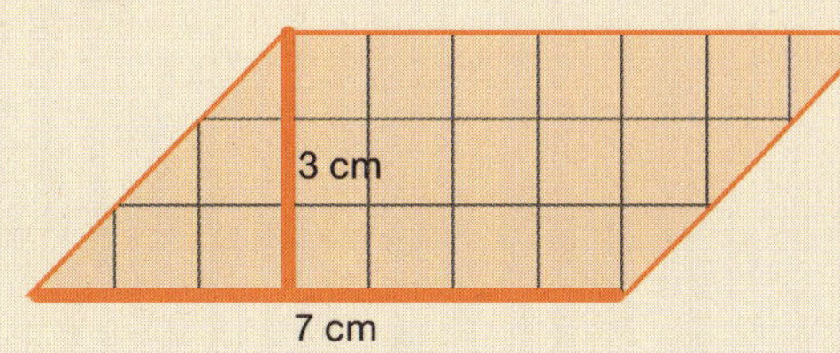

$A = 7 \text{ cm} \cdot 3 \text{ cm}$
$A = \textbf{21 cm}^2$

Parallelogram Pick (2-Player Game)

Practice

Find the area of each parallelogram.

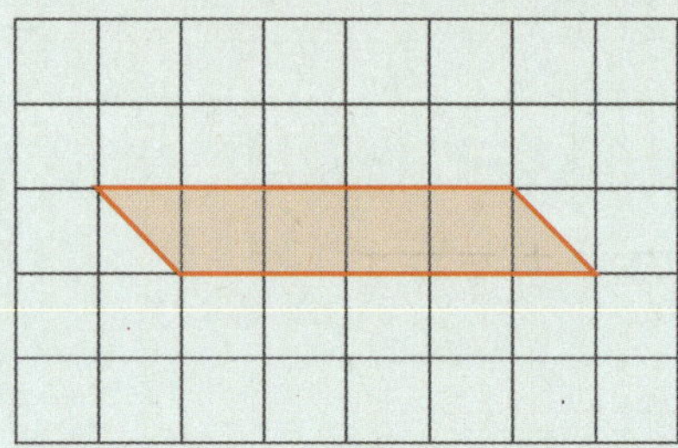

Area: _____________ units ^{2}

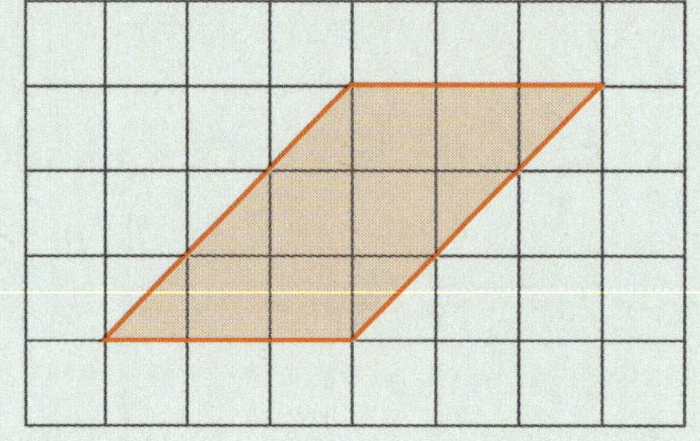

Area: _____________ units ^{2}

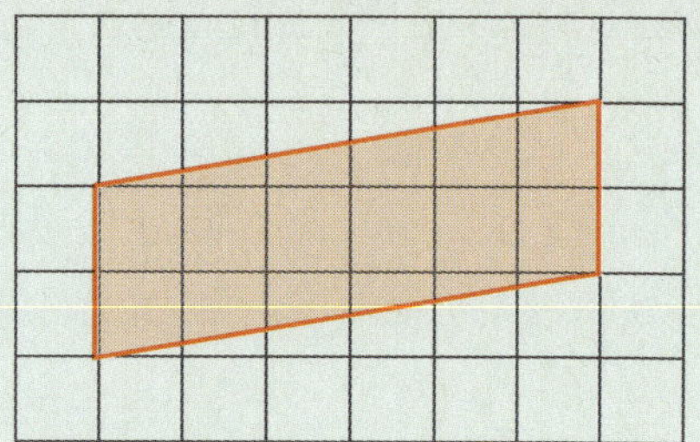

Area: _____________ units ^{2}

Draw a parallelogram with the given base and height. (Many different parallelograms are possible.) Then, find the area of your parallelogram.

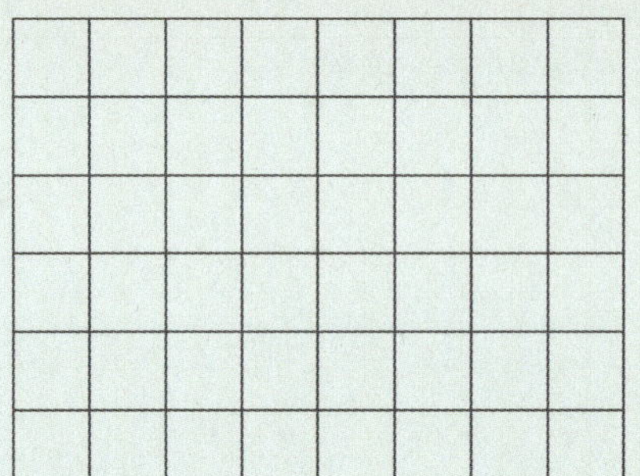

Base: 5 units

Height: 3 units

Area: _____________ units ^{2}

Base: 3 units

Height: 5 units

Area: _____________ units ^{2}

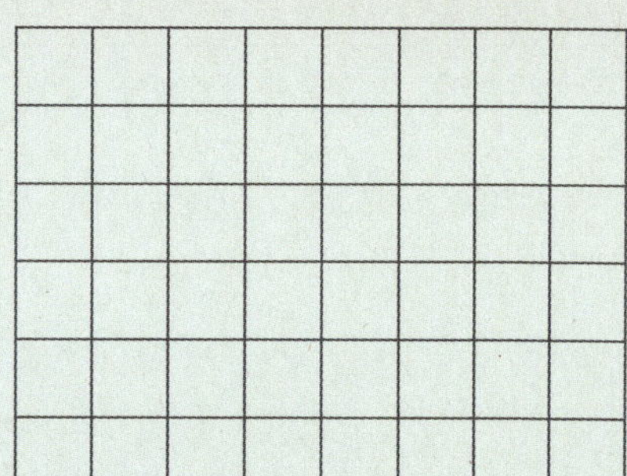

Base: 3 units

Height: 3 units

Area: _____________ units ^{2}

Solve. Write the equations you use.

The tile is shaped like a parallelogram. What is its area?

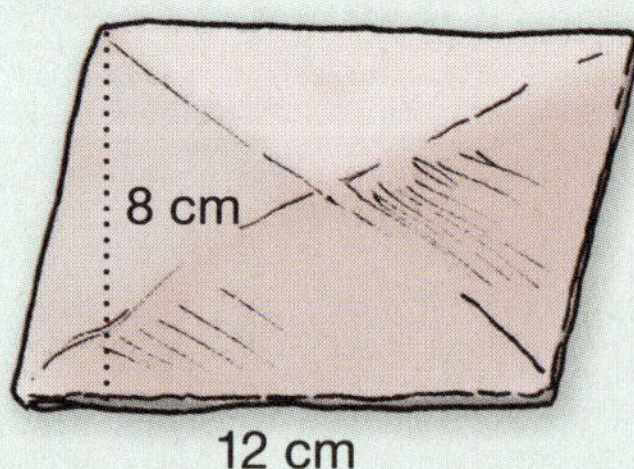

 The path is shaped like a parallelogram. What is its area?

Review 

Write each number in expanded form.

Standard Form	Expanded Form
1.671	$1 + \dfrac{6}{10} + \dfrac{7}{100} + \dfrac{1}{1{,}000}$
3.945	
2.06	
5.937	

Circle the prime numbers. X the numbers that are not prime.

1	2	3	4	5	6	7	8	9	10
11	12	13	14	15	16	17	18	19	20

Use mental math to complete.

	400	500	600	700	800	900	1,000	1,100
÷ 2	200							

Draw a triangle that matches each description.

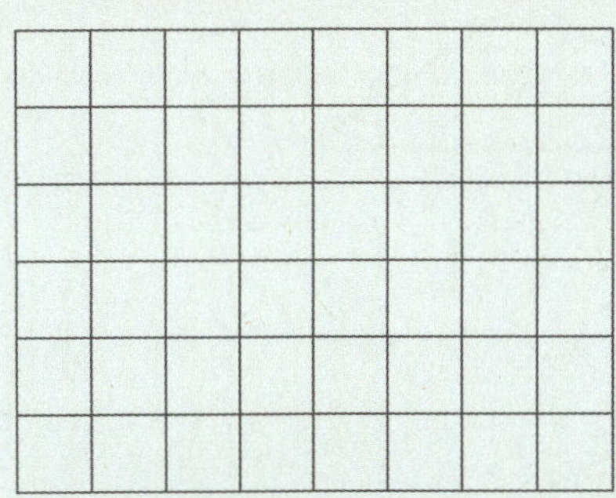

Right triangle
(1 right angle)

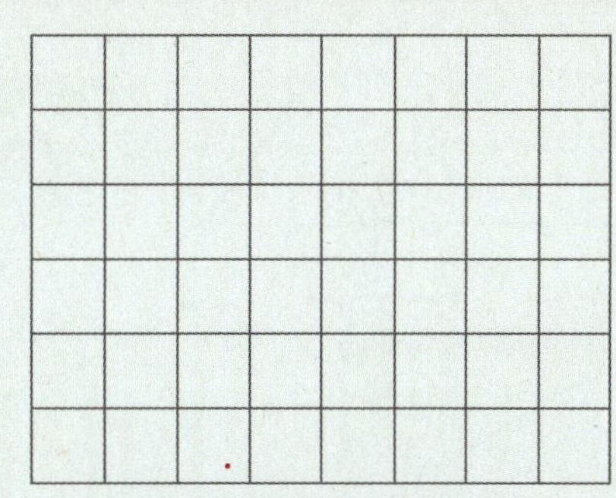

Obtuse triangle
(1 obtuse angle)

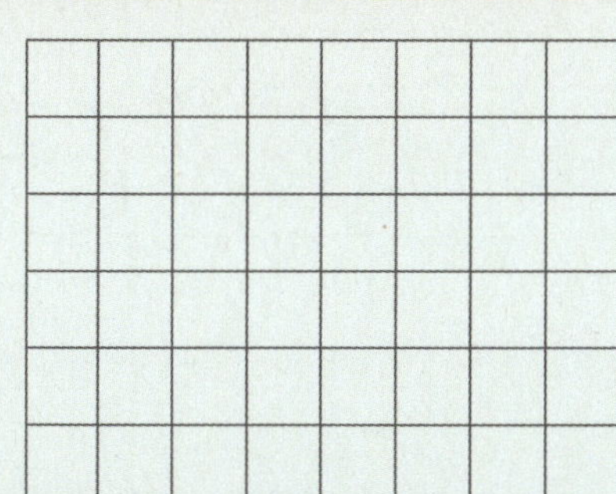

Acute triangle
(3 acute angles)

Lesson Activities

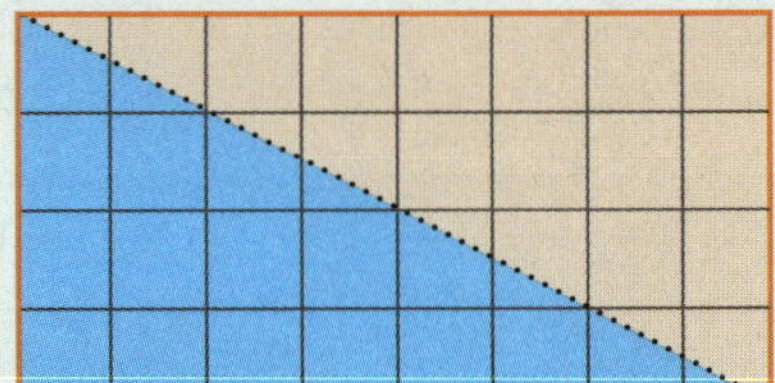

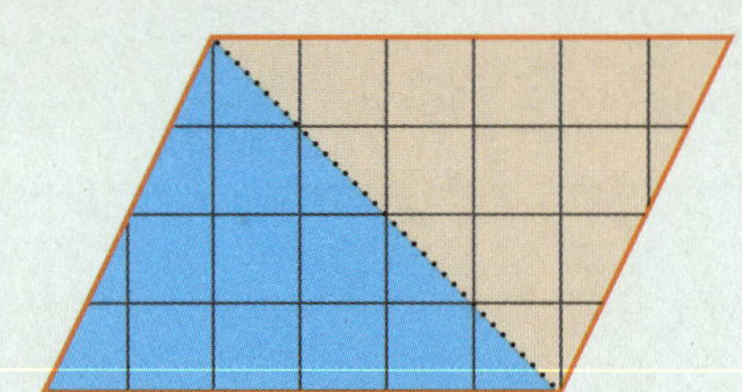

Area of the rectangle: __________ units²

Area of the blue triangle: __________ units²

Area of the parallelogram: __________ units²

Area of the blue triangle: __________ units²

A

B

Area of a Triangle

Every triangle is half of a matching parallelogram or rectangle.

To find the area of a triangle, multiply the base by the height. Then, divide the product by 2.

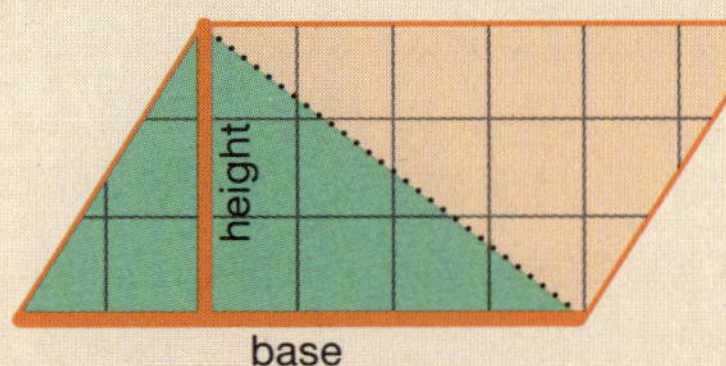

$$\text{Area} = \frac{\text{base} \cdot \text{height}}{2} \qquad A = \frac{b \cdot h}{2}$$

Ex. What is the area of this triangle?

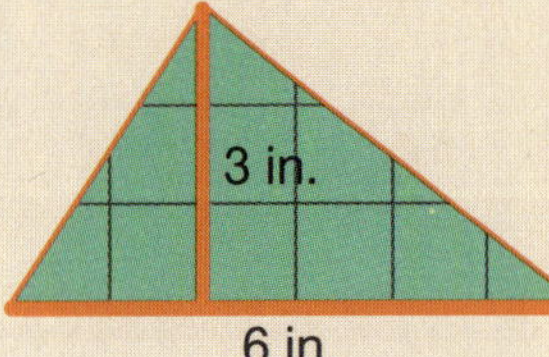

$$A = \frac{6 \text{ in.} \cdot 3 \text{ in.}}{2}$$

$$A = \textbf{9 in.}^2$$

C

	Area (units²)
A	
B	
C	
D	
E	

Practice

Find the area of each triangle.

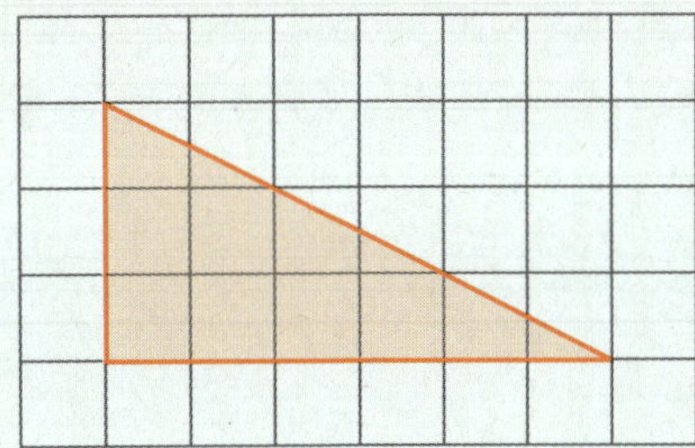

Area: _____________ units ^{2}

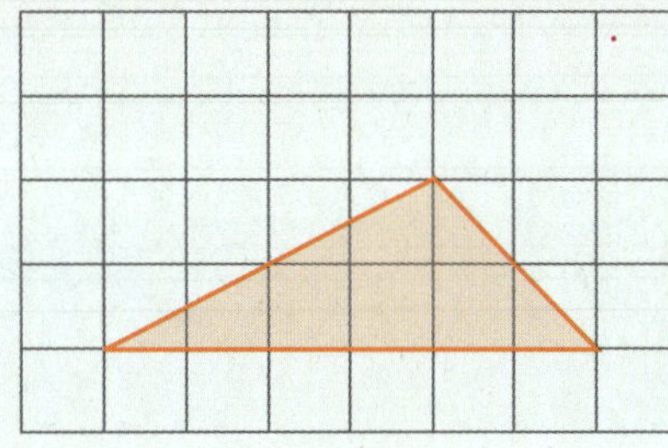

Area: _____________ units ^{2}

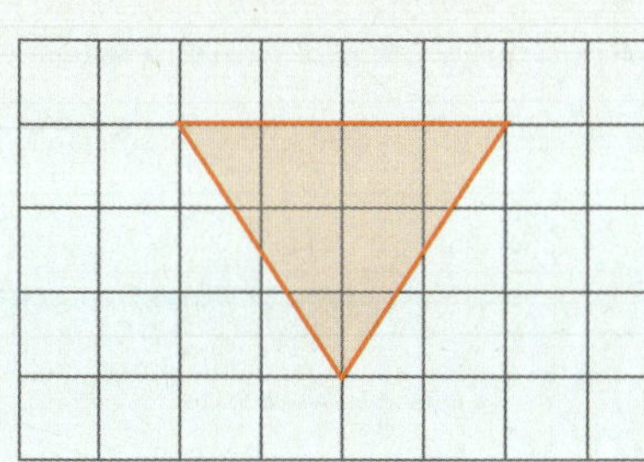

Area: _____________ units ^{2}

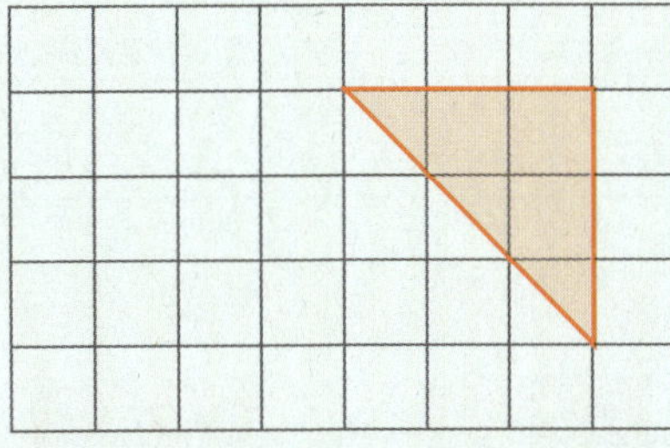

Area: _____________ units ^{2}

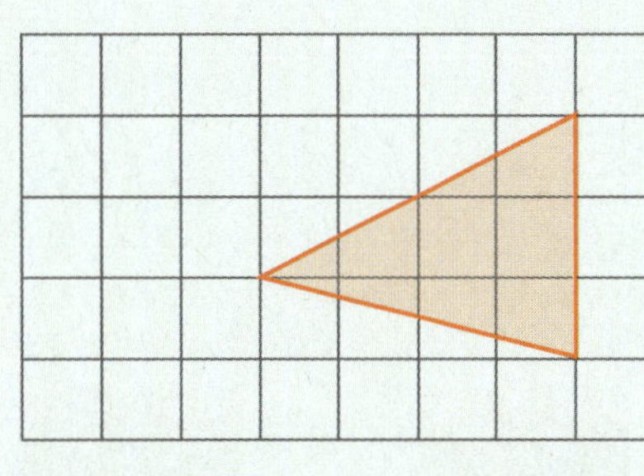

Area: _____________ units ^{2}

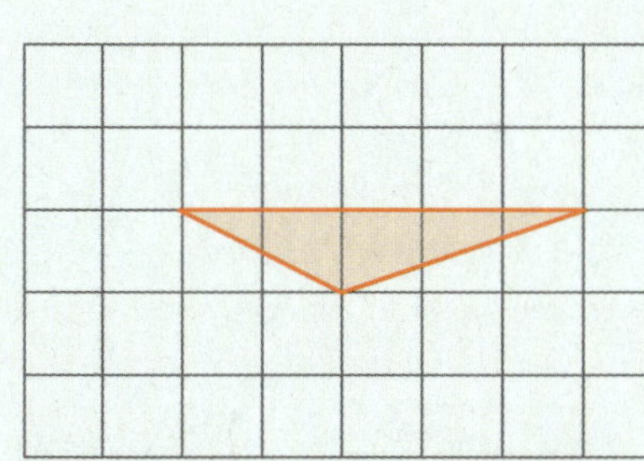

Area: _____________ units ^{2}

Draw a triangle with the given base and height. (Many different triangles are possible.) Then, find the triangle's area.

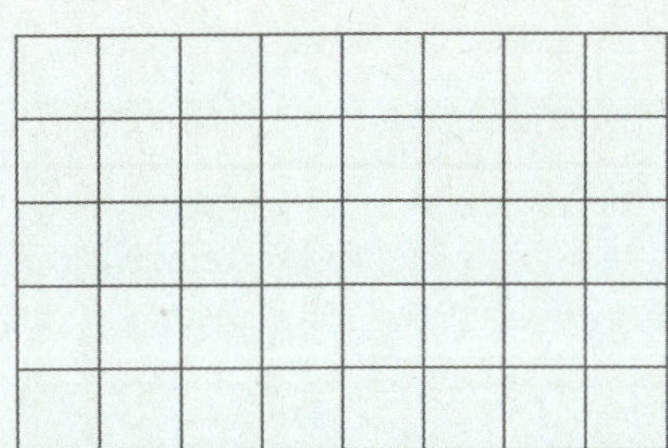

Base: 3 units

Height: 4 units

Area: _____________ units ^{2}

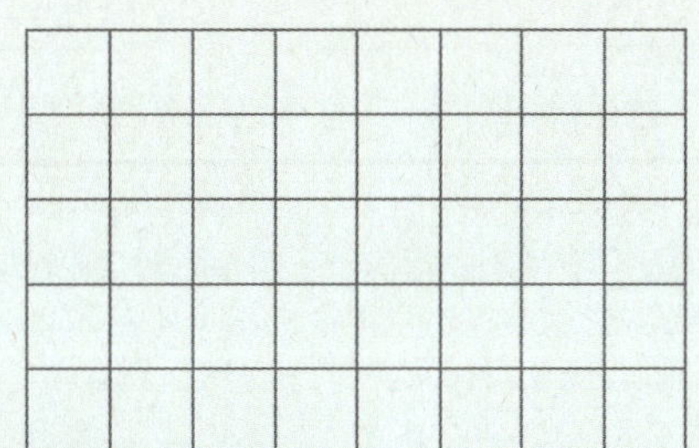

Base: 6 units

Height: 2 units

Area: _____________ units ^{2}

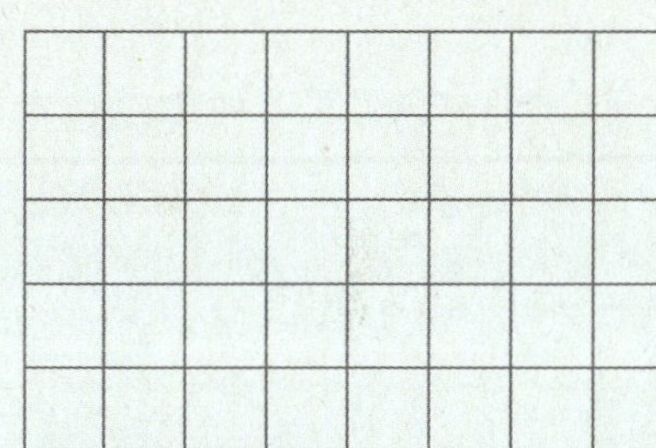

Base: 4 units

Height: 3 units

Area: _____________ units ^{2}

Solve. Write the equations you use.

What is the area of this flag?

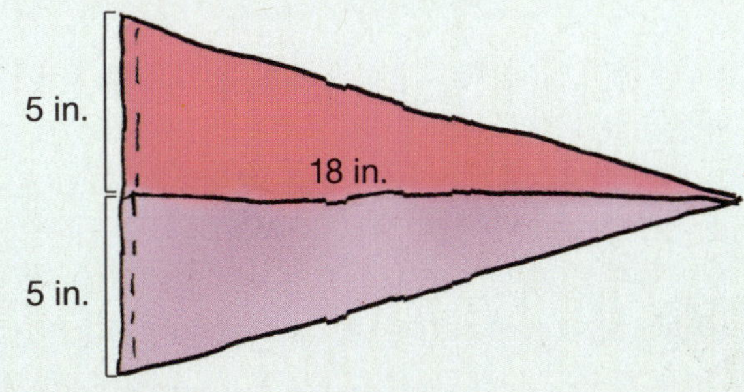

Review

Find the product or quotient.

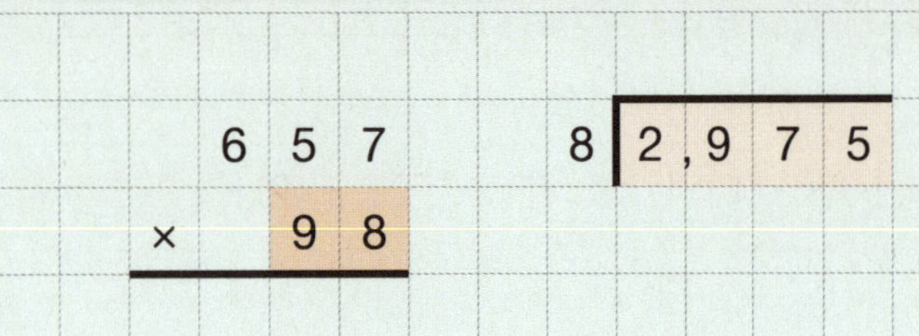

$$657 \times 98$$

$$8\overline{)2{,}975}$$

Evaluate.

$3^4 =$ _______________

$7^2 =$ _______________

$8^0 =$ _______________

$10^6 =$ _______________

$9 \times 10^4 =$ _______________

$6 \times 10^3 =$ _______________

$31 \times 10^5 =$ _______________

Match each number to its location on the number line.

| 0.3 | 0.7 | 0.8 |

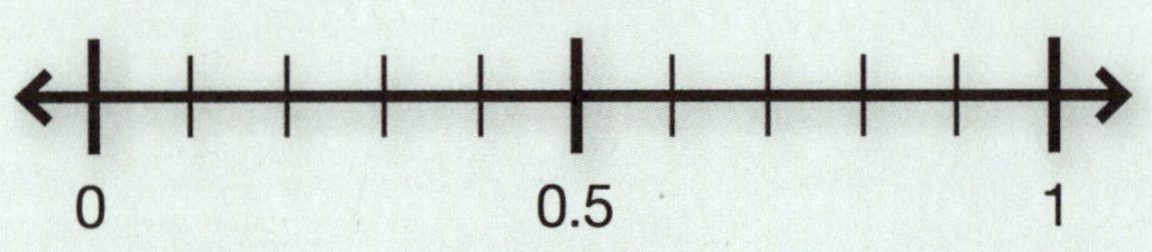

| 0.43 | 0.41 | 0.49 |

| 0.462 | 0.468 | 0.466 |

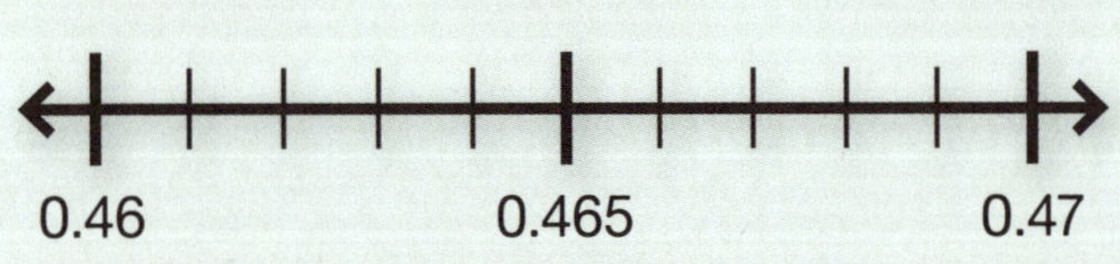

| 0.003 | 0.007 | 0.009 |

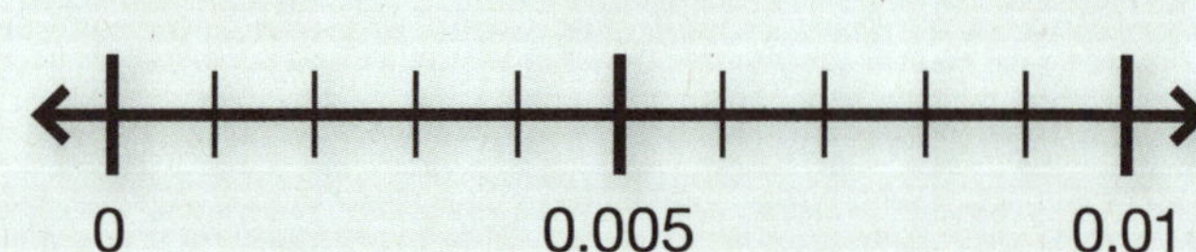

Solve. Write your answers in simplest form.

Annabelle is crocheting a blanket. The blanket will have 90 rows of stitches when she is finished. So far, Annabelle has crocheted 48 rows. What fraction of the blanket has she completed?

What fraction of the blanket does she have left to complete?

Charlie is also crocheting a blanket. So far, he has crocheted 40 rows. He has 60 rows left to crochet. What fraction of the blanket has he completed?

What fraction of the blanket does he have left to complete?

Lesson Activities 

Area of a Triangle, Part 2

The height of a triangle must always be perpendicular to its base. Sometimes, the line we use to measure height is outside of the triangle.

Obtuse triangles are triangles with one obtuse angle. We often measure their height outside of the triangle.

A

Ex. What is the area of this triangle?

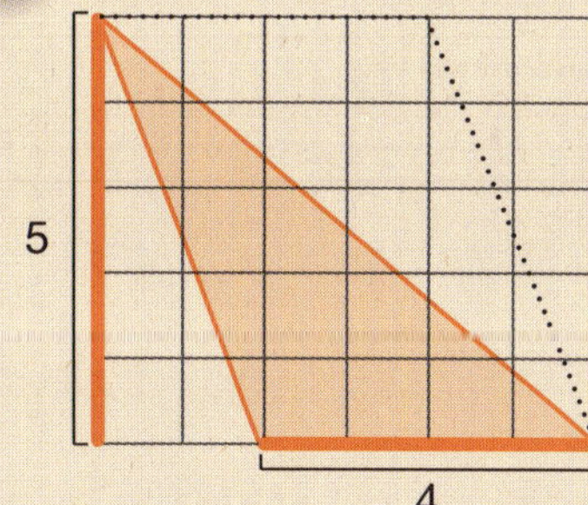

$$A = \frac{b \cdot h}{2}$$

$$A = \frac{4 \cdot 5}{2}$$

$$A = \textbf{10 units}^2$$

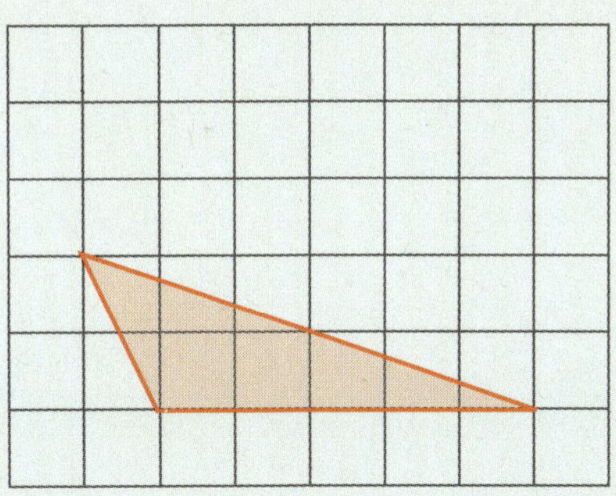

Area: ______________ units²

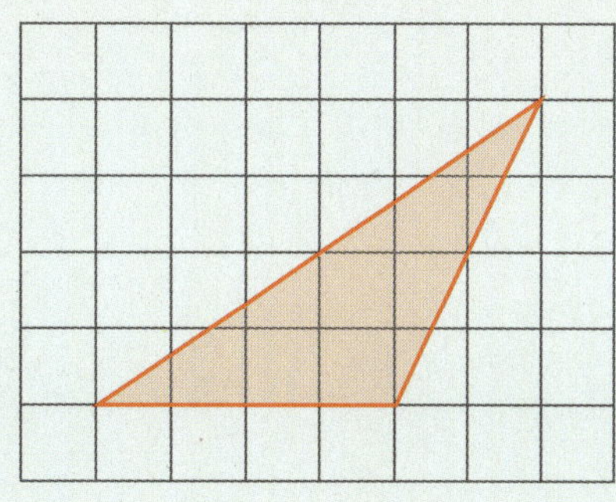

Area: ______________ units²

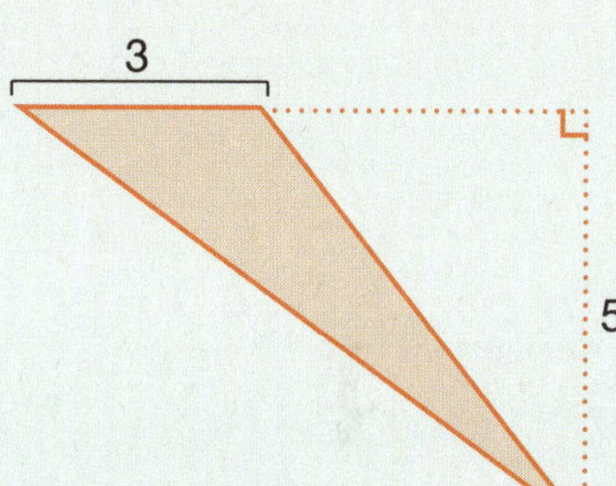

Area: ______________ units²

B

Triangle Roll (2-Player Game) 

Practice

Find the base, height, and area of each triangle.

	Base (units)	Height (units)	Area (units^2)
A			
B			
C			
D			
E			
F			
G			

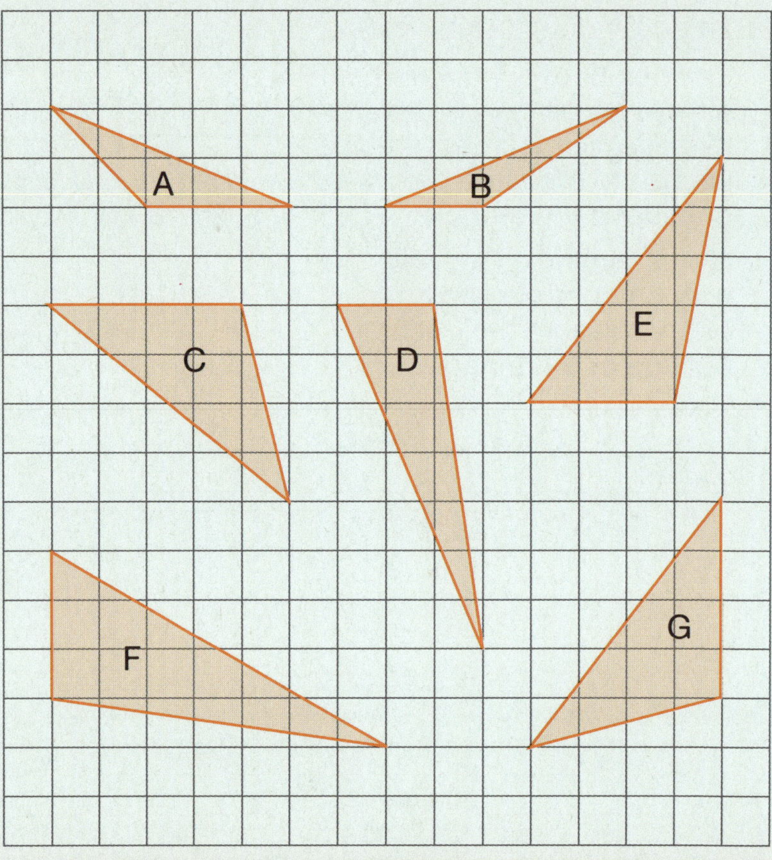

Draw a triangle that matches each definition, base, and height. (Many different triangles are possible.) Then, find the area of the triangle.

Right triangles have one right angle and two acute angles.

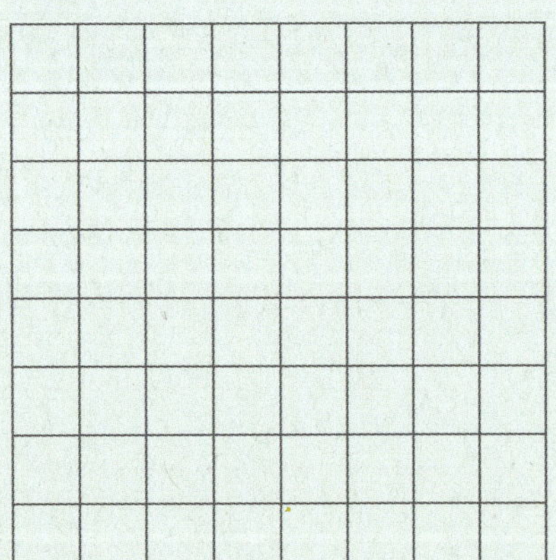

Base: 4 units

Height: 5 units

Area: ____________ units^2

Obtuse triangles have one obtuse angle and two acute angles.

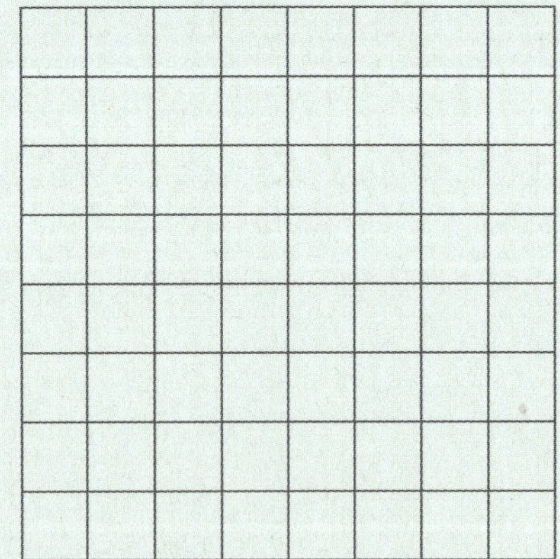

Base: 4 units

Height: 5 units

Area: ____________ units^2

Acute triangles have three acute angles.

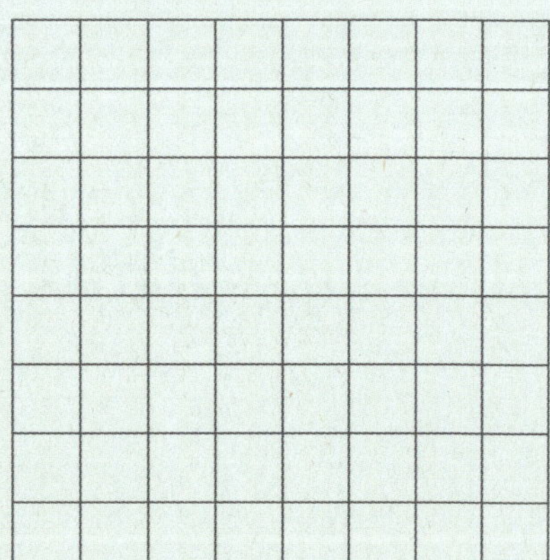

Base: 4 units

Height: 5 units

Area: ____________ units^2

Review

Match each number to its dot on the number line.
Then, round each number to the nearest whole number.

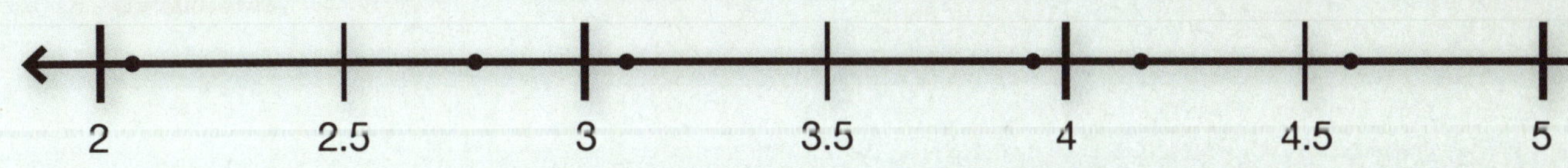

| 2.781 | 2.07 | 3.094 | 3.94 | 4.6 | 4.165 |

$2.07 \approx$ _____________ $4.165 \approx$ _____________ $2.781 \approx$ _____________

$3.94 \approx$ _____________ $4.6 \approx$ _____________ $3.094 \approx$ _____________

Complete.

$\dfrac{4}{7}$ of 42 = _______ $\dfrac{7}{8}$ of 64 = _______ $\dfrac{7}{9}$ of 63 = _______

$\dfrac{5}{6}$ of 54 = _______ $\dfrac{3}{8}$ of 72 = _______ $\dfrac{5}{9}$ of 81 = _______

Complete.

$5^2 =$ _______________ $10^2 =$ _______________ $9^2 =$ _______________

$7^2 =$ _______________ $2^2 =$ _______________ $4^2 =$ _______________

$8^2 =$ _______________ $3^2 =$ _______________ $6^2 =$ _______________

$11^2 =$ _______________ $1^2 =$ _______________ $12^2 =$ _______________

Bodie made a chart of how far he biked each day on a mountain biking trip. Use his chart to find the total distance he biked on the trip. Write the equations you use.

Day	Distance (km)
Friday	$5\dfrac{1}{2}$
Saturday	$6\dfrac{7}{10}$
Sunday	8
Total	

Lesson Activities

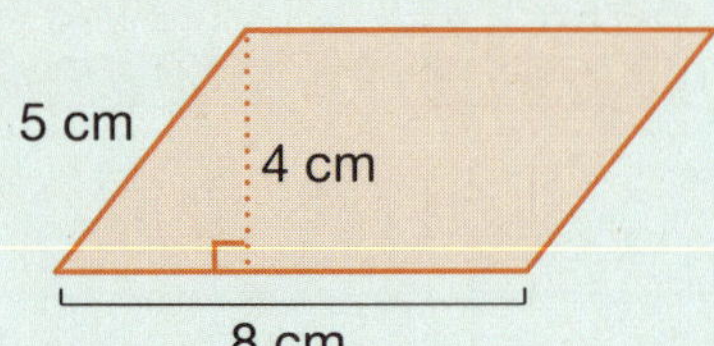

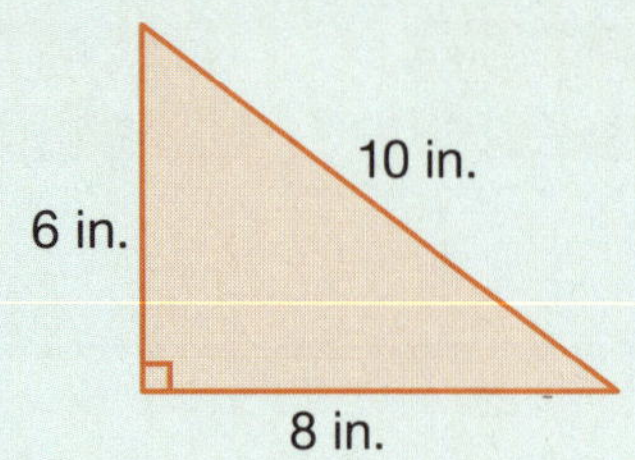

A

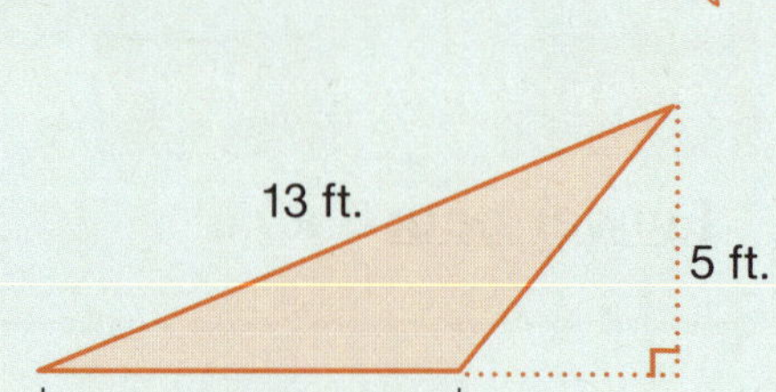

Area: _______________

Area: _______________

Area: _______________

B

Subtract to Find Area

Ex. What is the area of the grass?

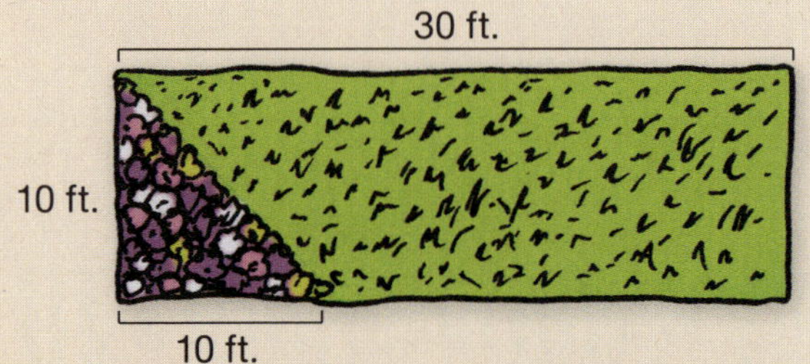

Area of the rectangle:
30 ft. × 10 ft. = **300 ft.^{2}**

Area of the flower bed:
$$\frac{10 \text{ ft.} \times 10 \text{ ft.}}{2} = \textbf{50 ft.}^2$$

Area of the grass:
300 ft.^{2} − 50 ft.^{2} = **250 ft.^{2}**

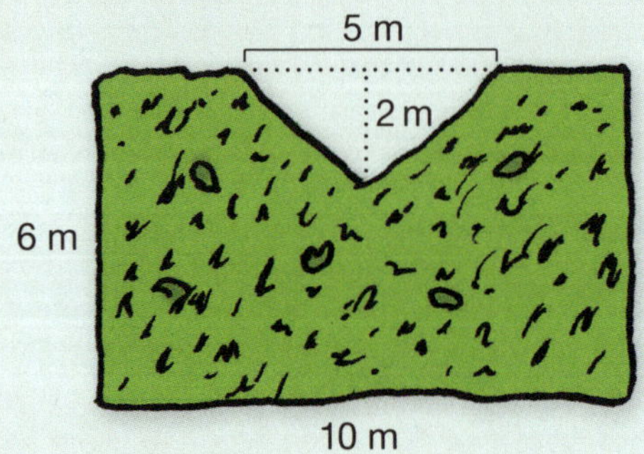

Area of the grass: _______________

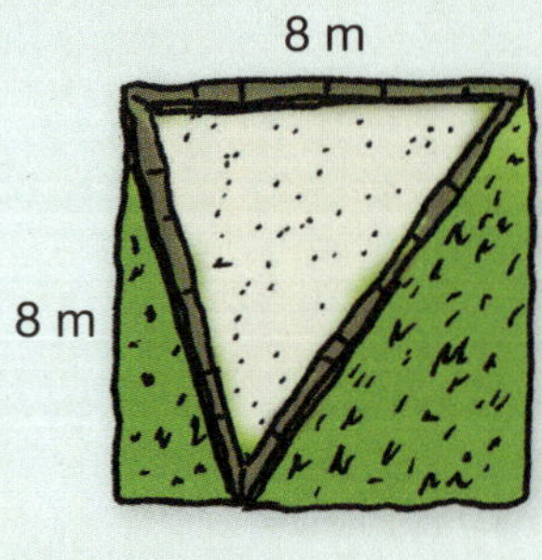

Area of the grass: _______________

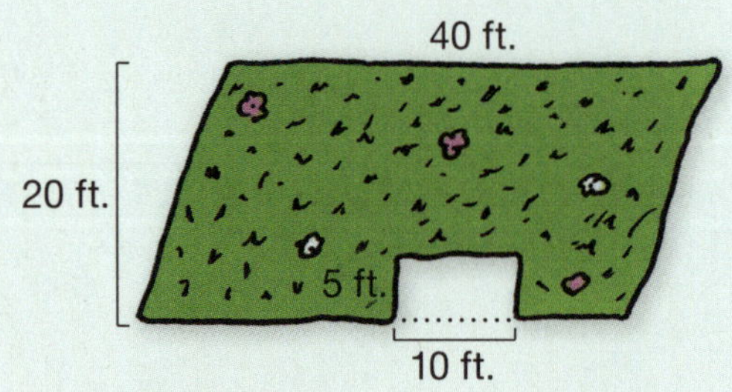

Area of the grass: _______________

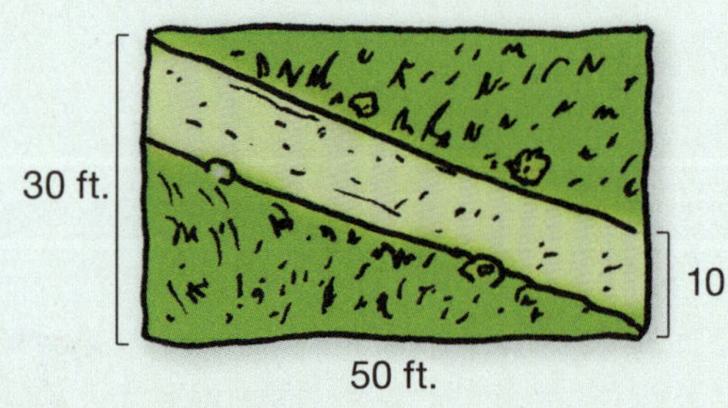

Area of the grass: _______________

Practice

Follow the directions to design a park.
(Each square represents 1 square foot.)

Design Your Own Park!

Flower bed: Draw a parallelogram. (Make sure to draw it so that the base and height align with the grid.) Color it red.

Sandbox: Draw a rectangle. Color it yellow.

Playground: Draw a triangle. (Make sure to draw it so that the base and height align with the grid.) Color it blue.

Grass: All the rest of the park is grass. Color it green.

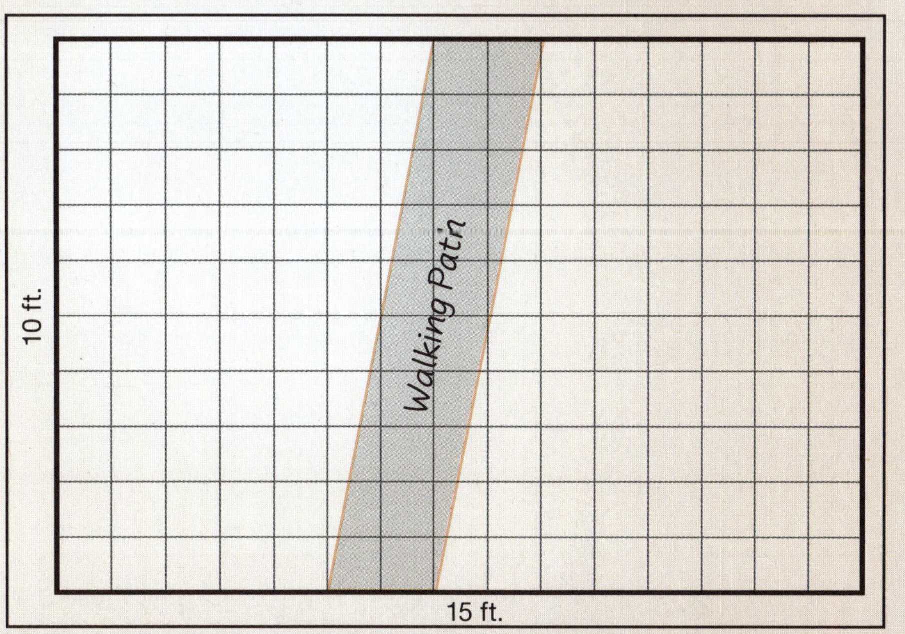

Complete the chart to match your park. Write your equations in the work space.

	Area (sq. ft.)
Whole Park	
Flower Bed	
Walking Path	
Sandbox	
Playground	
Grass	

WORK SPACE

Review 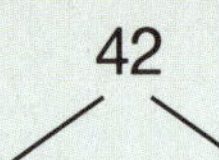

Create a factor tree to find the prime factorization for each number. Then, answer the questions.

21

42

What is the GCF of 21 and 42?

Use the GCF to write $\frac{21}{42}$ in simplest form.

Prime factorization of 21:

____

Prime factorization of 42:

____

$$\frac{21}{42} =$$

Match.

$5 \cdot 27 + 5 \cdot 3$	$7 \cdot (99 + 1)$	700
$4 \cdot 18 + 4 \cdot 2$	$5 \cdot (27 + 3)$	80
$7 \cdot 99 + 7 \cdot 1$	$4 \cdot (18 + 2)$	150

Use bar models to solve.

Cannon's goal is to collect 30 baseball hats. So far, he has reached $\frac{3}{5}$ of his goal. How many more baseball hats does he need to reach his goal?

A medium-sized humpback whale is 45 feet long. A medium-sized orca whale is $\frac{4}{9}$ as long as a humpback. How much longer is a humpback whale than an orca?

Humpback

Orca

Lesson Activities

A

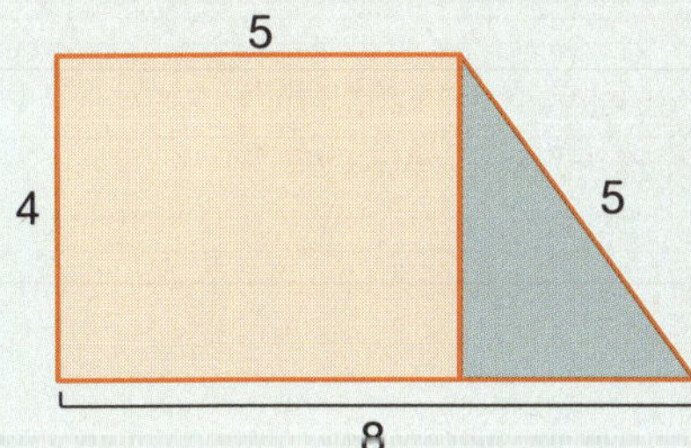

Area of the rectangle: _________ units^2

Area of the triangle: _________ units^2

Total area of the shape: _________ units^2

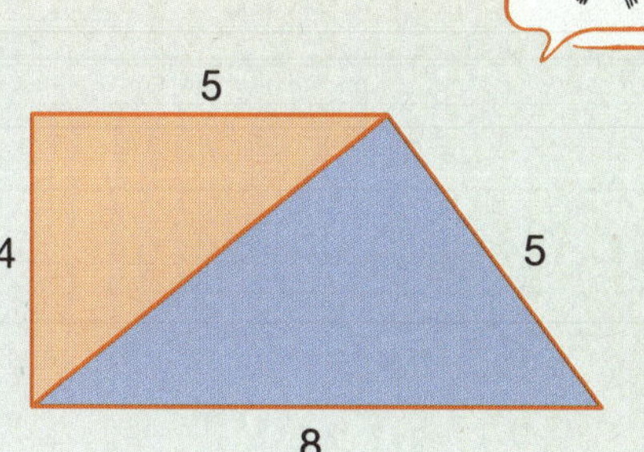

Area of the orange triangle: _________ units^2

Area of the blue triangle: _________ units^2

Total area of the shape: _________ units^2

B

Add to Find Area

 What is the area of the wall?

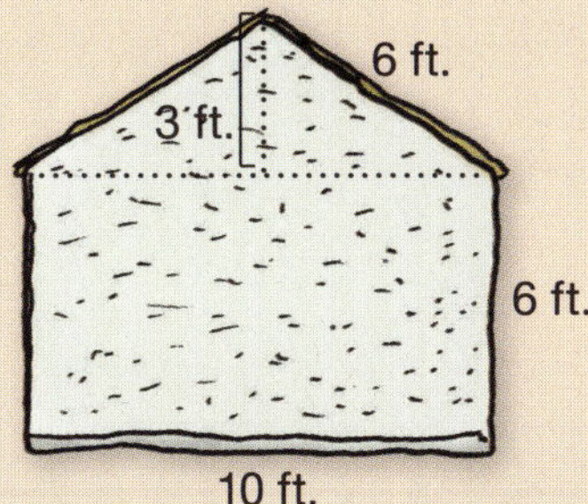

Area of the rectangle:
10 ft. · 6 ft. = **60 ft.^{2}**

Area of the triangle:
$$\frac{10 \text{ ft.} \cdot 3 \text{ ft.}}{2} = \textbf{15 ft.}^2$$

Total area of the wall:
60 ft.^{2} + 15 ft.^{2} = **75 ft.^{2}**

Rita is helping her mom lay tile in the bathroom. What is the area of one tile?

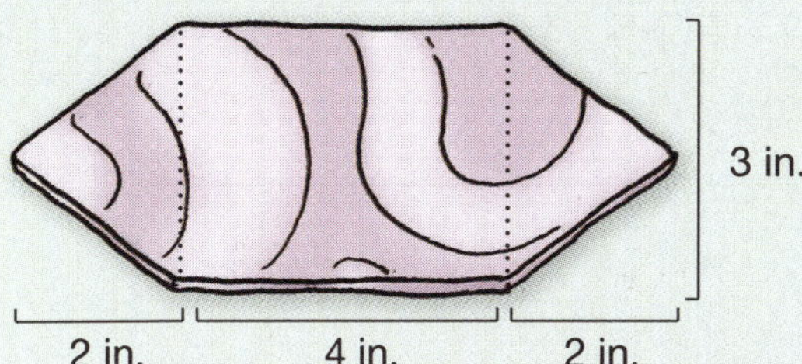

Krispin is following this design to make a kite. What is the area of the kite?

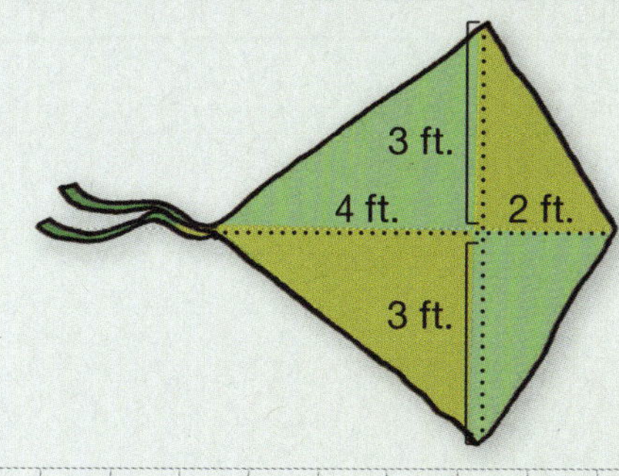

Practice

Find the area of each colored shape.
Write the equations you use in the work space.

WORK SPACE

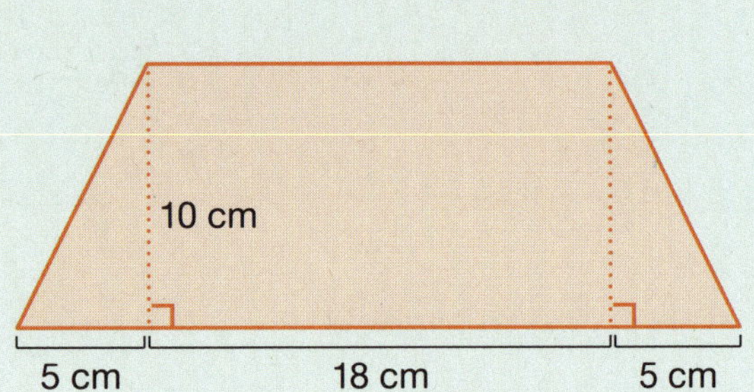

Area: _________________________

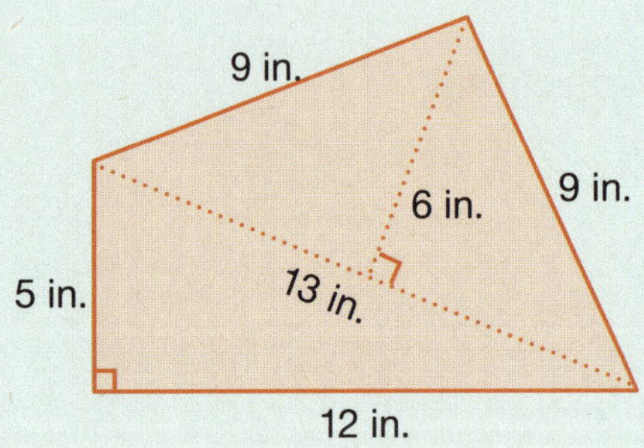

Area: _________________________

★

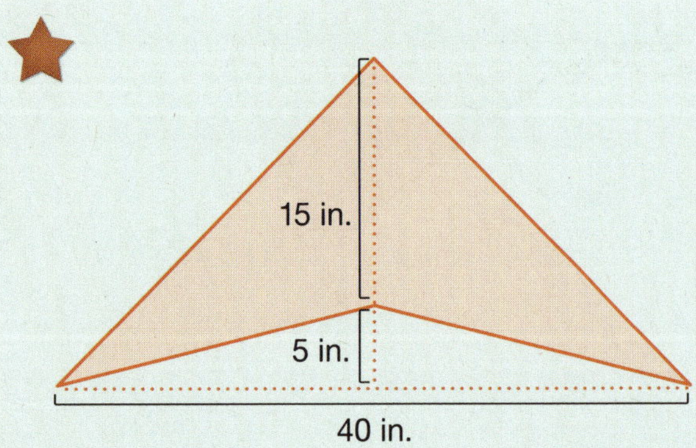

Area: _________________________

Review

Circle the fractions whose simplest form is the fraction in the star.

$\frac{1}{2}$ | $\frac{6}{10}$ $\frac{6}{12}$ $\frac{8}{16}$ $\frac{11}{20}$ $\frac{32}{64}$ $\frac{51}{100}$

$\frac{1}{3}$ | $\frac{4}{12}$ $\frac{3}{6}$ $\frac{3}{9}$ $\frac{7}{21}$ $\frac{6}{20}$ $\frac{15}{45}$

$\frac{1}{4}$ | $\frac{2}{6}$ $\frac{2}{8}$ $\frac{4}{12}$ $\frac{4}{16}$ $\frac{10}{40}$ $\frac{25}{100}$

$\frac{1}{5}$ | $\frac{2}{10}$ $\frac{5}{15}$ $\frac{4}{20}$ $\frac{15}{50}$ $\frac{20}{100}$ $\frac{5}{25}$

Evaluate.

$$\frac{6 \cdot 5}{2} + 5 \qquad\qquad (8 - 1)^2 \qquad\qquad 10 \cdot 7 - 4 \cdot 5$$

Solve. Write the equations you use.

Beatrix spends 45 minutes practicing the tuba each day. How many minutes does she practice in 30 days?

Last week, Ian practiced the fiddle for a total of 259 minutes. On average, how many minutes did he practice each day?

Unit Wrap-Up

Find the area of each shape.

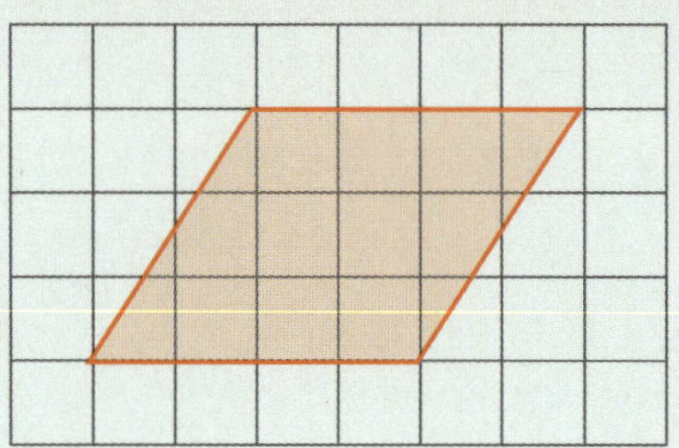

Area: _____________ units^2

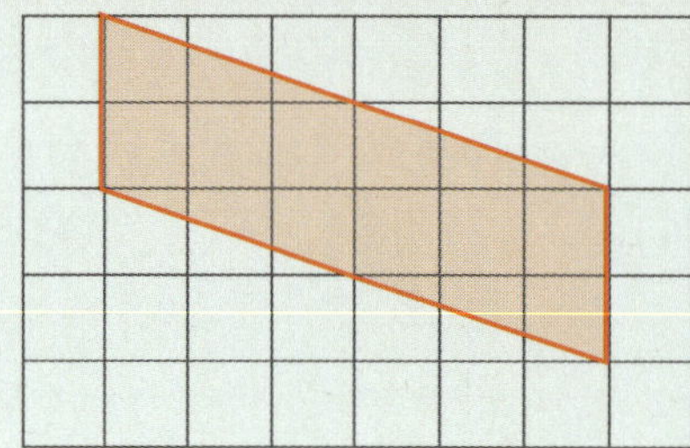

Area: _____________ units^2

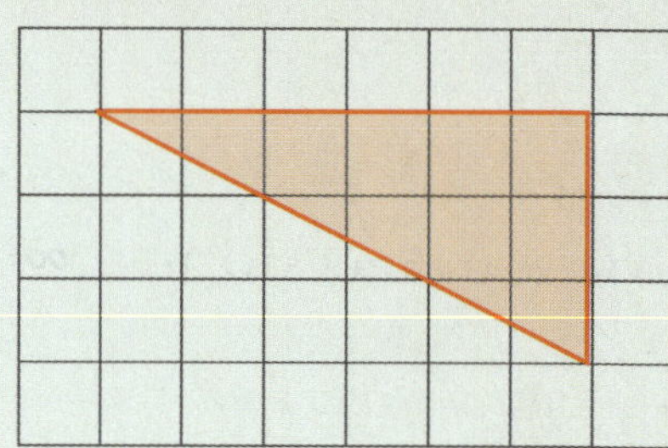

Area: _____________ units^2

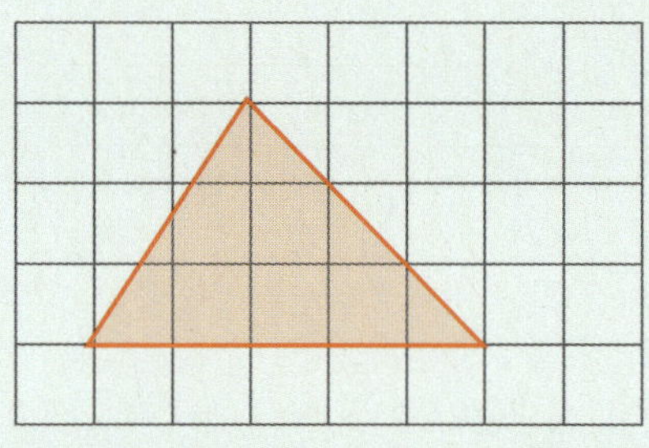

Area: _____________ units^2

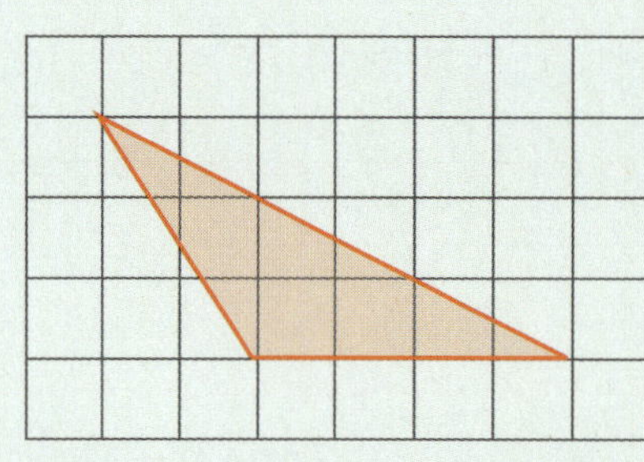

Area: _____________ units^2

Area: _____________ units^2

Find the area of each shape. All measurements are in centimeters.

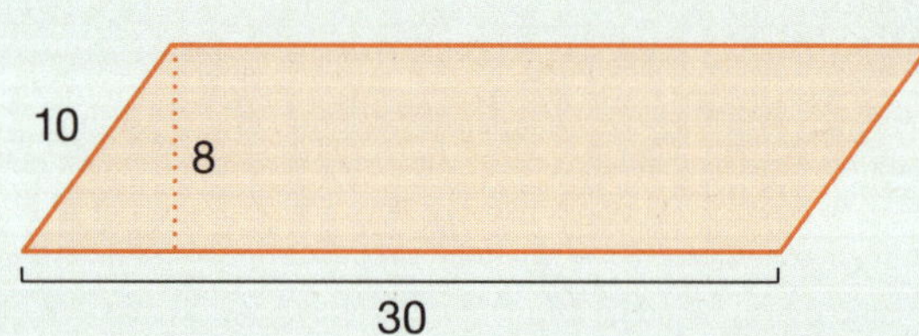

Area: _____________ cm^2

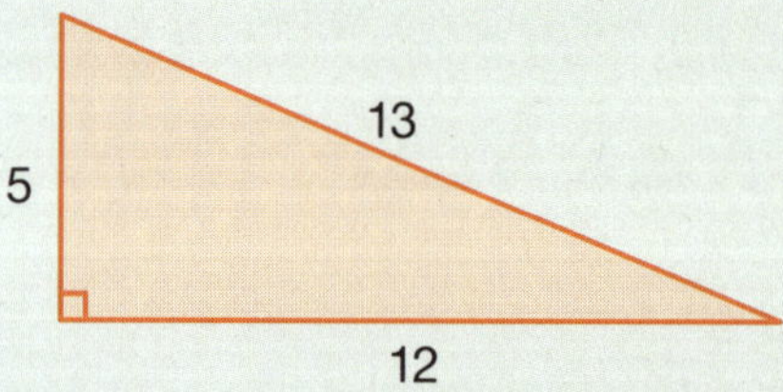

Area: _____________ cm^2

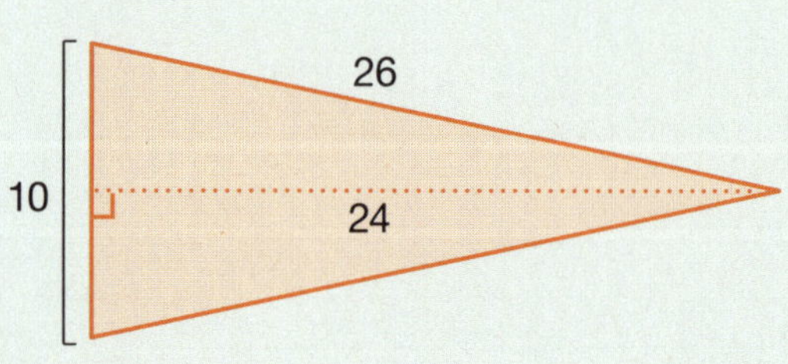

Area: _____________ cm^2

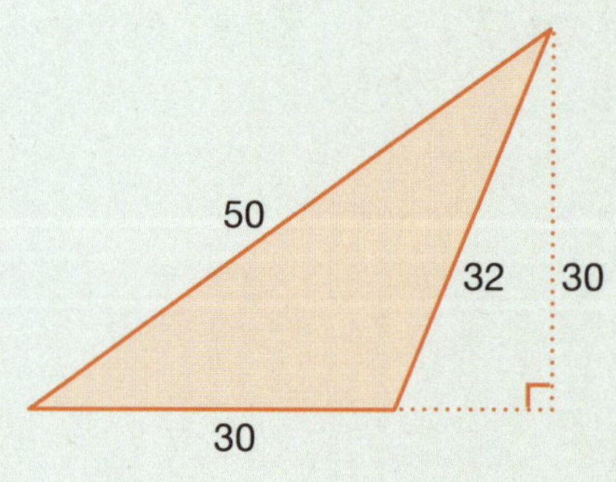

Area: _____________ cm^2

Unit Wrap-Up

Customers at home improvement stores sometimes have lots of questions! Use what you've learned about area to answer these customers' questions. Write the equations you use.

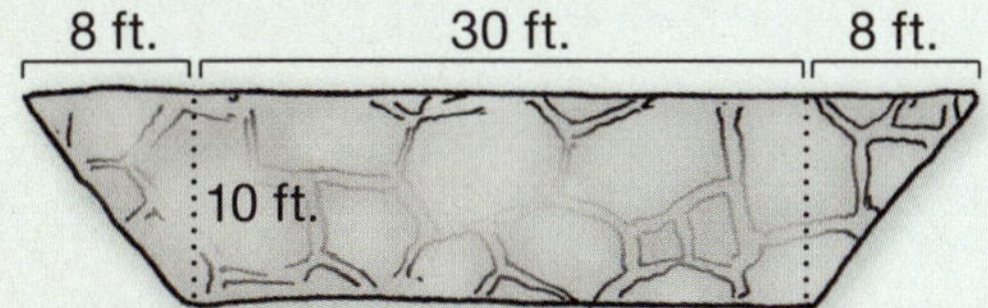

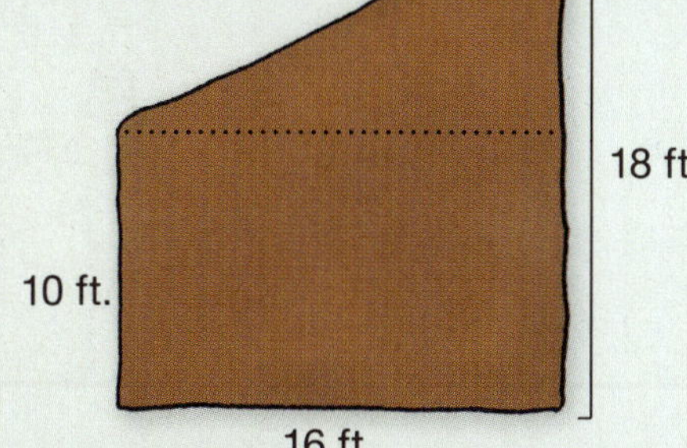

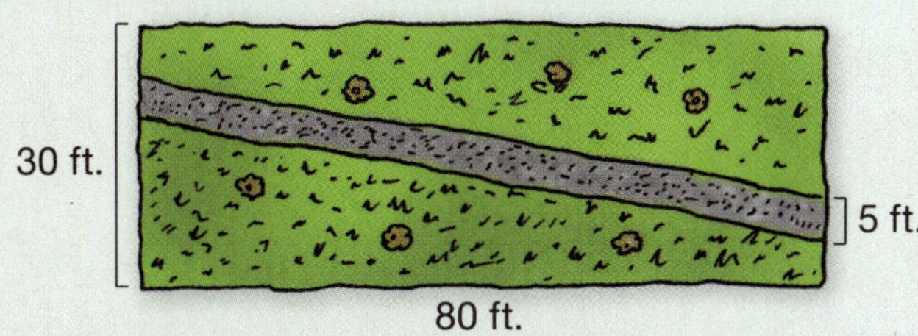

Lesson Activities 

Ratios

Ratios compare the size of one quantity to the size of another quantity. Some ratios compare two parts of a quantity. Others compare part of a quantity to the total quantity.

To write a ratio, write the size of each quantity in the order you want to compare them. Write a colon between the numbers.

 **Ex.** Abigail mixes 2 bottles of red paint and 3 bottles of white paint to make pink paint.

Part-to-Part Ratios	**Part-to-Whole Ratios**
Red paint : White paint	Red paint : Total paint
2 : 3	2 : 5
White paint : Red paint	White paint : Total paint
3 : 2	3 : 5

A

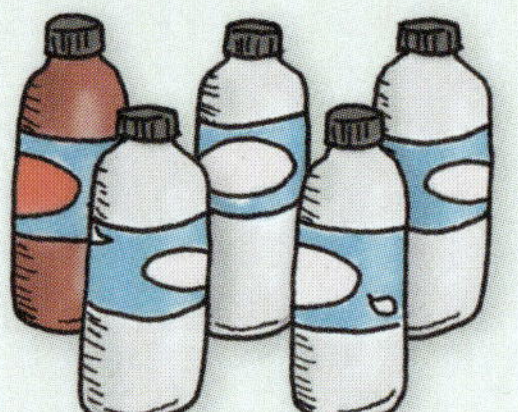

Red : White

______ : ______

Red : Total

______ : ______

B

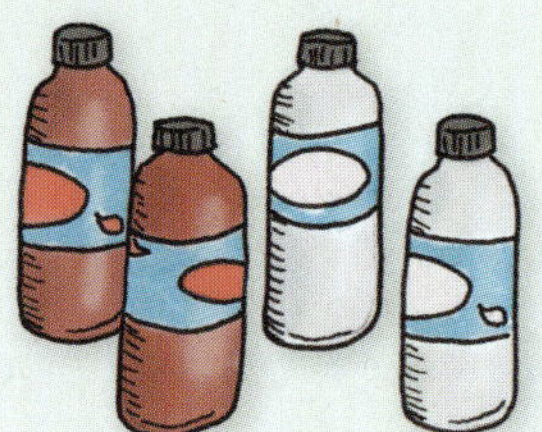

Red : White

______ : ______

Red : Total

______ : ______

C

Red : White

______ : ______

Red : Total

______ : ______

D

Red : White

______ : ______

Red : Total

______ : ______

E

Red : White

______ : ______

Red : Total

______ : ______

Which paint mix will look the darkest?

Which paint mix will look the lightest?

Which two paint mixes will look the same?

Practice

Use the diagrams to complete the ratios.

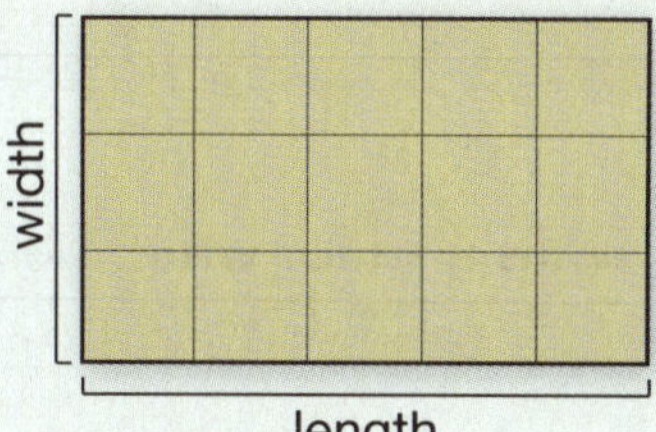

Brown : White	__ : __	Apples : Oranges	__ : __	Length : Width	__ : __
White : Brown	__ : __	Oranges : Apples	__ : __	Width : Length	__ : __
Brown : Total	__ : __	Apples : Total	__ : __	Length : Area	__ : __

Hamish's family has a small farm. Use the chart to answer the questions.

Ducks	3
Geese	7
Chickens	13
Goats	5
Horses	2
Total	30

What is the ratio of ducks to geese?

What is the ratio of geese to ducks?

What is the ratio of geese to chickens?

What is the ratio of goats to horses?

What is the ratio of birds to other animals?

What is the ratio of birds to the total number of animals?

Write your first name and last name in the blanks. Count how many vowels and consonants are in each name. Then, write ratios to complete the chart.

____
MY FIRST NAME

____
MY LAST NAME

	First Name	Last Name
Vowels : Consonants		
Consonants : Vowels		
Vowels : Total letters		
Consonants : Total letters		

Review

Write each fraction in simplest form.
If the fraction is already in simplest form, circle the fraction.

$$\frac{24}{64} =$$

$$\frac{29}{30} =$$

$$\frac{35}{40} =$$

$$\frac{48}{100} =$$

Find the area and perimeter of each shape.
Use the work space to write your equations, if needed.

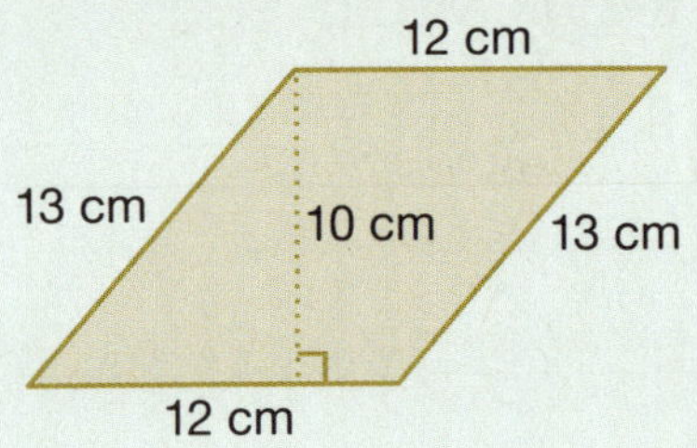

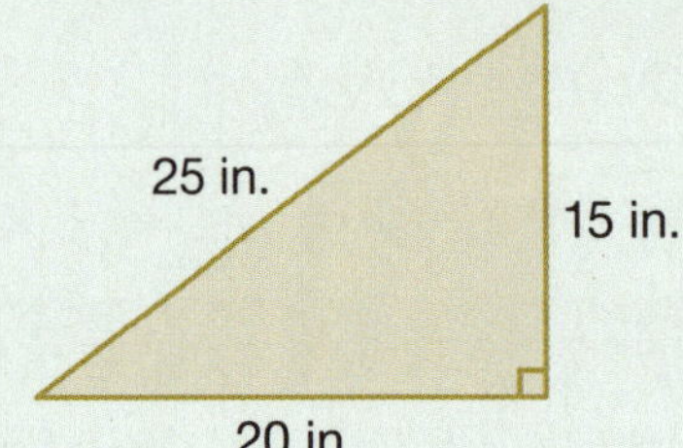

Perimeter: ___________________

Area: ___________________

Perimeter: ___________________

Area: ___________________

Katherine had a lemonade stand. Use the clues to complete the chart
and answer the questions. Write the equations you use.

- Katherine sold $\frac{3}{4}$ as many glasses on
  Friday as she sold on Thursday.

- Katherine sold $\frac{5}{6}$ as many glasses on
  Saturday as she sold on Friday.

Lemonade Stand Sales

Day	Glasses
Thursday	48
Friday	
Saturday	

How many glasses of lemonade did
Katherine sell in all?

What was the average number of glasses
Katherine sold each day?

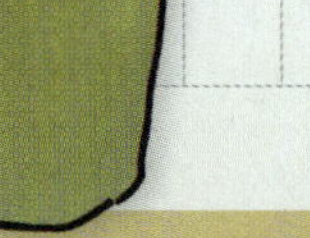

Lesson Activities 

What is the **ratio** of strawberries to grapes?

What **fraction** of the fruit pieces are strawberries?

What is the **ratio** of grapes to strawberries?

What **fraction** of the fruit pieces are grapes?

Simplify Ratios

Finding the simplest form of a ratio is just like finding the simplest form of a fraction. Divide both numbers by common factors until they have no common factor (other than 1).

Ratios that have the same simplest form are equivalent to each other.

Ex. Brandon is making fruit skewers for a party. He puts 3 strawberries and 6 grapes on each skewer. What is the ratio of strawberries to grapes in simplest form?

Strawberries : Grapes   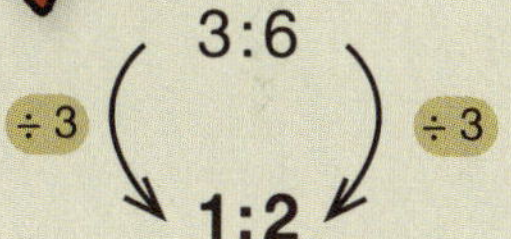

There is 1 strawberry for every 2 grapes.

Water : Vinegar

Money saved : Money spent

Campers : Counselors

Practice

Write a ratio to match each picture. Write each ratio in simplest form.

Brown : White

Apples : Oranges

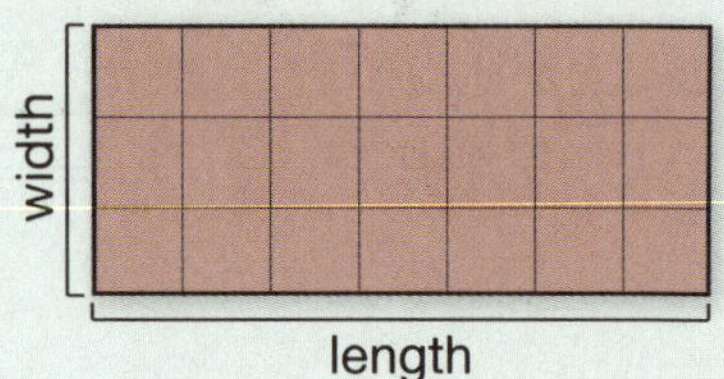

Length : Width

Write each ratio in simplest form.

15:20

15:6

15:15

9:27

27:9

27:36

Solve. Write the ratios in simplest form.

There are 4 instructors and 24 students at ice skating lessons. What is the ratio of instructors to students?

There are 10 boys and 14 girls at ice skating lessons. What is the ratio of boys to girls?

 The picture frame is 20 cm long. Its width is equal to its length. What is the ratio of its length to its width?

 The computer monitor is 32 in. wide. The sum of its width and length is 50 in. What is the ratio of its width to its length?

Review

Find the LCM. Then, use the LCM to evaluate the expressions. Write your answers in simplest form. If your answer is an improper fraction, convert it to a mixed number or whole number.

LCM of 2, 4, and 12: _______

$$\frac{3}{2} - \frac{7}{12} + \frac{3}{4}$$

$$\frac{11}{12} + \frac{5}{4} + \frac{1}{2}$$

Complete the missing units to answer the questions. Leave the blank empty if the number tells the number of groups or parts. Use exponents for square units.

The ribbon is 80 cm long. If you cut it into pieces that are each 20 cm long, how many pieces do you get?

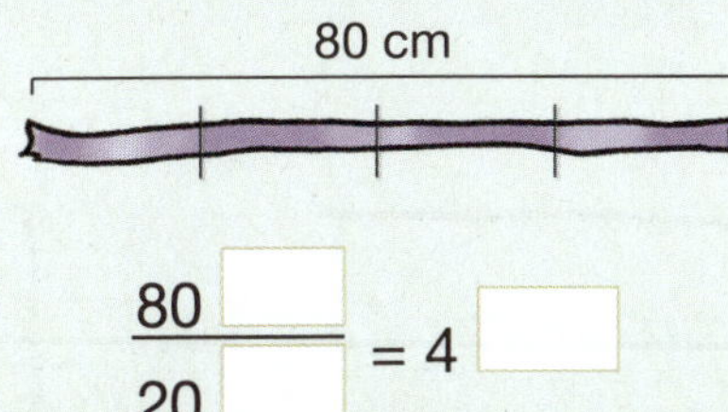

$$\frac{80 \quad \square}{20 \quad \square} = 4 \; \square$$

Each side of the square is 10 cm long. What is its area?

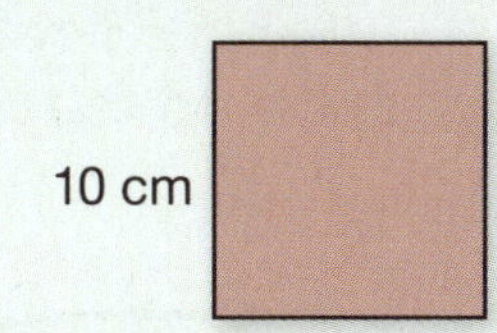

$10 \;\square \times 10 \;\square = 100 \;\square$

Each side of the square is 10 cm long. What is its perimeter?

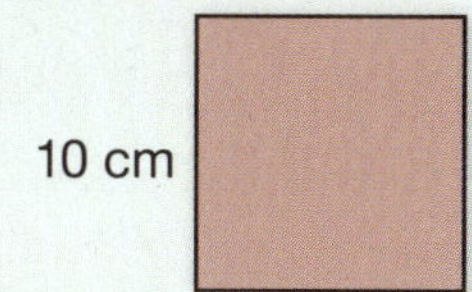

$4 \;\square \times 10 \;\square = 40 \;\square$

Complete the chart.

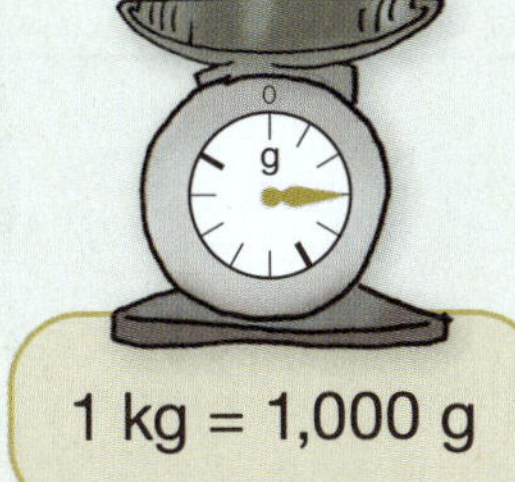

Fraction of a kilogram	$\frac{1}{10}$	$\frac{3}{10}$	$\frac{5}{10}$	$\frac{6}{10}$	$\frac{9}{10}$	$\frac{10}{10}$	$\frac{13}{10}$
Grams	100						

Find the area of the trapezoid. Write the equations you use.

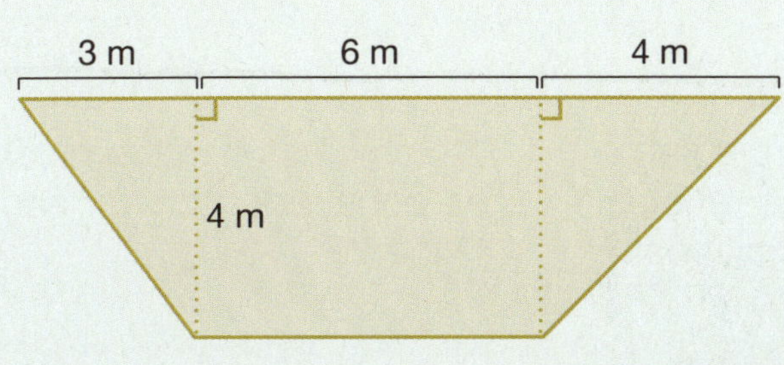

Lesson Activities

Salad Dressing
- 1 part vinegar
- 3 parts olive oil

A

Vinegar (Tablespoons)	1	2	3	4	5	6
Olive oil (Tablespoons)	3					

B

Use Ratio Tables to Find Equivalent Ratios

Ratios that have the same simplest form are equivalent to each other. To check whether two ratios are equivalent to each other, write each ratio in simplest form.

We can use ratio tables to organize the information in ratio problems. Make sure you write each number in the matching row.

Ex. Audrey used 30 mL of vinegar and 120 mL of olive oil. Jonathan used 25 mL of vinegar and 75 mL of olive oil. Who followed the salad dressing recipe (from part A) correctly?

Audrey ÷ 30

Vinegar	30	1
Olive oil	120	4

÷ 30

Jonathan ÷ 25

Vinegar	25	1
Olive oil	75	3

÷ 25

Jonathan's ratio simplifies to 1:3, so he followed the recipe correctly.

C

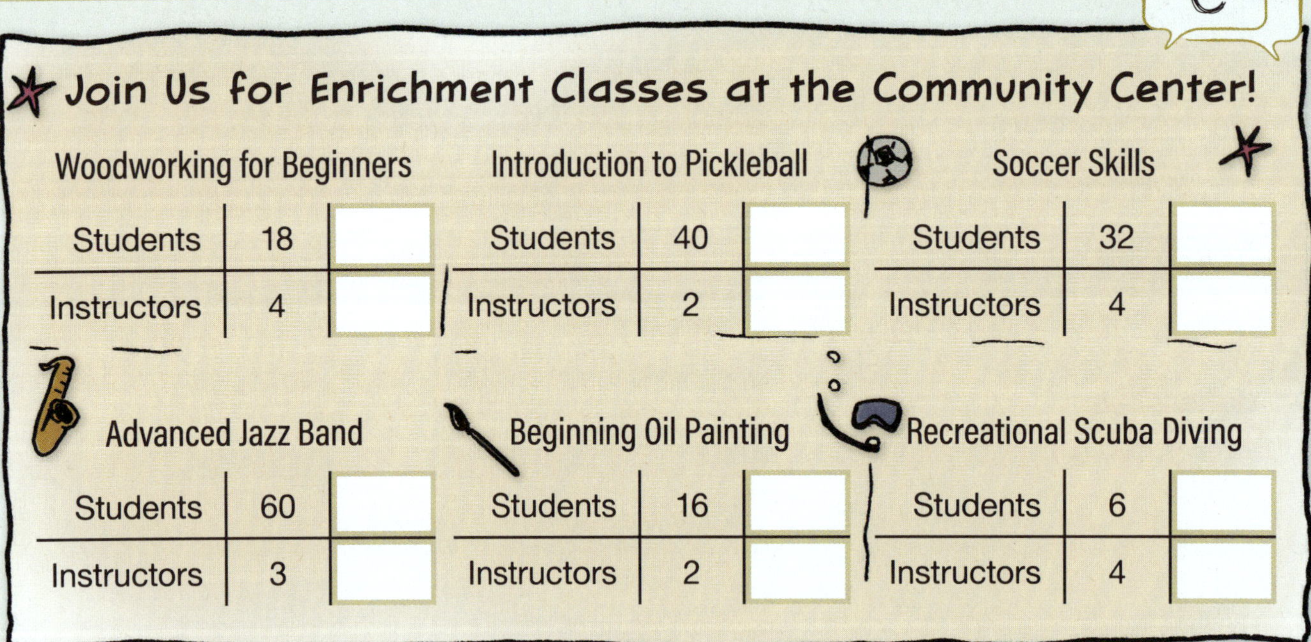

Which class has the same student-instructor ratio as Soccer Skills?

Which class has the same student-instructor ratio as Introduction to Pickleball?

Which class has the most personal attention for each student?

Practice

Use the information to complete the charts.

Carrot-Orange Juice
- 1 part carrot juice
- 4 parts orange juice

Carrot juice (fl. oz.)	1	2	3	4	5	6
Orange juice (fl. oz.)	4	8				

Cherry tomatoes	5	10	15	20	25	30
Cucumber slices	3					

Slime Recipe
- 2 parts cornstarch
- 3 parts water

Cornstarch (scoops)	2					
Water (scoops)	3	6	9	12	15	18

Write the simplest form of each ratio in the ratio tables.
Then, circle the two problems with equivalent ratios in each row.

Oil	90	
Vinegar	30	

Oil	60	
Vinegar	20	

Oil	30	
Vinegar	90	

9 cm
12 cm

Length	12	
Width	9	

15 cm
15 cm

Length	15	
Width	15	

15 cm
20 cm

Length	20	
Width	15	

Review

Find the area of each triangle.

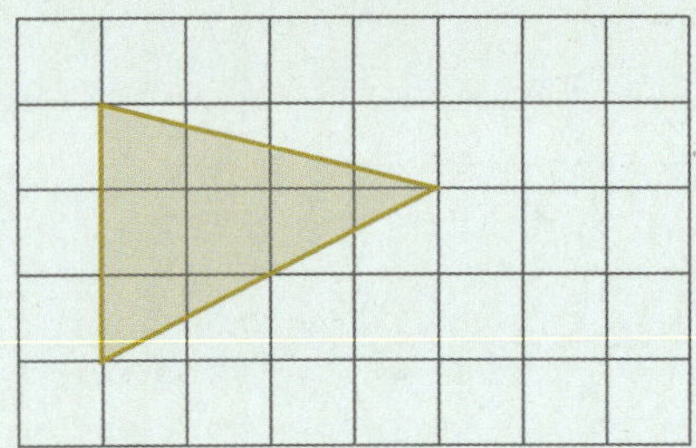

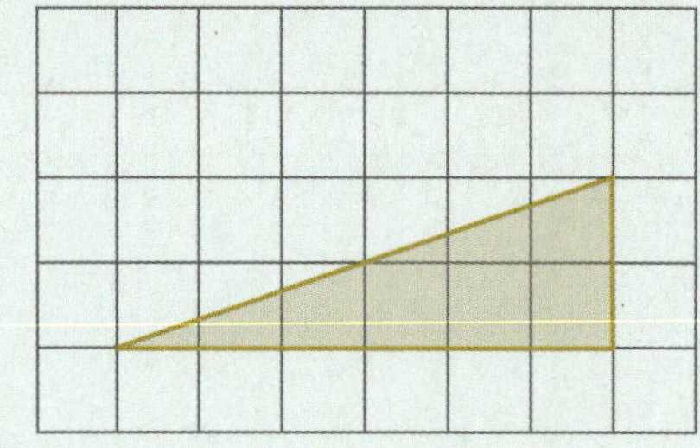

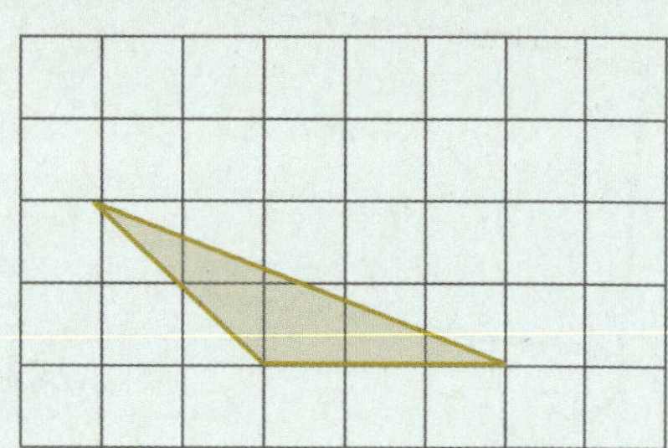

Area: ___________ sq. units

Area: ___________ sq. units

Area: ___________ sq. units

Complete.

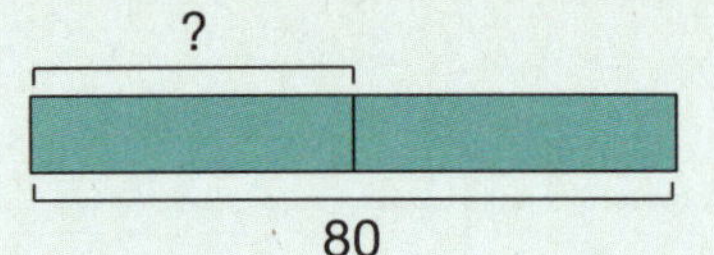

$\dfrac{1}{2}$ of 80 = ___________

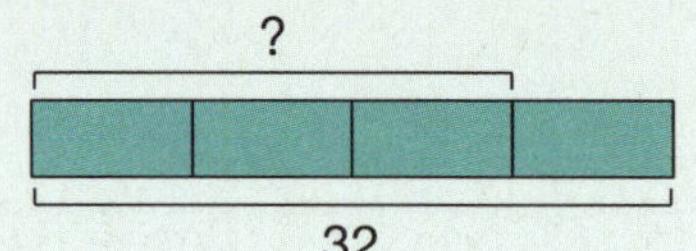

$\dfrac{3}{4}$ of 32 = ___________

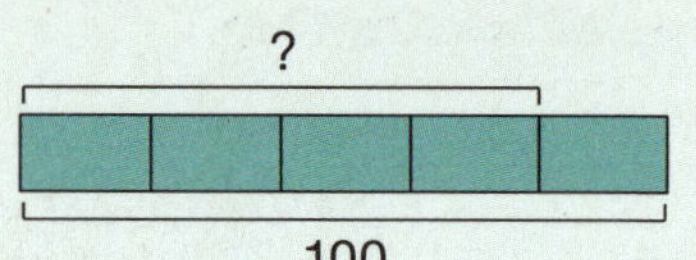

$\dfrac{4}{5}$ of 100 = ___________

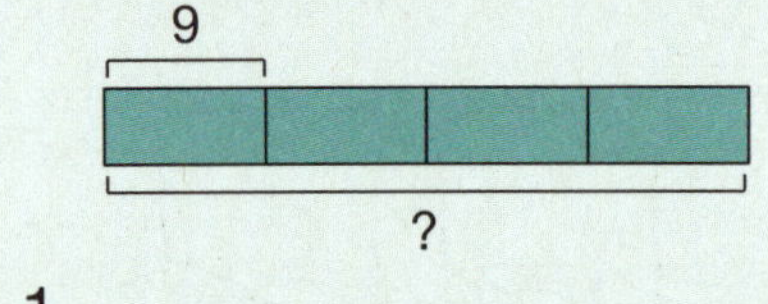

$\dfrac{1}{4}$ of ___________ = 9

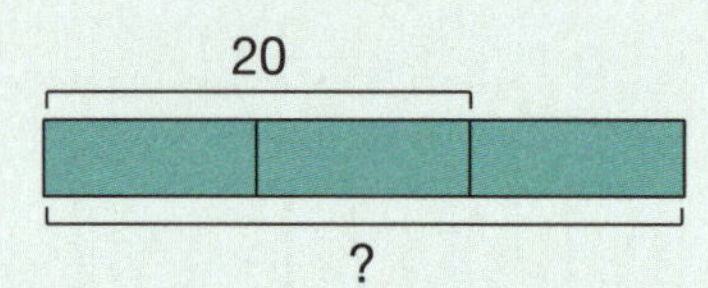

$\dfrac{2}{3}$ of ___________ = 20

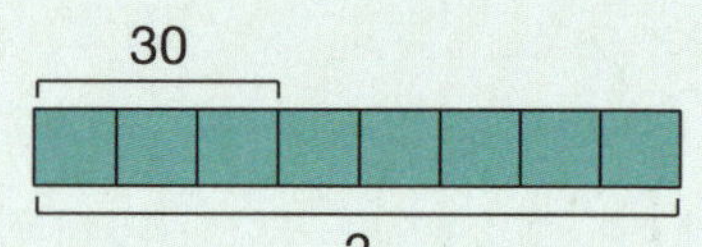

$\dfrac{3}{8}$ of ___________ = 30

Use Beatrice's scorecard from the diving meet to answer the questions.

Which dive earned Beatrice the highest score?

Which dive earned Beatrice the lowest score?

Dive	Score
1	28.74
2	31.09
3	30.70

How many more points did Beatrice earn for her second dive than for her first dive?

How many points did Beatrice earn for all three dives?

Lesson Activities

Counselors : Campers 1:8	Counselors	1	2	3	4	5	6	7
	Campers	8						

Use Ratio Tables to Find One of the Quantities

If you know the ratio between two quantities along with one of the quantities, you can use a ratio table to find the other quantity.

1. Set up the ratio table.

2. Use multiplication or division to describe the relationship between the columns.

3. Use the relationship to complete the missing number.

Ex. Canoe trips at Camp Adventure have a 2:9 ratio of counselors to campers. If 45 campers sign up for a canoe trip, how many counselors do they need?

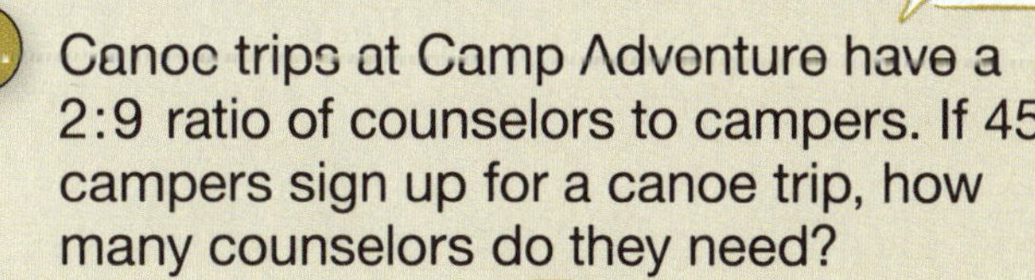

$\times 5$

Counselors	2	**10**
Campers	9	45

$\times 5$

$9 \times \underline{\ ?\ } = 45$

5 groups of 9 campers equal 45 campers. Each group needs 2 counselors, so they need a total of 10 counselors.

Backpacking trips at Camp Adventure have a 2:15 ratio of counselors to campers. If 8 counselors go on a trip, how many campers can go?

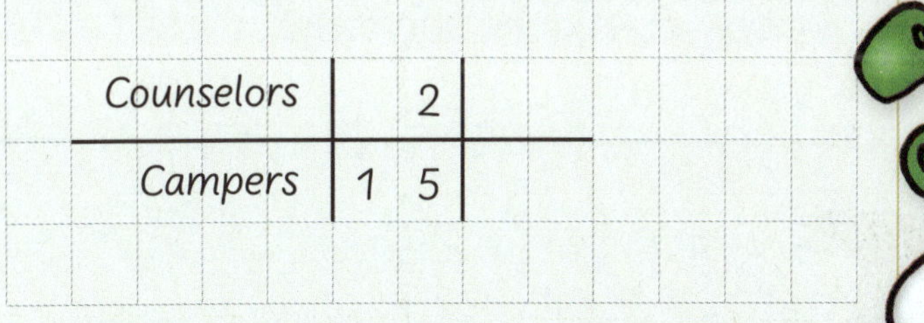

Counselors		2	
Campers	1	5	

During craft time, Erin makes a bracelet with 2 white beads for every 7 green beads. If she uses 50 white beads, how many green beads does she use?

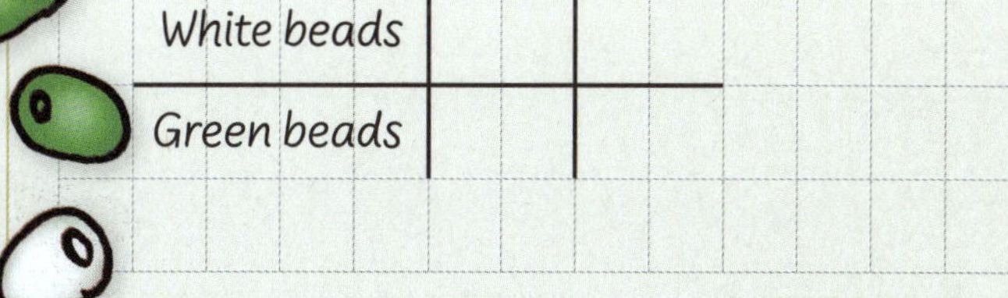

White beads		
Green beads		

Campers prefer blueberry pancakes and chocolate chip pancakes in a 3:4 ratio. If the camp chef makes 160 chocolate chip pancakes, how many blueberry pancakes should he make?

The camp chef uses a 2:3 ratio of rice to water to cook rice. If he uses 70 cups of rice, how many cups of water should he use?

Practice

Use ratio tables to solve the word problems.

The ratio of the length of Sarah's guinea pig to the length of her rabbit is 2:3. If her rabbit is 15 in. long, how long is her guinea pig?

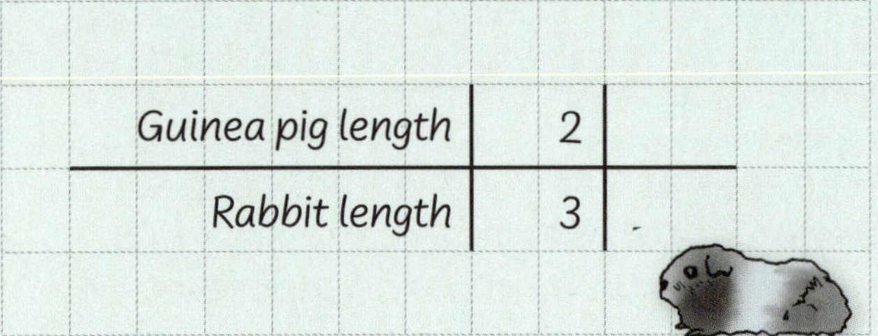

Guinea pig length	2	
Rabbit length	3	

The ratio of Vanshika's age to her mom's age is 1:3. If Vanshika is 14, how old is her mom?

Vanshika's age	1	
Mom's age	3	

Stephen is arranging balloons for a party. He puts 5 green balloons and 3 yellow balloons in each bunch. If he has 100 green balloons, how many yellow balloons does he need?

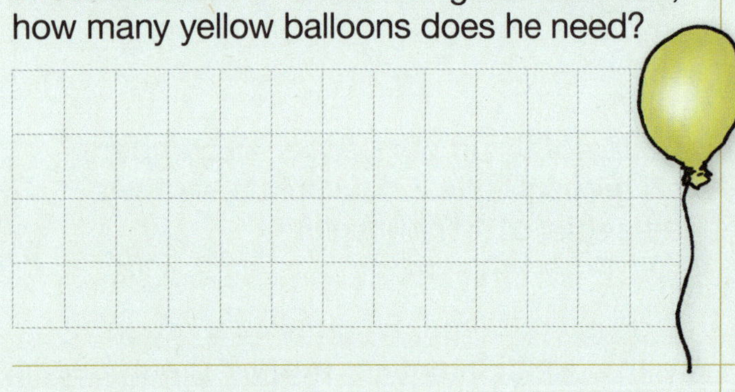

Jace saves $2 for every $7 he spends. In November, Jace spent $28. How much money did he save?

The ratio of adults to children at the magic show is 3:4. If there are 51 adults, how many children are there?

The ratio of fiction books to non-fiction books on Charis' bookshelf is 5:2. Charis owns 30 non-fiction books. How many fiction books does she own?

How many adults and children are there in total at the magic show?

How many more fiction books than non-fiction books does Charis own?

Review   Evaluate.

$5^3 \times 2 + 4$

$\dfrac{7^2 + 1}{10}$

$\dfrac{2^4}{2} + 3$

Use the numbers in the boxes to complete the equivalent fractions.

| 4 | 10 |

$\dfrac{\square}{8} = \dfrac{1}{2} = \dfrac{5}{\square}$

| 15 | 9 |

$\dfrac{\square}{12} = \dfrac{3}{4} = \dfrac{\square}{20}$

| 4 | 20 |

$\dfrac{6}{\square} = \dfrac{3}{2} = \dfrac{30}{\square}$

Draw a line to connect the numbers in order from Start to End. Follow the rule.

Rule: Add 15

Start →

15	30	25	35	170
20	45	40	55	150
65	60	50	150	165
80	75	90	135	180
95	100	105	120	125

END

Rule: Add 35

Start →

35	60	130	360	300
70	50	90	295	310
105	95	240	280	315
140	175	210	245	350
165	190	200	225	305

END

Write each measurement as a fraction of a foot. Write the fractions in simplest form.

4 in. = __________ ft.

$\dfrac{4}{12} = \dfrac{1}{3}$

5 in. = __________ ft.

6 in. = __________ ft.

2 in. = __________ ft.

8 in. = __________ ft.

11 in. = __________ ft.

Lesson Activities 👥

A

Pineapple-Orange Juice

- 3 parts orange juice
- 4 parts pineapple juice

Orange juice (fl. oz.)	3	12				
Pineapple juice (fl. oz.)	4		40			

B

Use Ratios to Scale Quantities

When two different combinations have the same ratio, we say that they are proportional to each other.

We use ratio tables with multiple columns to scale quantities up or down so that they are proportional to each other.

1. Set up the ratio table with the original amounts.

2. Simplify the ratio.

3. Use the simplified ratio to find the new amounts.

Ex. Anna mixes 9 fl. oz. of pomegranate juice with 6 fl. oz. of apple juice. She likes the flavor, so she decides to make a bigger batch. If she uses 14 fl. oz. of apple juice in the new batch, how much pomegranate juice should she use?

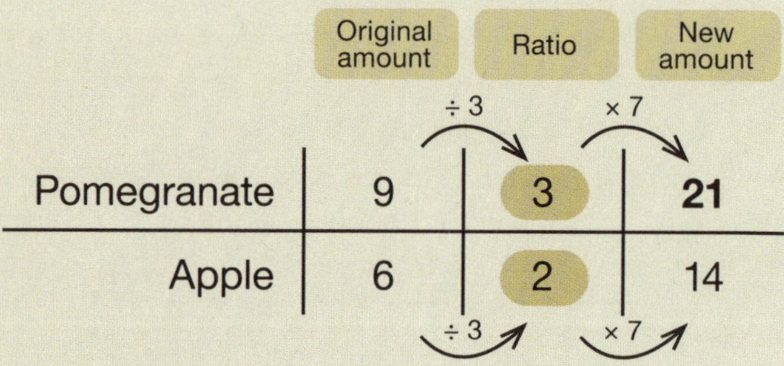

The original batch's ratio of pomegranate juice to apple juice was 3:2. So, the new batch must have the same ratio. She uses 21 fl. oz.

The recipe for a strawberry-banana smoothie calls for 20 oz. of frozen strawberries and 15 oz. of frozen bananas. Joshua only has 6 oz. of frozen bananas, so he scales the recipe down. How many ounces of frozen strawberries should he use?

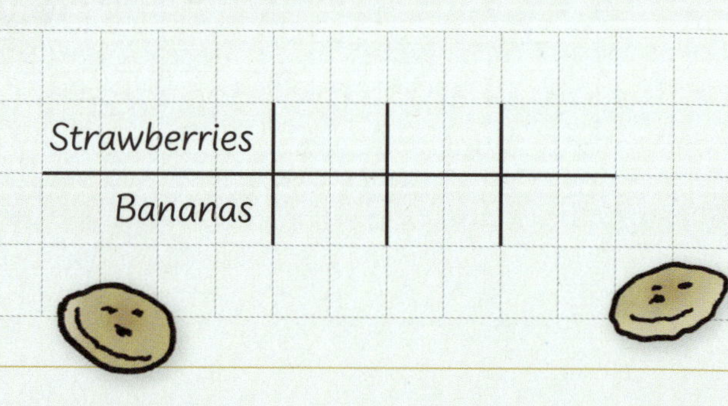

The photo has a length of 8 in. and a width of 12 in. Khadija enlarges the photo without changing the ratio of the length to the width. If the enlarged photo has a length of 20 in., what is its width?

Length				
Width				

Practice 

Complete the missing numbers in the ratio tables.

Dollars saved	5	1	
Dollars spent	20	4	36

Instructors	3	1	5
Students	36	12	

Chocolate cookies	100	5	
Sugar cookies		3	24

Sugar (lb.)	8		
Peaches (lb.)	4	1	14

Cranberry juice (mL)		3	30
Orange juice (mL)	24	4	

Length (ft.)	21		90
Width (ft.)	28	4	

Use ratio tables to solve the word problems.

Ella tries mixing 50 mL of purple paint with 75 mL of white paint to make light purple. She likes the color, so she decides to make more. If she uses 180 mL of purple paint, how much white paint should she use?

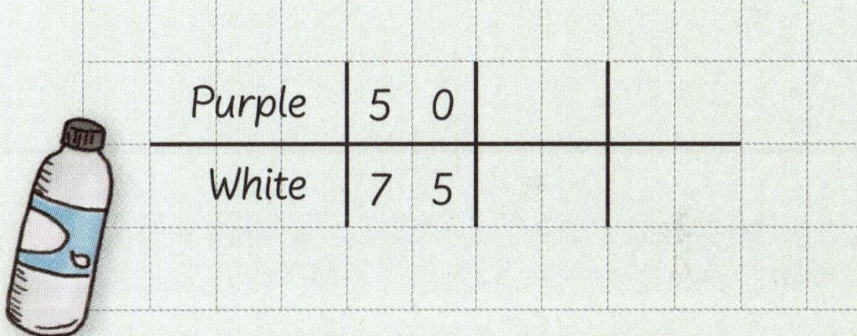

Purple	5	0					
White	7	5					

The photo has a length of 25 cm and a width of 20 cm. Stevie shrinks the photo without changing the ratio of the length to the width. If the smaller photo has a length of 10 cm, what is its width?

Length					
Width					

⭐ The soccer club has 6 coaches for 45 players. They decide to expand the club and hire 8 more coaches. If they keep the coach-to-player ratio the same, how many new players can join?

Coaches					
Players					

Review

Complete the missing units to answer the questions. Leave the blank empty if the number tells the number of groups or parts. Use exponents for square units.

The rectangle has an area of 30 ft.^{2} It is 5 ft. wide. What is its length?

$$\frac{30\ \boxed{}}{5\ \boxed{}} = 6\ \boxed{}$$

The rectangle has an area of 30 ft.^{2} If you split it into 5 equal pieces, what is the area of each piece?

$$\frac{30\ \boxed{}}{5\ \boxed{}} = 6\ \boxed{}$$

The rectangle has an area of 30 ft.^{2} If you cut it into pieces that each have an area of 5 ft.^{2}, how many pieces do you make?

$$\frac{30\ \boxed{}}{5\ \boxed{}} = 6\ \boxed{}$$

Find the perimeter and area.

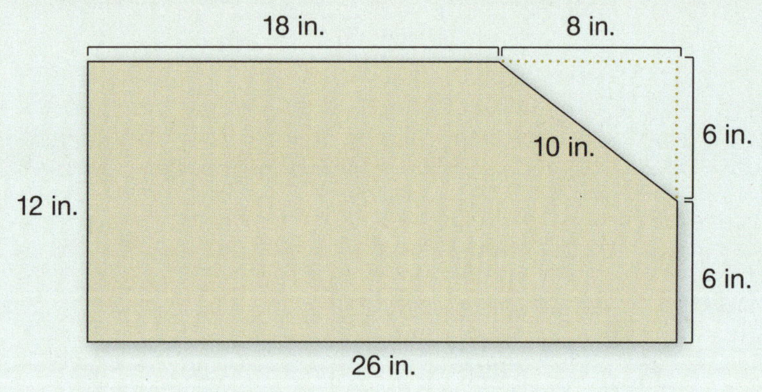

Perimeter: _______________   Area: _______________

Solve. Write the fractions in simplest form.

Truett collects baseball cards. He has 240 cards, and then he buys 30 more. How many cards does he have now?

What fraction of his cards are new?

What fraction of his cards did he already own?

Lily collects coins. She has 33 American coins. She has $\frac{1}{3}$ as many coins from other countries as American coins. How many coins from other countries does she have?

How many coins does she have in all?

What fraction of her coins are American coins?

Lesson Activities

What is the **ratio** of ducks to frogs?	What **fraction** of the prizes are ducks?
What is the **ratio** of frogs to ducks?	What **fraction** of the prizes are frogs?

Ratios and Fractions

 **Ex.** In a bag of marbles, the ratio of yellow marbles to green marbles is 1:3. What fraction of the marbles are yellow? What fraction of the marbles are green?

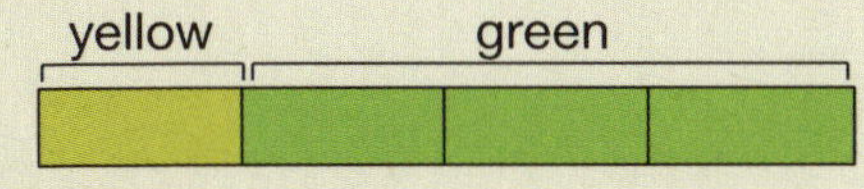

$\frac{1}{4}$ of the marbles are yellow.

$\frac{3}{4}$ of the marbles are green.

 **Ex.** In a different bag of marbles, $\frac{3}{5}$ of the marbles are red. The rest are orange. What is the ratio of red marbles to orange marbles?

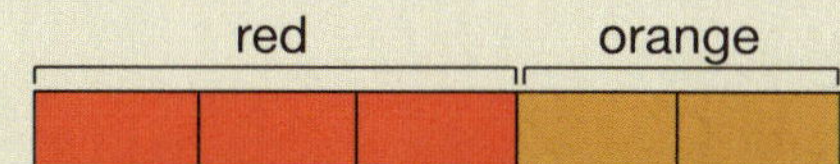

Red marbles : Orange marbles
3:2

Four in a Row (2-Player Game)

1:4	$\frac{1}{8}$ and $\frac{7}{8}$	5:1	$\frac{2}{5}$ and $\frac{3}{5}$
$\frac{5}{8}$ and $\frac{3}{8}$	3:4	$\frac{2}{7}$ and $\frac{5}{7}$	1:7
2:3	$\frac{5}{6}$ and $\frac{1}{6}$	1:2	$\frac{3}{4}$ and $\frac{1}{4}$
$\frac{1}{3}$ and $\frac{2}{3}$	5:3	$\frac{1}{2}$ and $\frac{1}{2}$	2:5
1:1	$\frac{1}{5}$ and $\frac{4}{5}$	3:1	$\frac{3}{7}$ and $\frac{4}{7}$

Practice   **Match.**

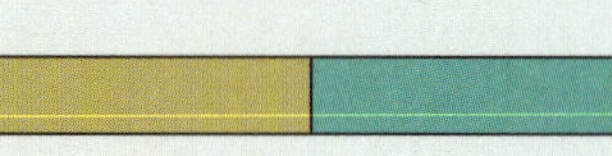

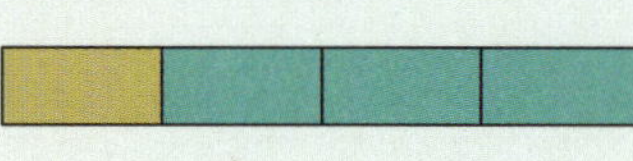

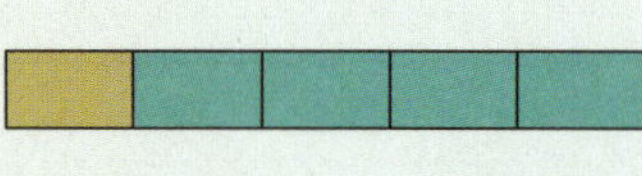

1:3		$\frac{1}{2}$ and $\frac{1}{2}$
1:1		$\frac{5}{6}$ and $\frac{1}{6}$
2:3		$\frac{1}{4}$ and $\frac{3}{4}$
5:1		$\frac{3}{7}$ and $\frac{4}{7}$
1:4		$\frac{2}{5}$ and $\frac{3}{5}$
3:4		$\frac{1}{5}$ and $\frac{4}{5}$

Draw bar models to match each question. Then, answer the questions.

Felicity saves and spends her money in a 1:6 ratio. What fraction of her money does she save?

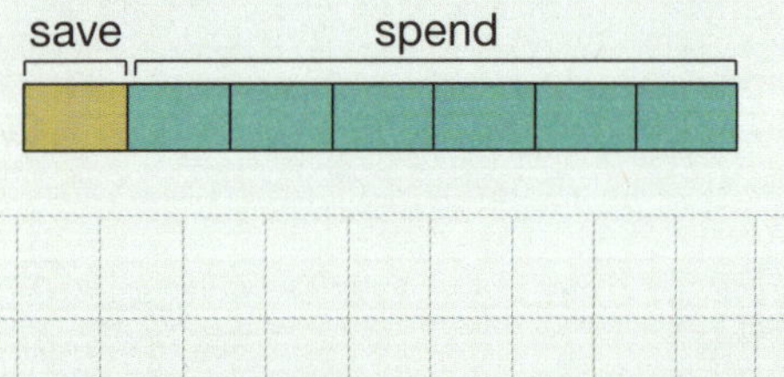

Michael mixes 1 part vinegar with 2 parts water to make a homemade cleaner. What fraction of the total amount is vinegar?

Esa and Malik share a chocolate bar. Esa gets $\frac{3}{5}$ of the chocolate bar, and Malik gets $\frac{2}{5}$ of the chocolate bar. What is the ratio of Esa's share of the chocolate bar to Malik's share of the chocolate bar?

At basketball practice, John Scott makes $\frac{3}{4}$ of his shots. He misses the rest. What is the ratio of shots he makes to shots he misses?

Review

Evaluate.

$1^3 =$ _______________

$2^3 =$ _______________

$3^3 =$ _______________

$4^3 =$ _______________

$5^3 =$ _______________

$7 \times 10^2 =$ _______________

$2 \times 10^4 =$ _______________

$8 \times 10^3 =$ _______________

$6 \times 10^1 =$ _______________

$4 \times 10^0 =$ _______________

Write in simplest form.

$\dfrac{50}{100} =$

$\dfrac{75}{100} =$

$\dfrac{25}{100} =$

$\dfrac{10}{100} =$

Use the information to complete the chart.

Lifeguards	2	4	6	8	10	12	14
Swimmers	25						

Use long division to solve. Write the remainder as a fraction. Use the example to help.

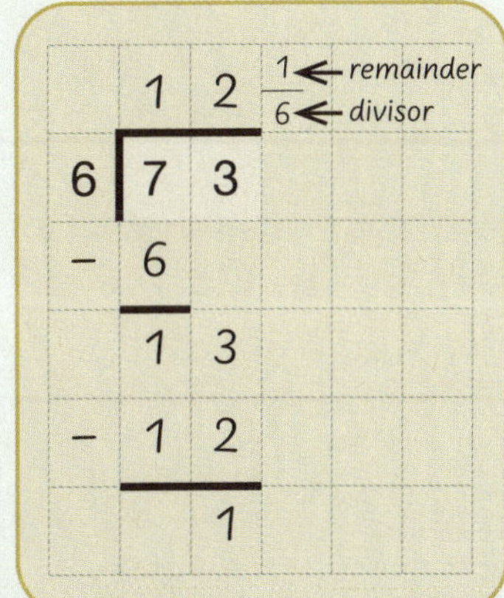

Use bar models to solve.

Adelaide's goal is to run 75 km this month. So far, she has run $\dfrac{3}{5}$ of her goal distance. How much farther does she need to run to reach her goal?

Goal distance

Distance run so far

Lesson Activities 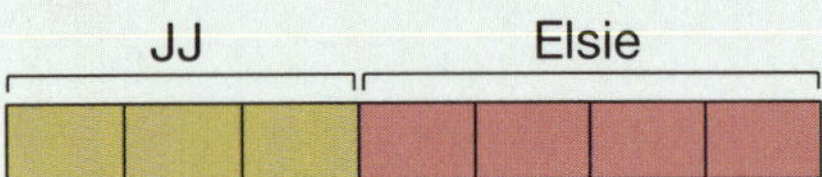

JJ and Elsie have a lemonade stand. JJ works 3 hours, and Elsie works 4 hours. So, they decide to share the money in a 3:4 ratio (with Elsie getting the bigger share).

JJ   Elsie

A

What fraction of the money does JJ get?

What fraction of the money does Elsie get?

B

Split a Sum According to a Ratio

If you know the sum of two quantities and the ratio between the quantities, you can find both quantities.

Ex. JJ and Elsie share their lemonade stand earnings in a 3:4 ratio. If the lemonade stand earns $42 in all, how much money does each person earn?

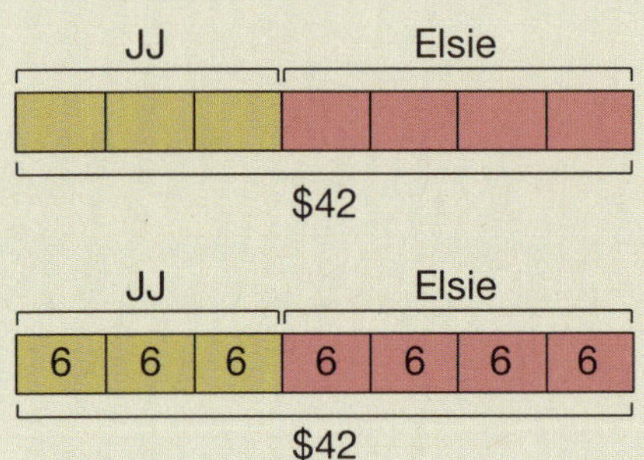

JJ and Elsie split the money into 7 shares.

$42 \div 7 = 6$. Each share is $6.

JJ gets 3 shares. $3 \times 6 = $ **$18**

Elsie gets 4 shares. $4 \times 6 = $ **$24**

C

Share the Wealth (2-Player Game)

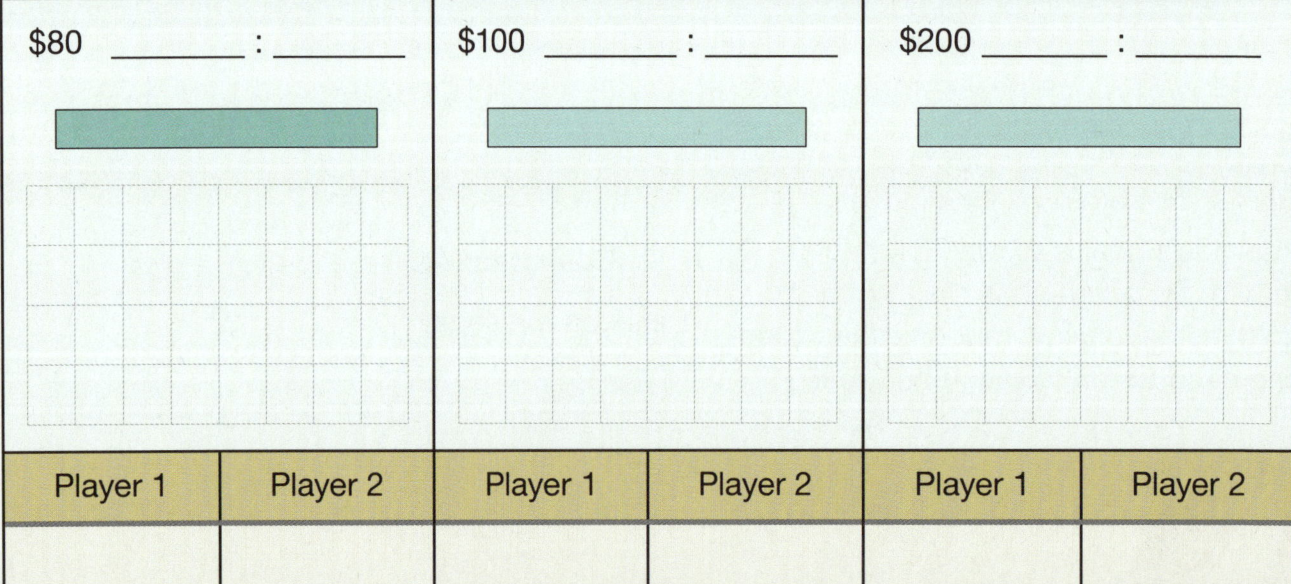

$80 ______ : ______		$100 ______ : ______		$200 ______ : ______	
Player 1	Player 2	Player 1	Player 2	Player 1	Player 2

Practice
Draw bar models to match each question. Then, complete the blanks.

Freya is arranging flowers for a party. She puts 4 yellow roses and 5 pink roses in each vase. She uses 72 roses in all.

yellow | pink

Number of yellow roses: _______________

Number of pink roses: _______________

David mixes red and blue paint in a 3:5 ratio to make purple paint. He makes a total of 64 fl. oz. of purple paint.

Fluid ounces of red paint: _______________

Fluid ounces of blue paint: _______________

The ratio of Owen's age to his dad's age is 2:7. The sum of their ages is 54.

Owen's age: _______________

Owen's dad's age: _______________

Avonlea saves $1 for every $5 she spends. In November, Avonlea earns $60. She spends or saves all of her earnings.

Money saved: _______________

Money spent: _______________

Eliana makes a friendship bracelet with blue and white beads. The ratio of blue beads to white beads is 4:1. She uses a total of 30 beads.

Number of blue beads: _______________

Number of white beads: _______________

There are 180 people at the ballet recital. The ratio of adults to children is 2:3.

Number of adults: _______________

Number of children: _______________

Review — Complete.

$7^2 =$ _______________ $1^2 =$ _______________ $6^2 =$ _______________

$5^2 =$ _______________ $3^2 =$ _______________ $4^2 =$ _______________

$9^2 =$ _______________ $8^2 =$ _______________ $2^2 =$ _______________

Write each measurement as a fraction or mixed number. Write the fractions in simplest form.

$10 \text{ cm} = \dfrac{1}{10}$ m

$\dfrac{10}{100} = \dfrac{1}{10}$

$25 \text{ cm} =$ _______________ m $60 \text{ cm} =$ _______________ m

$90 \text{ cm} =$ _______________ m $150 \text{ cm} =$ _______________ m $270 \text{ cm} =$ _______________ m

Find the product.

```
    3 7
×   8 6
```

Complete.

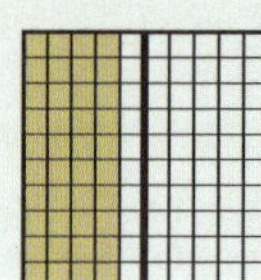

$0.4 +$ _________ $= 1$

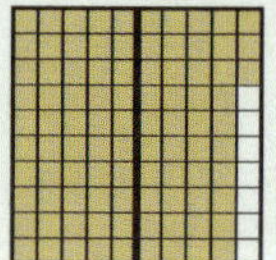

$0.93 +$ _________ $= 1$

Use bar models to solve.

The Eagles scored 45 points in the basketball game. The Eagles scored $\dfrac{5}{6}$ as many points as the Pumas. How many points did the Pumas score?

Eagles

Pumas

The bake sale earned $70 on Monday. It earned $\dfrac{2}{3}$ as much money on Monday as on Tuesday. How much money did it earn on Tuesday?

Monday

Tuesday

Lesson Activities 

Anja collects dolphin and whale figurines. She has 18 dolphins, and she has $\frac{2}{3}$ as many dolphins as whales.

Dolphins

Whales

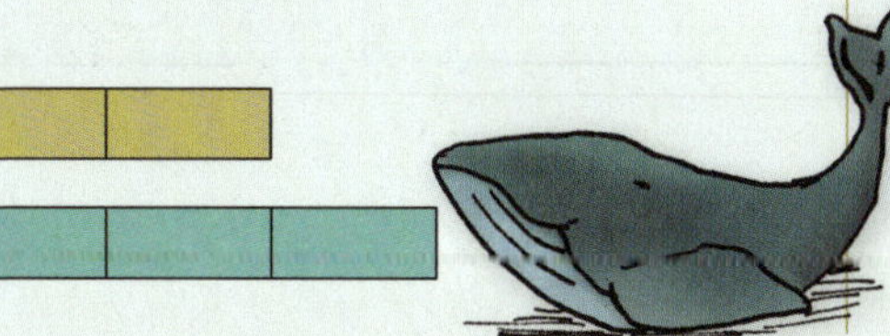

A

Dolphins : Whales

__________ : __________

How many whales does she have?

B

Use Ratios and Fractions to Solve Comparison Problems

Ex. Anja collects dolphin and whale figurines. She has $\frac{2}{3}$ as many dolphins as whales.

What is the ratio of dolphins to the total number of figurines?

Dolphins

Whales

$2 + 3 = 5$

Dolphins : Total
2:5

What fraction of the whole collection is dolphins?

Dolphins

Whales

$2 + 3 = 5$

$\dfrac{2}{5}$ ← Dolphin unit bars / Total unit bars

Porter collects football and baseball cards. He has $\frac{2}{5}$ as many football cards as baseball cards.

Football

Baseball

Football cards : Baseball cards

__________ : __________

Baseball cards : Football cards

__________ : __________

Football cards : Total cards

__________ : __________

Baseball cards : Total cards

__________ : __________

What fraction of the whole collection is football cards?

What fraction of the whole collection is baseball cards?

Porter owns a total of 140 cards. How many football cards does he own?

How many baseball cards does he own?

Practice

Draw bar models to match each description. Then, complete the ratios and answer the questions.

Olivia earns money by raking leaves and babysitting. One month, she earns $\frac{1}{3}$ as much raking leaves as she does babysitting.

Raking

Babysitting

Raking money : Babysitting money

______ : ______

Babysitting money : Raking money

______ : ______

Raking money : Total money

______ : ______

Babysitting money : Total money

______ : ______

What fraction of the total amount of money does she earn raking leaves?

What fraction of the total amount of money does she earn babysitting?

Olivia earns a total of $100. How much does she earn raking leaves?

How much does she earn babysitting?

Michael buys a remote control car and a drone. The remote control car costs $\frac{3}{4}$ as much as the drone.

Car

Drone

Car's price : Drone's price

______ : ______

Drone's price : Car's price

______ : ______

Car's price : Total price

______ : ______

Drone's price : Total price

______ : ______

What fraction of the total cost does Michael spend on the car?

What fraction of the total cost does Michael spend on the drone?

Michael spends a total of $140. How much does the car cost?

How much does the drone cost?

Review

Complete the chart.

	Base	Exponent	Repeated Multiplication	Value
2^5	2			32
3^3				
1^7				
0^4				
10^6				

Use long division to solve. Write the remainder as a fraction.

$$3\overline{)947} \qquad 7\overline{)2,462}$$

Complete the chart to find the perimeter and area of a rectangle with the given dimensions.

Length (l)	Width (w)	Perimeter (l + w + l + w)	Area (l · w)
8	7		
9	6		
10	5		
11	4		
12	3		

Use ratio tables to solve.

The chef mixes 3 parts ground beef with 2 parts ground pork to make meatballs. If she uses 16 lb. ground pork, how much ground beef should she use?

Ground beef			
Ground pork			

The photo has a length of 15 in. and a width of 10 in. Ruby enlarges the photo without changing the ratio of the length to the width. If the larger photo has a length of 24 in., what is its width?

Length			
Width			

Lesson Activities

The ratio of Ellie's age to Brayden's age is 5:3. If Ellie is 40, how old is Brayden?

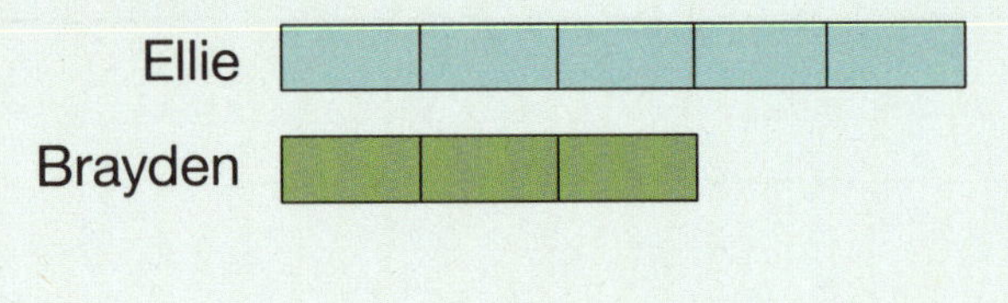

A

The ratio of Ellie's age to Brayden's age is 5:3. If Brayden is 6, how old is Ellie?

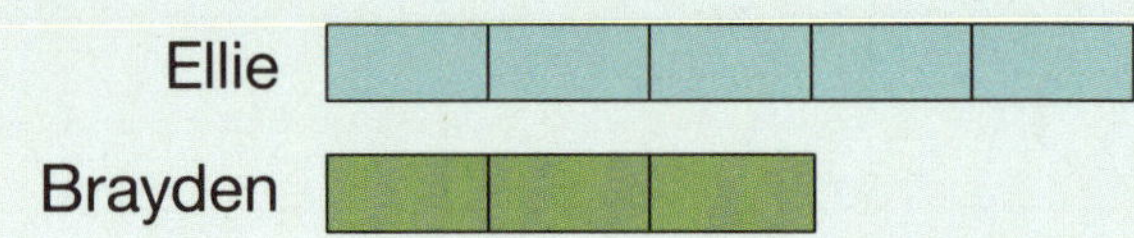

B

Use the Ratio and Difference to Find Quantities

If you know the difference between two quantities and the ratio between the quantities, you can find both quantities.

Ex. The ratio of Ellie's age to Brayden's age is 5:3. Ellie is 8 years older than Brayden. How old is Ellie? How old is Brayden?

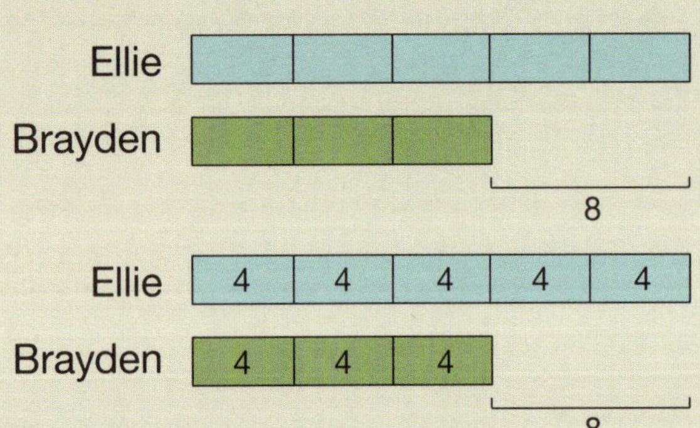

Ellie's bar is 2 units longer than Brayden's.

8 ÷ 2 = 4. Each unit stands for 4 years.

Ellie: 5 × 4 = **20 years old**

Brayden: 3 × 4 = **12 years old**

Rachel's cat is 2 years older than her dog. The ratio of the cat's age to the dog's age is 4:3. How old is her cat? How old is her dog?

Cat

Dog

The sweater costs $15 more than the T-shirt. The ratio of the sweater's price to the T-shirt's price is 7:4. How much does the sweater cost? How much does the T-shirt cost?

Sweater

T-shirt

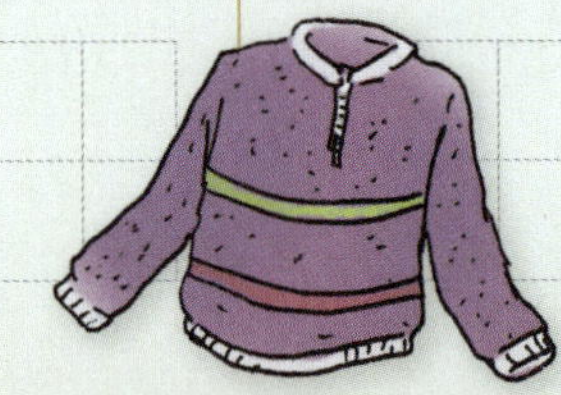

Practice

Use bar models to complete the blanks and answer the questions.

Jo mixed red and yellow paint in a 1:3 ratio to make orange paint. She used 60 fl. oz. more yellow paint than red paint.

Red

Yellow

Amount of red paint: _________________

Amount of yellow paint: _________________

The ratio of campers to counselors is 7:1. There are 90 more campers than counselors.

Campers

Counselors

Number of campers: _________________

Number of counselors: _________________

John and Livia both earned money for the library fundraiser. Livia earned $\frac{5}{7}$ as much as John. John earned $30 more than Livia.

Livia

John

Dollars earned by John: _________________

Dollars earned by Livia: _________________

Total dollars earned by both: _________________

Review

Use the distributive property to complete the blanks. (You do not need to evaluate.)

$7 \cdot (14 + 5) =$ _______ $\cdot 14 +$ _______ $\cdot 5$

$20 \cdot 88 + 20 \cdot 2 = 20 \cdot (88 +$ _______ $)$

$24 \cdot (8 + 50) = 24 \cdot 8 + 24 \cdot$ _______

$18 \cdot 1 + 18 \cdot 99 = 18 \cdot (1 +$ _______ $)$

$37 \cdot (22 + 9) = 37 \cdot$ _______ $+ 37 \cdot 9$

$13 \cdot 35 + 13 \cdot 5 =$ _______ $\cdot (35 + 5)$

Write each number in expanded form.

Standard Form	Expanded Form
3.872	$3 + \frac{8}{10} + \frac{7}{100} + \frac{2}{1,000}$
4.195	
37.4	
6.008	

Write <, >, or =.

1.2 $\bigcirc$ 2.1

3 $\bigcirc$ 0.945

1.7 $\bigcirc$ 1.78

0.3 $\bigcirc$ 0.30

4.651 $\bigcirc$ 3.651

0.87 $\bigcirc$ 0.9

Draw and label each point in the correct location on the coordinate plane. Then, follow the directions and answer the questions.

Point	Ordered Pair
S	(0,5)
T	(1,1)
U	(5,1)
V	(4,5)

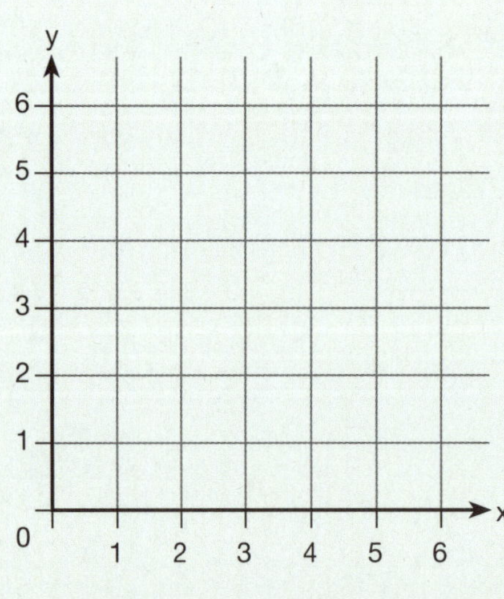

Draw straight lines to connect the points in order (S to T, T to U, U to V). Connect V to S, too. What shape do you create?

What is the area of the shape? (Each small box on the coordinate plane is 1 square unit.)

Unit Wrap-Up

Write the simplest form of each ratio in the ratio tables. Then, circle the tables that have the same ratio of adults to children.

Adults	6	
Children	8	

Adults	12	
Children	9	

Adults	15	
Children	20	

Adults	20	
Children	30	

Adults	75	
Children	100	

Adults	25	
Children	45	

Draw bar models to match each question. Then, answer the questions.

The soccer team's ratio of wins to losses is 3:1. What fraction of their games have they won?

The soccer team has won 12 games. How many games have they played in all?

There are $\frac{2}{3}$ as many oatmeal raisin cookies as chocolate chip cookies on the tray.

Oatmeal raisin

Chocolate chip

Oatmeal raisin : Chocolate chip

______ : ______

Chocolate chip : Oatmeal raisin

______ : ______

Oatmeal raisin : Total cookies

______ : ______

Chocolate chip : Total cookies

______ : ______

What fraction of the cookies are oatmeal raisin?

What fraction of the cookies are chocolate chip?

There are 24 oatmeal raisin cookies. How many more chocolate chip cookies than oatmeal raisin cookies are on the tray?

Unit Wrap-Up

Thelma's Bakery is deciding how many pies to bake for Thanksgiving week. Use ratio tables and bar models to answer the questions and complete the chart.

Thelma's Bakery

Type of pie	Number of pies sold last year	Number of pies we'll bake this year
Pumpkin	300	400
Pecan	120	
Apple		
Sweet potato		

For pumpkin pies, the bakery uses a ratio of 8 parts pumpkin puree to 3 parts sugar. If they use 320 lb. of pumpkin puree, how much sugar do they need?

Pumpkin puree					
Sugar					

Last year, the bakery sold 300 pumpkin pies and 120 pecan pies. They want to keep the ratio of pumpkin pies to pecan pies the same this year as last year. If they bake 400 pumpkin pies, how many pecan pies should they bake?

Pumpkin pies			
Pecan pies			

Last year, customers bought apple pies and sweet potato pies in a 4:1 ratio. They bought 90 more apple pies than sweet potato pies. How many of each kind did they buy?

Apple

Sweet potato

This year, the bakery wants to make apple and sweet potato pies in a 3:1 ratio. If they bake a total of 240 apple and sweet potato pies, how many of each kind should they bake?

Apple

Sweet potato

Lesson Activities 

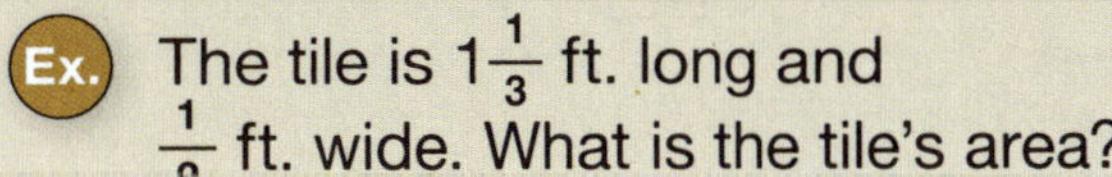

$$2\frac{3}{5} = \frac{\ }{5} \qquad 1\frac{7}{12} = \frac{\ }{12} \qquad 4 = \frac{\ }{1} \qquad 7 = \frac{\ }{1}$$

Multiply Fractions, Whole Numbers, or Mixed Numbers

Convert mixed numbers to improper fractions before multiplying. Write whole numbers with a denominator of 1.

1. Multiply the numerators.
2. Multiply the denominators.
3. Simplify or convert to a mixed number if needed.

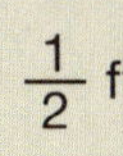 The tile is $1\frac{1}{3}$ ft. long and $\frac{1}{2}$ ft. wide. What is the tile's area?

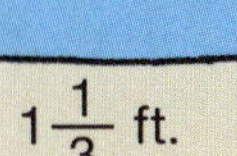

$$1\frac{1}{3} \times \frac{1}{2}$$

$$\frac{4}{3} \times \frac{1}{2} = \frac{4 \times 1}{3 \times 2} = \frac{4}{6} = \frac{2}{3} \text{ ft.}^2$$

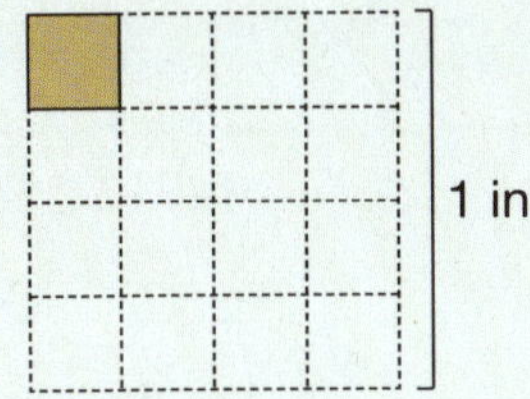

$$\frac{1}{4} \times \frac{1}{4} =$$

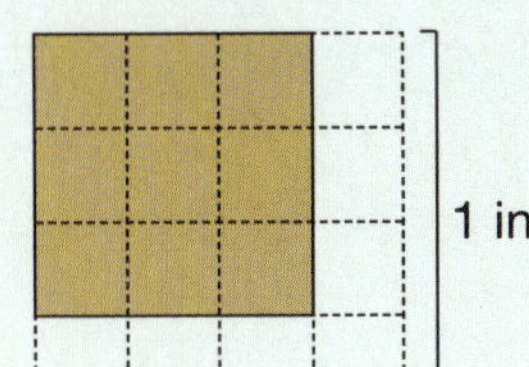

$$\frac{3}{4} \times \frac{3}{4} =$$

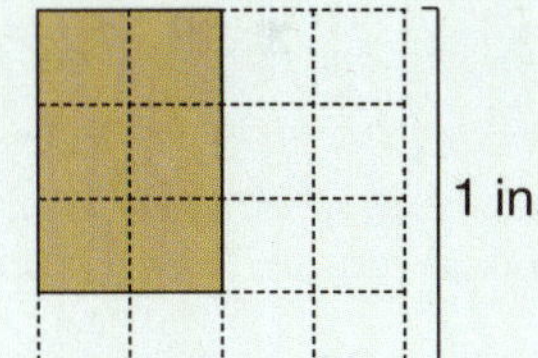

$$\frac{3}{4} \times \frac{1}{2} =$$

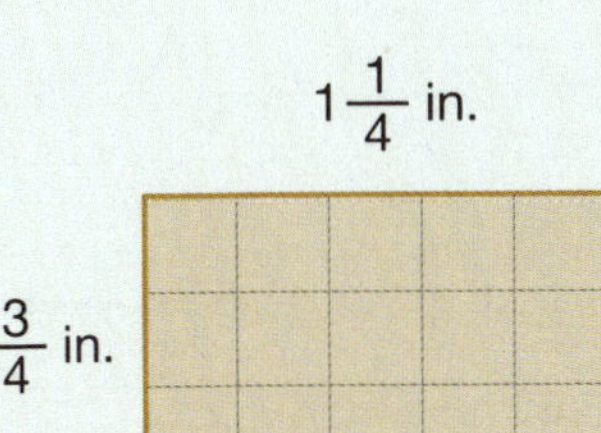

$$\frac{3}{4} \times 1\frac{1}{4}$$

$$1\frac{1}{4} \times 1\frac{1}{2}$$

$$2 \times 1\frac{1}{2}$$

Practice

Find the product. Write your answers in simplest form.

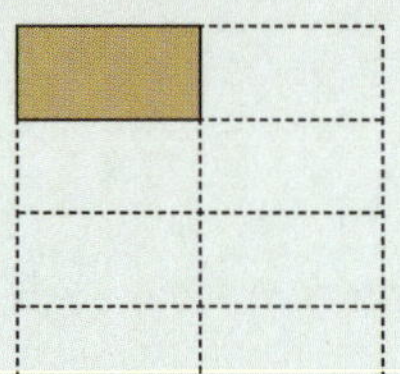

$$\frac{1}{4} \times \frac{1}{2} =$$

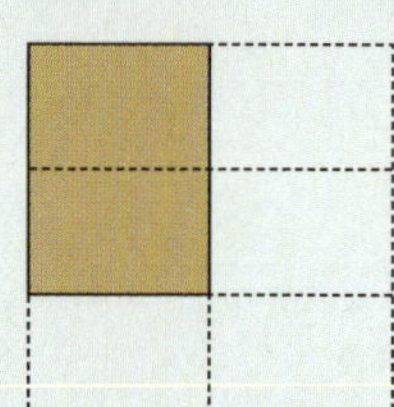

$$\frac{2}{3} \times \frac{1}{2} =$$

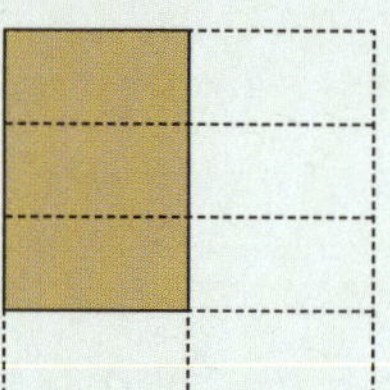

$$\frac{3}{4} \times \frac{1}{2} =$$

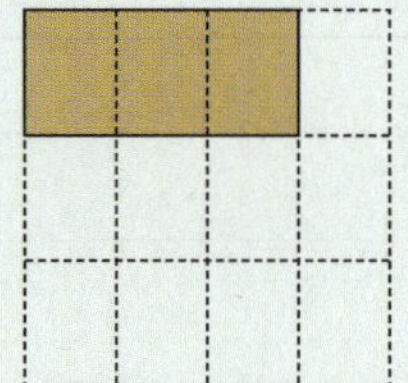

$$\frac{1}{3} \times \frac{3}{4} =$$

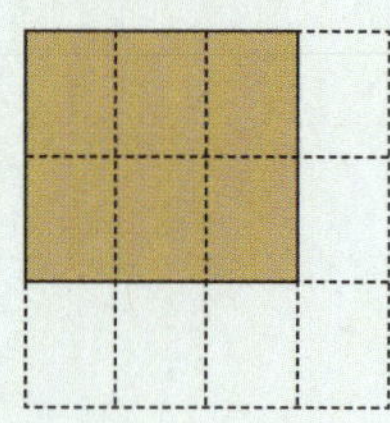

$$\frac{2}{3} \times \frac{3}{4} =$$

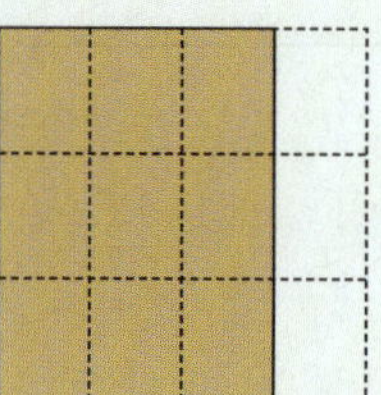

$$\frac{3}{3} \times \frac{3}{4} =$$

Find the area of each shape. Write the equations you use. Write your answers in simplest form. Include the correct units.

$\frac{2}{3}$ ft.

$1\frac{1}{8}$ ft.

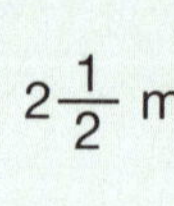

$1\frac{2}{3}$ in.

3 in.

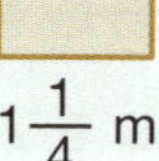

$2\frac{1}{2}$ m

$1\frac{1}{4}$ m

Solve. Write the equations you use. Write your answers in simplest form.

The garden bed is 4 m long and $1\frac{3}{4}$ m wide. What is the area of the bed?

Each side of the square sticky note is $2\frac{1}{2}$ in. long. What is the area of the sticky note?

Review 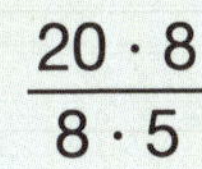 Evaluate. Use cancelling where possible.

$$\frac{20 \cdot 8}{8 \cdot 5}$$

$$\frac{6 \cdot 12}{6}$$

$$\frac{7 \cdot 4 \cdot 9}{9 \cdot 4}$$

$$\frac{6 \cdot 15}{15 \cdot 6}$$

$$\frac{3 \cdot 4}{1}$$

$$\frac{0 \cdot 7}{7}$$

Complete the missing numbers to write each decimal as a fraction.

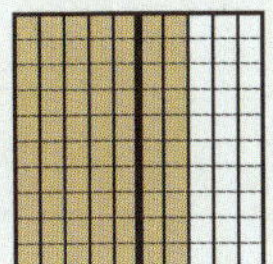

$$0.7 = \frac{}{10}$$

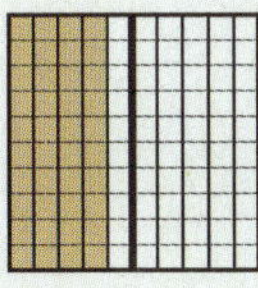

$$0.4 = \frac{}{10}$$

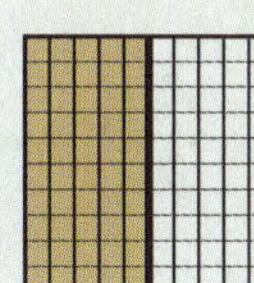

$$0.5 = \frac{}{10}$$

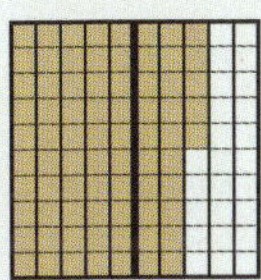

$$0.75 = \frac{}{100}$$

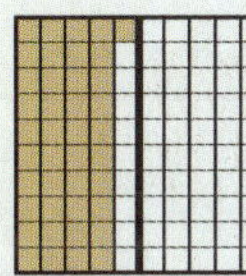

$$0.41 = \frac{}{100}$$

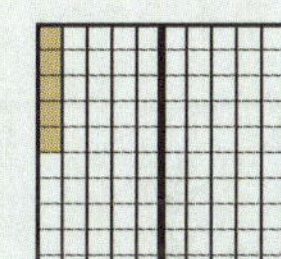

$$0.05 = \frac{}{100}$$

Use ratio tables to complete.

Two computer monitors have the same length-to-width ratio. The smaller monitor has a length of 28 in. and a width of 21 in. The larger monitor has a length of 40 in. What is the larger monitor's width?

Length			
Width			

Hanna's favorite punch recipe calls for 24 fl. oz. of pineapple juice and 40 fl. oz. of lemon-lime soda. She only has 30 fl. oz. of lemon-lime soda, so she decides to make a smaller batch. How much pineapple juice should she use?

Pineapple juice			
Lemon-lime soda			

5.2

Lesson Activities 

$$\frac{5}{10} \times \frac{1}{3} =$$ $$\frac{5}{3} \times \frac{3}{7} =$$ $$\frac{1}{4} \times \frac{8}{3} =$$ $$\frac{2}{9} \times \frac{6}{5} =$$

Simplify Before Multiplying

1. Look for a pair of numbers that have a common factor. One number must be above the fraction bar, and one number must be below the fraction bar. They do not have to be in the same fraction!

2. Divide both numbers by the common factor. Use cancelling to show the division.

3. Multiply like usual.

Ex. $$\frac{1}{5} \times \frac{\overset{3}{\cancel{6}}}{\underset{4}{\cancel{8}}} = \frac{3}{20}$$ $$\frac{1}{5} \times \frac{6}{8} = \frac{6}{40} \overset{\div 2}{\underset{\div 2}{=}} \frac{3}{20}$$

Ex. $$\frac{1}{\underset{2}{\cancel{14}}} \times \frac{\overset{1}{\cancel{7}}}{5} = \frac{1}{10}$$ $$\frac{1}{14} \times \frac{7}{5} = \frac{7}{70} \overset{\div 7}{\underset{\div 7}{=}} \frac{1}{10}$$

Ex. $$\frac{7}{\underset{1}{\cancel{5}}} \times \frac{\overset{1}{\cancel{5}}}{8} = \frac{7}{8}$$ $$\frac{7}{5} \times \frac{5}{8} = \frac{35}{40} \overset{\div 5}{\underset{\div 5}{=}} \frac{7}{8}$$

$$\frac{5}{10} \times \frac{1}{3} =$$ $$\frac{5}{3} \times \frac{3}{7} =$$ $$\frac{1}{4} \times \frac{8}{3} =$$ $$\frac{2}{9} \times \frac{6}{5} =$$

Dice Tic-Tac-Toe (2-Player Game)

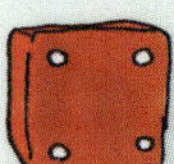

1	2	3	4	5
$\frac{20}{7} \times \frac{1}{100} =$	$\frac{3}{6} \times \frac{1}{4} =$	$\frac{5}{18} \times \frac{10}{7} =$	$\frac{8}{3} \times \frac{1}{10} =$	$\frac{12}{5} \times \frac{1}{12} =$
$\frac{3}{5} \times \frac{8}{8} =$	$\frac{3}{4} \times \frac{16}{25} =$	$\frac{4}{9} \times \frac{1}{4} =$	$\frac{16}{9} \times \frac{1}{8} =$	$\frac{50}{100} \times \frac{1}{3} =$
$\frac{1}{15} \times \frac{9}{4} =$	$\frac{6}{7} \times \frac{11}{11} =$	$\frac{0}{6} \times \frac{6}{8} =$	$\frac{9}{9} \times \frac{7}{10} =$	$\frac{12}{1} \times \frac{10}{3} =$
$\frac{2}{45} \times \frac{9}{5} =$	$\frac{7}{4} \times \frac{1}{7} =$	$\frac{4}{21} \times \frac{7}{5} =$	$\frac{36}{11} \times \frac{1}{24} =$	$\frac{1}{18} \times \frac{27}{4} =$

Practice

Find the product. Use cancelling where possible. Write your answers in simplest form. Then, find the blanks that match the answer. Write the matching letter in the blanks to solve the riddle.

G $\dfrac{3}{19} \times \dfrac{19}{8} =$

R $\dfrac{7}{1} \times \dfrac{1}{14} =$

D $\dfrac{23}{13} \times \dfrac{12}{23} =$

Y $\dfrac{4}{3} \times \dfrac{12}{1} =$

A $\dfrac{6}{7} \times \dfrac{4}{15} =$

L $\dfrac{7}{10} \times \dfrac{9}{7} =$

H $\dfrac{8}{16} \times \dfrac{1}{9} =$

T $\dfrac{1}{3} \times \dfrac{20}{25} =$

I $\dfrac{25}{2} \times \dfrac{1}{100} =$

E $\dfrac{1}{50} \times \dfrac{100}{1} =$

Why did the two 4s skip lunch?

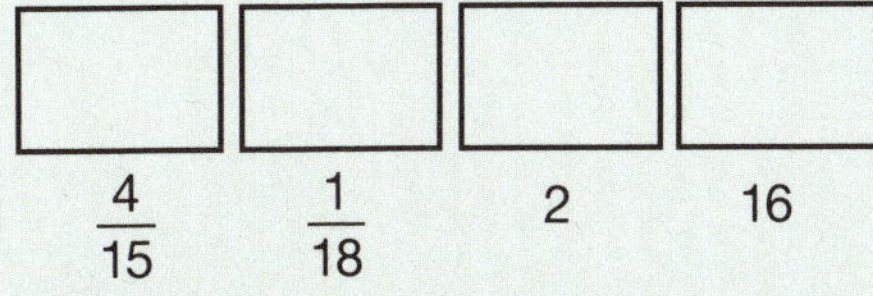

$\dfrac{4}{15}$	$\dfrac{1}{18}$	2	16

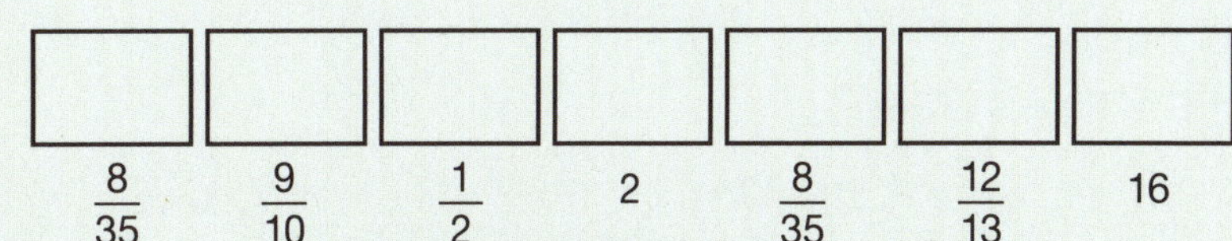

$\dfrac{8}{35}$	$\dfrac{9}{10}$	$\dfrac{1}{2}$	2	$\dfrac{8}{35}$	$\dfrac{12}{13}$	16

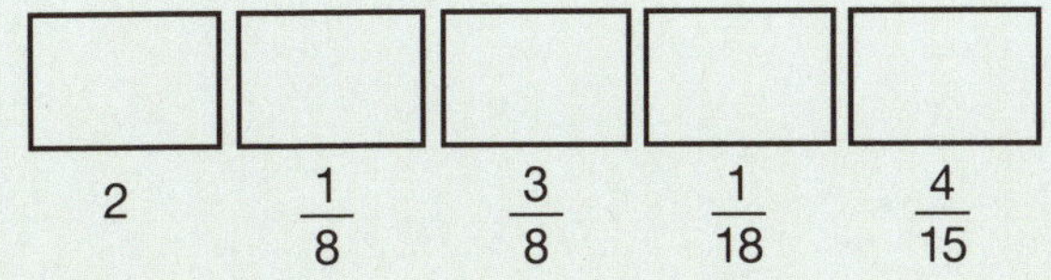

2	$\dfrac{1}{8}$	$\dfrac{3}{8}$	$\dfrac{1}{18}$	$\dfrac{4}{15}$

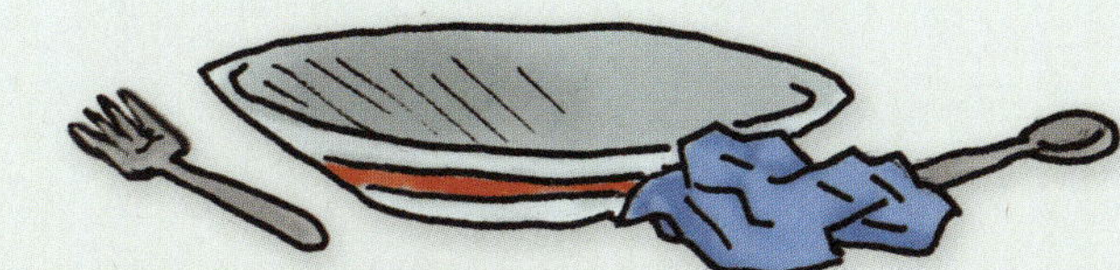

Review — Find the perimeter and area.

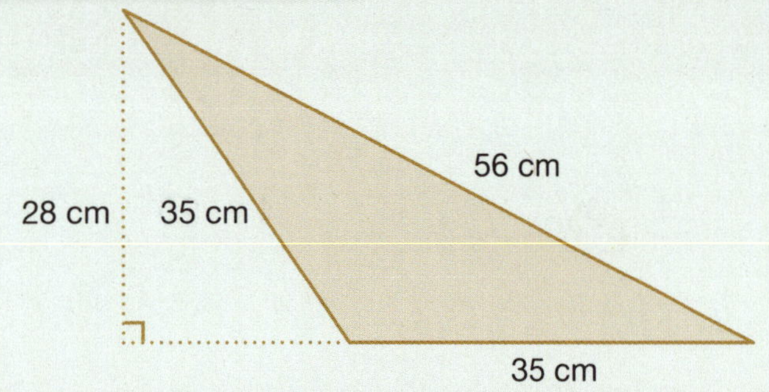

Perimeter: _________________   Area: _________________

Label the numbers on the number lines.

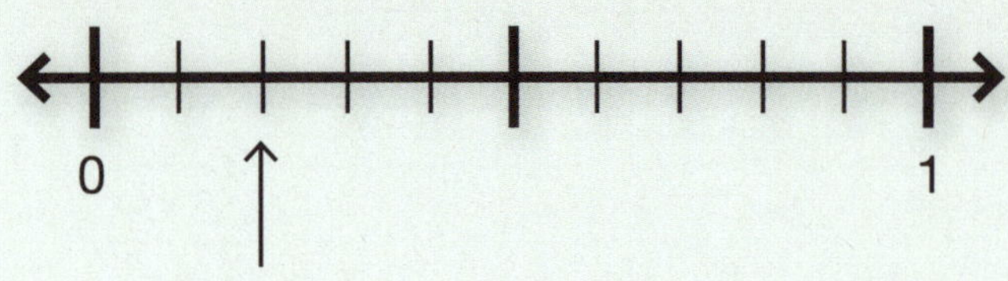

____

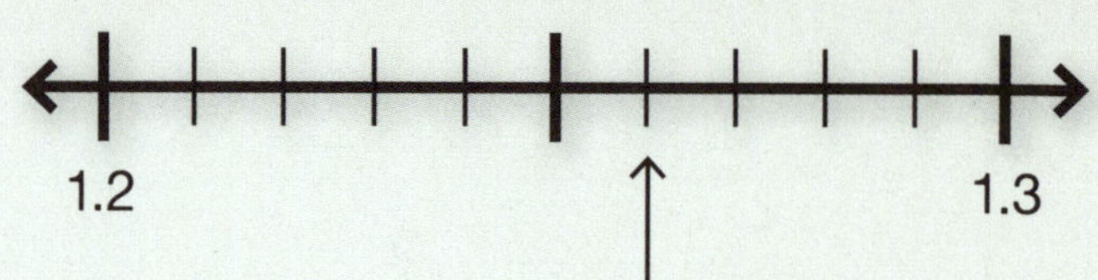

____

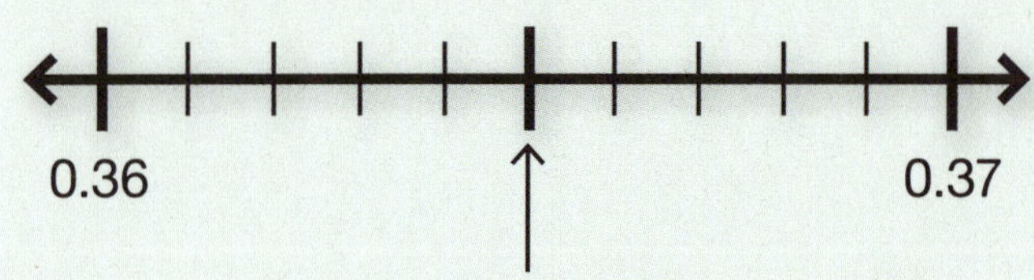

____

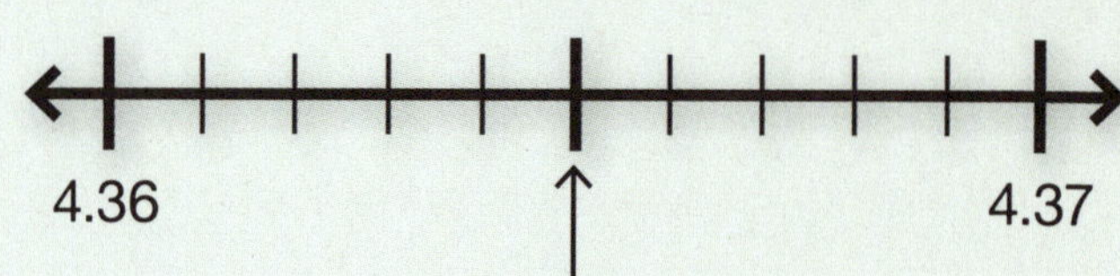

____

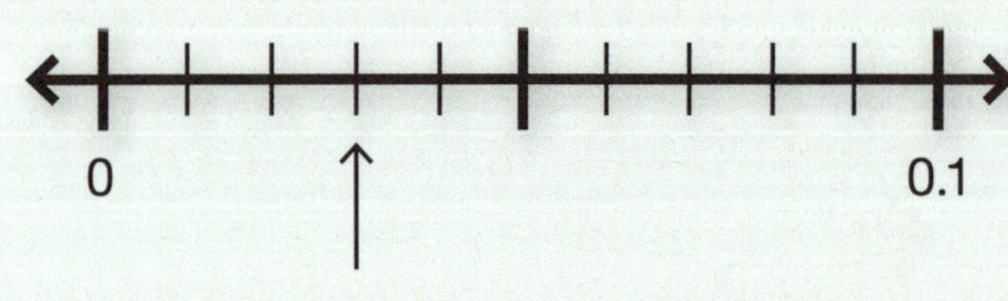

____

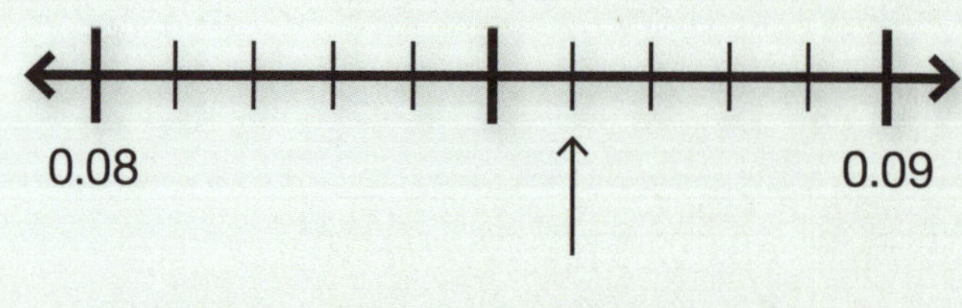

____

Use bar models to solve.

Camden's age is $\frac{4}{5}$ of Dash's age.
Camden is 12 years old.
How old is Dash?

Camden

Dash

Lesson Activities 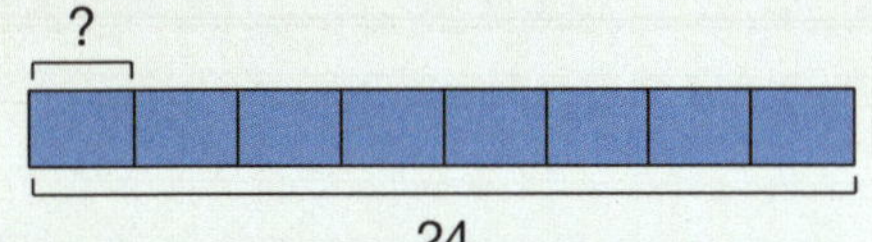

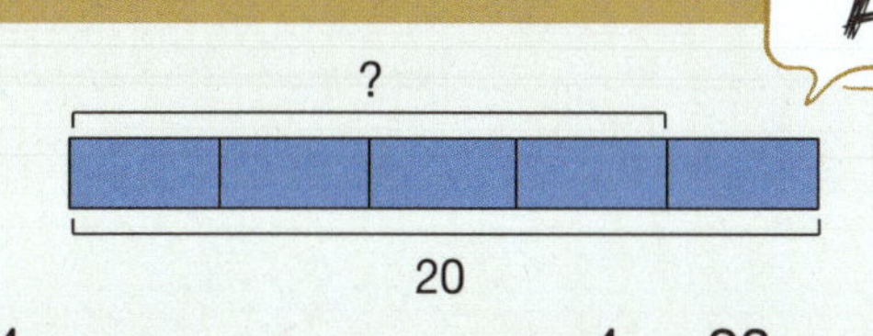

$\frac{1}{8}$ of 24 = _______ $\frac{1}{8} \times \frac{24}{1} =$

$\frac{4}{5}$ of 20 = _______ $\frac{4}{5} \times \frac{20}{1} =$

B

"Of" Means Multiply

In math, "of" usually means multiply. We multiply to find a fraction of a whole number.

Ex. Juniper bakes 36 cupcakes. She puts sprinkles on $\frac{3}{4}$ of the cupcakes. How many cupcakes have sprinkles?

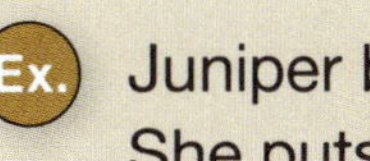

36

$\frac{3}{4}$ of 36 → $\frac{3}{4} \times 36$

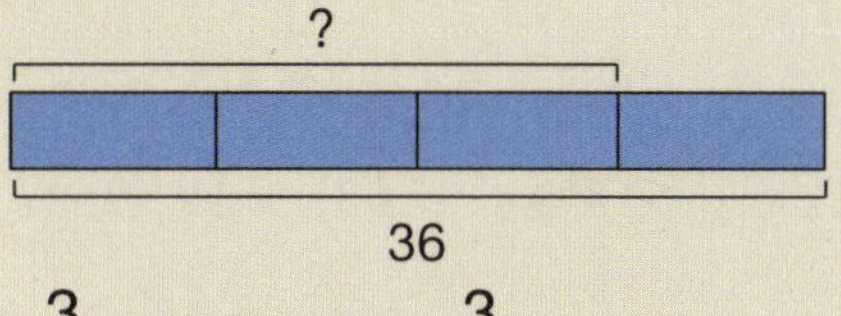

$$\frac{3}{\cancel{4}_{1}} \times \frac{\cancel{36}^{9}}{1} = \frac{27}{1} = \textbf{27 cupcakes}$$

C

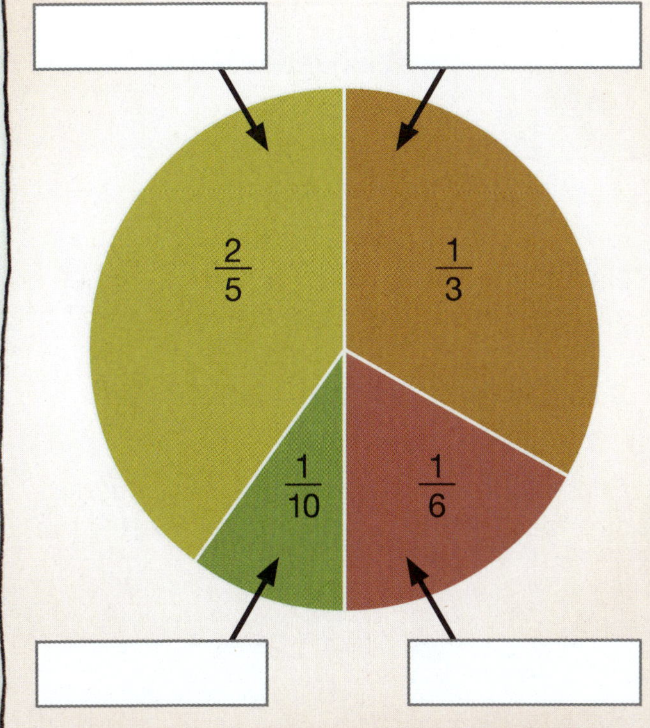

Activities

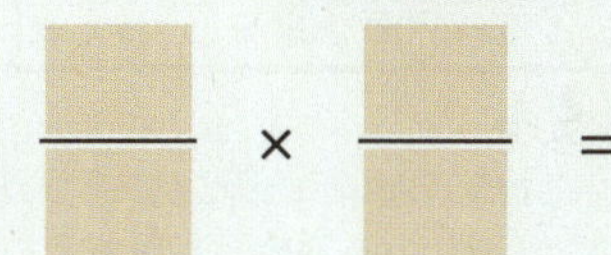

____ × ____ =

Decorations

____ × ____ =

Food

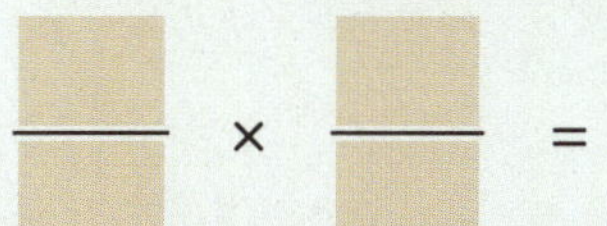

____ × ____ =

Party Favors

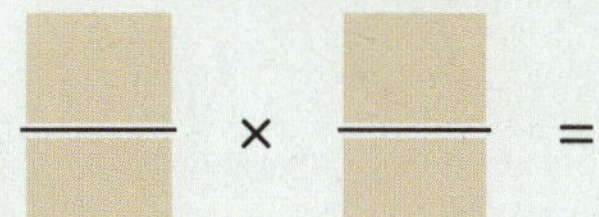

____ × ____ =

Practice

Write each "of" statement as a multiplication problem. Then, find the product. Use cancelling if possible.

$\frac{2}{3}$ of 27

$\frac{4}{5}$ of 100

$\frac{5}{8}$ of 64

Write a multiplication problem to match each question. Then, solve.

Ezra surveyed 40 people about their favorite fall activity.

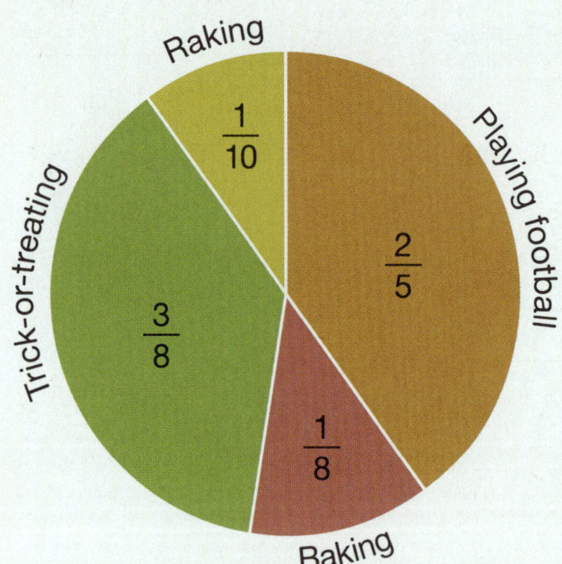

How many people chose playing football?

How many people chose baking?

How many people chose trick-or-treating?

How many people chose raking leaves?

Naomi earned $60 raking leaves. She made the following budget for her earnings.

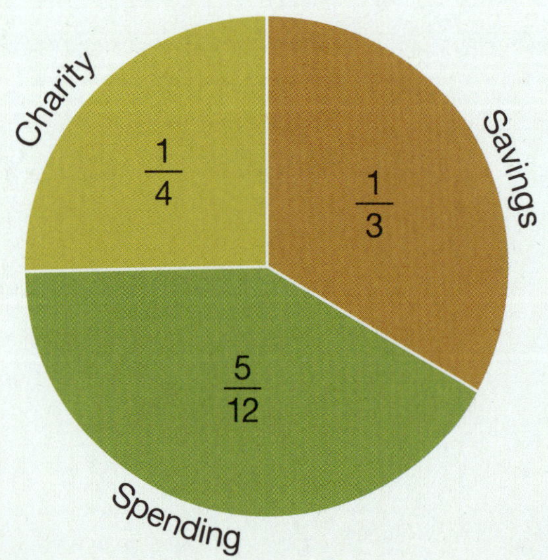

How much spending money does Naomi have?

Naomi spends $\frac{3}{5}$ of her spending money on a book. How much does the book cost?

After Naomi buys the book, how much spending money does she have left?

Review

Use the chart to answer the questions.
Write the ratios and fractions in simplest form.

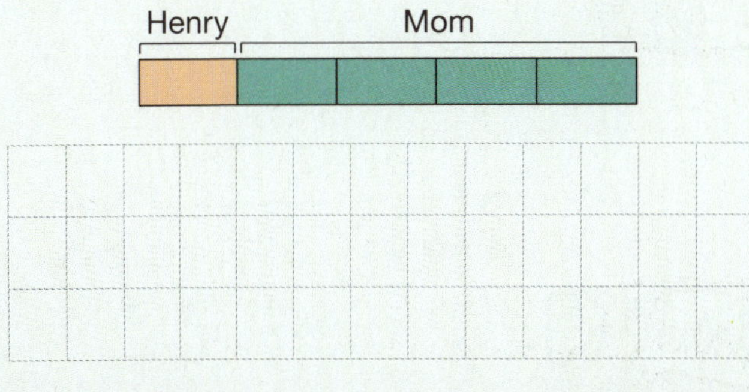

Tomatoes : Zucchini

________ : ________

What fraction of the total harvest was tomatoes?

____

Zucchini : Tomatoes

________ : ________

What fraction of the total harvest was zucchini?

____

Use long division to solve.
Use the multiplication table to help.

1 8 | 6 1 2   1 8 | 2 , 9 1 6

× 18	
1	18
2	36
3	54
4	72
5	90
6	108
7	126
8	144
9	162

Complete.

$10^2 =$ ________________

$8^2 =$ ________________

$9^2 =$ ________________

$7^2 =$ ________________

$12^2 =$ ________________

$11^2 =$ ________________

Use bar models to find the quantities.

The ratio of Henry's age to his mom's age is 1:4. The sum of their ages is 60.

Henry   Mom

Henry's age: ___________________________

Henry's mom's age: _______________________

Stella mixes 2 parts black paint with 5 parts white paint to make gray paint. She makes a total of 350 mL of paint.

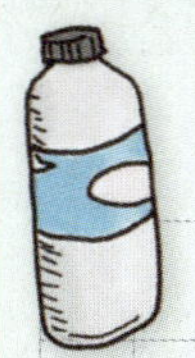

Milliliters of black paint: _______________

Milliliters of white paint: _______________

Lesson Activities 👥

A

$\dfrac{3}{5}$ of 200　　　$\dfrac{5}{6}$ of 300　　　$\dfrac{3}{25}$ of 100

$$\dfrac{3}{5} \times \dfrac{2\ 0\ 0}{1} =$$

B

Fraction Multiplication

We multiply to find a fraction of a quantity or equal groups of a quantity.

Ex. The racecourse is $3\frac{2}{3}$ mi. long. So far, Katya has run $\frac{3}{4}$ of the racecourse. How far has she already run?

$$\dfrac{3}{4} \text{ of } 3\dfrac{2}{3} \;\rightarrow\; \dfrac{3}{4} \times 3\dfrac{2}{3}$$

$$\dfrac{\cancel{3}^{\,1}}{4} \times \dfrac{11}{\cancel{3}_{\,1}} = \dfrac{11}{4} = 2\,\dfrac{3}{4}\text{ mi.}$$

Ex. Abby eats $2\frac{1}{2}$ bags of jellybeans. Each bag weighs $\frac{3}{10}$ lb. How many pounds of jellybeans does she eat?

$$2\dfrac{1}{2} \text{ of } \dfrac{3}{10} \;\rightarrow\; 2\dfrac{1}{2} \times \dfrac{3}{10}$$

$$\dfrac{\cancel{5}^{\,1}}{2} \times \dfrac{3}{\cancel{10}_{\,2}} = \dfrac{3}{4}\text{ lb.}$$

C

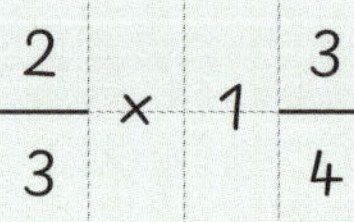

$$\dfrac{2}{3} \times 1\dfrac{3}{4}$$

Practice

Write each statement as a multiplication problem. Then, find the product. Use cancelling if possible. Write your answers in simplest form. If your answer is an improper fraction, convert it to a mixed number or whole number.

$\frac{1}{5}$ of $\frac{5}{6}$

$\frac{3}{4}$ of $\frac{5}{6}$

$1\frac{1}{2}$ groups of $\frac{5}{6}$

Solve. Write the equations you use. Write your answers in simplest form. If your answer is an improper fraction, convert it to a mixed number or whole number.

The ostrich's height is $\frac{2}{5}$ of the giraffe's height. The giraffe is $4\frac{1}{2}$ m tall. How tall is the ostrich?

Ollie buys 3 boxes of fudge. Each box weighs $1\frac{2}{3}$ lb. What is the total weight of the fudge?

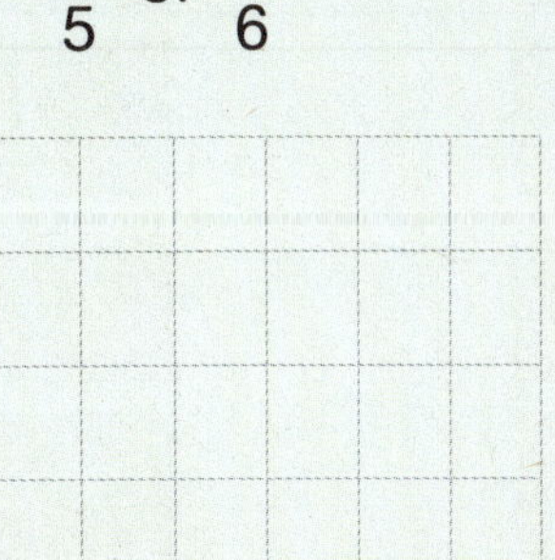

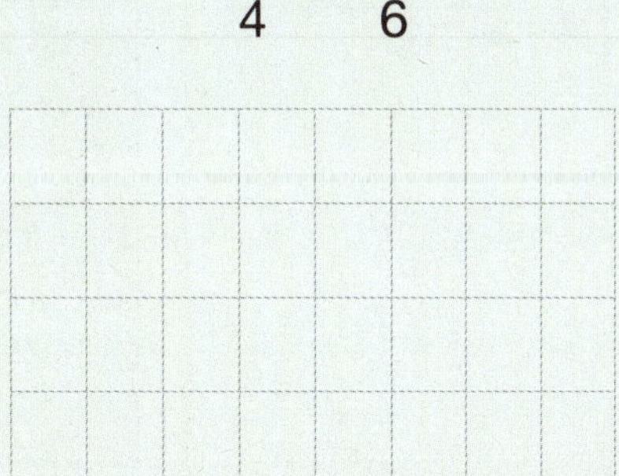

Lewis uses $1\frac{2}{3}$ bags of chocolate chips to make cookies. Each bag weighs 9 oz. How many ounces of chocolate chips does he use?

Poppy has $3\frac{1}{5}$ oz. of green wool to use for a felting project. She uses $\frac{3}{4}$ of the wool to make a frog. How many ounces of wool does she use?

Review :

Use long division to solve. Write the remainder as a fraction.

7) 1 8 0   6) 4 3 3

Match the pairs of numbers whose sum is 2.

Circle the numbers that match the description.
X the numbers that don't match the description.

This number is prime.

20	21	22
23	24	25

This number is composite.

20	21	22
23	24	25

This number is a factor of 100.

20	21	22
23	24	25

This number is divisible by 3.

20	21	22
23	24	25

The sum of this number and 3 is 27.

20	21	22
23	24	25

The product of this number and 3 is 60.

20	21	22
23	24	25

Find the perimeter and area.

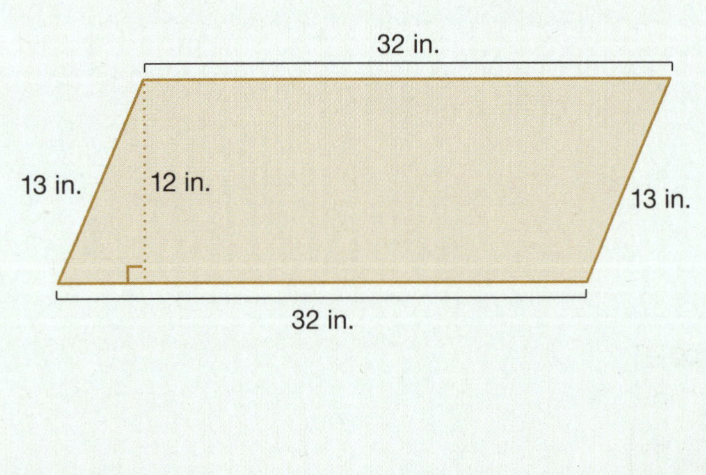

Perimeter: _____________   Area: _____________

Lesson Activities 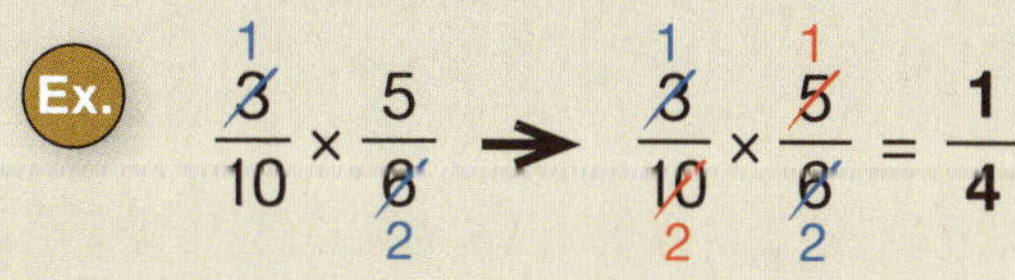

A

$$\frac{6}{7} \times \frac{8}{9} =$$

$$\frac{3}{4} \times \frac{4}{11} =$$

$$\frac{45}{50} \times \frac{1}{4} =$$

$$\frac{6}{12} \times \frac{5}{1} =$$

B

Simplify Before Multiplying

Sometimes, you can cancel more than one pair of numbers before multiplying fractions.

Always simplify the numbers in pairs. Make sure one number in the pair is above the fraction bar and the other number in the pair is below the fraction bar.

Ex. $\dfrac{3}{10} \times \dfrac{5}{6} \;\rightarrow\; \dfrac{\cancel{3}^{\,1}}{10_{\,2}} \times \dfrac{\cancel{5}^{\,1}}{\cancel{6}_{\,2}} = \dfrac{1}{4}$

Ex. $\dfrac{9}{5} \times \dfrac{8}{12} \;\rightarrow\; \dfrac{\cancel{9}^{\,3}}{5} \times \dfrac{\cancel{8}^{\,2}}{\cancel{12}_{\,4_{\,1}}} = \dfrac{6}{5} = 1\dfrac{1}{5}$

Multiply 3 or More Fractions

To multiply 3 or more fractions, simplify as much as possible. Then, multiply like usual.

Ex. $\dfrac{5}{8} \times \dfrac{4}{3} \times \dfrac{7}{15} \;\rightarrow\; \dfrac{\cancel{5}^{\,1}}{\cancel{8}_{\,2}} \times \dfrac{\cancel{4}^{\,1}}{3} \times \dfrac{7}{\cancel{15}_{\,3}} = \dfrac{7}{18}$

C

Slash It! (2-Player Game)

$\dfrac{21}{10} \times \dfrac{5}{3} =$	$\dfrac{5}{7} \times \dfrac{28}{10} =$
$\dfrac{1}{10} \times \dfrac{5}{2} \times \dfrac{6}{1} =$	$\dfrac{3}{4} \times \dfrac{4}{5} \times \dfrac{5}{6} =$
$\dfrac{1}{2} \times \dfrac{2}{4} \times \dfrac{4}{1} =$	$\dfrac{7}{3} \times \dfrac{5}{2} \times \dfrac{3}{7} =$
$\dfrac{9}{11} \times \dfrac{5}{3} \times \dfrac{11}{10} =$	$\dfrac{15}{16} \times \dfrac{3}{5} \times \dfrac{8}{3} =$

Practice

Find the product. Use cancelling where possible. Write your answers in simplest form. If your answer is an improper fraction, convert it to a mixed number or whole number.

$\dfrac{2}{9} \times \dfrac{3}{2} =$

$\dfrac{15}{14} \times \dfrac{7}{5} =$

$\dfrac{8}{16} \times \dfrac{7}{21} =$

$\dfrac{11}{7} \times \dfrac{7}{11} =$

$\dfrac{3}{2} \times \dfrac{6}{7} \times \dfrac{10}{5} =$

$\dfrac{6}{5} \times \dfrac{16}{3} \times \dfrac{10}{4} =$

$\dfrac{1}{2} \times \dfrac{1}{2} \times \dfrac{1}{2} \times \dfrac{1}{2} =$

$\dfrac{1}{2} \times \dfrac{2}{3} \times \dfrac{3}{4} \times \dfrac{4}{5} =$

Use the numbers to complete the equations.

| 4 | 5 | | 3 | 5 | | ★ | 9 | 2 |

 $\dfrac{7}{10} \times \dfrac{4}{5} \times \dfrac{\square}{\square} = \dfrac{7}{10}$

 $\dfrac{2}{\square} \times \dfrac{3}{5} \times \dfrac{\square}{7} = \dfrac{2}{7}$

 $\dfrac{8}{7} \times \dfrac{\square}{8} \times \dfrac{1}{\square} = \dfrac{9}{14}$

Solve. Write the equations you use. Write your answers in simplest form.

Gracy has a narrow strip of cardboard that is $4\dfrac{1}{2}$ ft. long. She uses $\dfrac{2}{3}$ of the cardboard strip to build a dragon. What length of cardboard does she use?

Each bag of flour weighs $1\dfrac{8}{10}$ kg. Norah uses $1\dfrac{1}{3}$ bags to make pizza dough. What weight of flour does she use?

Review   Evaluate.

$$6 \times 10^2 + 9 \times 10^1 + 4 \times 10^0 = \underline{\quad 694 \quad}$$
$$600 \quad + \quad 90 \quad + \quad 4$$

$$7 \times 10^2 + 3 \times 10^1 + 5 \times 10^0 = \underline{\hspace{3cm}}$$

$$2 \times 10^3 + 3 \times 10^2 + 8 \times 10^1 + 4 \times 10^0 = \underline{\hspace{3cm}}$$

$$8 \times 10^3 + 5 \times 10^2 + 6 \times 10^0 = \underline{\hspace{3cm}}$$

Write <, >, or =.

3.51 ◯ 3.6

0.92 ◯ 1.0

2.84 ◯ 2.83

4.5 ◯ 4.50

4.001 ◯ 4.002

3.87 ◯ 3.870

Use a factor tree to find the prime factorization for each number. Write the prime factors in order from least to greatest. Then, find the GCF.

36

80

Prime Factorizations

$36 = \underline{\hspace{4cm}}$

$80 = \underline{\hspace{4cm}}$

What is the GCF of 36 and 80?

Answer the questions.

Niall takes a spelling test. The ratio of words he spells correctly to words he spells incorrectly is 9:1. What fraction of the words does he spell correctly?

At field hockey practice, Evie makes $\frac{3}{5}$ of her shots. She misses the rest. What is the ratio of shots she makes to shots she misses?

There are 30 words on the spelling test. How many words does he spell correctly?

Evie takes a total of 25 shots. How many shots does she make?

Lesson Activities

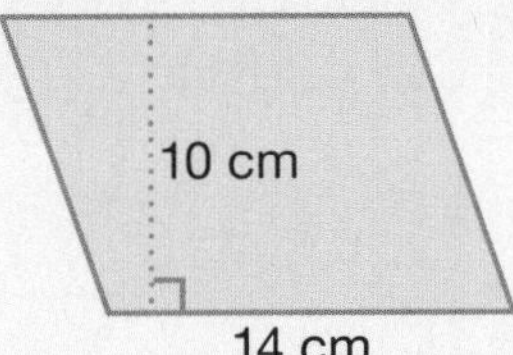

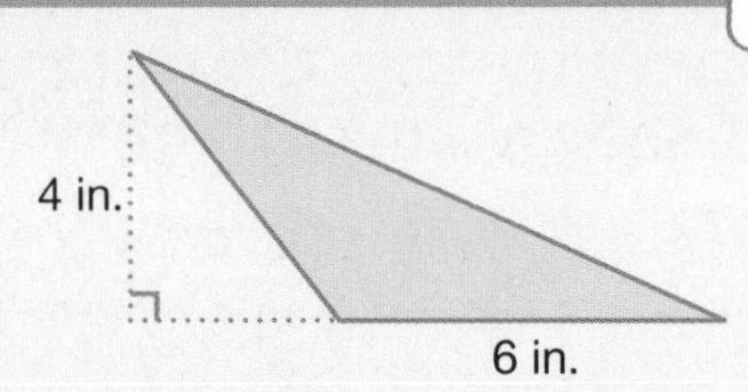

Area: ______________________

Area: ______________________

Area of Parallelograms and Triangles

We use the usual formulas to find the area of shapes with fractional bases or heights.

Parallelogram

Area = base × height

Ex. What is the area of the parallelogram?

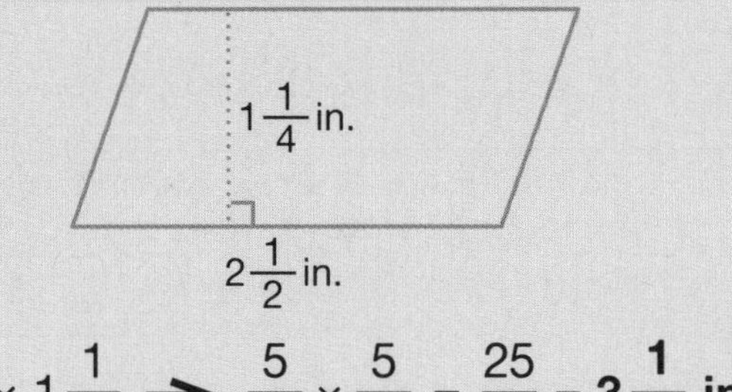

$$2\frac{1}{2} \times 1\frac{1}{4} \ \Rightarrow\ \frac{5}{2} \times \frac{5}{4} = \frac{25}{8} = 3\frac{1}{8} \text{ in.}^2$$

Dividing a number by 2 is the same as finding half of the number. We can use either of these formulas to find the area of a triangle.

Triangle

$$\text{Area} = \frac{\text{base} \times \text{height}}{2}$$

$$\text{Area} = \frac{1}{2} \times \text{base} \times \text{height}$$

Ex. What is the area of the triangle?

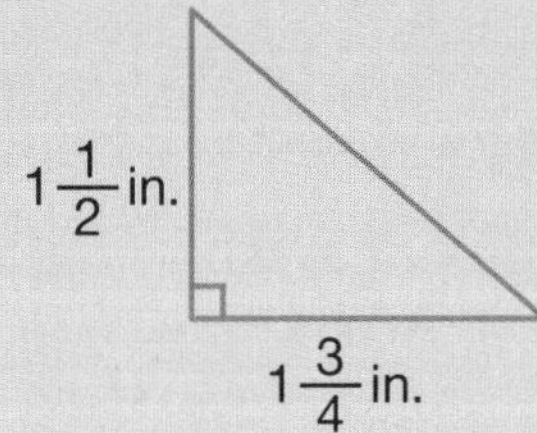

$$\frac{1}{2} \times 1\frac{3}{4} \times 1\frac{1}{2}$$

$$\frac{1}{2} \times \frac{7}{4} \times \frac{3}{2} = \frac{21}{16} = 1\frac{5}{16} \text{ in.}^2$$

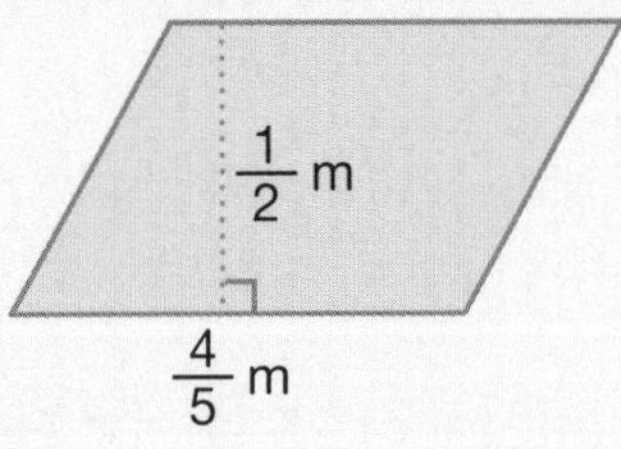

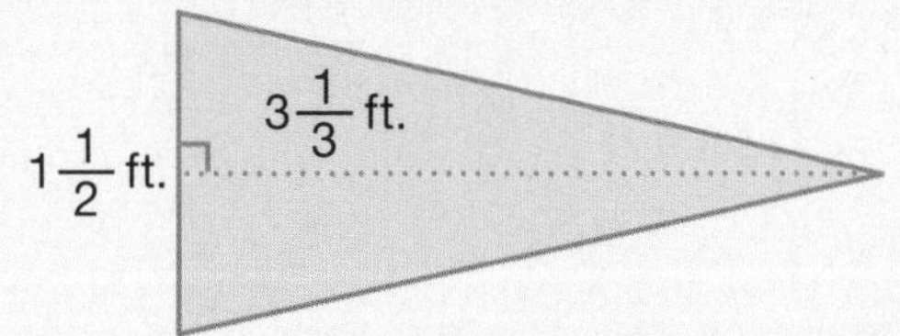

Practice

Find the area of each shape. Write your equations in the work space. Write your answers in simplest form, and include the correct units.

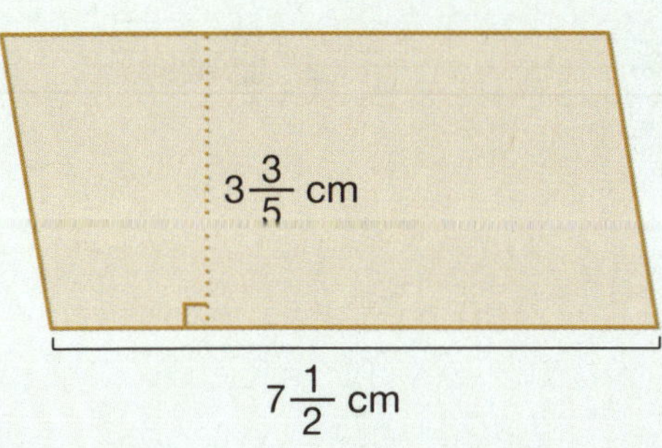

Area: __________________________

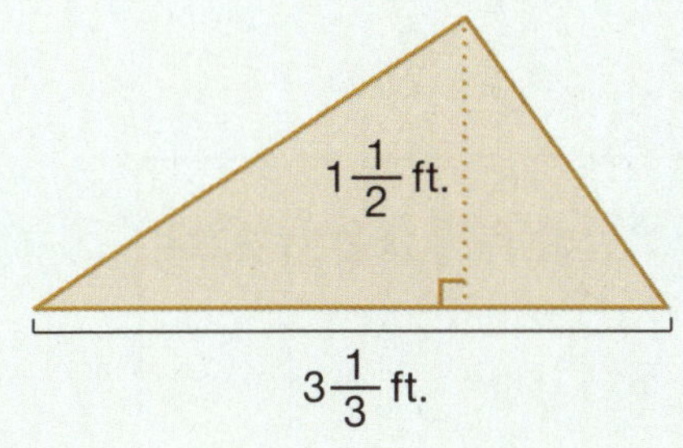

Area: __________________________

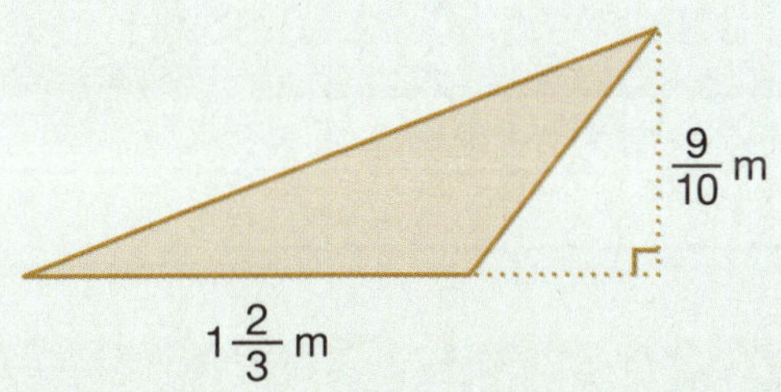

Area: __________________________

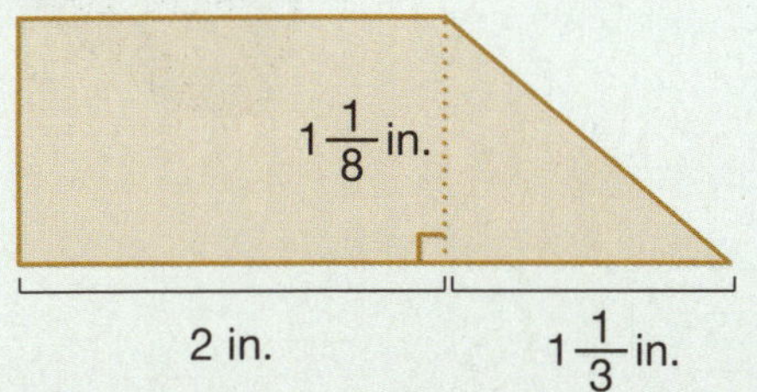

Area: __________________________

WORK SPACE

Review   Use mental math to complete.

$40 \cdot 60 =$ _____2,400_____ $\qquad$ $300 \cdot 90 =$ _________ $\qquad$ $20^2 =$ _________

$70 \cdot 70 =$ _________ $\qquad$ $600 \cdot 80 =$ _________ $\qquad$ $300^2 =$ _________

$\dfrac{400}{5} =$ _____80_____ $\qquad$ $\dfrac{1,000}{2} =$ _________ $\qquad$ $\dfrac{2,800}{700} =$ _________

$\dfrac{400}{50} =$ _________ $\qquad$ $\dfrac{1,000}{20} =$ _________ $\qquad$ $\dfrac{2,800}{70} =$ _________

Draw a line to connect the numbers in order from Start to End. Follow the rule.

Rule: Add 0.7

Start →

0.7	1.4	1.7	2.0	2.4
1.3	2.1	1.8	2.6	3.0
1.9	2.8	3.5	3.4	3.2
3.6	3.9	4.2	4.8	7.0
4.1	4.5	4.9	5.6	6.3

END

Rule: Add 0.08

Start →

0.08	0.10	0.18	0.20	0.82
0.16	0.22	0.26	0.38	0.66
0.24	0.34	0.42	0.52	0.69
0.32	0.36	0.64	0.72	0.80
0.40	0.48	0.56	0.70	0.84

END

Use bar models to complete the blanks.

The concession stand at the stadium sells hamburgers and hot dogs. At one game, they sell hamburgers and hot dogs in a 3 to 1 ratio. They sell 300 more hamburgers than hot dogs.

Hamburgers

Hot dogs

Number of hamburgers: _________________

Number of hot dogs: _________________

Unit Wrap-Up

Use the numbers to complete the equations. Multiple answers are possible.

$$\frac{\square}{\square} \times \frac{\square}{\square} = \frac{5}{6}$$

$$\frac{\square}{\square} \times \frac{\square}{\square} = \frac{6}{5}$$

$$\frac{\square}{\square} \times \frac{\square}{\square} = \frac{2}{15}$$

$$\frac{\square}{\square} \times \frac{\square}{\square} = 1$$

$$\frac{\square}{\square} \times \frac{\square}{\square} = \frac{4}{9}$$

$$\frac{\square}{\square} \times \frac{\square}{\square} = \frac{9}{4}$$

 $$\frac{\square}{\square} \times \frac{\square}{\square} = \frac{3}{5}$$

$$\frac{\square}{\square} \times \frac{\square}{\square} = 3$$

$$\frac{\square}{\square} \times \frac{\square}{\square} = 1$$

Find the area of each shape. Write the equations you use. Write your answers in simplest form. Include the correct units.

Area: _________________

Area: _________________

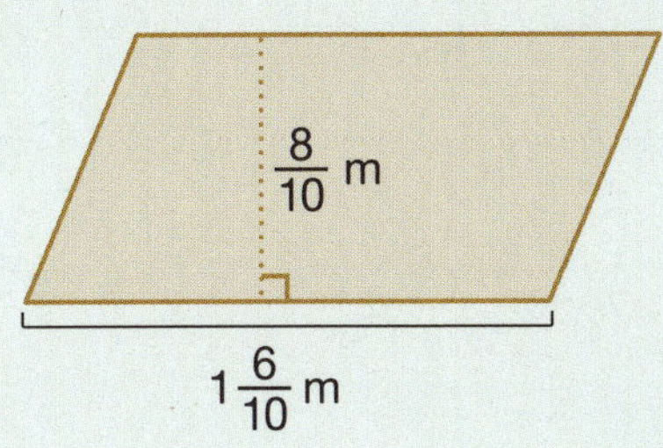

Area: _________________

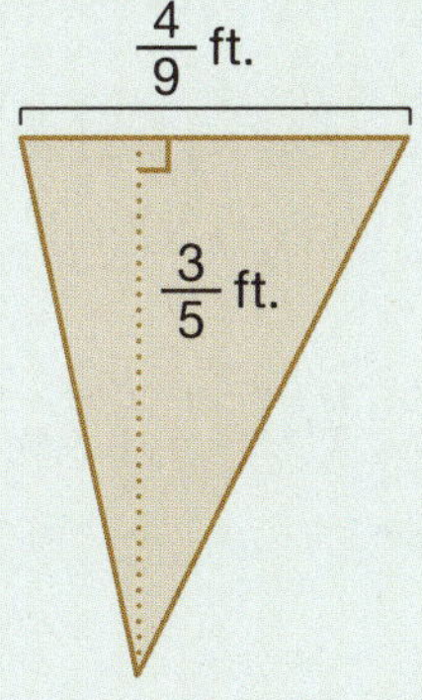

Unit Wrap-Up 👤

Roland is helping his aunt make an extra-large batch of tuna casserole. Multiply $2\frac{1}{4}$ by each quantity to find how much of each ingredient they need. Write your equations in the work space.

Aunt Wanda's Tuna Casserole
(Original)

3 c. noodles

2 small cans of tuna

$1\frac{1}{3}$ c. chopped celery

$\frac{2}{3}$ c. chopped onion

$\frac{1}{3}$ c. mayonnaise

$\frac{1}{4}$ lb. shredded cheese

1 can of cream of celery soup

$\frac{1}{2}$ c. milk

Aunt Wanda's Tuna Casserole
($2\frac{1}{4}$ times the original)

______ c. noodles

______ small cans of tuna

______ c. chopped celery

______ c. chopped onion

______ c. mayonnaise

______ lb. shredded cheese

______ cans of cream of celery soup

______ c. milk

WORK SPACE

Lesson Activities

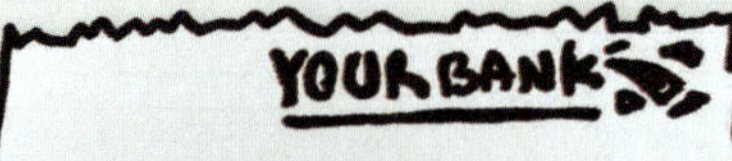

A

B

Positive and Negative Numbers on the Number Line

Positive numbers are numbers greater than zero. Negative numbers are numbers less than zero. Zero is neither positive nor negative.

A number's sign tells us whether the number is greater than or less than zero. The numeral itself tells how far the number is from zero.

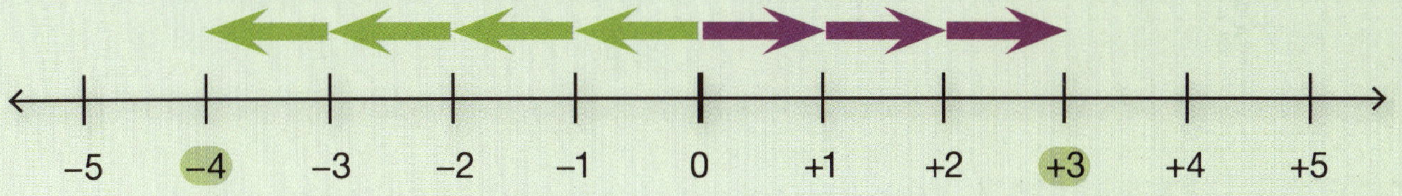

−4 means "4 units less than zero"   +3 means "3 units greater than zero"

We write a minus sign to show that a number is negative. We sometimes write a plus sign in front of a positive number to emphasize that it is positive.

To compare positive and negative numbers, plot them on the number line. Numbers farther to the left are less than numbers farther to the right.

+5 ◯ +1	−5 ◯ 1	+4 ◯ −4	−3 ◯ −2
3 ◯ −5	−2 ◯ 2	+2 ◯ 0	−2 ◯ 0

C

Guess My Number (2-Player Game)

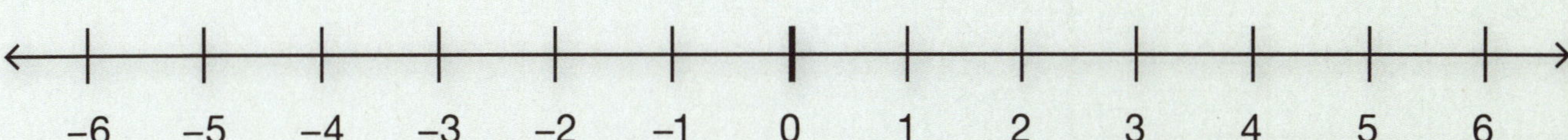

Practice

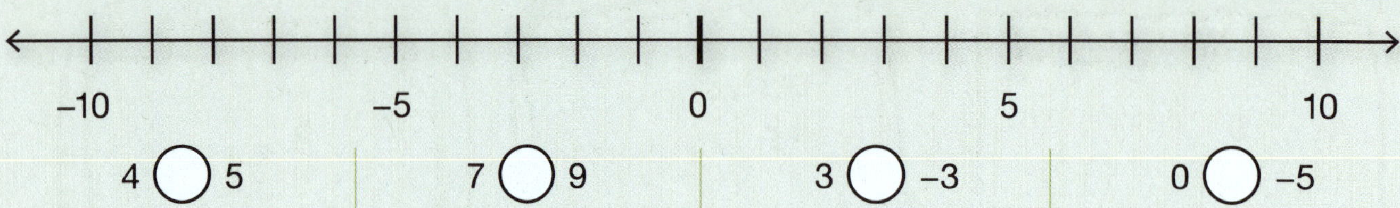

Write <, >, or = to compare the numbers. Use the number line to help.

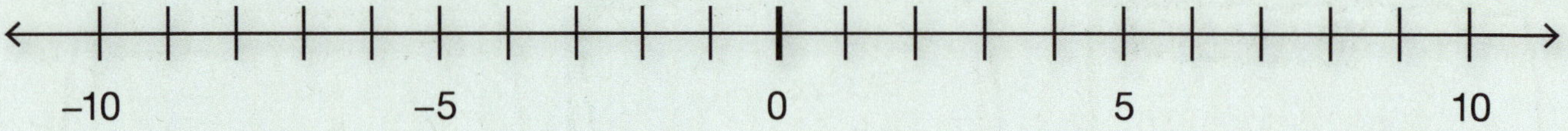

4 ◯ 5	7 ◯ 9	3 ◯ –3	0 ◯ –5
–6 ◯ –2	–7 ◯ 9	–3 ◯ 3	0 ◯ +5
1 ◯ –4	–7 ◯ –9	3 ◯ +3	5 ◯ 0

Connect each number to its position on the number line.

–25   –23   –28

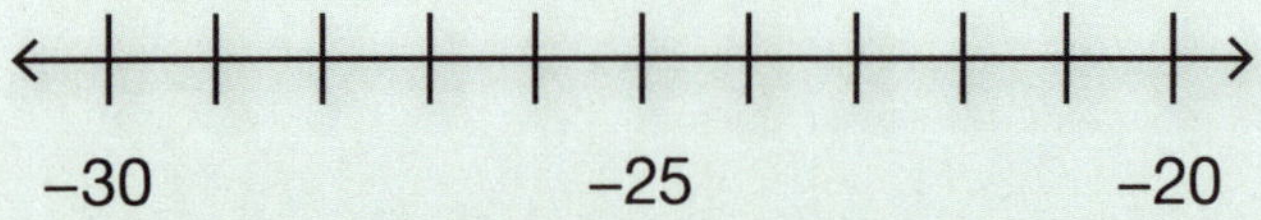

–40   –70   –10

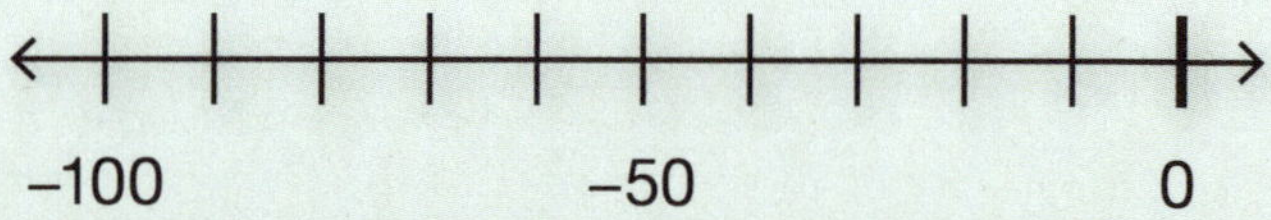

Use the charts to answer the questions.

Golf Tournament Scores	
Tim	0
Meredith	–2
Ella	–4
Gabriel	7
Milo	3
Audrey	–1

Write the scores in order from least to greatest.

_______ _______ _______ _______ _______ _______
least greatest

In golf, the lowest score wins. Who won the tournament?

Who came in second place?

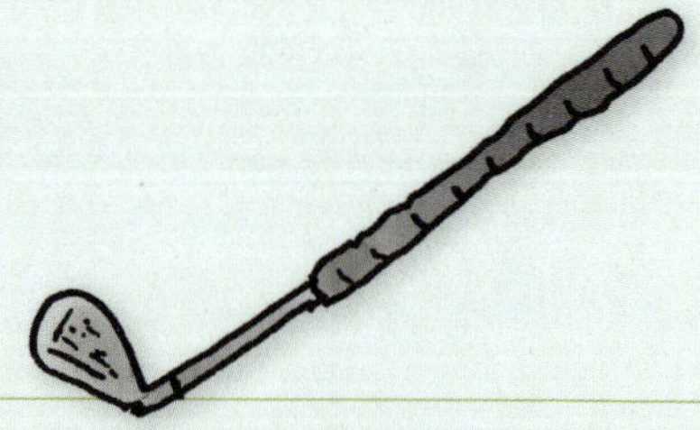

Daily Temperature (°F) at Noon	
Monday	12
Tuesday	–5
Wednesday	–3
Thursday	1
Friday	5

Write the temperatures in order from least to greatest.

_______ _______ _______ _______ _______
least greatest

Which day had the warmest temperature at noon?

Which day had the coolest temperature at noon?

Review

Find the product. Use cancelling where possible.

$$\frac{5}{8} \times \frac{4}{15} =$$

$$\frac{3}{4} \times \frac{3}{2} =$$

$$\frac{5}{6} \times \frac{6}{5} =$$

$$\frac{10}{3} \times \frac{9}{5} =$$

$$\frac{7}{1} \times \frac{2}{7} =$$

$$\frac{7}{7} \times \frac{5}{9} =$$

Find the perimeter and area.

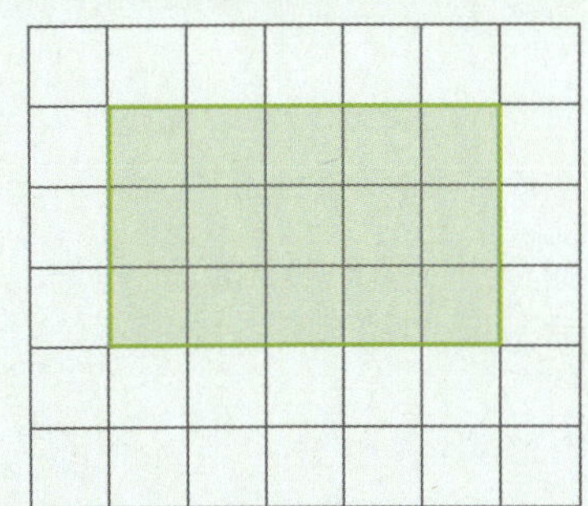

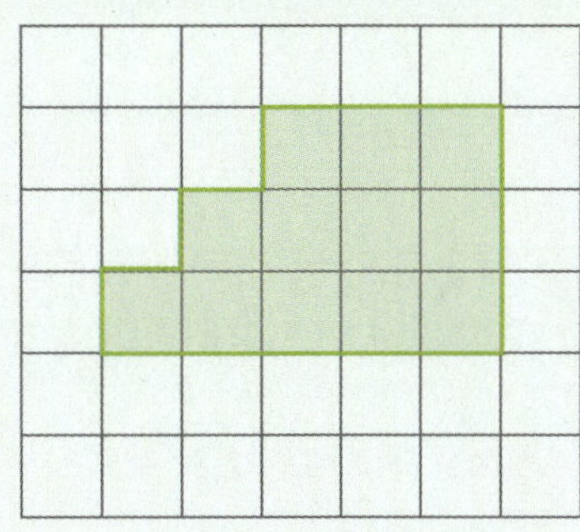

Perimeter: __________ units

Perimeter: __________ units

Area: __________ units ^{2}

Area: __________ units ^{2}

Use mental math to complete.

$100 \div 25 =$ __________

$120 \div 40 =$ __________

$200 \div 50 =$ __________

$150 \div 10 =$ __________

$30 \div 15 =$ __________

$75 \div 25 =$ __________

Some friends competed to see who could jump the farthest. Use the clues to complete the chart.

- Jay jumped $1\frac{1}{4}$ times Adley's distance.

- Eawyn jumped $\frac{2}{3}$ of Jay's distance.

- Rebekah jumped $1\frac{2}{5}$ times Eawyn's distance.

- Kory jumped $\frac{5}{7}$ of Rebekah's distance.

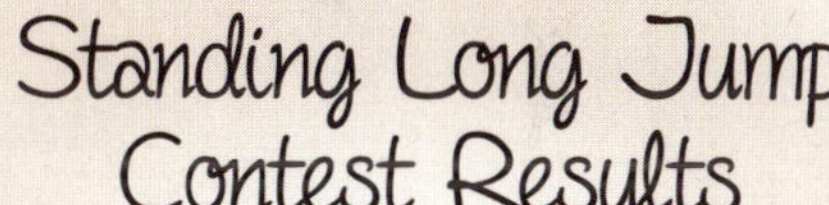

Standing Long Jump Contest Results

Adley	60 in.
Jay	
Eawyn	
Rebekah	
Kory	

Lesson Activities

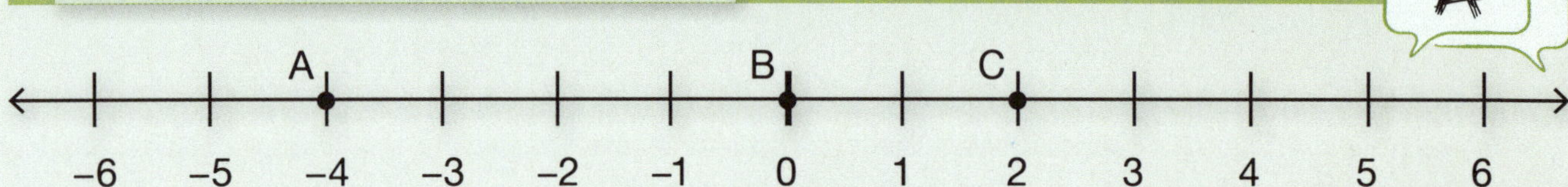

How far is point A from 0?

___________ units

How far is point B from 0?

___________ units

How far is point C from 0?

___________ units

Absolute Value

The absolute value of a number is the number's distance from zero on the number line. The symbol for absolute value is two parallel vertical lines around the number.

Ex. What is the absolute value of –4?

$$|-4| = 4$$

The absolute value of negative 4 is 4.

Ex. What is the absolute value of 0?

$$|0| = 0$$

The absolute value of zero is zero.

Ex. What is the absolute value of +2?

$$|+2| = 2$$

The absolute value of positive 2 is 2.

Words	Symbols	Value
absolute value of +3	$|+3|$	
absolute value of –1		
absolute value of 1		
absolute value of –6		

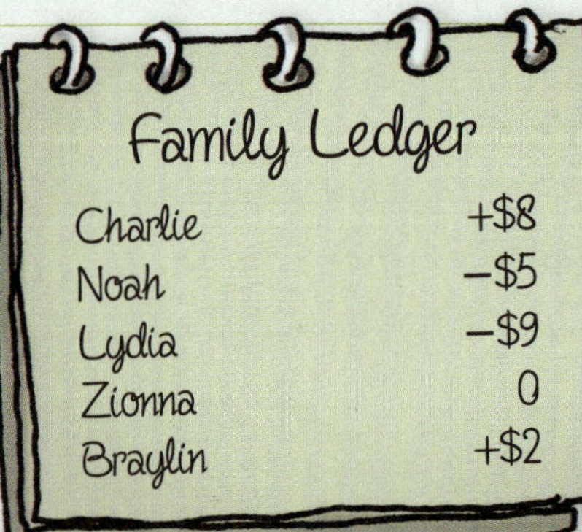

$|+8| =$ ___________

$|-5| =$ ___________

$|-9| =$ ___________

$|0| =$ ___________

$|+2| =$ ___________

Who has the most money?

Who owes the most money?

Practice   **Complete the chart.**

Words	Symbols	Value
absolute value of 2	$\lvert 2 \rvert$	2
absolute value of −8		
absolute value of 0		
absolute value of +6		
	$\lvert 23 \rvert$	
	$\lvert -23 \rvert$	
absolute value of −9		
absolute value of 9		

Compare with <, >, or =.

−3 ◯ 1	−8 ◯ −4	7 ◯ 2	5 ◯ −5
$\lvert -3 \rvert$ ◯ $\lvert 1 \rvert$	$\lvert -8 \rvert$ ◯ $\lvert -4 \rvert$	$\lvert 7 \rvert$ ◯ $\lvert 2 \rvert$	$\lvert 5 \rvert$ ◯ $\lvert -5 \rvert$

Complete each blank with positive, negative, or zero.

The absolute value of a positive number is

_______________________.

The absolute value of a negative number is

_______________________.

The absolute value of zero is

_______________________.

Answer the questions.

What two numbers both have an absolute value of 5?

What two numbers both have an absolute value of 17?

What number has an absolute value of 0?

Review

Find the area of each shape. Write the equations you use.
Write your answers in simplest form. Include the correct units.

Area: _______________________

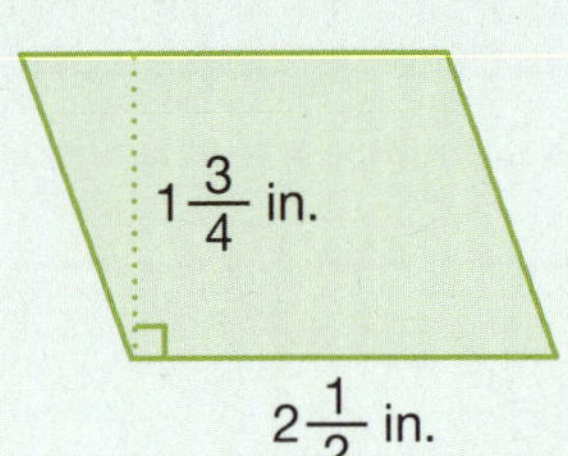

Area: _______________________

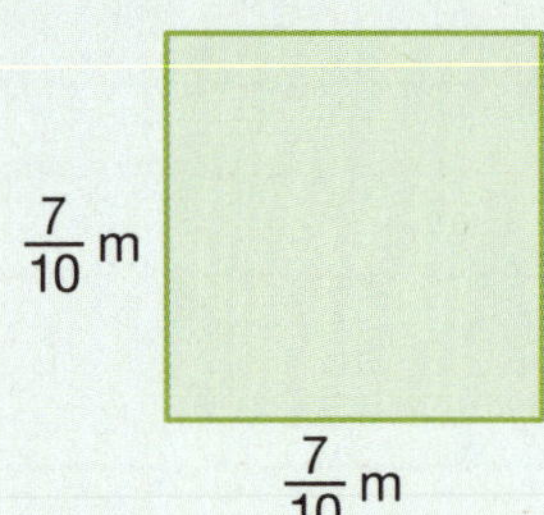

Area: _______________________

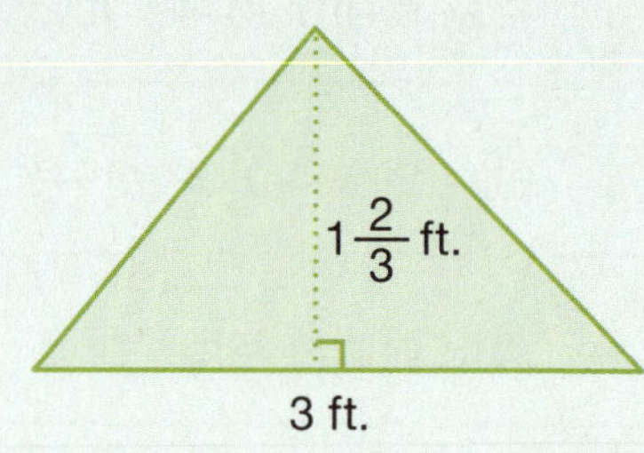

Use subtraction or logical reasoning to find the distances between the numbers on the number line.

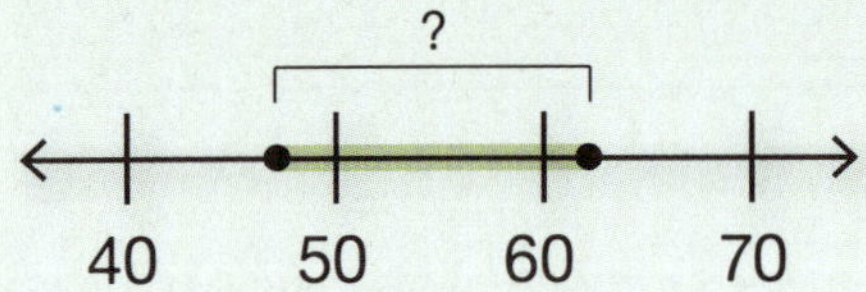

What's the distance between 47 and 62?

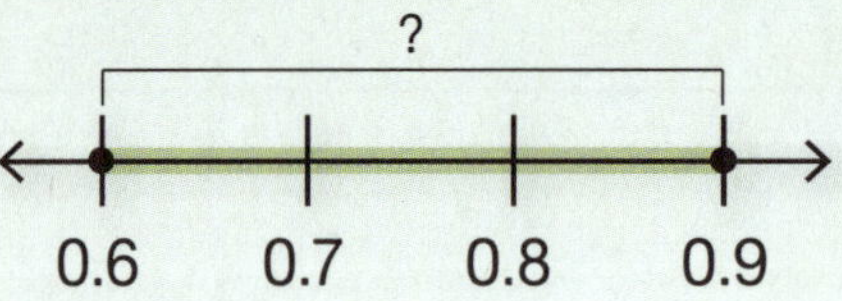

What's the distance between 0.6 and 0.9?

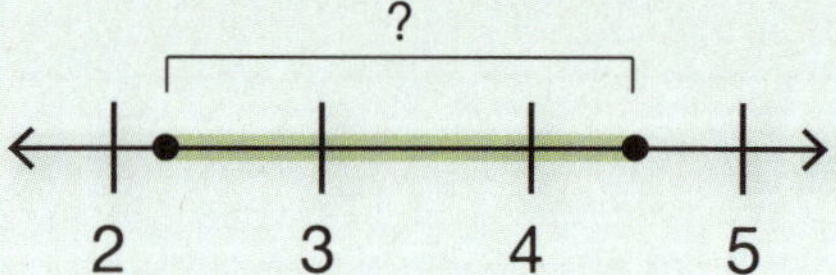

What's the distance between $2\frac{1}{4}$ and $4\frac{1}{2}$?

Solve. Write the equations you use.

Sonia runs $4\frac{1}{2}$ km each day. How far does she run in 30 days?

Asher swims $1\frac{7}{8}$ km at swim practice. Evie swims $\frac{4}{5}$ of the distance that Asher swims. How far does Evie swim?

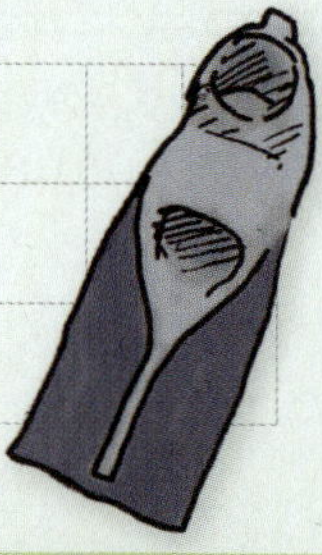

Lesson Activities

A

All 3 ants start at 0.

- Ant A walks 5 units to the left.
- Ant B walks 2 units to the left.
- Ant C walks 4 units to the right.

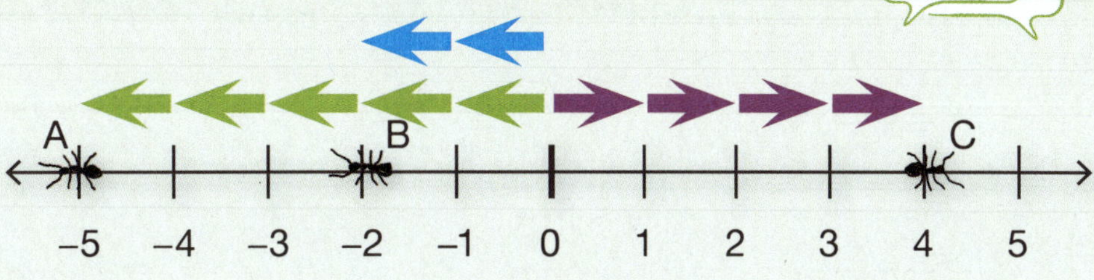

How far apart are ants A and B?	How far apart are ants B and C?	How far apart are ants C and A?
__________ units	__________ units	__________ units

B

Distances on the Number Line

 **Ex.** How far apart are 1 and 4 on the number line?

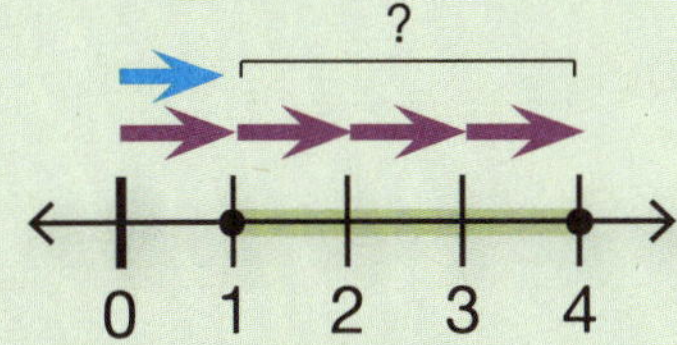

4 – 1 = **3 units**

 **Ex.** How far apart are –3 and –1 on the number line?

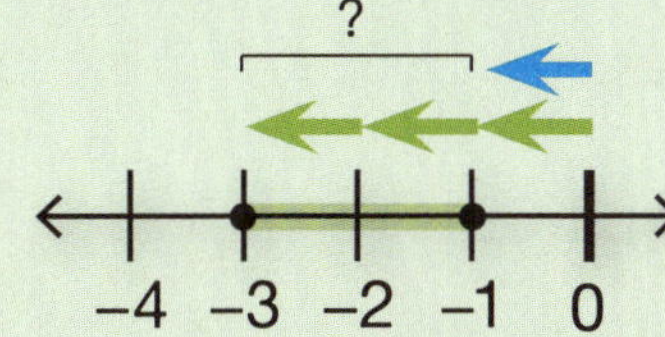

3 – 1 = **2 units**

 **Ex.** How far apart are –3 and 2 on the number line?

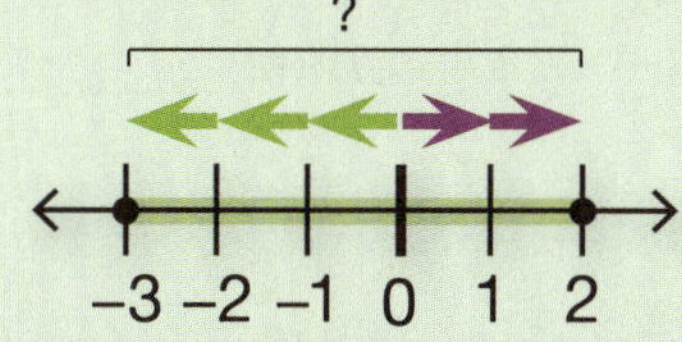

3 + 2 = **5 units**

C

What's the Distance?  (2-Player Game)

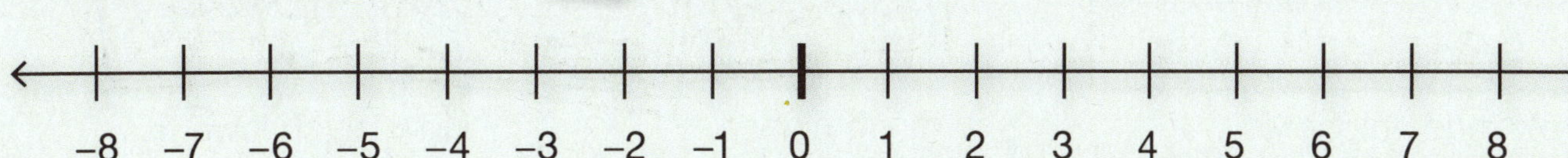

		Round 1	Round 2	Round 3	Round 4	Round 5
Player 1	Numbers					
	Distance					
Player 2	Numbers					
	Distance					

Practice

Find the distance between each pair of points.
(Not all tick marks are shown on the number lines.)

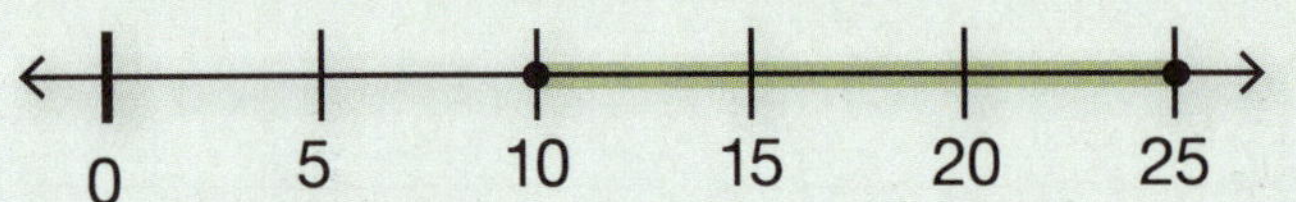

Distance: ___________ units

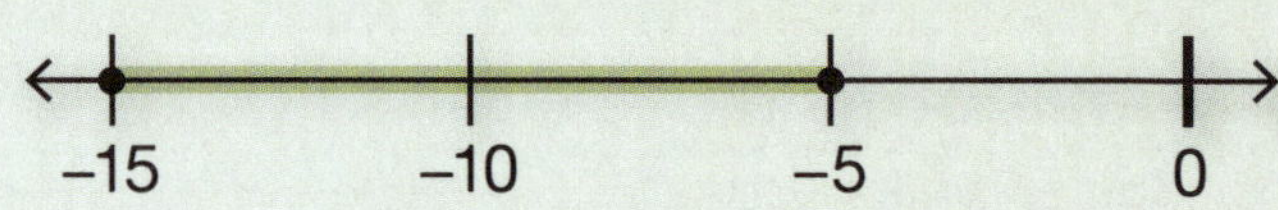

Distance: ___________ units

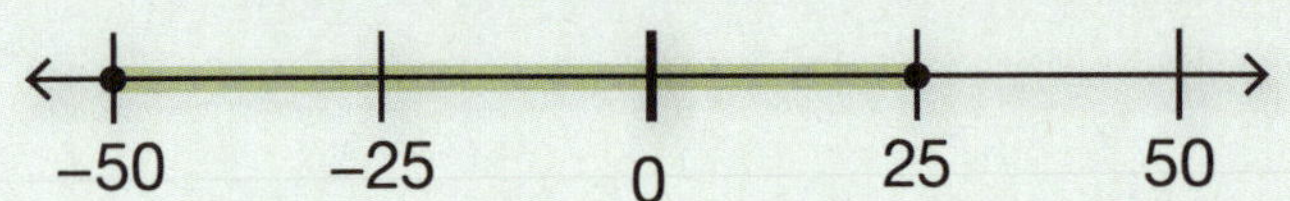

Distance: ___________ units

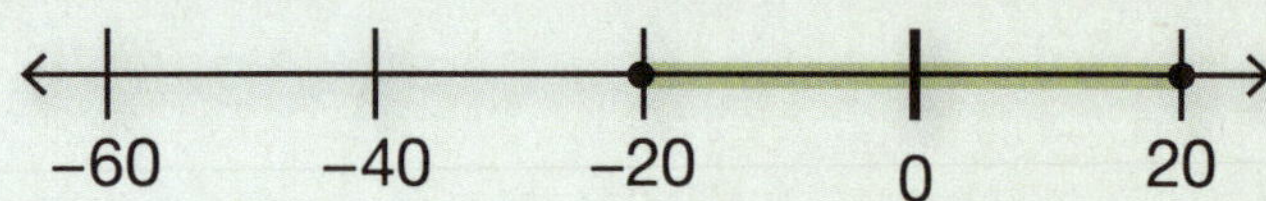

Distance: ___________ units

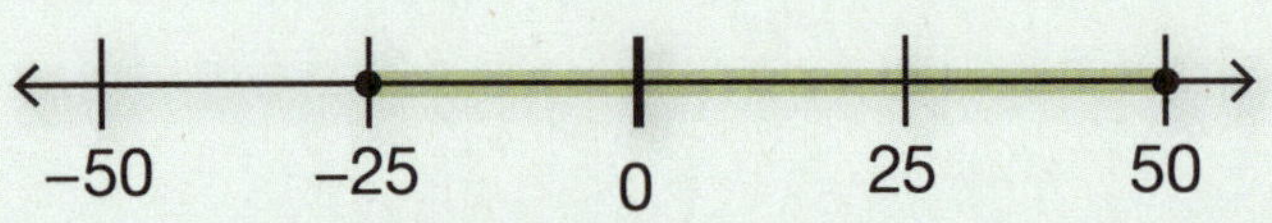

Distance: ___________ units

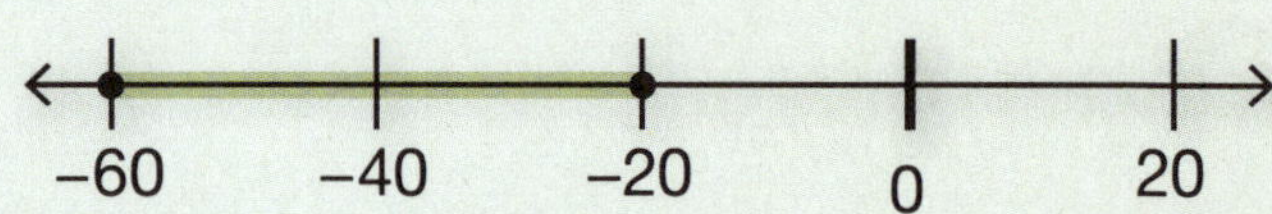

Distance: ___________ units

The chart shows how far each body of water's surface is above or below sea level.
(Positive numbers are above sea level, and negative numbers are below sea level.)
Use the chart to answer the questions.

Body of Water	Elevation (m)
Lake Michigan	176
Caspian Sea	−28
Dead Sea	−430

How much higher is Lake Michigan than the Caspian Sea?

How much higher is Lake Michigan than the Dead Sea?

How much lower is the Dead Sea than the Caspian Sea?

Review  Match each number to its position on the number line.

$4\frac{1}{2}$ $4\frac{3}{4}$ $4\frac{1}{10}$ $4\frac{9}{10}$ 4.5   4.75   4.1   4.9

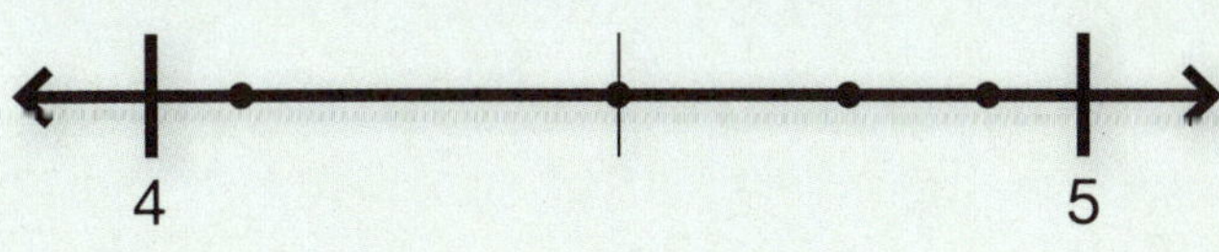

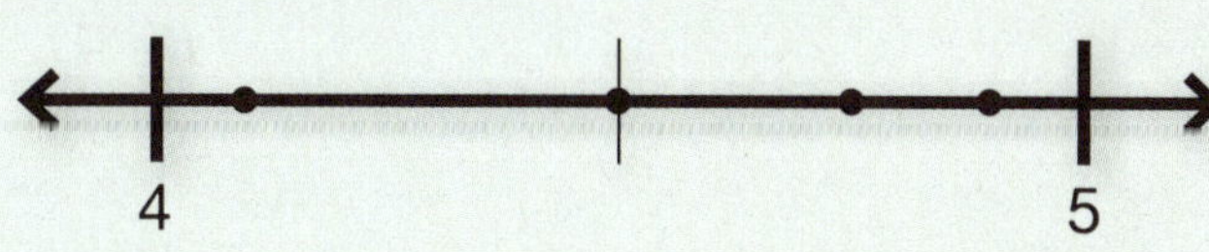

Find the products. Write your answers in simplest form. If the answer is an improper fraction, convert it to a mixed number or whole number.

$$\frac{3}{5} \times \frac{10}{9} =$$

$$\frac{8}{7} \times \frac{5}{2} =$$

$$\frac{11}{3} \times \frac{3}{11} =$$

$$\frac{9}{10} \times \frac{4}{3} \times \frac{0}{7} =$$

$$\frac{6}{5} \times \frac{4}{6} \times \frac{5}{4} =$$

$$\frac{3}{5} \times \frac{7}{8} \times \frac{4}{14} =$$

Draw a bar model to match the description.
Then, complete the ratios and answer the questions.

Adelaine buys a longboard and a helmet. The helmet costs $\frac{1}{3}$ as much as the longboard.

Longboard

Helmet

Longboard's price : Helmet's price

_______ : _______

Helmet's price : Longboard's price

_______ : _______

Longboard's price : Total price of both

_______ : _______

Adelaine spends a total of $216. How much does the longboard cost? How much does the helmet cost?

How much more does the longboard cost than the helmet?

Lesson Activities

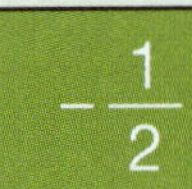 $-\dfrac{1}{2}$ 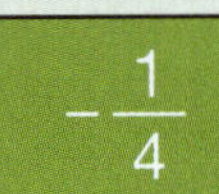 $-\dfrac{1}{4}$ 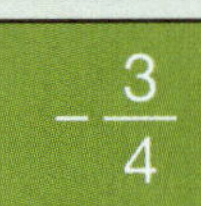 $-\dfrac{3}{4}$  -3.5 -3.8 -3.1

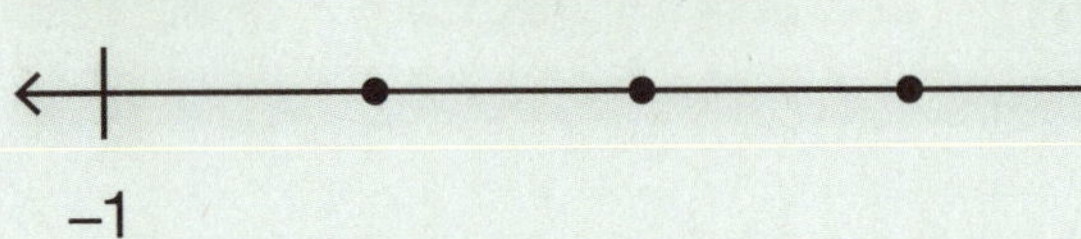

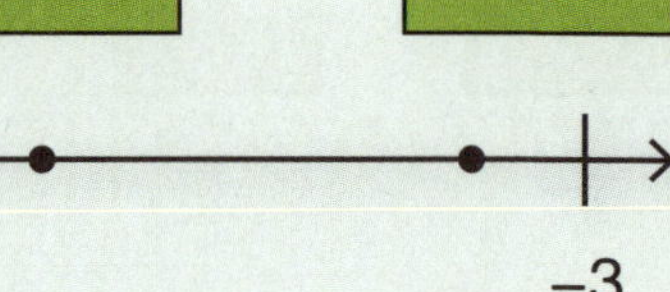

A

B

Opposites

The opposite of a number is the number that is the same distance from zero, in the opposite direction. The opposite of a positive number is the matching negative number. The opposite of a negative number is the matching positive number. The opposite of zero is zero.

We use a minus sign and parentheses to show that we want to find the opposite of a number.

Ex. What is the opposite of 3?

$$-(3) = -3$$

The opposite of 3 is −3.

Ex. What is the opposite of −1?

$$-(-1) = 1$$

The opposite of −1 is 1.

C

Dice Tic-Tac-Toe (2-Player Game)

1	2	3	4	5
$-\left(\dfrac{9}{10}\right)$	$\lvert -2 \rvert$	$-(6.321)$	$\lvert 3.75 \rvert$	$-\left(-3\dfrac{1}{4}\right)$
$\lvert -0.01 \rvert$	$-\left(2\dfrac{5}{6}\right)$	$\left\lvert -\dfrac{1}{8}\right\rvert$	$-(-0.65)$	$\lvert 4 \rvert$
$-(-2)$	$\left\lvert -7\dfrac{1}{2}\right\rvert$	$-\left(-\dfrac{1}{4}\right)$	$\left\lvert 2\dfrac{1}{3}\right\rvert$	$-(9)$
$\lvert 0 \rvert$	$-(5)$	$\left\lvert -\dfrac{3}{4}\right\rvert$	$-\left(-\dfrac{7}{8}\right)$	$\lvert -4.67 \rvert$
$-(-4.8)$	$\lvert 1.2 \rvert$	$-(1.04)$	$\lvert -5 \rvert$	$-(-10)$

Practice

Find the opposite of each number. Label the opposite on the number line.

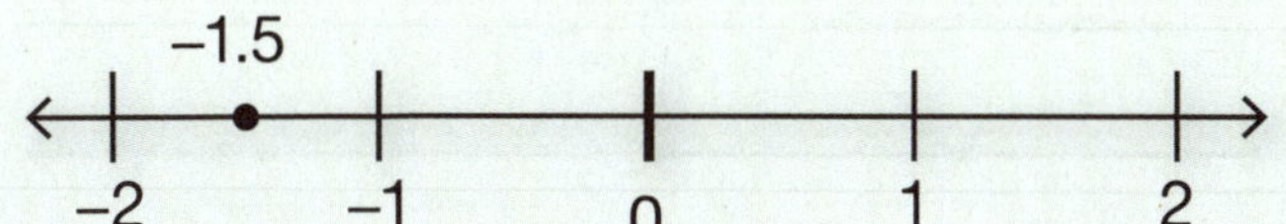

$-(-1.5) =$ _______

$-(0.4) =$ _______

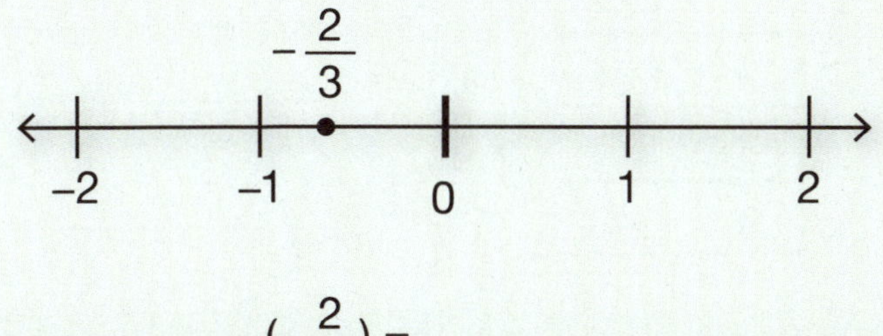

$-(-\frac{2}{3}) =$ _______

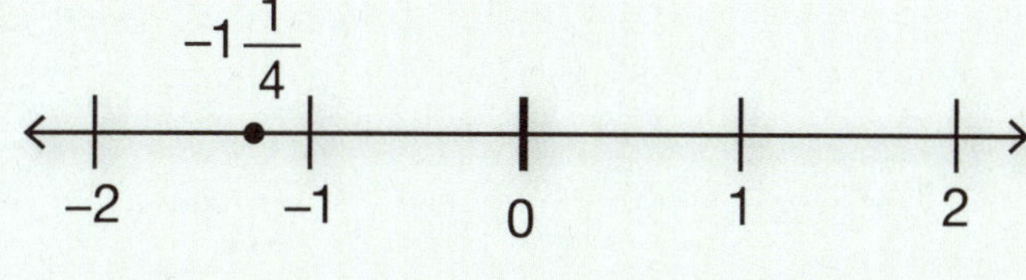

$-(-1\frac{1}{4}) =$ _______

Complete the chart.

Words	Symbols	Value
opposite of −4	−(−4)	
opposite of +2.72		
opposite of 0		
opposite of $-\frac{7}{8}$		
opposite of $\frac{7}{8}$		
	−(−3)	
	−(−1)	

Complete each blank with positive, negative, or zero.

The opposite of a positive number is

_________________ .

The opposite of a negative number is

_________________ .

The opposite of zero is

_________________ .

Review

Use long division to solve.
Use the multiplication table to help.

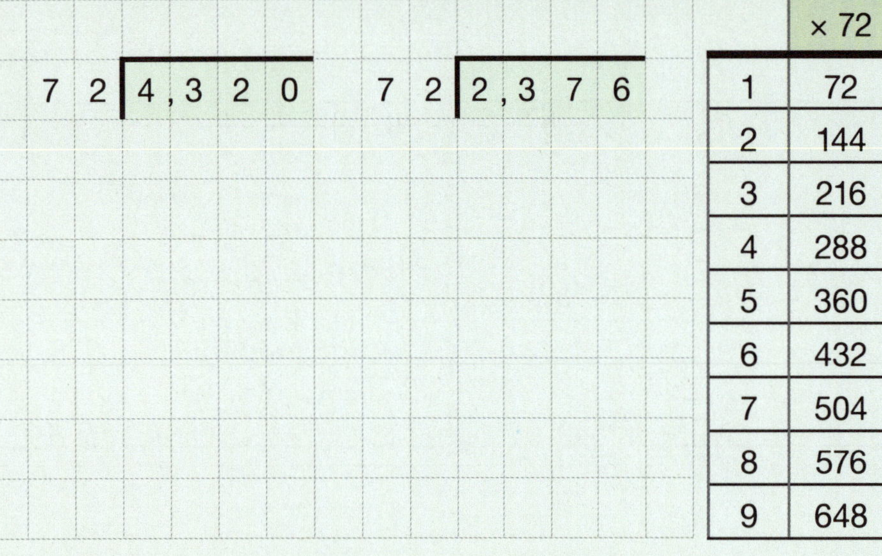

$$7\,2\,\overline{)\,4,3\,2\,0}\qquad 7\,2\,\overline{)\,2,3\,7\,6}$$

	× 72
1	72
2	144
3	216
4	288
5	360
6	432
7	504
8	576
9	648

Evaluate.

$4^2 = $ ___________

$3^2 = $ ___________

$1^2 = $ ___________

$2^2 = $ ___________

$0^2 = $ ___________

$5^2 = $ ___________

Write the ordered pair that describes the location of each point.

Point	Ordered Pair
W	
X	
Y	
Z	

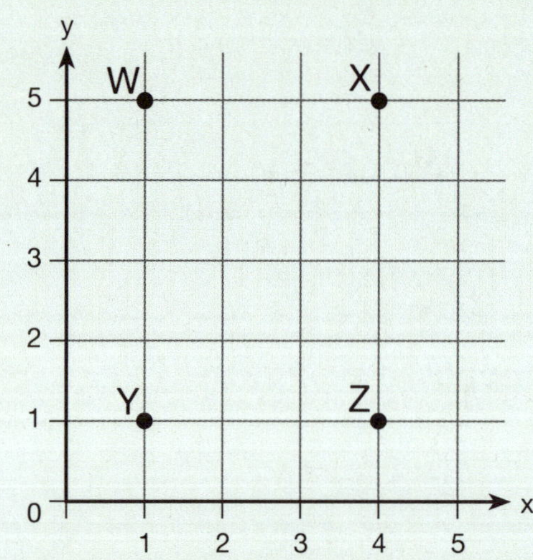

Solve. Write the equations you use.

Adelheid mixes $\frac{2}{3}$ c. melon, $\frac{1}{2}$ c. strawberries, and $\frac{1}{4}$ c. blueberries to make 1 serving of fruit salad. How many cups of fruit does she use to make 1 serving?

Adelheid makes 4 servings of fruit salad. How many cups of fruit does she use in all?

Lesson Activities 👥

Ordered Pairs

An ordered pair tells a location on the coordinate plane.

$$(-3, 2)$$

x-coordinate   y-coordinate

The x-coordinate tells the horizontal distance and direction from the origin. The y-coordinate tells the vertical distance and direction from the origin.

Each section of the coordinate plane is called a quadrant.

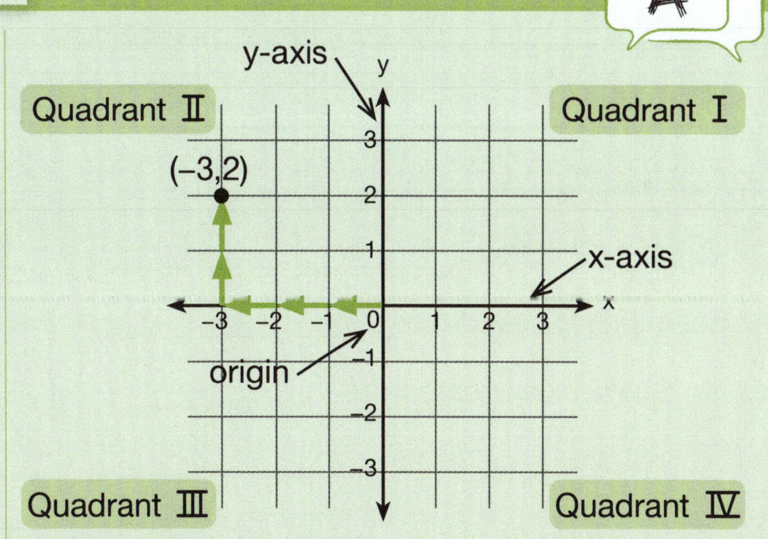

Point	Ordered Pair	Quadrant or Axis
A	(2,−1)	
B	(−3,0)	
C	(−4,−1)	
D		
E		
F		
G		

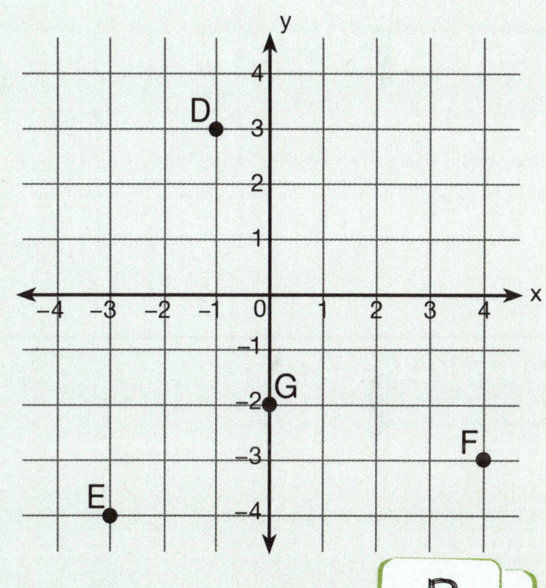

Hot and Cold (2-Player Game)

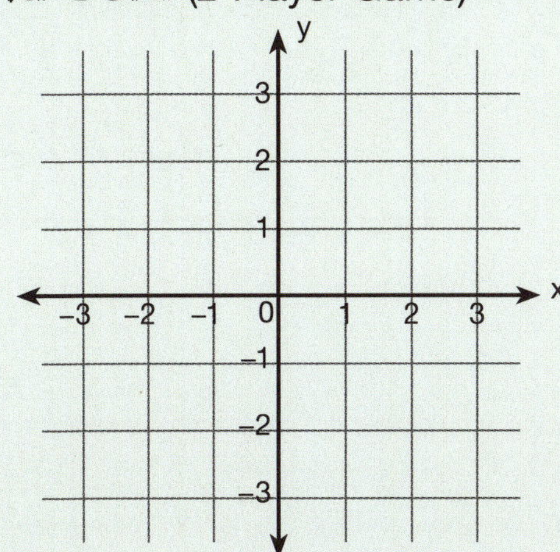

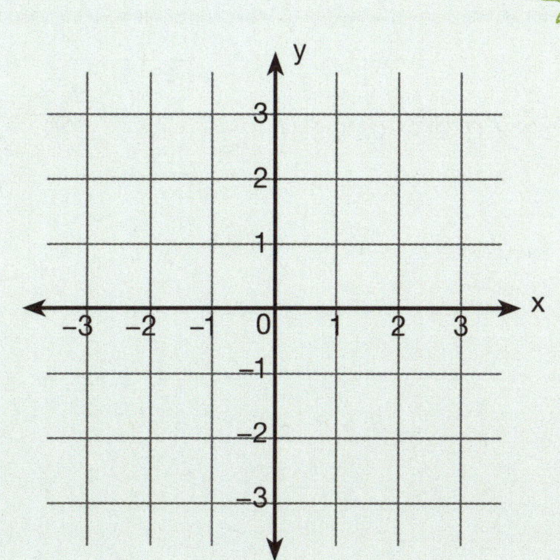

Practice

Use the words and phrases in the word bank to fill in the blanks. You will use each word or phrase once.

(3,–2) is called an ________________________ .

In (3,–2), the 3 is the ________________________ .

In (3,–2), the –2 is the ________________________ .

The point (0,0) is called the ________________ .

The horizontal axis is called the ____________ .

The vertical axis is called the ______________ .

x-axis	y-axis
origin	ordered pair
x-coordinate	y-coordinate

Complete the chart for each point.

Point	Ordered Pair	Quadrant or Axis
L		
M		
N		
O		
P		

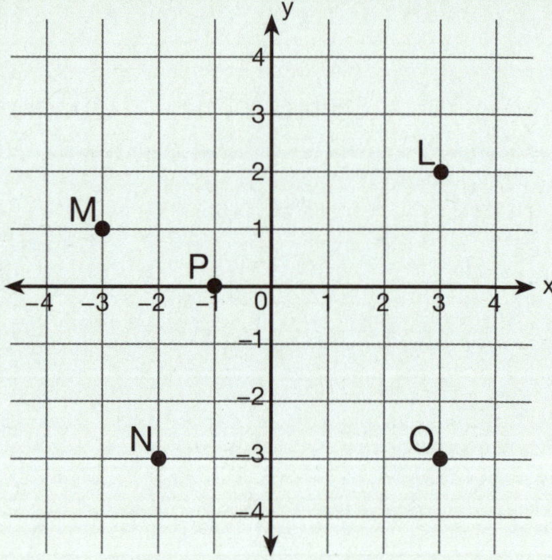

Draw and label each point in the correct location on the coordinate plane.

Point	Ordered Pair
Q	(3,–1)
R	(–4,0)
S	(0,–3)
T	(–3,–1)
U	(–1,3)

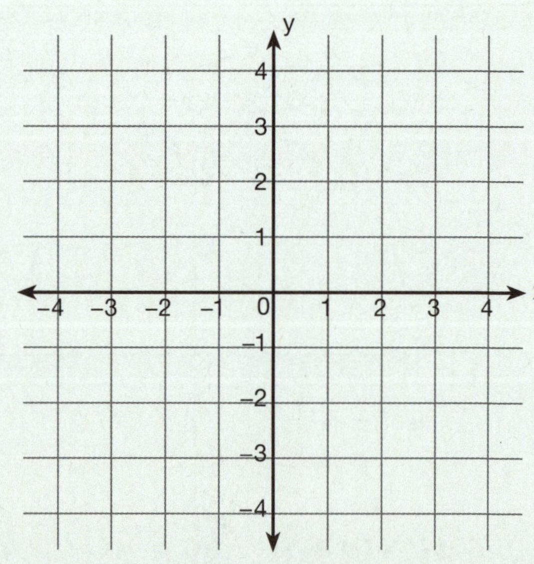

Review

Find the sum or difference.

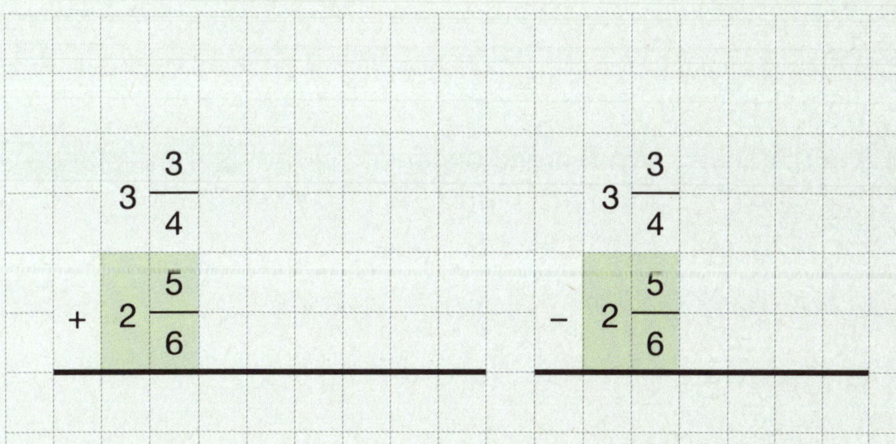

$3\dfrac{3}{4}$

$+\;2\dfrac{5}{6}$

$3\dfrac{3}{4}$

$-\;2\dfrac{5}{6}$

Evaluate.

$|\,4\,| =$ ________________

$|\,-3\,| =$ ________________

$|\,0\,| =$ ________________

$-(4) =$ ________________

$-(-3) =$ ________________

$-(0) =$ ________________

Find the distance between each pair of points.

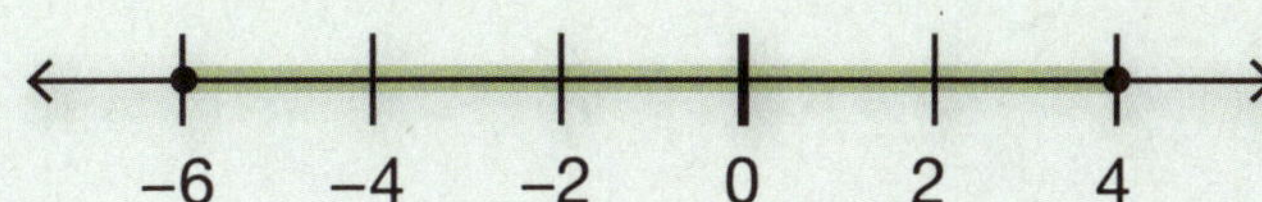

Distance: ______________ units

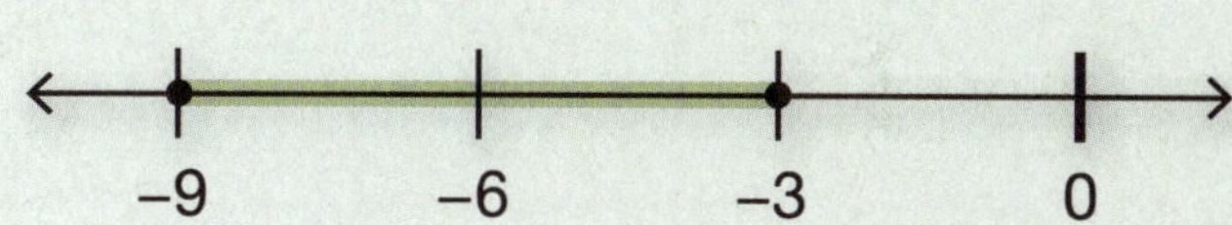

Distance: ______________ units

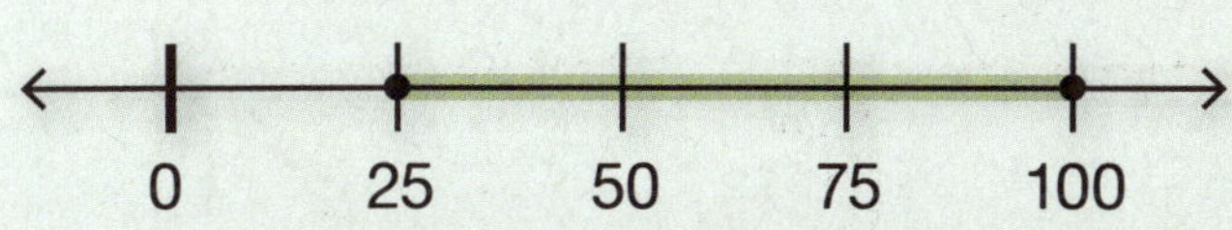

Distance: ______________ units

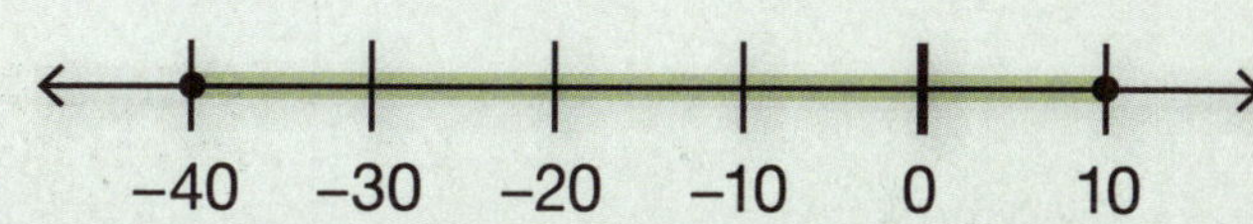

Distance: ______________ units

Use a bar model to complete the blanks.

Mihika plays badminton. This year, her ratio of wins to losses is 4 to 3. She has won 6 more games than she has lost.

Wins

Losses

Number of wins: ________________________

Number of losses: ________________________

Total number of games: ____________________

Lesson Activities 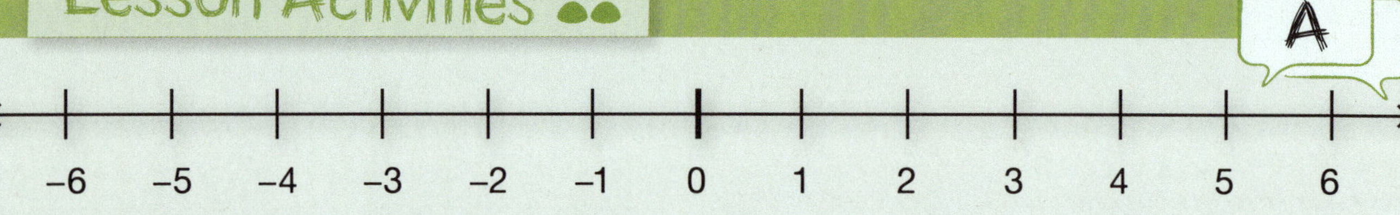

A

What is the distance between 6 and 2?

__________ units

What is the distance between –5 and –1?

__________ units

What is the distance between 0 and –3?

__________ units

What is the distance between –1 and 2?

__________ units

B

Distance on the Coordinate Plane

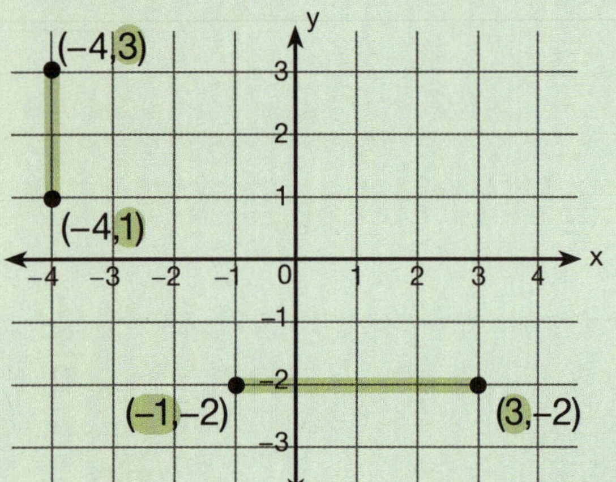

Ex. What is the distance between (–4,3) and (–4,1)?

$3 - 1 = $ **2 units**

Ex. What is the distance between (–1,–2) and (3,–2)?

$1 + 3 = $ **4 units**

C

Location	Ordered Pair
Park	(–6,3)
Hospital	(–2,3)
Library	(–2,–1)
Fire station	(4,–1)
City hall	(4,–4)

What is the distance between the park and hospital?

__________ blocks

What is the distance between the hospital and library?

__________ blocks

What is the distance between the fire station and city hall?

__________ blocks

Practice

**Write the coordinates for each point.
Then, answer the questions.**

Point	Coordinates
A	(−8,2)
B	
C	
D	
E	
F	

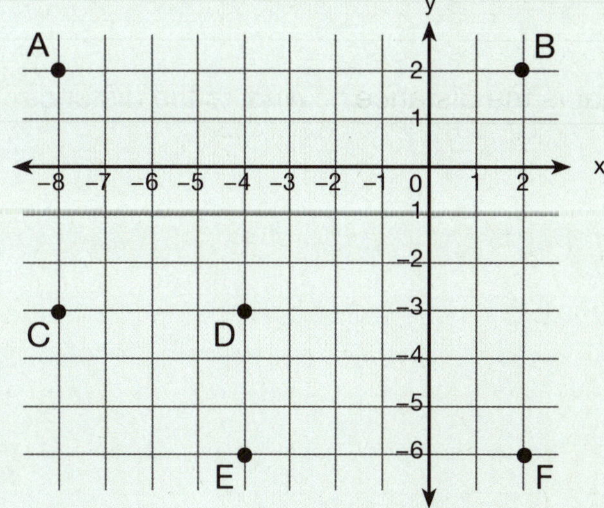

What is the distance between points A and B?

What is the distance between points A and C?

What is the distance between points C and D?

What is the distance between points D and E?

What is the distance between points E and F?

What is the distance between points F and B?

**The treasure is beneath one of the palm trees on the pirate map.
Use the directions to draw the matching path and answer the question.**

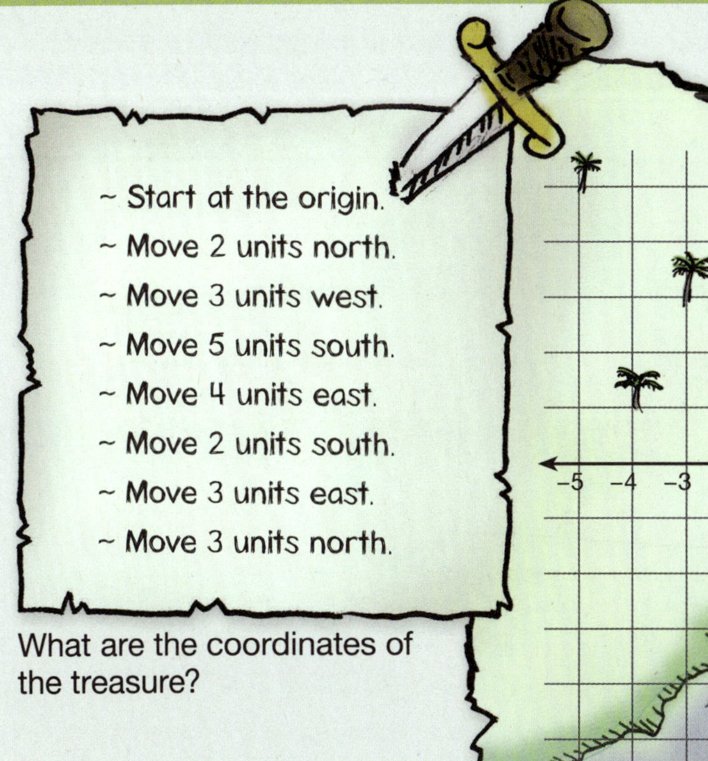

What are the coordinates of the treasure?

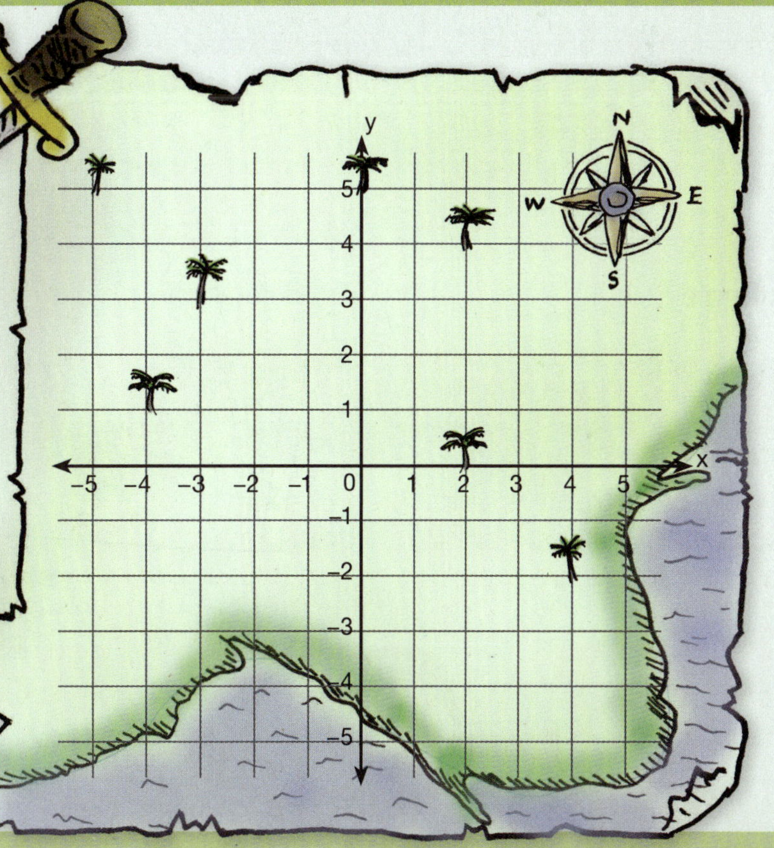

Review

Use logical reasoning to complete the circles with <, >, or =. (You do not need to find the products.)

$\dfrac{3}{5} \bigcirc 1$

$\dfrac{5}{5} \bigcirc 1$

$\dfrac{6}{5} \bigcirc 1$

$\dfrac{3}{5} \times \dfrac{8}{9} \bigcirc \dfrac{8}{9}$

$\dfrac{5}{5} \times \dfrac{8}{9} \bigcirc \dfrac{8}{9}$

$\dfrac{6}{5} \times \dfrac{8}{9} \bigcirc \dfrac{8}{9}$

Find the area of each shape.

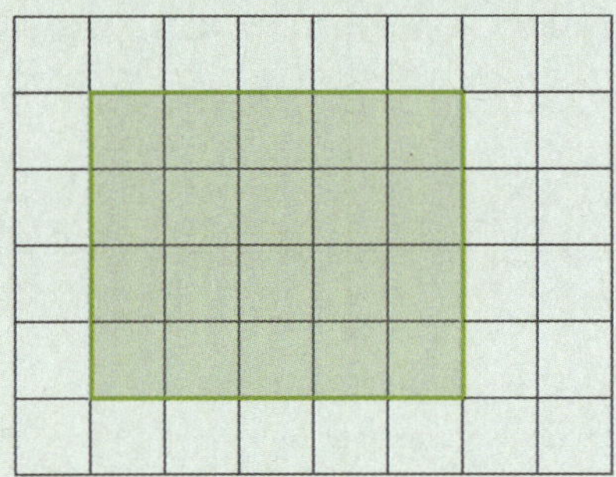

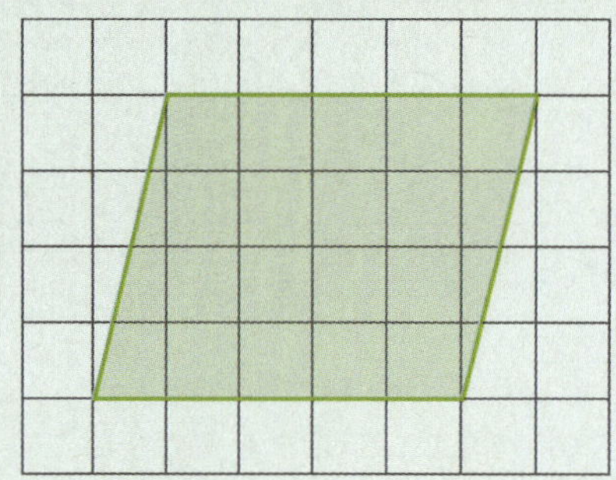

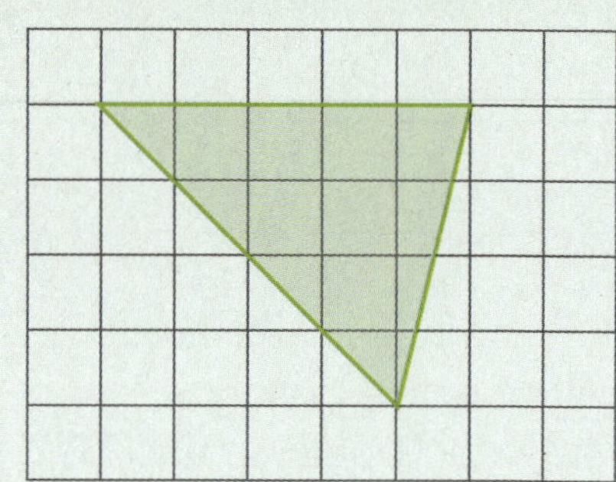

Area: _____________ units^2

Area: _____________ units^2

Area: _____________ units^2

Draw a shape that matches each description.

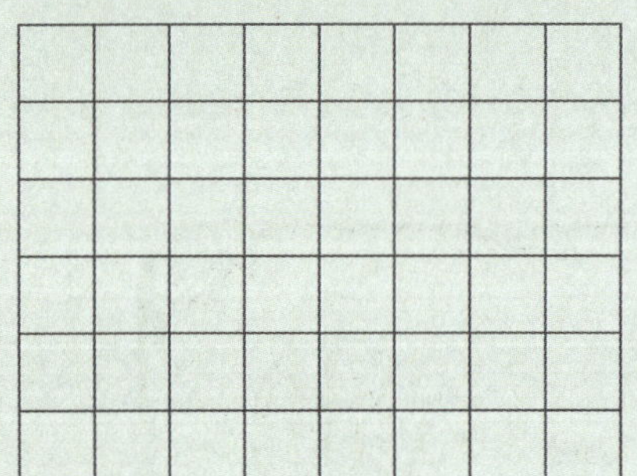

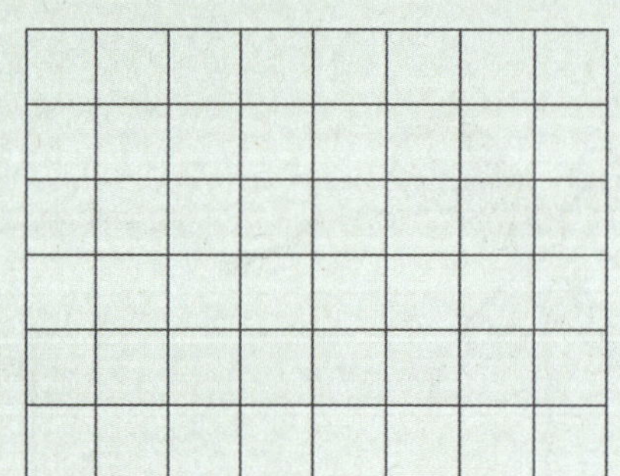

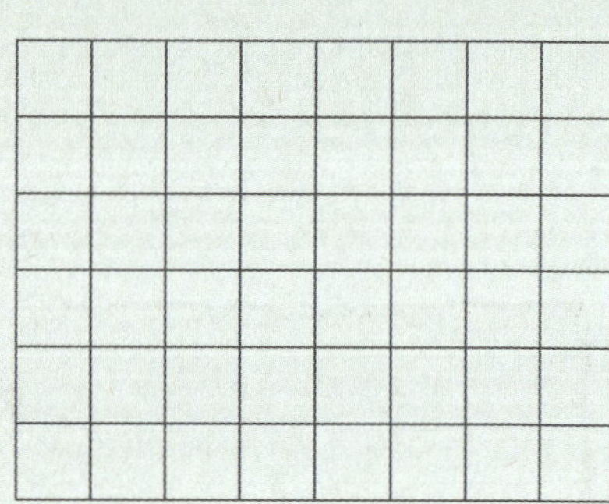

Rectangle

Area: 12 units^2

Parallelogram

Area: 12 units^2

Triangle

Area: 6 units^2

Use the ratio table to solve.

The ratio of instructors to children at swim lessons is 1:6. If there are 42 children, how many instructors are there?

Instructors		
Children		

Lesson Activities 

A

Find Perimeter and Area on the Coordinate Plane

Ex. What are the perimeter and area of this rectangle?

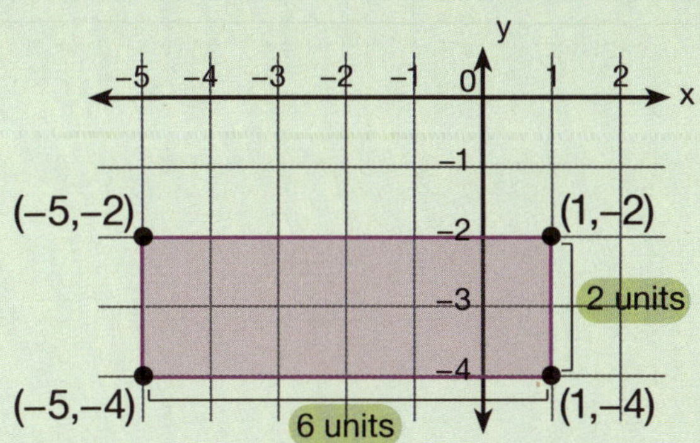

Length:
5 + 1 = 6 units

Width:
4 − 2 = 2 units

Perimeter: 6 + 2 + 6 + 2 = **16 units**

Area: 6 × 2 = **12 units²**

Plot the points. Then, connect them with straight lines to form a rectangle.

| (4,2) | (−4,2) | (−4,−2) | (4,−2) |

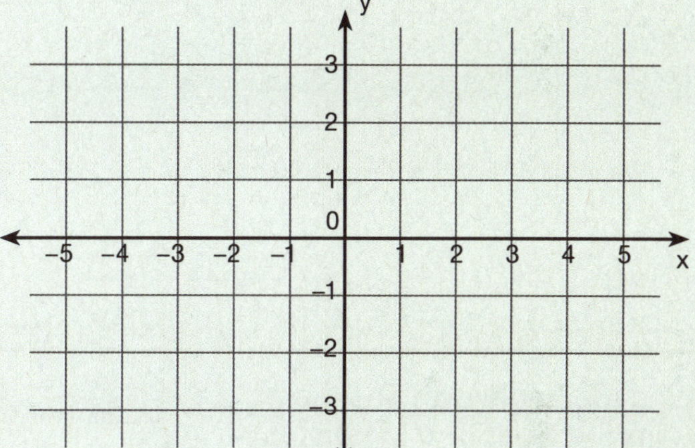

Length: ___________ units

Width: ___________ units

Perimeter: ___________ units

Area: ___________ units²

Plot the points. Then, connect them with straight lines to form a parallelogram.

| (−3,0) | (−4,−3) | (1,−3) | (2,0) |

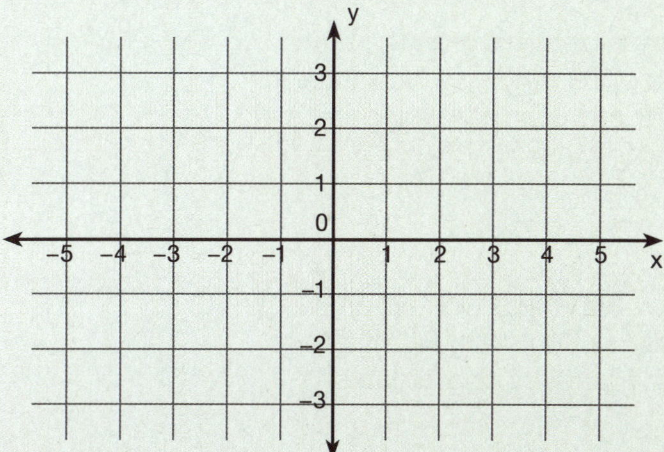

Base: ___________ units

Height: ___________ units

Area: ___________ units²

Practice

Find the area of each shape.

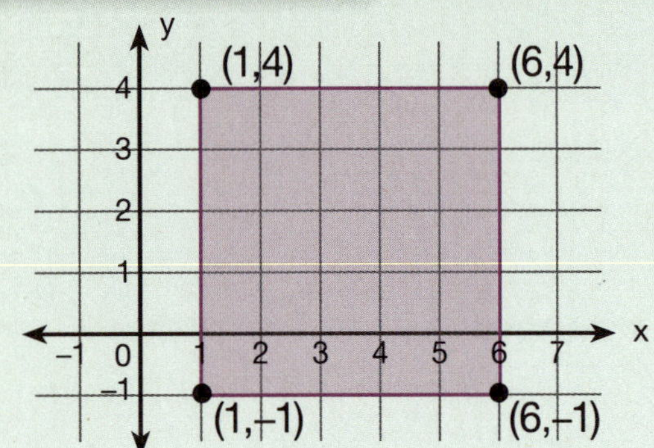

Area: _________________ units²

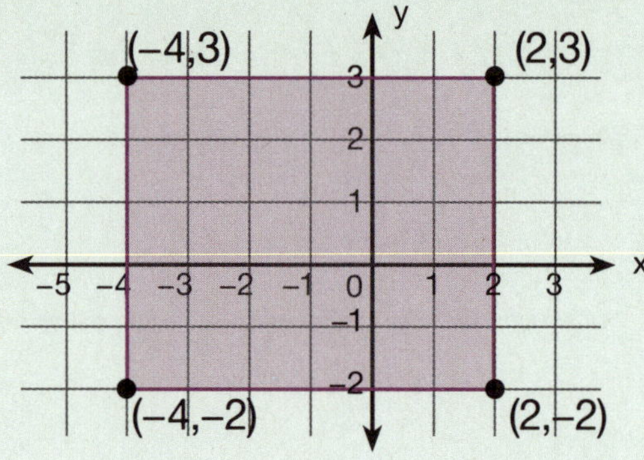

Area: _________________ units²

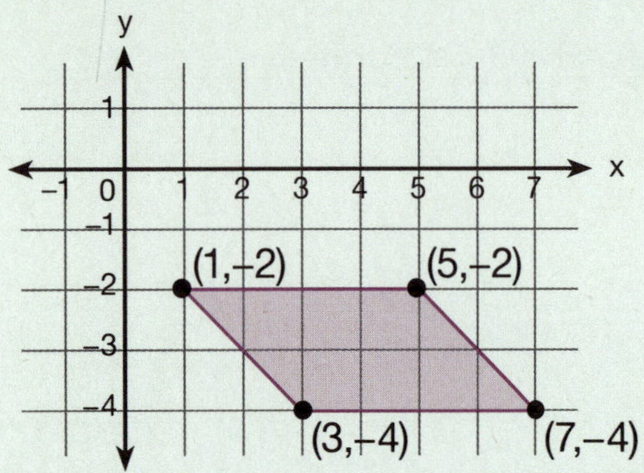

Area: _________________ units²

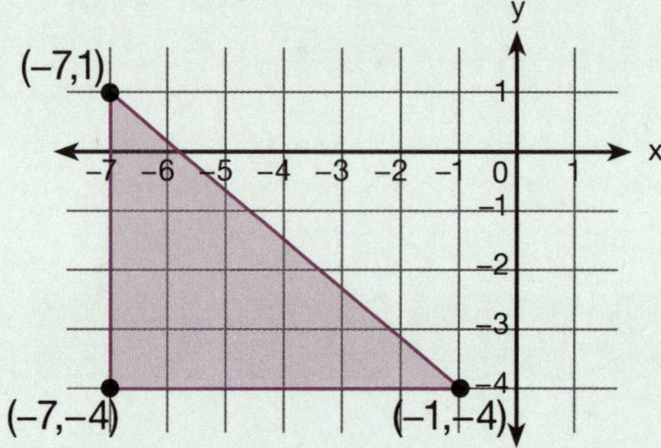

Area: _________________ units²

Follow the directions and answer the questions.

Draw a rectangle with an area of 12 units² in Quadrant II. What are your rectangle's coordinates?

Draw a parallelogram with an area of 20 units² in Quadrant III. What are your parallelogram's coordinates?

Draw a triangle with an area of 6 units² in Quadrant IV. What are your triangle's coordinates?

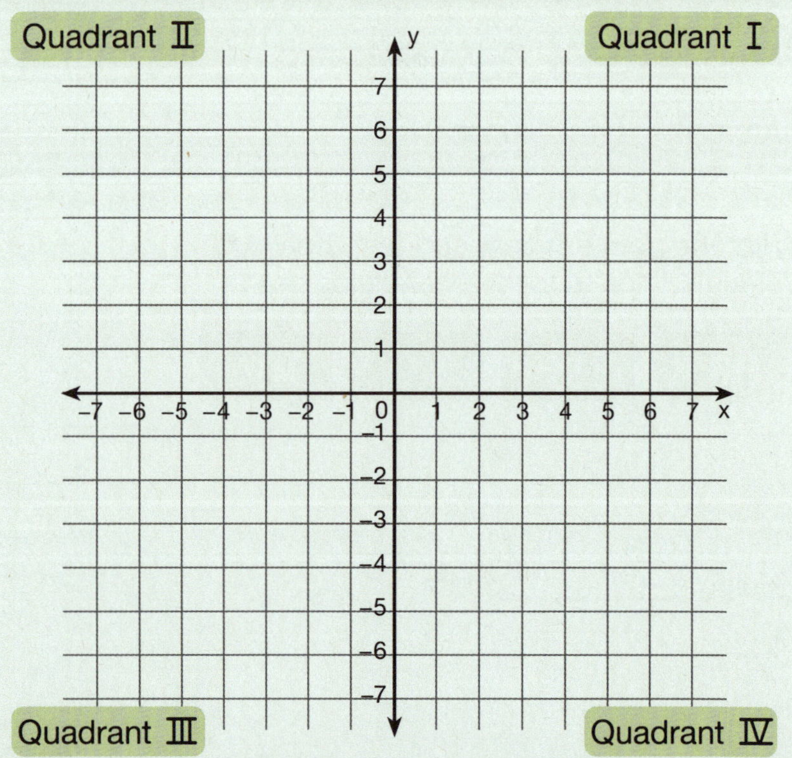

Review

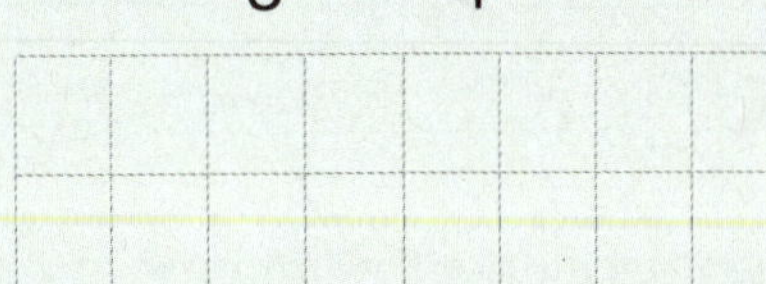

Find the products. Write your answers in simplest form. If the answer is an improper fraction, convert it to a mixed number or whole number.

$\frac{1}{3} \times 1\frac{3}{4} =$

$\frac{2}{3} \times 1\frac{3}{4} =$

$\frac{3}{3} \times 1\frac{3}{4} =$

$\frac{4}{3} \times 1\frac{3}{4} =$

$\frac{5}{3} \times 1\frac{3}{4} =$

$\frac{6}{3} \times 1\frac{3}{4} =$

Find the product.

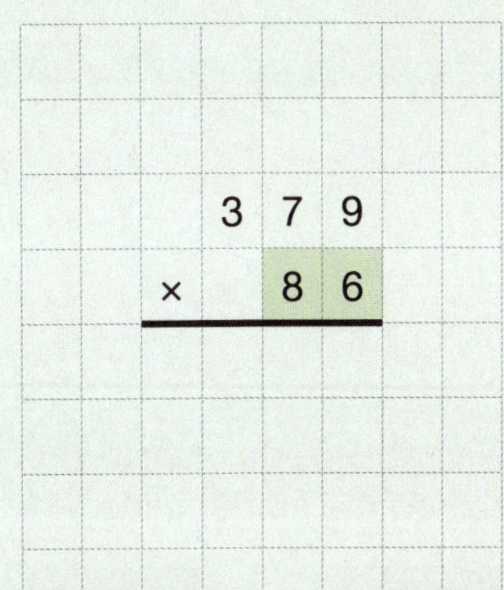

```
      3 7 9
  ×     8 6
  ___________
```

Compare the numbers with <, >, or =.

$\frac{1}{3} \bigcirc \frac{1}{4}$

$\frac{1}{2} \bigcirc \frac{5}{8}$

$\frac{6}{6} \bigcirc \frac{9}{10}$

$\frac{1}{5} \bigcirc \frac{1}{100}$

$\frac{0}{8} \bigcirc \frac{0}{12}$

$5.2 \bigcirc 3.81$

$+5.2 \bigcirc +3.81$

$-5.2 \bigcirc -3.81$

$-5.2 \bigcirc 3.81$

$5.2 \bigcirc -3.81$

Solve. Write the equations you use.

Charlie bikes $15\frac{1}{3}$ miles on Saturday and $10\frac{3}{4}$ miles on Sunday. How much farther does he bike on Saturday than on Sunday?

Abram participates in a triathlon. He swims $\frac{7}{10}$ km, bikes $12\frac{3}{4}$ km, and runs $5\frac{1}{2}$ km. What is the triathlon's total distance?

Unit Wrap-Up

Complete each blank with positive, negative, or zero.

The absolute value of a positive number is ________.	The absolute value of a negative number is ________.	The absolute value of zero is ________.
The opposite of a positive number is ________.	The opposite of a negative number is ________.	The opposite of zero is ________.

Compare the numbers with <, >, or =.

3 ◯ 0	3 ◯ −2
−2 ◯ 0	−2 ◯ −1.7
−1.7 ◯ 0	−1.7 ◯ $2\frac{3}{4}$
$2\frac{3}{4}$ ◯ 0	3 ◯ $2\frac{3}{4}$

Complete.

$\lvert 3 \rvert$ = ________	−(3) = ________
$\lvert -2 \rvert$ = ________	−(−2) = ________
$\lvert -1.7 \rvert$ = ________	−(−1.7) = ________
$\lvert 2\frac{3}{4} \rvert$ = ________	$-(2\frac{3}{4})$ = ________

Use the chart to answer the questions about the average low temperatures.

Average Low Temperatures in Fairbanks, Alaska (°C)	
January	−27
March	−20
July	11
October	−9

Match each temperature to its point on the number line.

−27 −20 11 −9

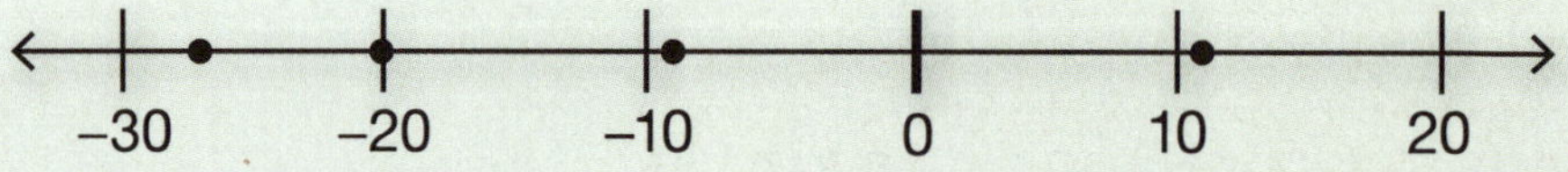

Which month has the coldest temperature?

Which month has the warmest temperature?

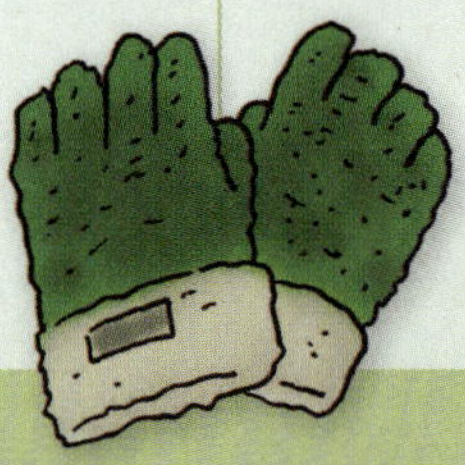

How many degrees warmer is the October temperature than the March temperature?

How many degrees warmer is the July temperature than the January temperature?

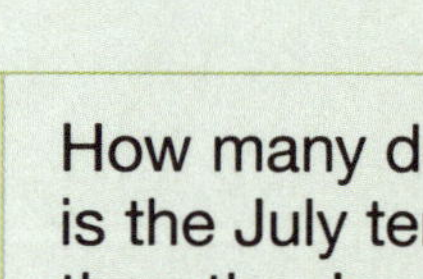

Unit Wrap-Up

Write the correct letter in the blank.

Point __________ is at the origin.

Point __________ is on the x-axis.

Point __________ is on the y-axis.

Point __________ is in Quadrant I.

Point __________ is in Quadrant II.

Point __________ is in Quadrant III.

Point __________ is in Quadrant IV.

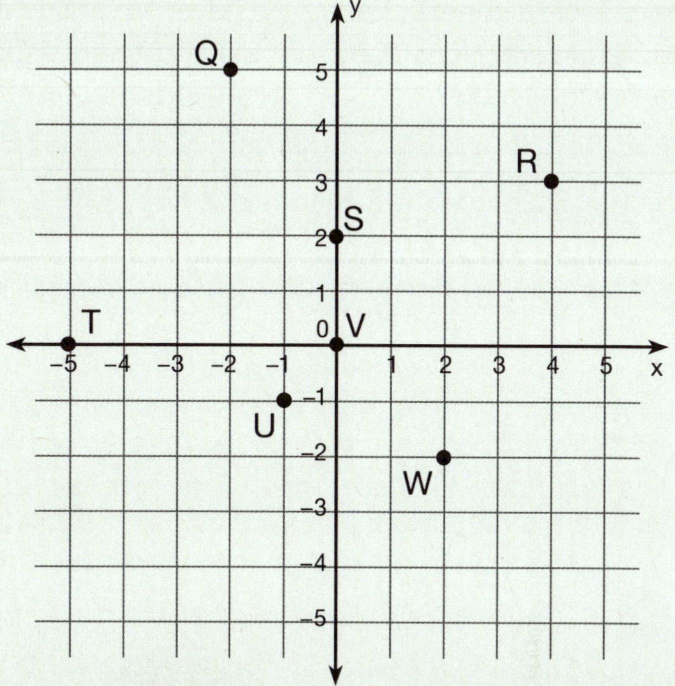

Follow the directions and complete the blanks.

Plot the points. Then, connect them with straight lines to form a rectangle.

| (–1,1) | (–1,–3) | (5,–3) | (5,1) |

Length: __________ units

Width: __________ units

Perimeter: __________ units

Area: __________ units²

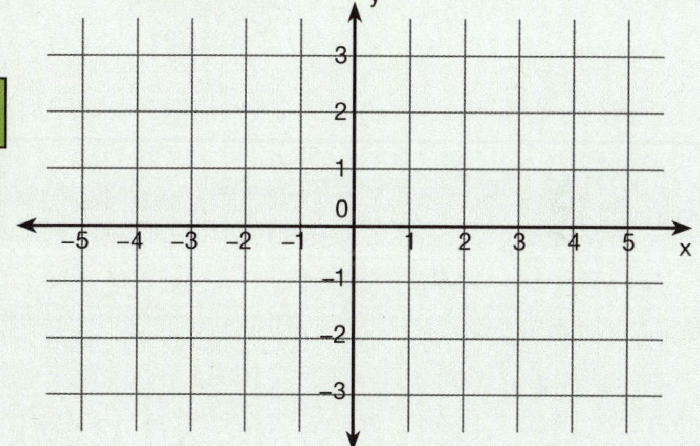

Plot the points. Then, connect them with straight lines to form a triangle.

| (–4,–2) | (0,3) | (2,–2) |

Base: __________ units

Height: __________ units

Area: __________ units²

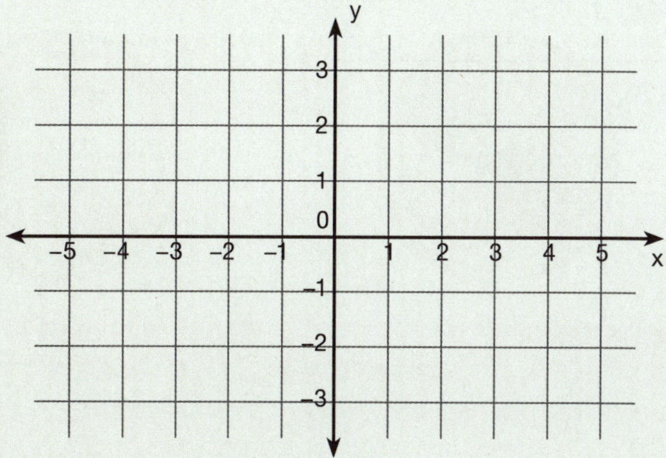

Lesson Activities 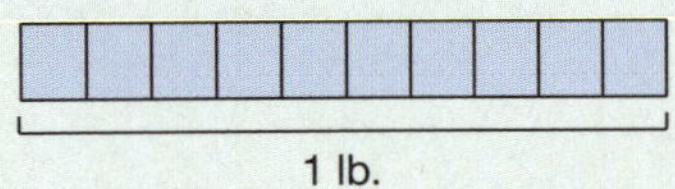

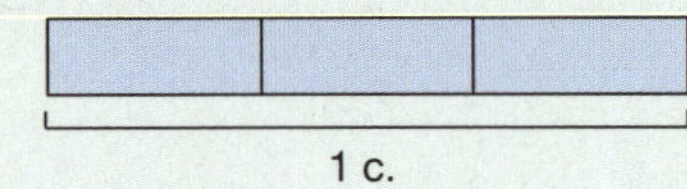

I have 1 lb. of cheese. Each serving is $\frac{1}{10}$ lb. How many servings do I have?

I have 1 c. of rice. Each serving is $\frac{1}{3}$ c. How many servings can I make?

I have 1 liter of juice. Each serving is $\frac{1}{4}$ L. How many servings can I pour?

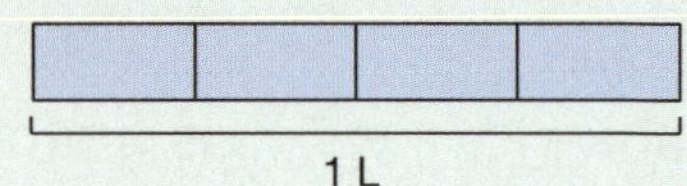

A

1 lb.

1 c.

1 L

$1 \text{ lb.} \div \frac{1}{10} \text{ lb.} = \underline{\quad}$ servings

$1 \text{ c.} \div \frac{1}{3} \text{ c.} = \underline{\quad}$ servings

$1 \text{ L} \div \frac{1}{4} \text{ L} = \underline{\quad}$ servings

B

Reciprocals

The reciprocal tells how many times the number "goes into" 1.
To find the reciprocal of a fraction, flip the numerator and denominator.

Ex. How many servings are in 1 pie?

Serving size:
$\frac{1}{6}$ of the pie

$\frac{1}{6} \quad \frac{6}{1}$

$\frac{6}{1} = 6$, so 6 is the reciprocal.

$1 \text{ pie} \div \frac{1}{6} = \mathbf{6 \text{ servings}}$

Ex. How many servings are in 1 pizza?

Serving size:
$\frac{2}{5}$ of the pizza

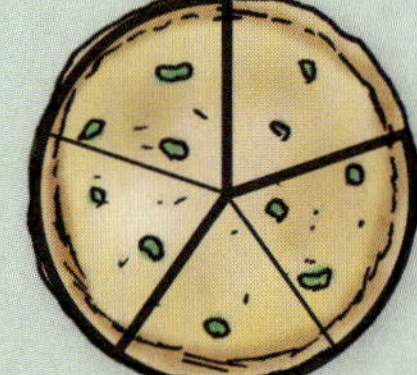

$\frac{2}{5} \quad \frac{5}{2}$

$\frac{5}{2} = 2\frac{1}{2}$, so $2\frac{1}{2}$ is the reciprocal.

$1 \text{ pizza} \div \frac{2}{5} = \frac{5}{2} = \mathbf{2\frac{1}{2} \text{ servings}}$

I have 1 pizza. If each serving is $\frac{1}{8}$ of a pizza, how many servings are there?

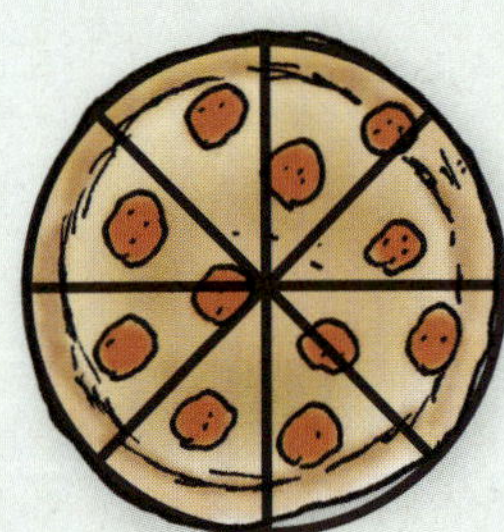

Reciprocal of $\frac{1}{8}$: _______

$1 \div \frac{1}{8} =$

I have 1 pizza. If each serving is $\frac{3}{8}$ of a pizza, how many servings are there?

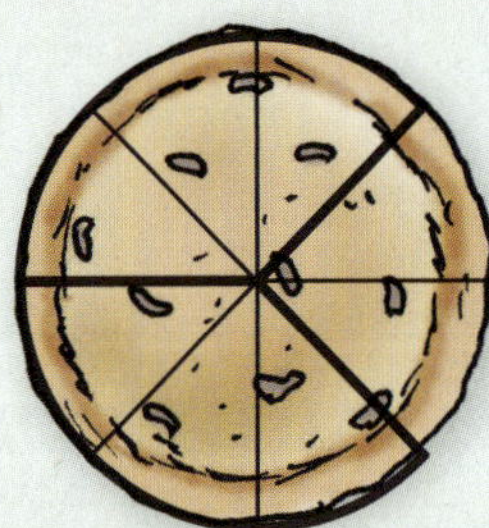

Reciprocal of $\frac{3}{8}$: _______

$1 \div \frac{3}{8} =$

I have 1 pizza. If each serving is $\frac{5}{8}$ of a pizza, how many servings are there?

Reciprocal of $\frac{5}{8}$: _______

$1 \div \frac{5}{8} =$

Practice

Find the reciprocal of each number. Write the reciprocals in simplest form. Convert improper fractions to whole numbers or mixed numbers.

Reciprocal of $\frac{1}{4}$: _________

Reciprocal of $\frac{1}{10}$: _________

Reciprocal of $\frac{1}{7}$: _________

Reciprocal of $\frac{3}{4}$: _________

Reciprocal of $\frac{5}{10}$: _________

Reciprocal of $\frac{2}{7}$: _________

Reciprocal of $\frac{2}{3}$: _________

Reciprocal of $\frac{9}{10}$: _________

Reciprocal of $\frac{4}{7}$: _________

Use reciprocals to answer the questions and complete the division problems.

I have 1 large chocolate bar. If each serving is $\frac{1}{12}$ of the bar, how many servings are there?

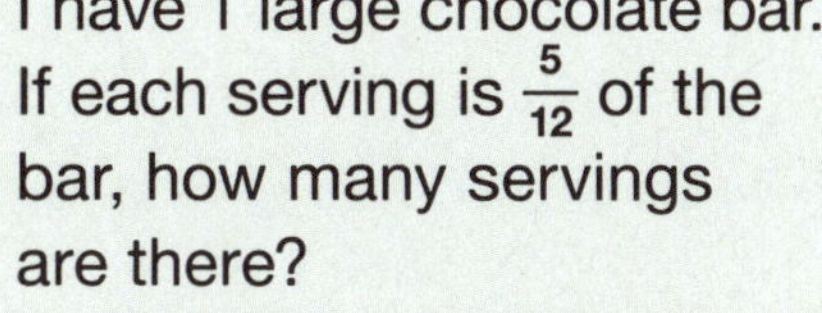

$1 \div \frac{1}{12} =$

I have 1 large chocolate bar. If each serving is $\frac{5}{12}$ of the bar, how many servings are there?

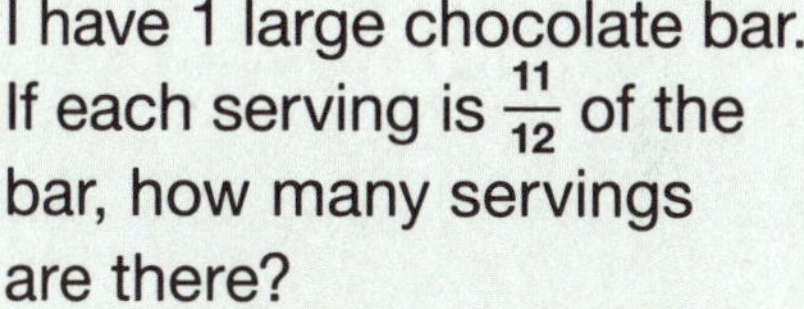

$1 \div \frac{5}{12} =$

I have 1 large chocolate bar. If each serving is $\frac{11}{12}$ of the bar, how many servings are there?

$1 \div \frac{11}{12} =$

I have 1 sub sandwich. If each serving is $\frac{1}{5}$ of the sandwich, how many servings are there?

$1 \div \frac{1}{5} =$

I have 1 sub sandwich. If each serving is $\frac{2}{5}$ of the sandwich, how many servings are there?

$1 \div \frac{2}{5} =$

I have 1 sub sandwich. If each serving is $\frac{4}{5}$ of the sandwich, how many servings are there?

$1 \div \frac{4}{5} =$

Review

Find the products.

```
    7 4          8 6          5 3 1        2,1 8 8
  × 8 8        × 4 0        ×   8 4      × 7,0 0 0
```

Compare with <, >, or =.

−4 ◯ −3   5 ◯ 2   −7 ◯ 1   0 ◯ −6

4 ◯ −3   −5 ◯ 2   7 ◯ −1   0 ◯ 6

Complete the chart.

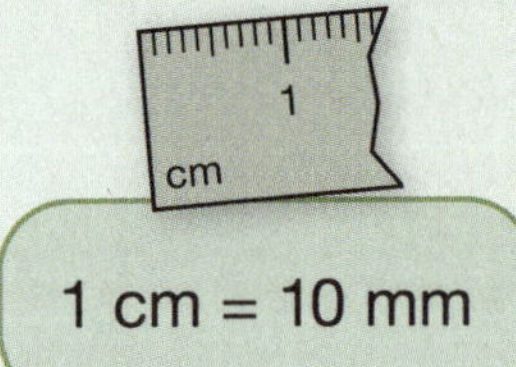

1 cm = 10 mm

	$1\frac{7}{10}$	$2\frac{5}{10}$	$3\frac{4}{10}$	$3\frac{9}{10}$			
Centimeters							
Millimeters	17				47	51	109

Solve. Write the equations you use.

Andrew mixed $3\frac{1}{2}$ c. chopped melon, $2\frac{2}{3}$ c. grapes, and $1\frac{3}{4}$ c. sliced strawberries to make fruit salad for a party. How many cups of fruit did he use in all?

Genevieve used $2\frac{3}{4}$ lb. sliced turkey and $4\frac{1}{2}$ lb. sliced ham to make sandwiches for a party. How much more ham did she use than turkey?

Lesson Activities 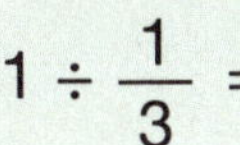

If each serving is $\frac{1}{3}$ of a pizza, how many servings are in 1 pizza?

$1 \div \dfrac{1}{3} =$

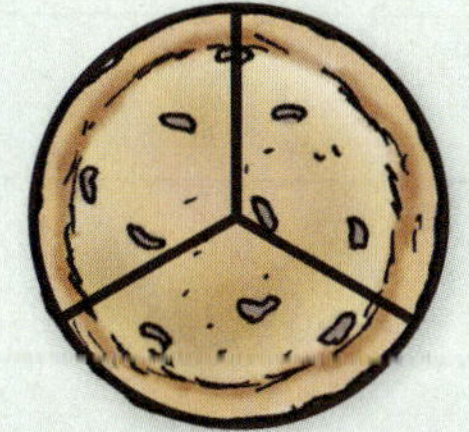

If each serving is $\frac{2}{3}$ of a pizza, how many servings are in 1 pizza?

$1 \div \dfrac{2}{3} =$

Divide by a Fraction

To divide a number by a fraction, we multiply the number by the reciprocal of the fraction.

1. Keep the dividend the same.

2. Change the division sign to a multiplication sign.

3. Flip the divisor's numerator and denominator and write its reciprocal.

Keep ➜ Change ➜ Flip

Ex. I have 3 pizzas. If each serving is $\frac{1}{3}$ of a pizza, how many servings are there?

$3 \div \dfrac{1}{3} = ?$

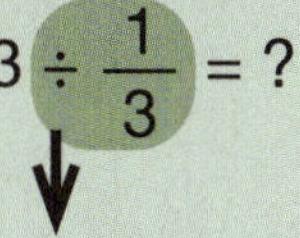   

$3 \times 3 = $ **9 servings**

Ex. I have 3 pizzas. If each serving is $\frac{2}{3}$ of a pizza, how many servings are there?

$3 \div \dfrac{2}{3} = ?$

$\dfrac{3}{1} \times \dfrac{3}{2} = \dfrac{9}{2} = 4\dfrac{1}{2}$ **servings**

How Much Pizza? (2-Player Game)

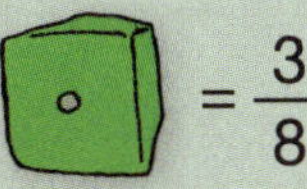 $= \dfrac{3}{8}$ 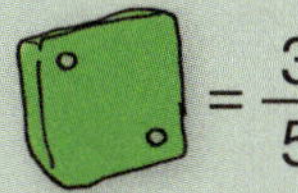 $= \dfrac{3}{5}$ 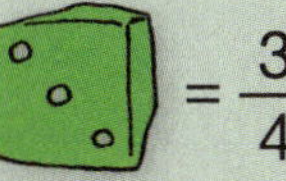 $= \dfrac{3}{4}$ 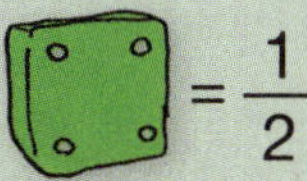 $= \dfrac{1}{2}$  $= \dfrac{3}{10}$ 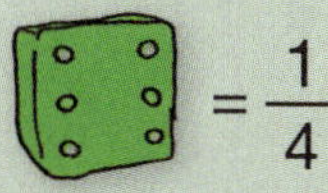 $= \dfrac{1}{4}$

Player 1

$2 \div \underline{\hspace{2cm}} = $ $3 \div \underline{\hspace{2cm}} = $ $4 \div \underline{\hspace{2cm}} = $

Player 2

$2 \div \underline{\hspace{2cm}} = $ $3 \div \underline{\hspace{2cm}} = $ $4 \div \underline{\hspace{2cm}} = $

Practice

Rewrite each division problem as a multiplication problem and solve. Write your answers in simplest form. Convert improper fractions to whole numbers or mixed numbers.

$1 \div \dfrac{1}{3}$	$1 \div \dfrac{5}{8}$	$1 \div \dfrac{4}{5}$
$\dfrac{1}{1} \times \dfrac{3}{1} = \dfrac{3}{1} = 3$		

$2 \div \dfrac{1}{3}$	$2 \div \dfrac{5}{8}$	$2 \div \dfrac{4}{5}$

$3 \div \dfrac{1}{3}$	$3 \div \dfrac{5}{8}$	$3 \div \dfrac{4}{5}$

Complete the blanks to match each word problem. Then, rewrite each problem as a multiplication problem and solve. Simplify your answers if needed. Write improper fractions as whole numbers or mixed numbers.

Kate makes 4 lb. of granola. She packages the granola in bags that each weigh $\dfrac{2}{3}$ lb. How many bags does she fill?

$$\underline{\quad 4 \quad} \div \underline{\quad \tfrac{2}{3} \quad}$$

Soren makes 3 kg of trail mix. He packages the trail mix in bags that each weigh $\dfrac{3}{8}$ kg. How many bags does he fill?

$$\underline{\qquad} \div \underline{\qquad}$$

Joseph buys 4 kg of hamburger. He freezes it in packs that each weigh $\dfrac{8}{10}$ kg. How many packs does he make?

$$\underline{\qquad} \div \underline{\qquad}$$

Kascia-Maria makes 9 L of lemonade. She pours $\dfrac{3}{4}$ L in each pitcher. How many pitchers does she fill?

$$\underline{\qquad} \div \underline{\qquad}$$

Review   Plot the points.

(0,4)	(0,−4)
(2,4)	(−2,4)
(4,2)	(−4,2)
(4,−2)	(−4,−2)
(2,−2)	(−2,−2)

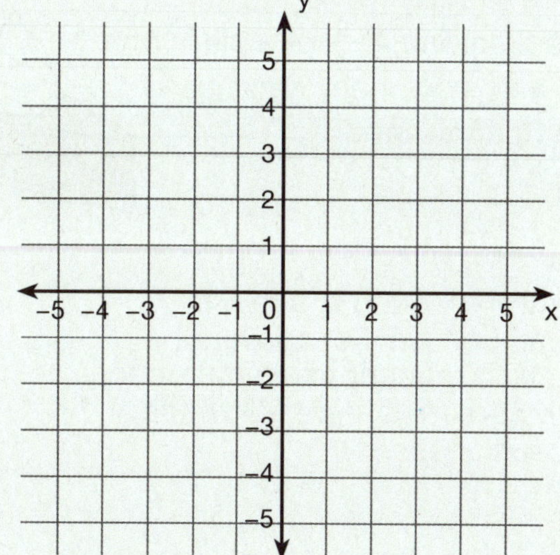

Convert the improper fractions to whole numbers or mixed numbers. Convert the mixed numbers to improper fractions.

$\frac{12}{5} =$	$\frac{11}{4} =$	$\frac{13}{7} =$	$\frac{23}{10} =$
$1\frac{9}{10} =$	$5\frac{2}{3} =$	$3\frac{5}{8} =$	$2\frac{5}{6} =$

Use bar models to complete the blanks.

There are 80 marbles in the bag. The ratio of green marbles to blue marbles is 1 to 3.

Number of green marbles: _______________

Number of blue marbles: _______________

There are 200 visitors at the zoo. The ratio of adults to children is 2 to 3.

Number of adults: _______________

Number of children: _______________

Lesson Activities

Clara's family makes 3 pies for Thanksgiving. If $\frac{1}{8}$ of a pie is one serving, how many servings of pie do they have?

Divide Mixed Numbers

If the dividend is a mixed number, we first convert the mixed number to an improper fraction. Then, we follow the usual steps.

Ex. After Thanksgiving, Clara's family has $1\frac{1}{2}$ pies left over. If $\frac{1}{8}$ of a pie is one serving, how many servings do they have?

$$1\frac{1}{2} \div \frac{1}{8} = ?$$

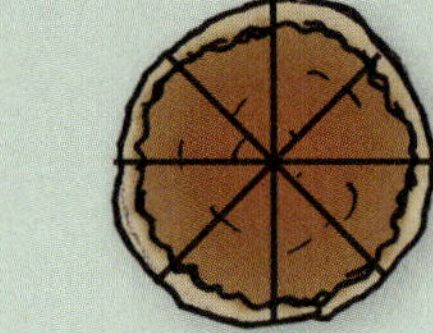

$$\frac{3}{2} \div \frac{1}{8} = ?$$

$$\frac{3}{\cancel{2}_1} \times \frac{\cancel{8}^4}{1} = \frac{12}{1} = \textbf{12 servings}$$

The bag of potatoes weighs $7\frac{1}{2}$ lb. How many servings is that?

Uncle Joe's stuffing recipe makes $8\frac{1}{2}$ c. How many servings is that?

Grandma's gravy recipe makes $4\frac{1}{2}$ c. How many servings is that?

Aunt Mary's cranberry sauce recipe makes $3\frac{3}{4}$ c. How many servings is that?

Thanksgiving Planning for 10 People

Food	Amount per person
Cranberry sauce	$\frac{1}{4}$ c.
Stuffing	$\frac{3}{4}$ c.
Potatoes	$\frac{1}{2}$ lb.
Gravy	$\frac{1}{3}$ c.

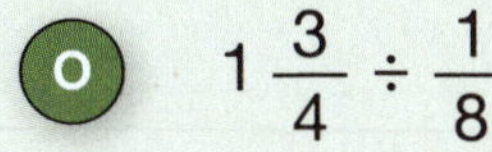

Practice

Rewrite each division problem as a multiplication problem and solve. Write your answers as mixed numbers in simplest form. Then, find the blanks that match the answers. Write the matching letters in the blanks to solve the riddle.

O $\quad 1\frac{3}{4} \div \frac{1}{8}$

H $\quad 1\frac{3}{4} \div \frac{5}{8}$

A $\quad 1\frac{3}{4} \div \frac{7}{8}$

S $\quad 2\frac{1}{2} \div \frac{1}{5}$

G $\quad 2\frac{1}{2} \div \frac{3}{5}$

I $\quad 2\frac{1}{2} \div \frac{4}{5}$

P $\quad 4\frac{1}{6} \div \frac{1}{6}$

T $\quad 4\frac{1}{6} \div \frac{3}{6}$

N $\quad 4\frac{1}{6} \div \frac{5}{6}$

Did you hear about the mathematician who's scared of negative numbers?

She will □ □ □ □ □ □

$12\frac{1}{2}$ $\quad$ $8\frac{1}{3}$ $\quad$ 14 $\quad$ 25 $\quad\quad$ 2 $\quad$ $8\frac{1}{3}$

□ □ □ □ □ □ □ $\quad$ to avoid them.

5 $\quad$ 14 $\quad$ $8\frac{1}{3}$ $\quad$ $2\frac{4}{5}$ $\quad$ $3\frac{1}{8}$ $\quad$ 5 $\quad$ $4\frac{1}{6}$

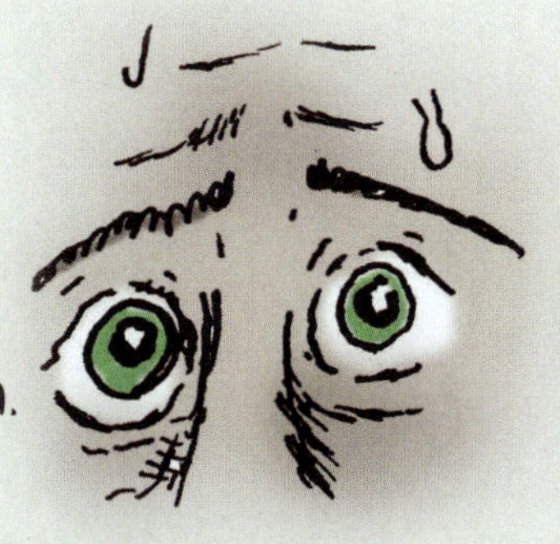

Review

Compare with <, >, or =.

$\frac{1}{4}$ ◯ $\frac{1}{3}$	$\frac{1}{5}$ ◯ $\frac{1}{8}$	$\frac{8}{9}$ ◯ 1	$\frac{4}{5}$ ◯ $\frac{5}{4}$
$\frac{2}{4}$ ◯ $\frac{2}{3}$	$\frac{3}{5}$ ◯ $\frac{3}{8}$	$\frac{9}{8}$ ◯ 1	$\frac{8}{3}$ ◯ $\frac{3}{8}$
$\frac{3}{4}$ ◯ $\frac{3}{3}$	$\frac{5}{5}$ ◯ $\frac{8}{8}$	$\frac{9}{9}$ ◯ 1	$\frac{7}{10}$ ◯ $\frac{10}{7}$

Use long division to solve. Write the remainders as fractions.

5 | 4 3 9

7 | 3 0 6

8 | 6 5 6

Complete.

$4 \times 10^3 =$ ___________

$4 \times 10^1 =$ ___________

$4 \times 10^4 =$ ___________

$4 \times 10^2 =$ ___________

$4 \times 10^0 =$ ___________

$4 \times 10^6 =$ ___________

Complete the chart.

100 cm = 1 m

Centimeters	137	201	299	313			
Meters	$1\frac{37}{100}$				$3\frac{51}{100}$	$4\frac{7}{100}$	$4\frac{73}{100}$

Draw a bar model to match the problem. Then, answer the questions.

In a bag of candy, the ratio of chocolate candy to fruit-flavored candy is 2:5.

What fraction of the candy is chocolate?

What fraction of the candy is fruit-flavored?

Lesson Activities 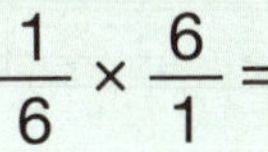

A

$$\frac{1}{6} \times \frac{6}{1} =$$

$$\frac{3}{4} \times \frac{4}{3} =$$

$$\frac{5}{8} \times \frac{8}{5} =$$

B

Reciprocals

To find the reciprocal of a whole number or mixed number, write the number as a fraction. Then, flip the numerator and denominator.

The product of a number and its reciprocal is 1.

Ex.  What is the reciprocal of $1\frac{1}{2}$?

$$1\frac{1}{2} = \frac{3}{2} \qquad \frac{2}{3} \text{ is the reciprocal}$$

$$\frac{\cancel{3}^{1}}{\cancel{2}_{1}} \times \frac{\cancel{2}^{1}}{\cancel{3}_{1}} = \frac{1}{1} = 1$$

Reciprocal of $1\frac{3}{4}$: ______

Reciprocal of $2\frac{3}{10}$: ______

Reciprocal of 8 : ______

C

Divide by Mixed Numbers or Whole Numbers

Ex. Ali has $2\frac{1}{3}$ c. of flour. The cookie recipe calls for $1\frac{3}{4}$ c. of flour for each batch. How many batches can he make?

$$2\frac{1}{3} \div 1\frac{3}{4} = ? \quad \longrightarrow \quad \frac{7}{3} \div \frac{7}{4} = ?$$

$$\frac{\cancel{7}^{1}}{3} \times \frac{4}{\cancel{7}_{1}} = \frac{4}{3} = 1\frac{1}{3} \text{ batches}$$

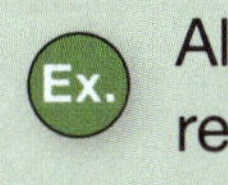

Ex. Josiah has $2\frac{1}{2}$ kg of clay. He divides the clay into 8 equal lumps to make 8 small bowls. How much does each lump weigh?

$$2\frac{1}{2} \div 8 = ? \quad \longrightarrow \quad \frac{5}{2} \div \frac{8}{1} = ?$$

$$\frac{5}{2} \times \frac{1}{8} = \frac{5}{16} \text{ kg}$$

I have $4\frac{1}{2}$ L of orange juice. I pour the orange juice into containers that each hold $1\frac{1}{4}$ L. How many containers do I fill?

I have $4\frac{1}{2}$ L of apple juice. I divide the apple juice evenly between 6 glasses. How much apple juice is in each glass?

Practice

Find the reciprocal of each number. Simplify your answers if needed. Convert improper fractions to whole numbers or mixed numbers.

Reciprocal of $1\frac{1}{4}$: _______

Reciprocal of $1\frac{7}{8}$: _______

Reciprocal of 2 : _______

Reciprocal of $2\frac{1}{3}$: _______

Reciprocal of $3\frac{1}{2}$: _______

Reciprocal of 5 : _______

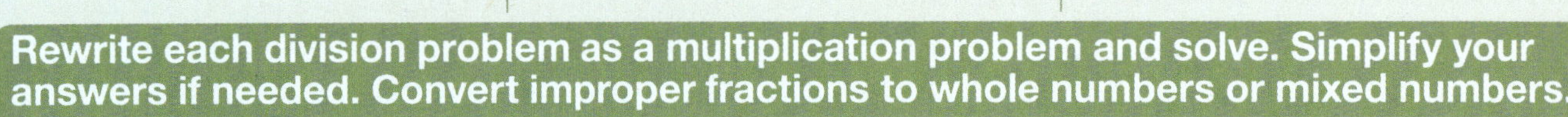

Rewrite each division problem as a multiplication problem and solve. Simplify your answers if needed. Convert improper fractions to whole numbers or mixed numbers.

$$2\frac{1}{7} \div 1\frac{2}{3}$$

$$3\frac{3}{5} \div 2\frac{1}{4}$$

$$5\frac{1}{2} \div 3$$

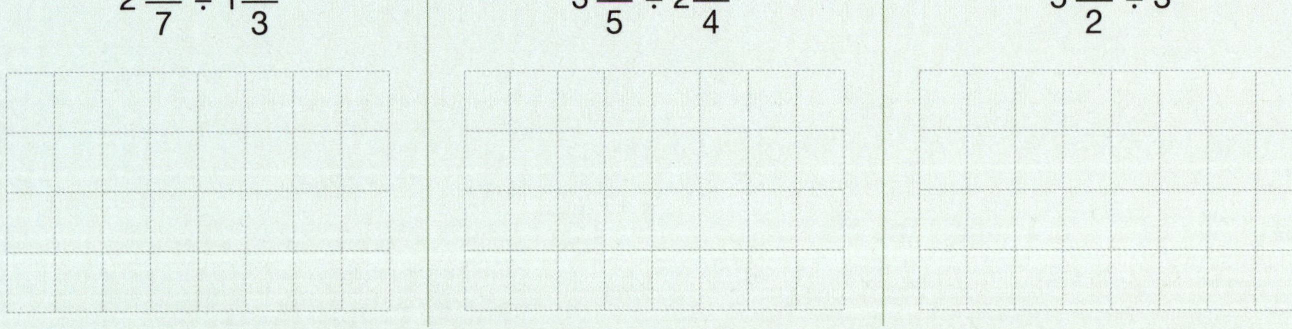

Complete the blanks to match each word problem. Then, solve. Simplify your answers if needed. Convert improper fractions to whole numbers or mixed numbers.

Elizabeth went to 3 swim team practices last week. She swam a total of $4\frac{3}{4}$ km. On average, how many kilometers did she swim at each practice?

_________ ÷ _________

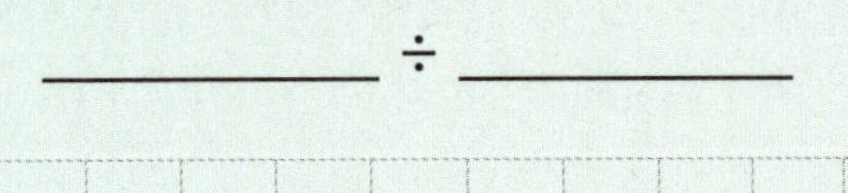

The bag of almonds weighs 5 oz. Each serving of almonds weighs $1\frac{1}{2}$ oz. How many servings are in the bag?

 _________ ÷ _________

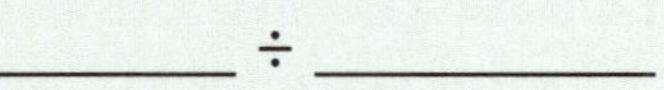

Review

Complete the equivalent fractions.

$\dfrac{1}{2} = \dfrac{}{20}$ $\dfrac{1}{2} = \dfrac{}{40}$ $\dfrac{1}{2} = \dfrac{}{100}$ $\dfrac{1}{2} = \dfrac{}{1,000}$

$\dfrac{1}{4} = \dfrac{}{20}$ $\dfrac{1}{4} = \dfrac{}{40}$ $\dfrac{1}{4} = \dfrac{}{100}$ $\dfrac{1}{4} = \dfrac{}{1,000}$

$\dfrac{3}{4} = \dfrac{}{20}$ $\dfrac{3}{4} = \dfrac{}{40}$ $\dfrac{3}{4} = \dfrac{}{100}$ $\dfrac{3}{4} = \dfrac{}{1,000}$

Complete the chart.

Standard Form	Expanded Form
7.04	
5.189	
	$6 + \dfrac{3}{10} + \dfrac{8}{100} + \dfrac{7}{1,000}$
	$4 + \dfrac{6}{100}$

Evaluate.

$|\,7\,| = \rule{3cm}{0.4pt}$

$|\,-4\,| = \rule{3cm}{0.4pt}$

$-(5) = \rule{3cm}{0.4pt}$

$-(0) = \rule{3cm}{0.4pt}$

$-(-3) = \rule{3cm}{0.4pt}$

Circle the numbers that could be the secret number.
X the numbers that can't be the secret number.

My secret number is greater than 1 and less than 2.

0.74	1.902	3.2
1.5	1.99	2.001

My secret number is prime. It's greater than 10 and less than 20.

17	29	15
23	13	20

My secret number is divisible by 6 and divisible by 5.

120	60	50
30	40	100

Complete the chart.

The pizzeria uses a 3 : 8 ratio of water to flour in its pizza crust recipe. If the chef uses 48 c. flour, how many cups of water should she use?

Water					
Flour					

Lesson Activities 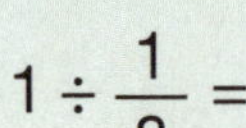

$1 \div \dfrac{1}{8} =$

$5 \div \dfrac{3}{4} =$

$4\dfrac{1}{5} \div 1\dfrac{1}{2} =$

Divide Fractions by Fractions

 **Ex.** $\dfrac{3}{8}$ of a pizza equals one serving. If I have $\dfrac{7}{8}$ of a pizza, how many servings do I have?

How many times does $\dfrac{3}{8}$ go into $\dfrac{7}{8}$?

$\dfrac{7}{8} \div \dfrac{3}{8} = ?$

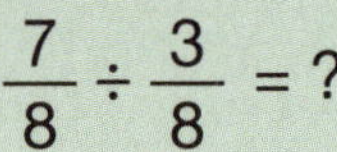

$\dfrac{7}{\cancel{8}^{1}} \times \dfrac{\cancel{8}^{1}}{3} = \dfrac{7}{3} = \mathbf{2}\,\dfrac{\mathbf{1}}{\mathbf{3}}$ **servings**

 **Ex.** I have $\dfrac{3}{4}$ c. of molasses. I need $\dfrac{1}{2}$ c. for each batch of gingerbread cookies. How many batches of cookies can I make?

How many times does $\dfrac{1}{2}$ go into $\dfrac{3}{4}$?

$\dfrac{3}{4} \div \dfrac{1}{2} = ?$

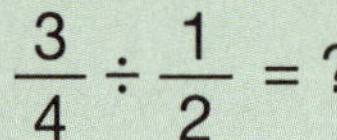
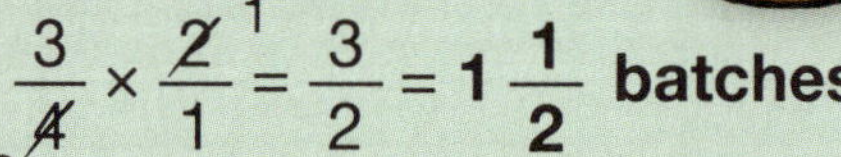
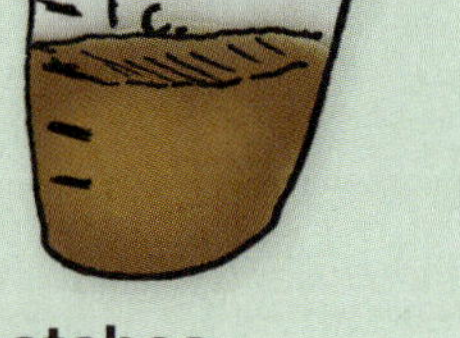

$\dfrac{3}{\cancel{4}^{2}} \times \dfrac{\cancel{2}^{1}}{1} = \dfrac{3}{2} = \mathbf{1}\,\dfrac{\mathbf{1}}{\mathbf{2}}$ **batches**

Roll and Divide (2-Player Game) 

Player 1

$\dfrac{}{6} \div \dfrac{}{6}$ 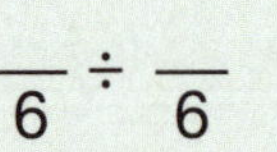

$\dfrac{}{8} \div \dfrac{}{8}$ 

$\dfrac{}{10} \div \dfrac{}{10}$ 

Player 2

$\dfrac{}{6} \div \dfrac{}{6}$ 

$\dfrac{}{8} \div \dfrac{}{8}$ 

$\dfrac{}{10} \div \dfrac{}{10}$

Practice

Find the quotients. Write your answers in simplest form. Convert improper fractions to whole numbers or mixed numbers.

$\dfrac{5}{6} \div \dfrac{1}{6}$ 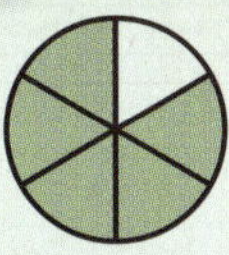

$\dfrac{5}{6} \div \dfrac{2}{6}$ 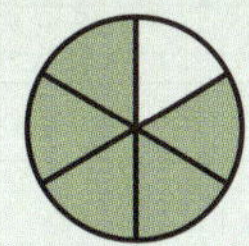

$\dfrac{5}{6} \div \dfrac{3}{6}$ 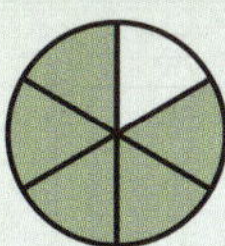

$\dfrac{6}{10} \div \dfrac{3}{10}$ 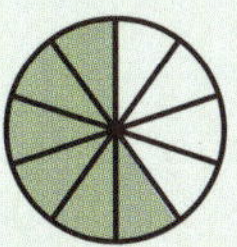

$\dfrac{7}{10} \div \dfrac{3}{10}$ 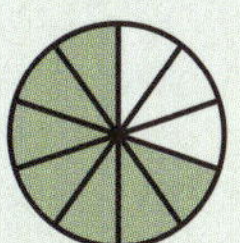

$\dfrac{8}{10} \div \dfrac{3}{10}$ 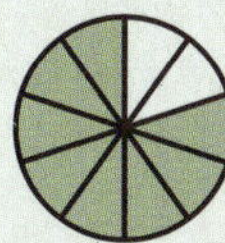

$\dfrac{2}{3} \div \dfrac{1}{3}$ 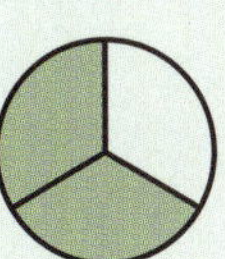

$\dfrac{2}{3} \div \dfrac{1}{6}$ 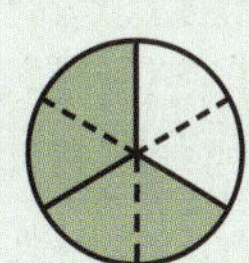

$\dfrac{2}{3} \div \dfrac{1}{2}$ 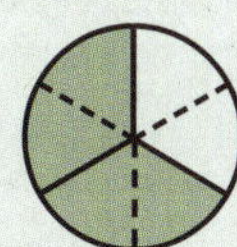

$\dfrac{3}{4} \div \dfrac{1}{4}$ 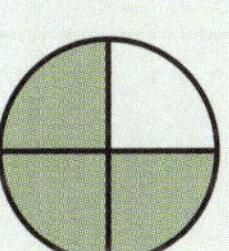

$\dfrac{3}{4} \div \dfrac{1}{8}$ 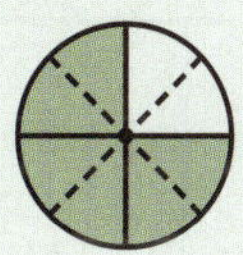

$\dfrac{3}{4} \div \dfrac{3}{8}$ 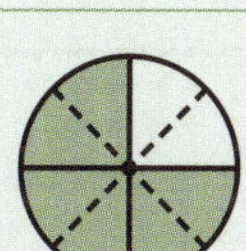

Solve. Write the equations you use. Simplify your answers if needed. Convert improper fractions to whole numbers or mixed numbers.

Harper has $\dfrac{9}{10}$ kg of flour. She needs $\dfrac{4}{10}$ kg for each batch of brownies. How many batches of brownies can she make?

Holden has $\dfrac{7}{12}$ of a large chocolate bar. One serving is $\dfrac{1}{6}$ of the whole bar. How many servings does he have?

Review

Find the distance between each pair of numbers.

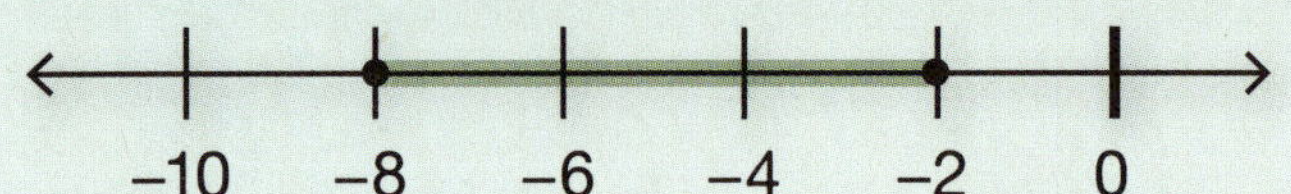

Distance: __________ units

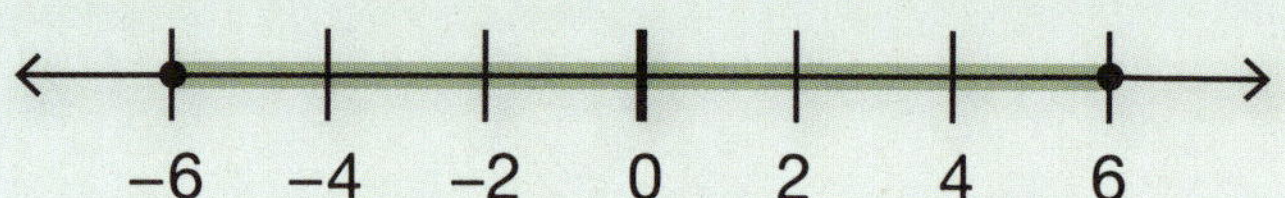

Distance: __________ units

Match pairs that equal 0.5.

0.2	0.15
0.02	0.3
0.35	0.48
0.305	0.01
0.49	0.001
0.499	0.195

Complete.

$47 \cdot 100 =$ __________________

$362 \cdot 10 =$ __________________

$875 \cdot 1{,}000 =$ __________________

$300 \cdot 70 =$ __________________

$800 \cdot 500 =$ __________________

$9{,}000 \cdot 800 =$ __________________

Write the numbers in order from least to greatest.

0.2	0.08	0.6	0.347

______ ______ ______ ______
least   greatest

3	−14	20	−5

______ ______ ______ ______
least   greatest

$\dfrac{1}{4}$	$\dfrac{1}{100}$	$\dfrac{1}{10}$	$\dfrac{1}{2}$

______ ______ ______ ______
least   greatest

$\dfrac{1}{5}$	$\dfrac{99}{100}$	$\dfrac{7}{10}$	$\dfrac{1}{2}$

______ ______ ______ ______
least   greatest

Solve. Write the ratios in simplest form.

There are 6 instructors and 28 children at ski lessons. What is the ratio of instructors to students?

The poster is 54 in. long and 36 in. wide. What is the ratio of its length to its height?

Lesson Activities 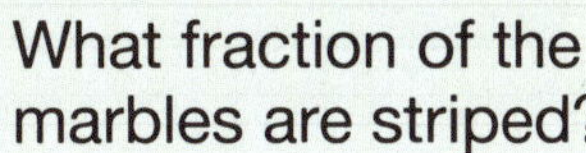

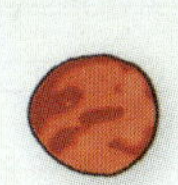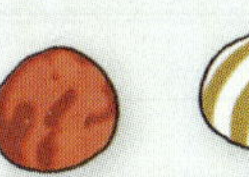

What fraction of the marbles are striped?

What fraction of the marbles are not striped?

A

B

Divide to Find a Fraction of a Quantity

To find a fraction of a quantity, we divide the partial amount by the whole amount.

Ex. The track race is 4 km long. Ramona has run 3 km so far. What fraction of the race has she completed?

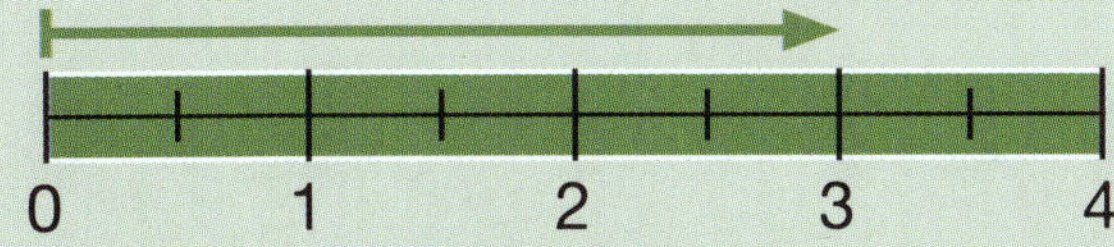

$$3 \div 4 = \frac{3}{4} \text{ of the race}$$

$$\text{dividend} \div \text{divisor} = \frac{\text{dividend}}{\text{divisor}}$$

Ex. The track race is 4 km long. Beatrice has run $2\frac{1}{2}$ km so far. What fraction of the race has she completed?

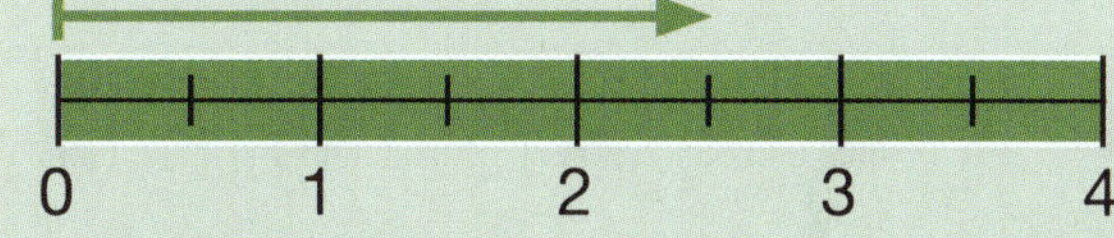

$$2\frac{1}{2} \div 4 = ?$$

$$\frac{5}{2} \div \frac{4}{1} = ?$$

$$\frac{5}{2} \times \frac{1}{4} = \frac{5}{8} \text{ of the race}$$

C

Fraction Race (2-Player Game) 

	Player 1		Player 2	
	Distance (mi.)	Fraction complete	Distance (mi.)	Fraction complete

Practice

Write each question as a division problem and solve. Simplify your answers if needed. Convert improper fractions to whole numbers or mixed numbers.

$1\frac{1}{3}$ is what fraction of $2\frac{2}{3}$?

__________ ÷ __________

$\frac{3}{4}$ is what fraction of $2\frac{1}{2}$?

__________ ÷ __________

$1\frac{7}{8}$ is what fraction of 5?

__________ ÷ __________

2 is what fraction of $3\frac{1}{3}$?

__________ ÷ __________

$3\frac{1}{4}$ is what fraction of $3\frac{3}{4}$?

__________ ÷ __________

4 is what fraction of 6?

__________ ÷ __________

Solve. Write the equations you use. Simplify your answers if needed. Convert improper fractions to whole numbers or mixed numbers.

Zeinab's family bought $5\frac{1}{2}$ lb. of apples. They used $3\frac{1}{2}$ lb. of apples to make applesauce. What fraction of the apples did they use to make applesauce?

Jack's family went on a 6 mi. hike. They stopped after $3\frac{3}{4}$ mi. to have a snack. What fraction of the hike had they completed at that point?

Review   Use the shapes to answer the questions.

What is the area of the rectangle?

What is the area of the parallelogram?

What is the area of the triangle?

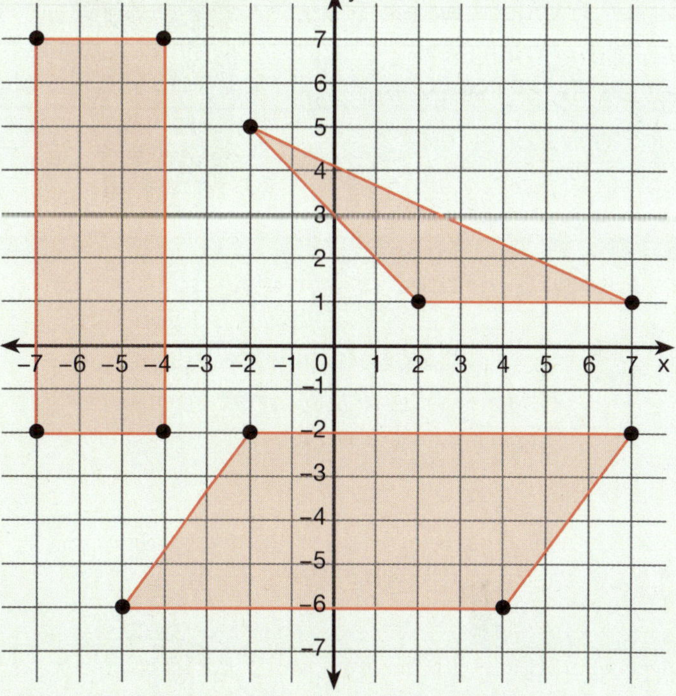

Write the fractions in simplest form.

$\dfrac{50}{100} =$	$\dfrac{70}{100} =$	$\dfrac{20}{100} =$	$\dfrac{24}{100} =$
$\dfrac{25}{100} =$	$\dfrac{75}{100} =$	$\dfrac{45}{100} =$	$\dfrac{82}{100} =$

Use bar models to complete the blanks.

At the fun run, the participants can choose whether to run or walk. The ratio of runners to walkers is 7:2. There are 450 more runners than walkers.

Runners

Walkers

Number of runners: _______________

Number of walkers: _______________

Total number of participants:

____

Lesson Activities 

A

The soccer team's water cooler holds 6 gal. of water. After halftime, there are $2\frac{1}{2}$ gal. of water left. What fraction of the water is left?

B

Divide Fractions by Fractions

Ex. $\frac{3}{8}$ of a pizza equals one serving. If I have $\frac{1}{8}$ of a pizza, what fraction of a serving do I have?

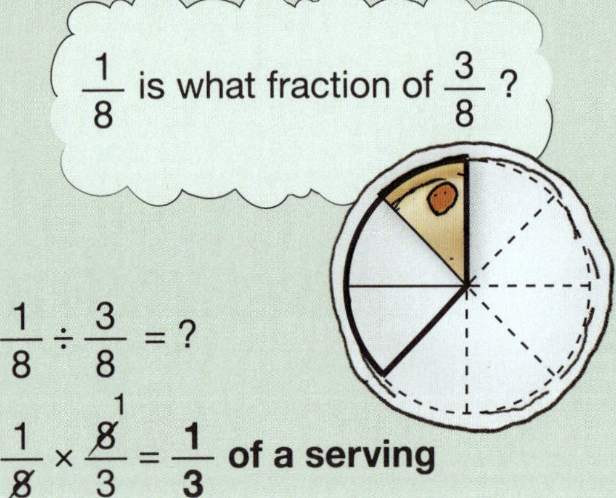

$$\frac{1}{8} \div \frac{3}{8} = ?$$

$$\frac{1}{\cancel{8}} \times \frac{\cancel{8}^{\,1}}{3} = \frac{1}{3} \text{ of a serving}$$

Ex. The cookie recipe calls for $\frac{3}{4}$ c. of brown sugar, but I only have $\frac{1}{2}$ c. What fraction of a batch can I make?

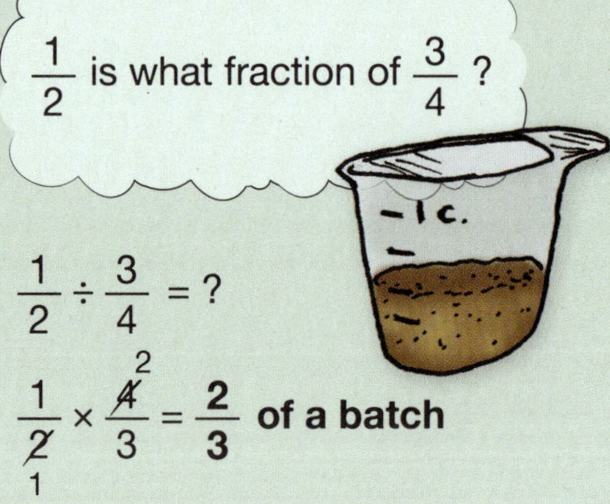

$$\frac{1}{2} \div \frac{3}{4} = ?$$

$$\frac{1}{\cancel{2}} \times \frac{\cancel{4}^{\,2}}{3} = \frac{2}{3} \text{ of a batch}$$

C

Roll and Divide (2-Player Game) 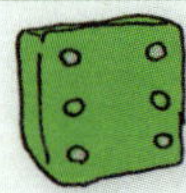

Player 1

$$\frac{}{6} \div \frac{}{6}$$ 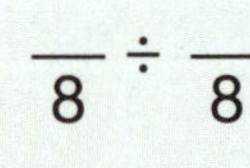

$$\frac{}{8} \div \frac{}{8}$$

$$\frac{}{10} \div \frac{}{10}$$

Player 2

$$\frac{}{6} \div \frac{}{6}$$ 

$$\frac{}{8} \div \frac{}{8}$$

$$\frac{}{10} \div \frac{}{10}$$

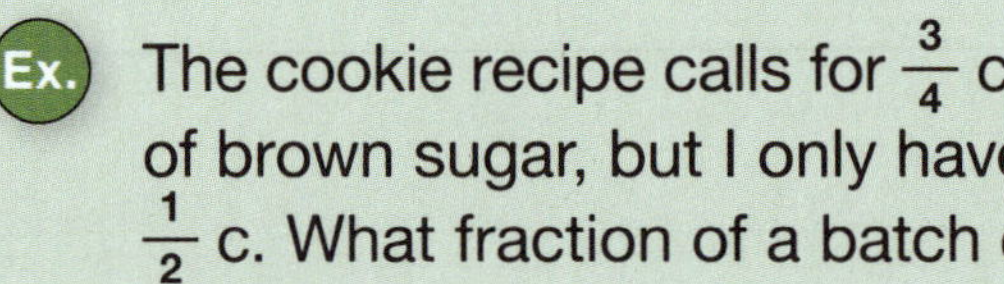
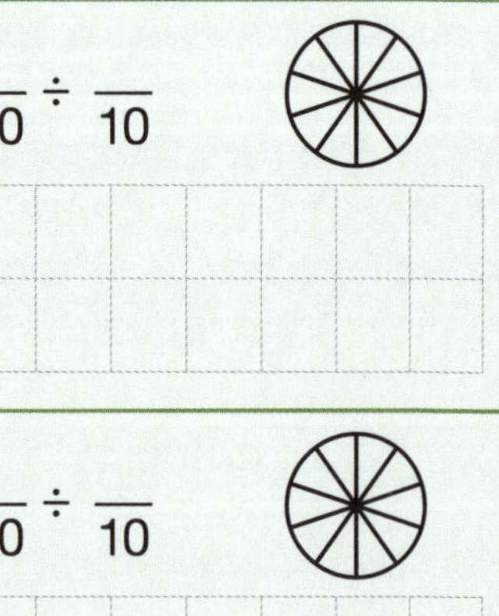

Practice 

Find the quotients. Write your answers in simplest form. Convert improper fractions to whole numbers or mixed numbers.

$\frac{1}{5} \div \frac{2}{5}$ 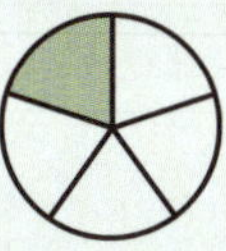

$\frac{1}{5} \div \frac{3}{5}$ 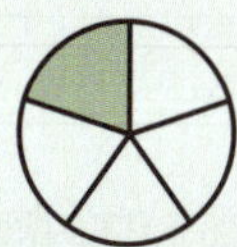

$\frac{1}{5} \div \frac{4}{5}$ 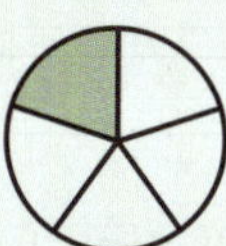

$\frac{1}{4} \div \frac{3}{8}$ 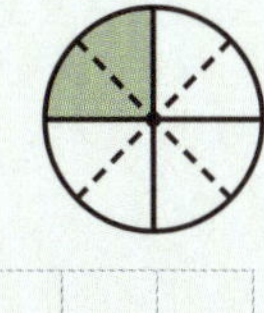

$\frac{1}{4} \div \frac{5}{8}$ 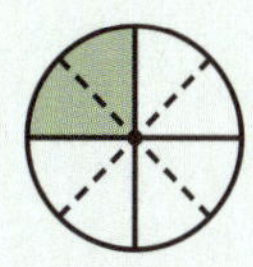

$\frac{1}{4} \div \frac{7}{8}$ 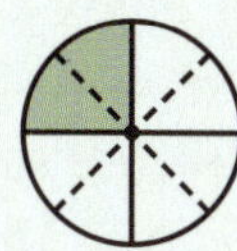

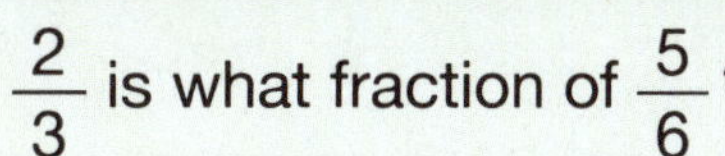

Write each question as a division problem and solve. Simplify your answers if needed. Convert improper fractions to whole numbers or mixed numbers.

$\frac{1}{10}$ is what fraction of $\frac{7}{10}$?

$\frac{2}{3}$ is what fraction of $\frac{5}{6}$?

$\frac{3}{10}$ is what fraction of $\frac{4}{5}$?

__________ ÷ __________

__________ ÷ __________

__________ ÷ __________

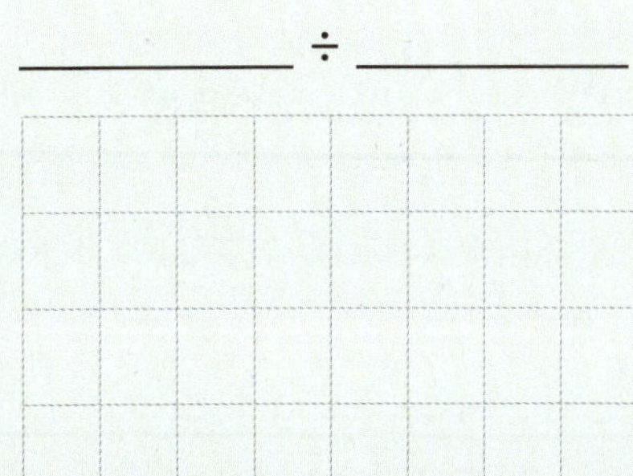
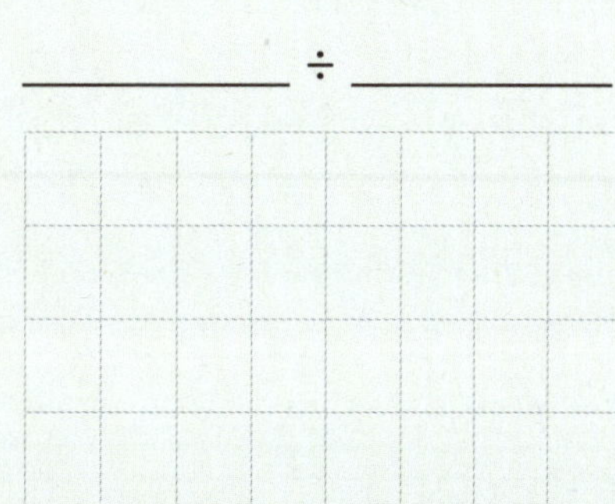
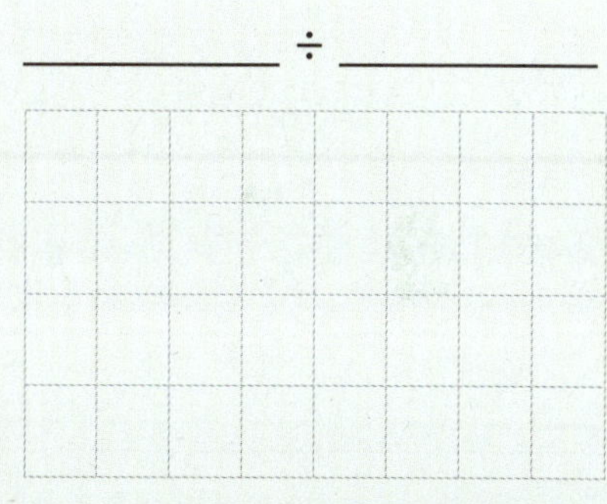

Solve. Write the equations you use. Simplify your answers if needed. Convert improper fractions to whole numbers or mixed numbers.

Rosie fills her water bottle with $\frac{9}{10}$ L of water. After she drinks some, $\frac{2}{5}$ L of water is left. What fraction of the water is left?

Tom has a ribbon that is $\frac{7}{8}$ yd. long. He cuts a piece that is $\frac{1}{3}$ yd. long to use for a craft project. What fraction of the ribbon does he use?

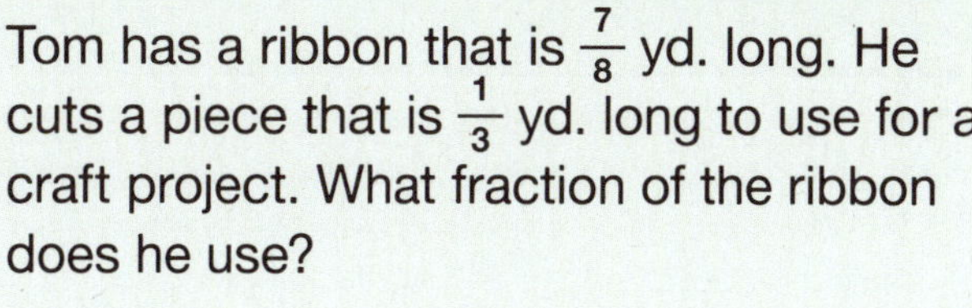

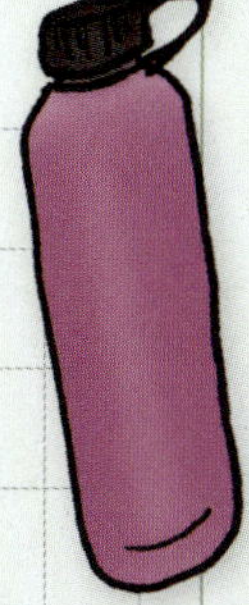

Review   Evaluate.

$6^2 + 5 \cdot 2$

$7 \cdot (8 + 5 - 4)$

$\dfrac{4^2}{2} \times \dfrac{10^2}{2}$

Complete the missing units to answer the questions. Leave the blank empty if the number tells the number of groups or parts. Use exponents for square units.

The string is 40 in. long. If you cut it into 5 pieces, how long is each piece?

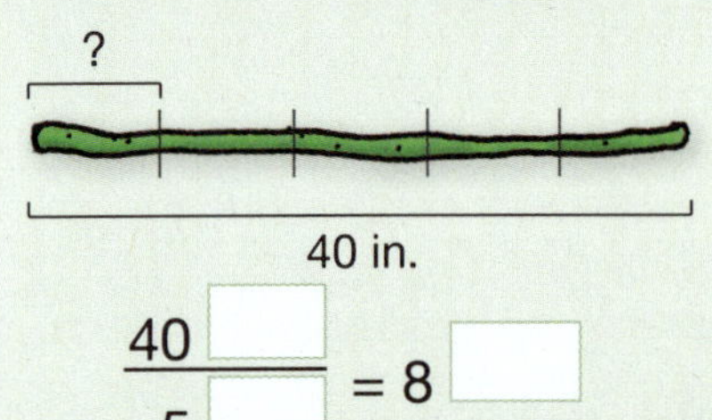

$\dfrac{40\ \boxed{}}{5\ \boxed{}} = 8\ \boxed{}$

The rectangle has a length of 9 ft. and a width of 4 ft. What is its area?

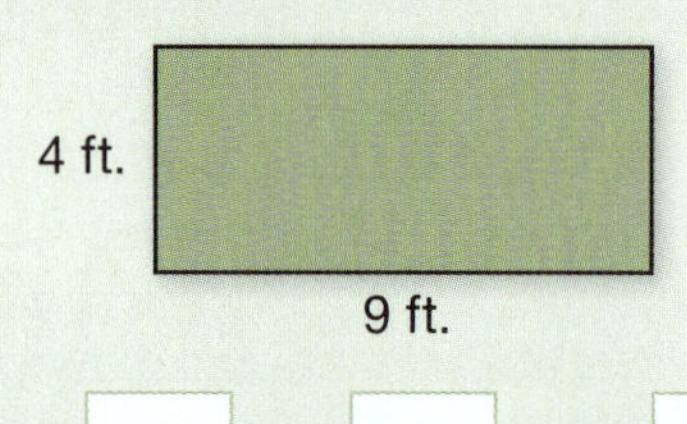

$9\ \boxed{} \times 4\ \boxed{} = 36\ \boxed{}$

Each side of the triangle is 20 cm long. What is its perimeter?

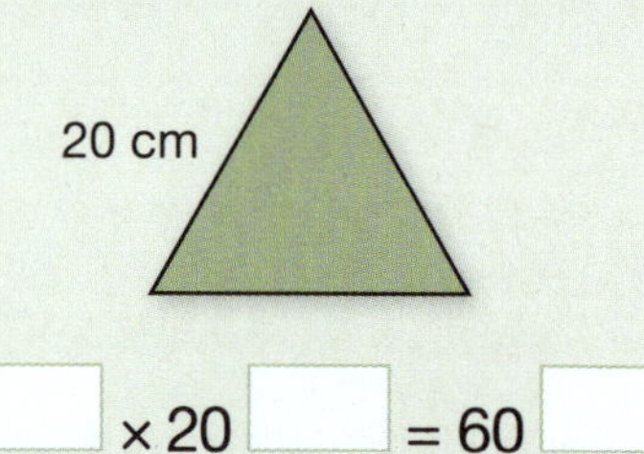

$3\ \boxed{} \times 20\ \boxed{} = 60\ \boxed{}$

Complete the chart.

	Base	Exponent	Repeated Multiplication	Value
1^5	1			
4^3				
8^2				
10^5				

Find the products. Use cancelling where possible. Write your answers in simplest form. If your answer is an improper fraction, convert it to a mixed number or whole number.

$\dfrac{5}{3} \times \dfrac{3}{5} \times \dfrac{1}{4} =$

$\dfrac{5}{7} \times \dfrac{3}{2} \times \dfrac{2}{3} =$

$\dfrac{8}{7} \times \dfrac{7}{8} \times \dfrac{6}{1} =$

$\dfrac{3}{4} \times \dfrac{7}{11} \times \dfrac{4}{3} =$

Lesson Activities

Fraction Division Word Problems

To find the **number** of pieces, divide the total by the size of each piece.	To find the **size** of each piece, divide the total by the number of pieces.	To find a **fractional amount**, divide the partial amount by the total amount.

Ex. I have 3 yd. of ribbon. I cut the ribbon into pieces that are each $\frac{3}{4}$ yd. long. How many pieces do I get?

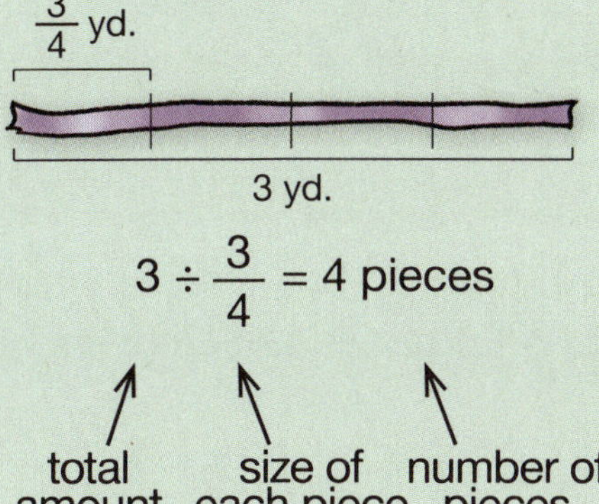

$\frac{3}{4}$ yd.

3 yd.

$$3 \div \frac{3}{4} = 4 \text{ pieces}$$

total amount   size of each piece   number of pieces

Ex. I have $\frac{3}{4}$ m of rope. I cut the rope into 3 equal pieces. How long is each piece?

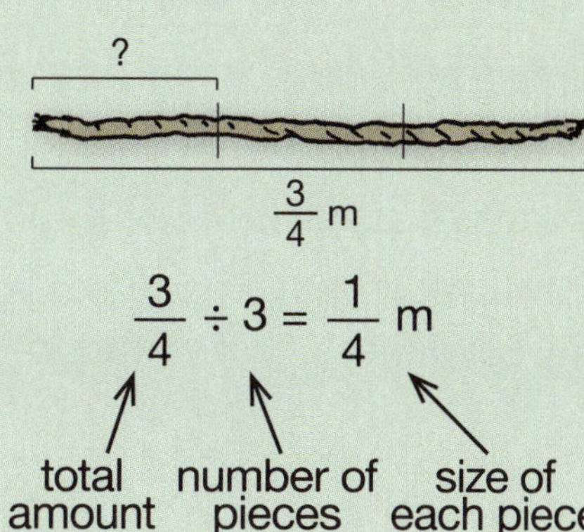

?

$\frac{3}{4}$ m

$$\frac{3}{4} \div 3 = \frac{1}{4} \text{ m}$$

total amount   number of pieces   size of each piece

Ex. The hiking trail is 3 mi. long. So far, I've hiked $\frac{3}{4}$ mi. What fraction of the trail have I completed?

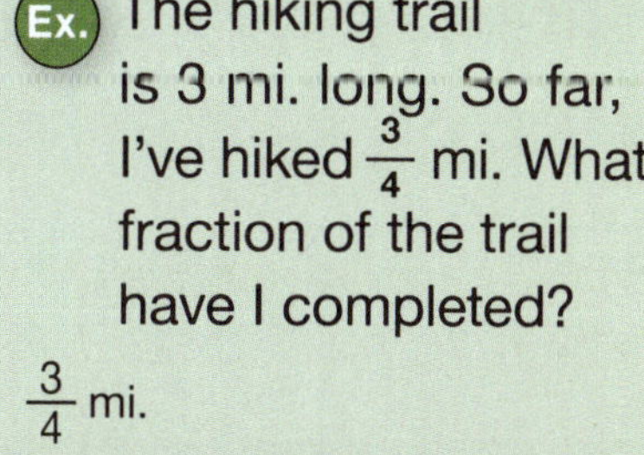

$\frac{3}{4}$ mi.

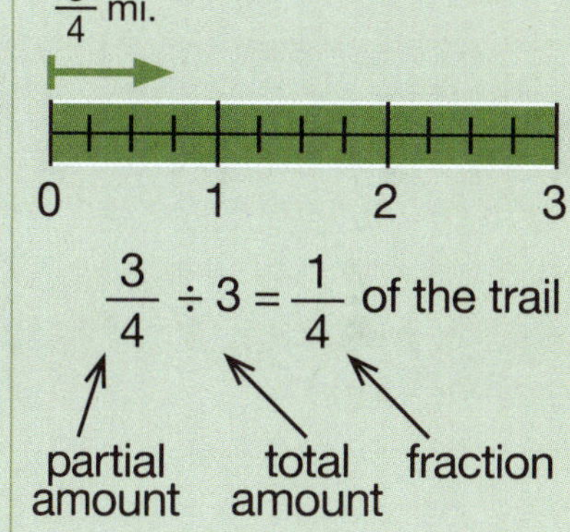

0   1   2   3

$$\frac{3}{4} \div 3 = \frac{1}{4} \text{ of the trail}$$

partial amount   total amount   fraction

Callie has a piece of ribbon that is $\frac{9}{10}$ m long. She cuts the ribbon into pieces that are each $\frac{1}{5}$ m long. How many pieces does she get?

Each spool of wire holds 4 m of wire. Sammy uses $1\frac{2}{5}$ m of wire for a project. What fraction of the spool does he use?

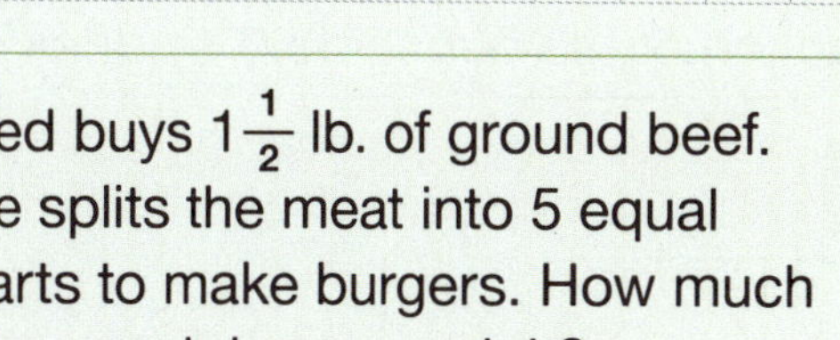

Brielle is making a friendship bracelet. So far, the bracelet is 3 in. long. She wants the finished bracelet to be $7\frac{1}{2}$ in. long. What fraction of the bracelet has she completed?

Ned buys $1\frac{1}{2}$ lb. of ground beef. He splits the meat into 5 equal parts to make burgers. How much does each burger weigh?

Practice

Use logical reasoning to circle the words that describe the quotient. (Think about whether the dividend is greater than or less than the divisor.) You do not need to find the exact answer.

$\frac{1}{2} \div \frac{1}{3}$	$\frac{1}{2} \div \frac{3}{4}$	$\frac{1}{2} \div \frac{9}{10}$
Less than 1 Greater than 1	Less than 1 Greater than 1	Less than 1 Greater than 1
$1\frac{3}{4} \div 2\frac{2}{3}$	$1\frac{3}{4} \div 1\frac{1}{4}$	$1\frac{3}{4} \div 4$
Less than 1 Greater than 1	Less than 1 Greater than 1	Less than 1 Greater than 1

Circle the division problem that you can use to solve each word problem. Then, solve. Simplify your answers if needed. Convert improper fractions to whole numbers or mixed numbers.

The bag of candy weighs $\frac{1}{2}$ lb. One serving of candy weighs $\frac{1}{10}$ lb. How many servings are in the bag?

$\frac{1}{10} \div \frac{1}{2}$ $\frac{1}{2} \div \frac{1}{10}$

The tub of yogurt has $\frac{1}{2}$ c. left. One serving of yogurt is $\frac{5}{8}$ c. What fraction of a serving is left?

$\frac{1}{2} \div \frac{5}{8}$ $\frac{5}{8} \div \frac{1}{2}$

Annie makes $3\frac{1}{4}$ L of punch. Then, her family drinks $1\frac{3}{4}$ L of the punch. What fraction of the punch do they drink?

$3\frac{1}{4} \div 1\frac{3}{4}$ $1\frac{3}{4} \div 3\frac{1}{4}$

The square picture frame has a perimeter of $3\frac{1}{2}$ ft. How long is each side?

$3\frac{1}{2} \div 4$ $4 \div 3\frac{1}{2}$

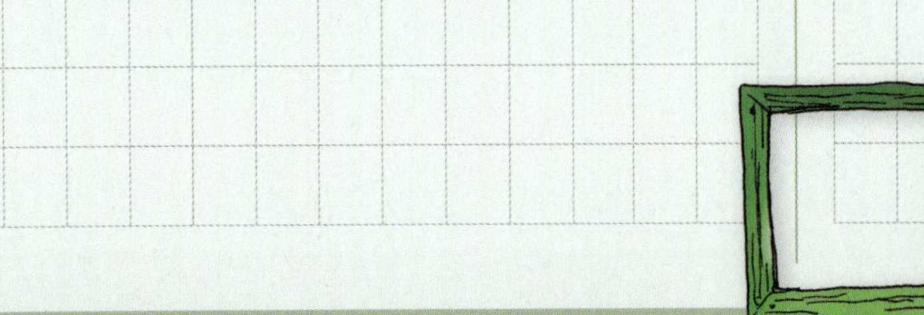

Review

Find the products.

```
    7 9          6 8
  ×  3 1        × 7 7
  -------       -------
```

Circle the prime numbers. X the composite numbers.

1	2	3	4	5	6
7	8	9	10	11	12
13	14	15	16	17	18
19	20	21	22	23	24

Follow the directions to find the mean and median for the data set. Write the equations you use.

How to Find the Mean (Average)

1. Add up all the numbers in the data set.
2. Divide by the number of numbers in the data set.

How to Find the Median

1. Write the numbers in order from least to greatest.
2. Choose the number in the middle.
3. If there are an even number of numbers, find the mean of the two numbers in the middle.

Number of Children in Each Family

3, 3, 2, 4, 1, 6, 2, 2, 1, 4, 5

Mean: __________   Median: __________

Answer the questions.

At basketball practice, Simon makes $\frac{5}{8}$ of his free throws. He misses the rest. What is the ratio of free throws he makes to free throws he misses?

Francesca is memorizing the state capitals. The ratio of state capitals she knows to state capitals she doesn't yet know is 7:3. What fraction of the state capitals does she know?

Simon attempts a total of 40 free throws. How many free throws does he make?

There are a total of 50 state capitals. How many of them does Francesca know?

Unit Wrap-Up

Find the reciprocal of each number. Simplify your answers if needed. Convert improper fractions to whole numbers or mixed numbers.

Reciprocal of $\frac{5}{6}$: _______

Reciprocal of 3 : _______

Reciprocal of $2\frac{3}{5}$: _______

Use logical reasoning to circle the words that describe the quotient. You do not need to find the exact answer.

$5 \div 6$

| Less than 1 | Greater than 1 |

$\frac{7}{10} \div \frac{1}{2}$

| Less than 1 | Greater than 1 |

$3\frac{1}{10} \div 4$

| Less than 1 | Greater than 1 |

$5 \div \frac{1}{6}$

| Less than 1 | Greater than 1 |

$\frac{1}{2} \div \frac{7}{10}$

| Less than 1 | Greater than 1 |

$3\frac{1}{10} \div 2$

| Less than 1 | Greater than 1 |

Find the quotients. Simplify your answers if needed. Convert improper fractions to whole numbers or mixed numbers.

$\frac{7}{9} \div \frac{2}{3}$

$2\frac{1}{12} \div \frac{5}{6}$

$\frac{3}{5} \div 4$

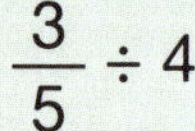

$\frac{3}{4} \div \frac{1}{6}$

$3 \div 1\frac{4}{5}$

$1\frac{1}{4} \div 3\frac{1}{3}$

Unit Wrap-Up 

Use the pizza recipe to solve. Write the equations you use. Write your answers in simplest form. Convert improper fractions to whole numbers or mixed numbers.

Joe's Pizzeria

Ingredients for a Medium Pepperoni Pizza

- $\frac{7}{8}$ lb. pizza dough
- $\frac{3}{5}$ lb. shredded mozzarella cheese
- $\frac{3}{8}$ lb. pizza sauce
- $\frac{1}{4}$ lb. pepperoni

Cut each pizza into 8 slices.

Each bag of shredded mozzarella weighs 5 lb. How many medium pizzas can the chef make from one bag of cheese?

Each can of pizza sauce holds $2\frac{5}{8}$ lb. How many medium pizzas can the chef make from one can of sauce?

The pizza chef makes 35 lb. of pizza dough at a time. How many medium pizzas can he make from one batch of dough?

The chef spreads the pepperoni evenly across each pizza. If you eat one slice of pizza, how much pepperoni do you eat?

Lesson Activities 👥

A

Decimals

tens	ones	tenths	hundredths	thousandths	ten thousandths
	2.	4	5	0	9

Decimals
- divide by 10 to create places with a smaller value
- expanded form expresses the number as the sum of the value of each digit

$$2.4509 = 2 + \frac{4}{10} + \frac{5}{100} + \frac{9}{10{,}000}$$

Digit Vocabulary
- decimal digits are digits to the right of the decimal point
- leading zeros come before the first non-zero digit
- trailing zeros come after the final non-zero digit

2.4509
4 decimal digits

0.067
2 leading zeros

1.40
1 trailing zero

Decimal → Fraction
- write decimal digits as the numerator (ignore leading zeros)
- the number of decimal digits equals the number of zeros in the denominator

$$2.4509 = 2\frac{4{,}509}{10{,}000}$$

$$0.067 = \frac{67}{1{,}000}$$

Round Decimals
- round down if the next digit is less than 5
- round up if the next digit is greater than or equal to 5
- drop the digits after the place you round to

$2.4509 \approx 2$
$2.4509 \approx 2.5$
$2.4509 \approx 2.45$
$2.4509 \approx 2.451$

Add and Subtract Decimals
- line up the decimal points
- tack on trailing zeros so both numbers have the same number of decimal digits
- write the decimal point in the answer below the other decimal points

$2.31 + 6.5243 = ?$

```
  2.3100
+ 6.5243
  8.8343
```

Practice

Complete the chart. Then, write the widths in order from least to greatest. (The pictures are not to scale.)

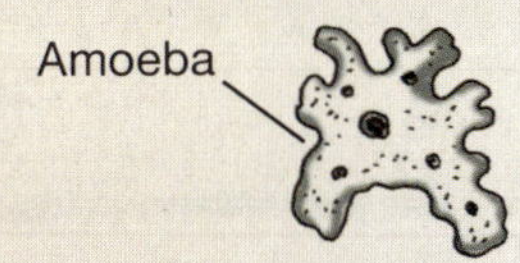
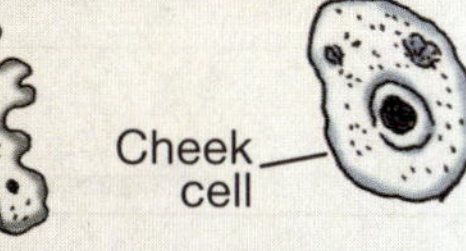
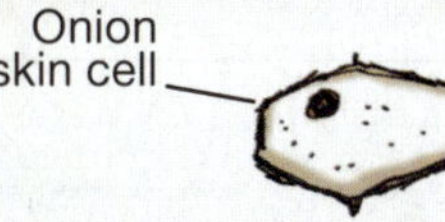
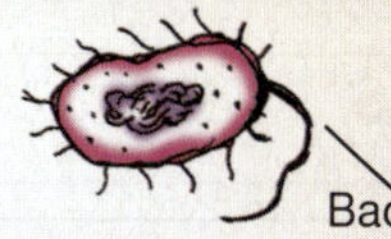
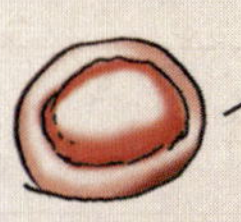

Type of Cell	Width (mm)	Expanded Form	Fraction
Amoeba	0.38		
Cheek	0.0614		
Onion skin	0.405		
Bacteria	0.0006		
Red blood	0.007		

______ ______ ______ ______ ______

least   greatest

Write a number that matches each description. (Many answers are possible.)

Has 4 decimal digits and 2 leading zeros.

Has 3 decimal digits and 1 leading zero.

Has 2 leading zeros and 1 trailing zero.

Round to the underlined place.

1.7809 ≈ ________________

1.7809 ≈ ________________

1.7809 ≈ ________________

2.9555 ≈ ________________

2.9555 ≈ ________________

2.9555 ≈ ________________

Find the sum or difference.

5.3 + 0.9781
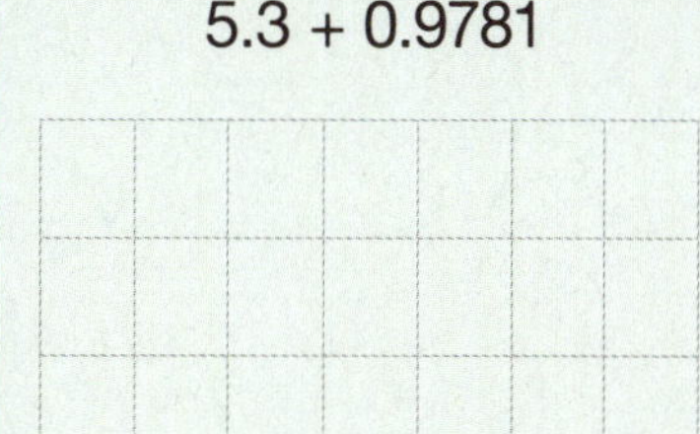

1.678 + 9.7004
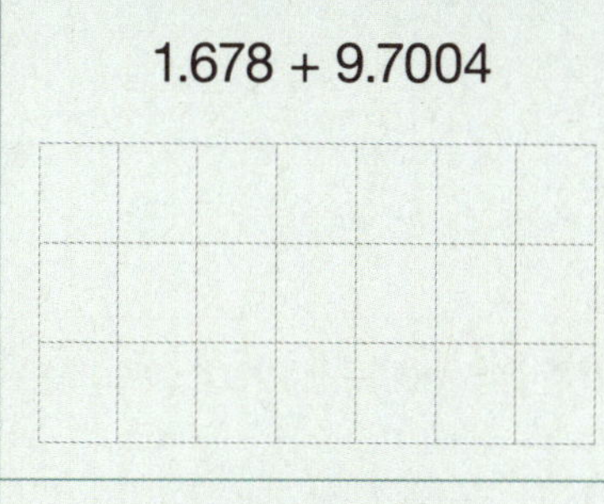

8.569 − 4.38
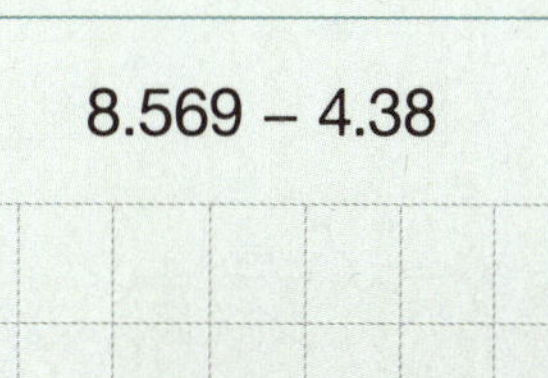

7.6 − 4.0329
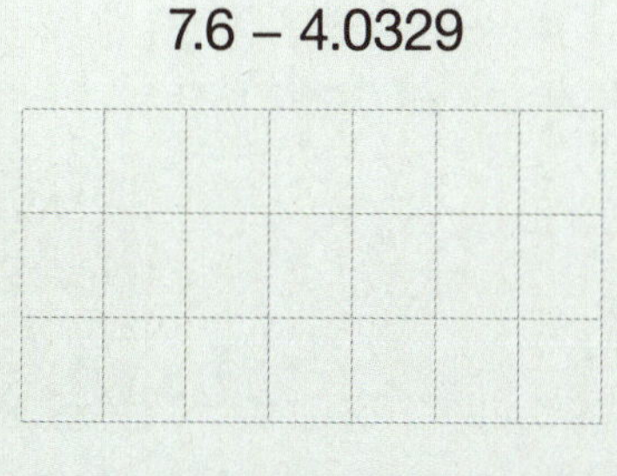

Review

Complete the equivalent fractions.
Then, use the equivalent fractions to compare the fractions.

$\frac{1}{4} = \frac{}{12}$	$\frac{1}{6} = \frac{}{12}$	$\frac{1}{3} = \frac{}{12}$
$\frac{3}{4} = \frac{}{12}$	$\frac{5}{6} = \frac{}{12}$	$\frac{2}{3} = \frac{}{12}$
$\frac{1}{4}$ ◯ $\frac{1}{6}$	$\frac{1}{4}$ ◯ $\frac{1}{3}$	$\frac{1}{6}$ ◯ $\frac{1}{3}$
$\frac{3}{4}$ ◯ $\frac{5}{6}$	$\frac{5}{6}$ ◯ $\frac{2}{3}$	$\frac{3}{4}$ ◯ $\frac{2}{3}$

Complete the charts.

centimeters	millimeters
3	30
8	
94	
200	

centimeters	meters
100	1
500	
1,000	
1,400	

milliliters	liters
1,000	1
3,000	
6,000	
10,000	

Solve. Write the equations you use.

The community center's basketball court is 84 ft. long and 53 ft. wide. What is its area?

The pickleball court is 20 ft. wide and has an area of 880 sq. ft. What is the pickleball court's length? (Use the multiplication chart to help.)

WORK SPACE

20 ft. ?

	× 20
1	20
2	40
3	60
4	80
5	100
6	120
7	140
8	160
9	180

Lesson Activities

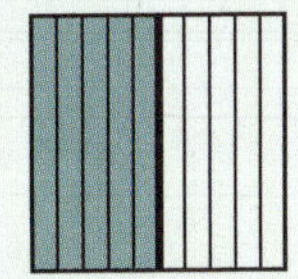

$$\frac{1}{2} = \underline{\ 0.5\ }$$

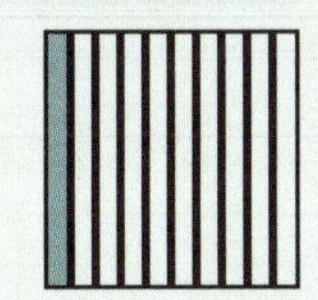

$$\frac{1}{10} = \underline{\hspace{2cm}}$$

$$\frac{1}{5} = \underline{\hspace{2cm}}$$

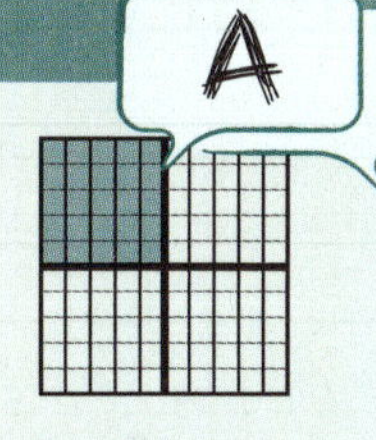

$$\frac{1}{4} = \underline{\hspace{2cm}}$$

A

B

Convert Fractions to Decimals

We can use either a fraction or a decimal to represent part of a whole. If the fraction has a base-ten denominator (like 10, 100, or 1,000), the number of zeros in the denominator equals the number of decimal digits.

For other fractions, try writing an equivalent fraction with a base-ten denominator. Then, use the equivalent fraction to write the matching decimal.

 **Ex.** Write $\frac{49}{1,000}$ as a decimal.

$$\frac{49}{1,000} = \mathbf{0.049}$$

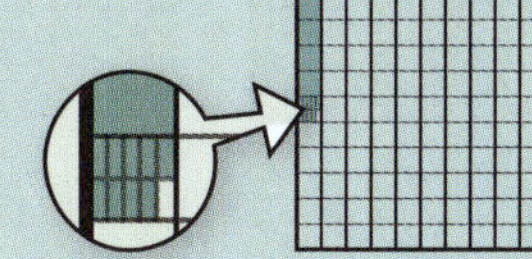

1,000 has 3 zeros, so the matching decimal has 3 decimal places.

 **Ex.** Write $\frac{1}{20}$ as a decimal.

$$\overset{\times 5}{\frac{1}{20}} = \frac{5}{100} = \mathbf{0.05}$$

$$\times 5$$

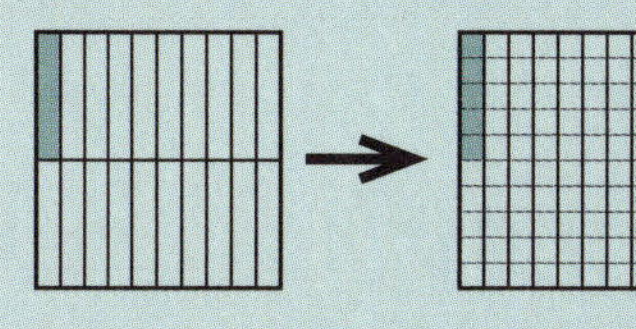

C

Four in a Row (2-Player Game)

$\frac{1}{25} = $ —	0.06	$\frac{3}{5} = $ —	0.8	$\frac{19}{20} = $ —
0.32	$\frac{49}{50} = $ —	0.4	$\frac{8}{25} = $ —	0.04
$\frac{2}{5} = $ —	0.95	$\frac{3}{50} = $ —	0.35	$\frac{13}{50} = $ —
0.98	$\frac{7}{20} = $ —	0.26	$\frac{4}{5} = $ —	0.6

Practice

Match the equivalent fractions and decimals.

| $\frac{1}{2}$ | $\frac{1}{4}$ | $\frac{3}{4}$ | $\frac{1}{5}$ | $\frac{2}{5}$ | $\frac{4}{5}$ | $\frac{9}{10}$ | $\frac{7}{10}$ |

| 0.75 | 0.2 | 0.5 | 0.8 | 0.25 | 0.7 | 0.4 | 0.9 |

Convert the fractions to decimals. (Use equivalent fractions with a base-ten denominator as needed.) Then, find the blank that matches each answer. Write the matching letter in the blank to solve the riddle.

E $\dfrac{3}{1,000}$	**L** $\dfrac{3}{10}$	**E** $\dfrac{3}{100}$
T $\dfrac{49}{100}$	**E** $\dfrac{187}{1,000}$	**R** $\dfrac{31}{1,000}$
H $\dfrac{3}{20}$	**L** $\dfrac{11}{20}$	**E** $\dfrac{9}{20}$
Y $\dfrac{16}{50}$	**E** $\dfrac{41}{50}$	**T** $\dfrac{12}{50}$
V $\dfrac{3}{25}$	**N** $\dfrac{24}{25}$	**M** $\dfrac{11}{25}$

Why is it sad when two parallel lines fall in love? Because...

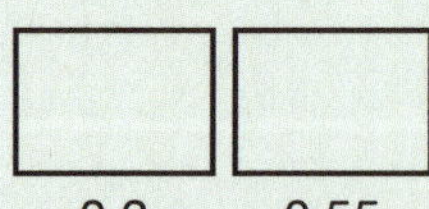

0.49	0.15	0.187	0.32	0.3	0.55

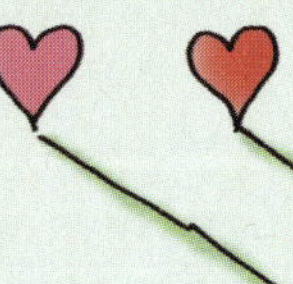

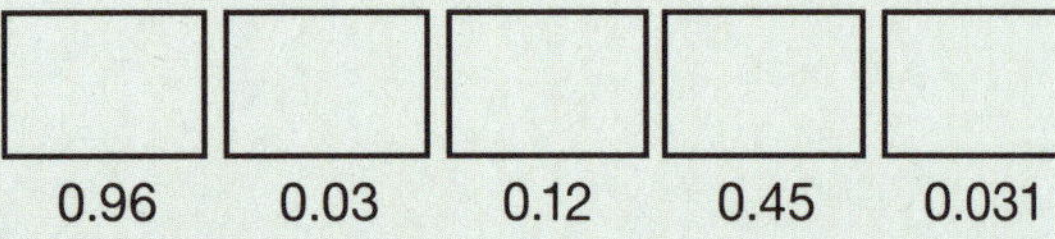

0.96	0.03	0.12	0.45	0.031		0.44	0.003	0.82	0.24

Review

Rewrite as a multiplication problem and solve. Write your answers in simplest form. Convert improper fractions to whole numbers or mixed numbers.

$$\frac{2}{3} \div \frac{2}{9} =$$

$$1\frac{2}{3} \div \frac{2}{9} =$$

$$3 \div \frac{2}{9} =$$

Choose the more sensible measurement for each item.

Width of a pencil tip

| 0.7 mm | 0.7 cm |

Capacity of a vase

| 3.2 mL | 3.2 L |

Weight of a pear

| 0.178 g | 0.178 kg |

Evaluate.

$$\frac{12 \cdot 7}{4 \cdot 7}$$

$$(8 - 1)^2 + 1^3$$

$$\frac{60 \cdot 5}{10^2}$$

Use Lucca's time card from the ski competition to answer the questions. Write the equations you use in the work space.

How much faster was Run 2 than Run 3?

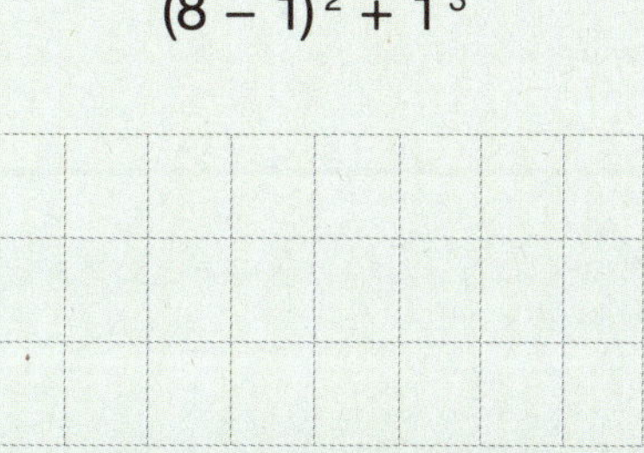

What was the total time for all 3 of Lucca's runs?

What was Lucca's average time for each run?

Lesson Activities 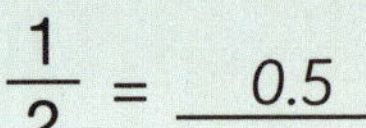

A

$\frac{1}{2}$ = ___0.5___

$\frac{1}{4}$ = _______

$\frac{3}{4}$ = _______

$\frac{1}{5}$ = _______

$\frac{2}{5}$ = _______

$\frac{3}{5}$ = _______

$\frac{4}{5}$ = _______

B

Use Decimals to Compare

Ex. Which is greater, $\frac{1}{4}$ or 0.23?

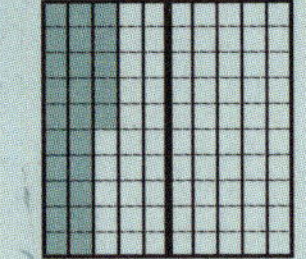 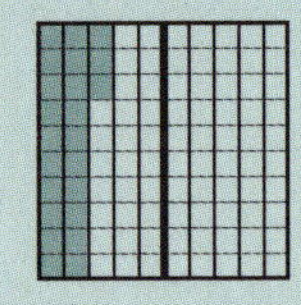

$\frac{1}{4}$ = 0.25   0.23

0.25 is greater than 0.23, so $\frac{1}{4}$ is greater than 0.23.

Ex. Which is greater, $\frac{1}{4}$ or $\frac{3}{10}$?

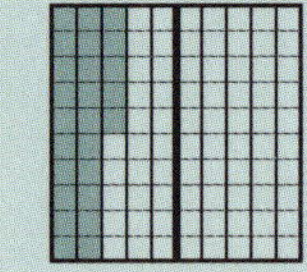 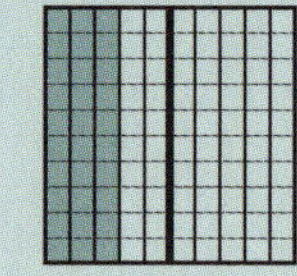

$\frac{1}{4}$ = 0.25 $\frac{3}{10}$ = 0.3

0.3 is greater than 0.25, so $\frac{3}{10}$ is greater than $\frac{1}{4}$.

$\frac{1}{2}$ ◯ 0.5001

$\frac{1}{5}$ ◯ 0.19

$\frac{3}{4}$ ◯ $\frac{4}{5}$

C

Hit the Target (2-Player Game)

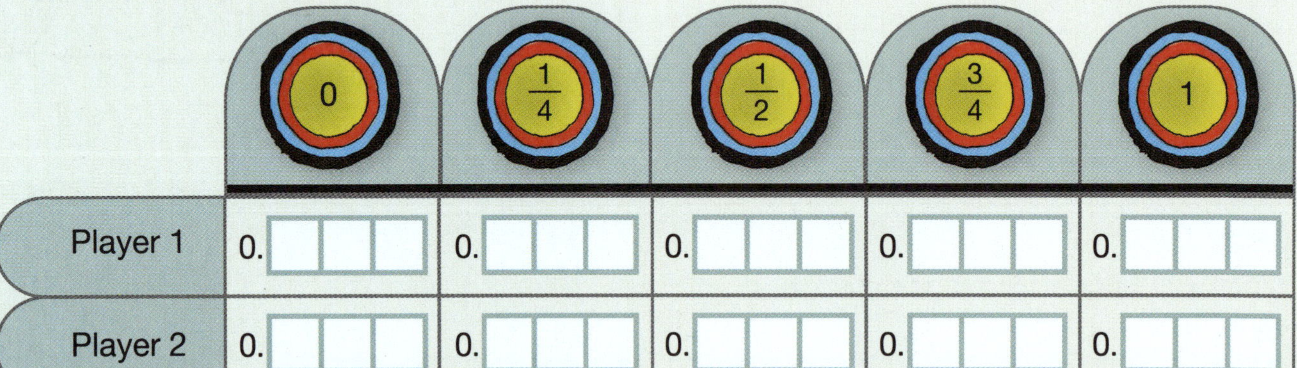

Practice 

Use the digits to complete the blanks and create a decimal number.

| 4 | 0 | 0 |

$\dfrac{4}{10} = 0.\square\square\square$

| 4 | 0 | 0 |

$\dfrac{4}{100} = 0.\square\square\square$

| 4 | 0 | 0 |

$\dfrac{4}{1,000} = 0.\square\square\square$

| 8 | 4 | 1 |

$\dfrac{3}{4} < 0.\square\square\square$

| 8 | 4 | 1 |

$\dfrac{1}{2} > 0.\square\square\square$

| 8 | 4 | 1 |

$\dfrac{1}{5} > 0.\square\square\square$

Use the charts and pictures to answer the questions.

Who swam the farthest distance?

Who swam the shortest distance?

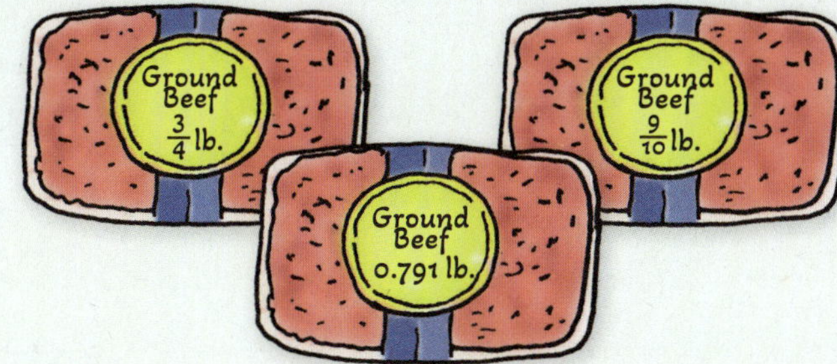

What is the weight of the heaviest package?

What is the weight of the lightest package?

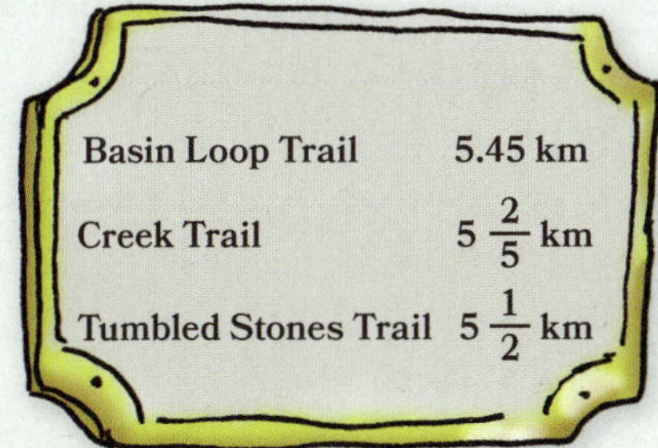

Which trail is the longest?

Which trail is the shortest?

Which bottle has the greatest capacity?

Which bottle has the lowest capacity?

Review

Match.

$\frac{7}{10}$ m	25 cm		$\frac{1}{10}$ cm	5 mm		$\frac{1}{2}$ kg	250 g
$\frac{1}{4}$ m	70 cm		$\frac{3}{10}$ cm	6 mm		$\frac{1}{4}$ kg	815 g
$\frac{99}{100}$ m	80 cm		$\frac{1}{2}$ cm	1 mm		$\frac{7}{10}$ kg	500 g
$\frac{4}{5}$ m	99 cm		$\frac{3}{5}$ cm	3 mm		$\frac{815}{1,000}$ kg	700 g

Find the product or quotient.

$$2\ 7\ 4 \times 3\ 6$$

$$7\ 5\ \overline{)\ 2{,}8\ 5\ 0}$$

	× 75
1	75
2	150
3	225
4	300
5	375
6	450
7	525
8	600
9	675

Complete.

$94 \times 10^2 =$ _____________

$17 \times 10^3 =$ _____________

$364 \times 10^0 =$ _____________

$48 \times 10^1 =$ _____________

$250 \times 10^3 =$ _____________

$6 \times 10^6 =$ _____________

Solve. Write the equations you use.

The bag of candy weighs $5\frac{1}{4}$ oz. One serving of candy weighs $\frac{3}{4}$ oz. How many servings are in the bag?

Elian mixes 3 parts potting soil with 2 parts compost for his planters. If he uses 12 lb. of compost, how much potting soil should he use?

potting soil	
compost	

Lesson Activities 

4.9 × 100 = ?

Estimate

4.9 ≈ _________

____ × 100 = ____

13.624 × 10 = ?

Estimate

13.624 ≈ _________

____ × 10 = ____

1.023 × 1,000 = ?

Estimate

1.023 ≈ _________

____ × 1,000 = ____

Multiply Decimals by 10, 100, or 1,000

1. Find the number of zeros in 10, 100, or 1,000.

2. Move the decimal point the same number of places to the right.

3. Tack on trailing zeros as needed.

Ex. Each box of blueberries weighs 0.8 lb. How much do 100 boxes of blueberries weigh?

0.8 × 100 = **80 lb.**

080.

The soccer field is 68.4 m wide and 100 m long. What is the area of the soccer field?

The python is 6.3 m long. How many centimeters long is it? (1 meter equals 100 centimeters.)

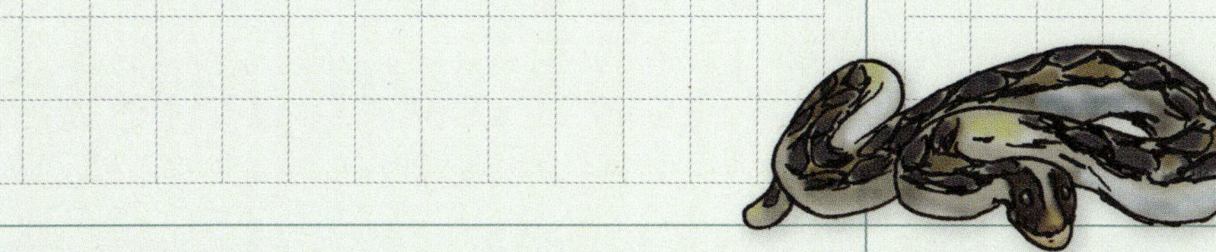

The unit price for 1 pack of markers is $3.19. How much do 100 packs of markers cost?

A newborn kangaroo weighs 0.0016 kg when it goes into its mother's pouch. It weighs 1,000 times more when it comes out of the pouch! How many kilograms does it weigh then?

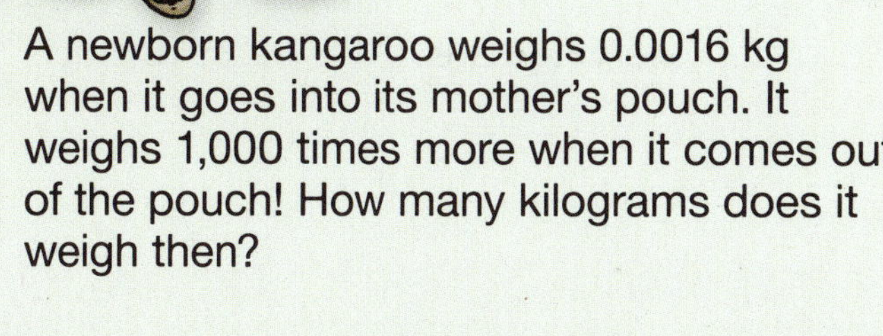

Practice

Move the decimal point to find the product.

3.678 × 10 = _______	0.49 × 10 = _______	6.1 × 10 = _______
3.678 × 100 = _______	0.49 × 100 = _______	6.1 × 100 = _______
3.678 × 1,000 = _______	0.49 × 1,000 = _______	6.1 × 1,000 = _______
1.704 × 10 = _______	3.44 × 10 = _______	10.2 × 10 = _______
1.704 × 100 = _______	3.44 × 100 = _______	10.2 × 100 = _______
1.704 × 1,000 = _______	3.44 × 1,000 = _______	10.2 × 1,000 = _______

Write 10, 100, or 1,000 to make the equations true.

0.367 × _______ = 36.7	0.43 × _______ = 4.3	0.201 × _______ = 201
0.007 × _______ = 7	0.008 × _______ = 0.08	0.006 × _______ = 0.6

Complete the metric conversion factors in the chart.
Then, use the chart to complete the conversions.

Metric Conversion Factors

1 m = _______ cm

1 cm = _______ mm

1 km = _______ m

1 L = _______ mL

1 kg = _______ g

5.62 m = _______ cm

5.62 × 100 =

0.4 m = _______ cm

35.8 cm = _______ mm

0.09 km = _______ m

2.8 L = _______ mL

0.005 kg = _______ g

Review

Complete the chart to find the perimeter and area of a square with the given side length.

Side length (s)	Perimeter ($4 \cdot s$)	Area (s^2)
1	4	1
2		
3		
4		
5		

Rewrite as a multiplication problem and solve. Write your answers in simplest form. Convert improper fractions to whole numbers or mixed numbers.

$$1 \div \frac{3}{8} =$$

$$\frac{7}{8} \div \frac{3}{8} =$$

$$\frac{1}{8} \div \frac{3}{8} =$$

Solve. Write the equations you use.

The walrus pup weighs 120 pounds. Its mother weighs 88 times as much as the pup. How much does the walrus mother weigh?

Rachel uses $2\frac{1}{2}$ c. almonds, $5\frac{1}{3}$ c. pecans, and $3\frac{3}{4}$ c. walnuts to make spiced nuts. How many cups of nuts does she use in all?

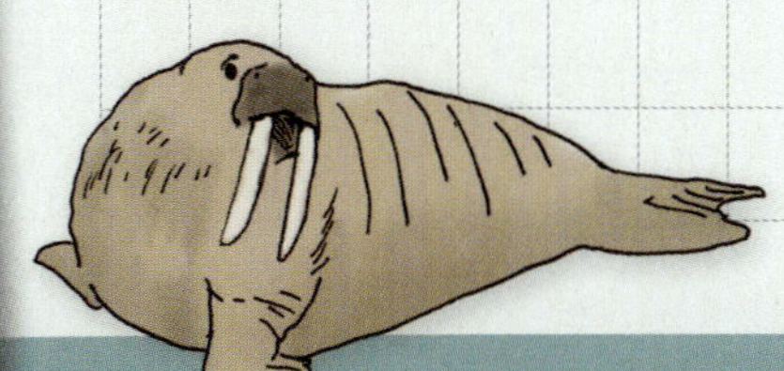

Lesson Activities 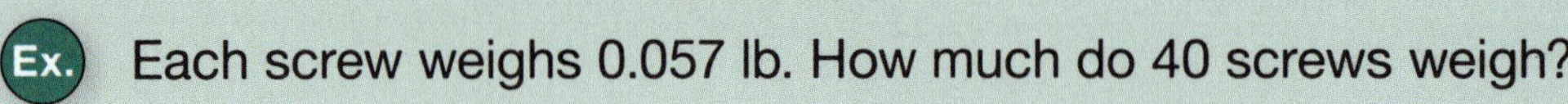

A

97.62 × 8 = ?

Estimate

9̲7.62 ≈ _________

____ × 8 = ____

3.75 × 40 = ?

Estimate

3̲.75 ≈ _________

____ × 40 = ____

0.89 × 65 = ?

Estimate

0̲.89 ≈ _________

____ × 65 = ____

B

Multiply Decimals by Whole Numbers

Ex. Each screw weighs 0.057 lb. How much do 40 screws weigh? 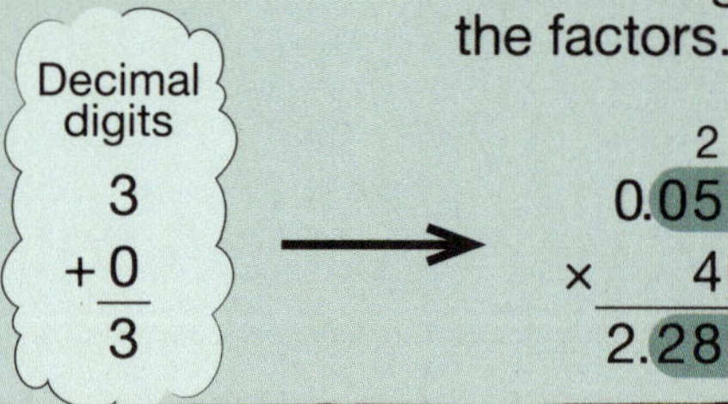

1. Multiply like usual. Ignore the decimal point and any leading zeros.

2. Find the total number of decimal digits in the factors.

3. Write a decimal point so the product has the same number of decimal digits as the factors.

$$
\begin{array}{r}
2 \\
0.057 \\
\times \quad 40 \\
\hline
2280
\end{array}
$$

$\longrightarrow$

$$
\begin{array}{r}
2 \\
0.057 \\
\times \quad 40 \\
\hline
2280
\end{array}
$$

Decimal digits

$$
\begin{array}{r}
3 \\
+0 \\
\hline
3
\end{array}
$$

$\longrightarrow$

$$
\begin{array}{r}
2 \\
0.057 \\
\times \quad 40 \\
\hline
2.280
\end{array}
$$

Decimal digits

$$
\begin{array}{r}
3 \\
+0 \\
\hline
3
\end{array}
$$

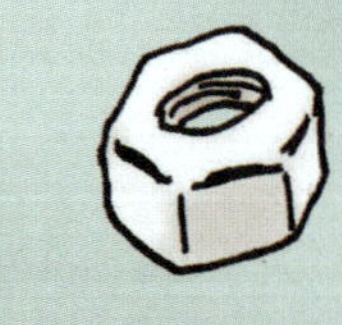
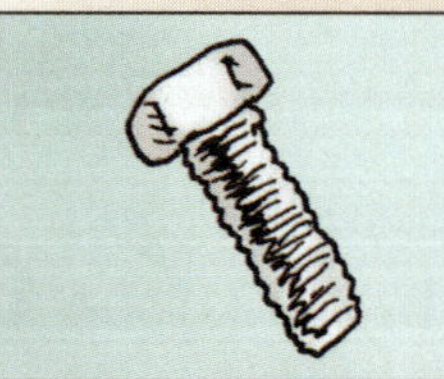

1 hinge: 0.46 lb.

8 hinges: ______ lb.

1 nut: 0.036 lb.

30 nuts: ______ lb.

1 bolt: 0.14 lb.

25 bolts: ______ lb.

WORK SPACE

Practice

Round each decimal to the nearest whole number and estimate the product. Circle the most reasonable product for each problem.

7.6 × 3	7.6 × 400	7.6 × 48
2.28 22.8 228	304 3,040 30,400	3.648 36.48 364.8
3.87 × 21	38.7 × 21	★ 3.87 × 2.1
8.127 81.27 812.7	8.127 81.27 812.7	0.8127 8.127 81.27

Find the products.

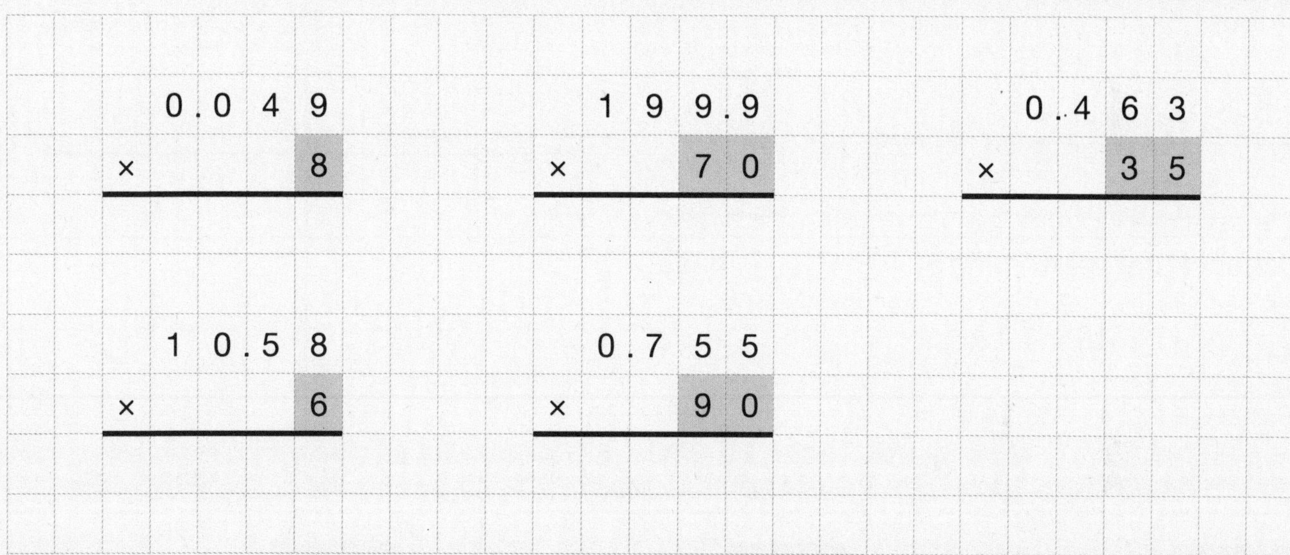

```
  0 . 0  4  9        1  9  9 . 9        0 . 4  6  3
×          8      ×          7  0    ×          3  5
```

```
  1  0 . 5  8        0 . 7  5  5
×          6      ×          9  0
```

Solve. Write the equations you use.

The state park is 5 miles long and 2.7 miles wide. What is its area?

The Statue of Liberty has a height of 93 m. The Empire State Building's height is 4.8 times the Statue of Liberty's height. What's the height of the Empire State Building?

Review

Compare with <, >, or =.

−2 ◯ −3	5.6 ◯ 2.31	−8.45 ◯ 0.1	$\frac{2}{3}$ ◯ $\frac{2}{3}$
$\lvert -2 \rvert$ ◯ $\lvert -3 \rvert$	$\lvert 5.6 \rvert$ ◯ $\lvert 2.31 \rvert$	$\lvert -8.45 \rvert$ ◯ $\lvert 0.1 \rvert$	$\left\lvert \frac{2}{3} \right\rvert$ ◯ $\left\lvert -\frac{2}{3} \right\rvert$

Write the coordinates for each point in the chart.
Then, find the distance between each pair of points.

Point	Coordinates
E	
F	
G	
H	

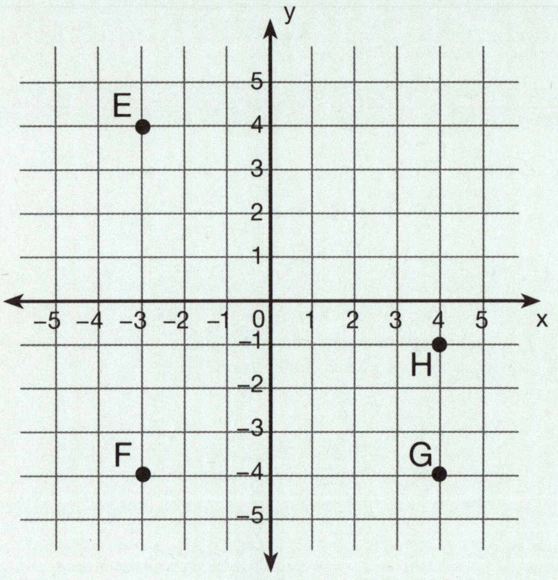

Distance between E and F: __________ units

Distance between F and G: __________ units

Distance between G and H: __________ units

Match.

50 cm	$\frac{1}{4}$ m	5 mm	$\frac{4}{5}$ cm	500 mL	$\frac{3}{5}$ L
25 cm	$\frac{1}{2}$ m	1 mm	$\frac{1}{5}$ cm	100 mL	$\frac{999}{1,000}$ L
75 cm	$\frac{73}{100}$ m	2 mm	$\frac{1}{10}$ cm	600 mL	$\frac{1}{2}$ L
10 cm	$\frac{3}{4}$ m	8 mm	$\frac{1}{2}$ cm	999 mL	$\frac{3}{4}$ L
73 cm	$\frac{1}{10}$ m	4 mm	$\frac{2}{5}$ cm	750 mL	$\frac{1}{10}$ L

Lesson Activities

37 ÷ 10
| Less than 1 | Greater than 1 |

37 ÷ 100
| Less than 1 | Greater than 1 |

37 ÷ 1,000
| Less than 1 | Greater than 1 |

196 ÷ 10
| Less than 1 | Greater than 1 |

196 ÷ 100
| Less than 1 | Greater than 1 |

196 ÷ 1,000
| Less than 1 | Greater than 1 |

Divide Decimals by 10, 100, or 1,000

1. Find the number of zeros in 10, 100, or 1,000.

2. Move the decimal point the same number of places to the left.

3. Fill in leading zeros as needed.

Ex. A stack of 1,000 sheets of copy paper is 12.7 cm thick. How thick is 1 sheet of copy paper?

$12.7 ÷ 1{,}000 = \textbf{0.0127 cm}$

0.0127

The food pantry has 78 kg of rice. The volunteers want to split the rice equally into 100 bags. How much should each bag weigh?

The giant anteater is 194 cm long. How many meters long is it? (100 centimeters equal 1 meter.)

The crate of 10 watermelons weighs 67 kg. On average, how much does each watermelon weigh?

1,000 stickers cost $38.95. What is the unit price for 1 sticker? Round your answer to the nearest cent.

Practice 👤 Move the decimal point to find the quotient.

134 ÷ 10 = ______________   6.3 ÷ 10 = ______________   29.7 ÷ 10 = ______________

134 ÷ 100 = ______________   6.3 ÷ 100 = ______________   29.7 ÷ 100 = ______________

134 ÷ 1,000 = ______________   6.3 ÷ 1,000 = ______________   29.7 ÷ 1,000 = ______________

6 ÷ 10 = ______________   297 ÷ 10 = ______________   73.1 ÷ 10 = ______________

6 ÷ 100 = ______________   297 ÷ 100 = ______________   73.1 ÷ 100 = ______________

6 ÷ 1,000 = ______________   297 ÷ 1,000 = ______________   73.1 ÷ 1,000 = ______________

Write 10, 100, or 1,000 to make the equations true.

8 ÷ __________ = 0.08   8 ÷ __________ = 0.8   8 ÷ __________ = 0.008

31.5 ÷ __________ = 3.15   146.9 ÷ __________ = 1.469   0.27 ÷ __________ = 0.027

Complete the metric conversion factors in the chart. Then, use the chart to complete the conversions.

Metric Conversion Factors

__________ mm = 1 cm

__________ cm = 1 m

__________ m = 1 km

__________ mL = 1 L

__________ g = 1 kg

13.8 cm = __________ m

13.8 ÷ 100 =

2 cm = __________ m

27 mm = __________ cm

1,950 m = __________ km

25 mL = __________ L

155.7 g = __________ kg

Review  Complete the chart.

Decimal	Expanded Form	Fraction or Mixed Number
0.803		
	$3 + \dfrac{5}{100} + \dfrac{7}{1{,}000}$	
		$2\dfrac{47}{1{,}000}$
1.71		
	$\dfrac{2}{10} + \dfrac{3}{100} + \dfrac{9}{1{,}000}$	

Find the product. Write your answers in simplest form. Convert improper fractions to whole numbers or mixed numbers.

$\dfrac{3}{2} \times \dfrac{4}{9} =$ | $\dfrac{5}{4} \times \dfrac{3}{10} =$ | $\dfrac{8}{1} \times \dfrac{1}{8} =$

$\dfrac{7}{4} \times \dfrac{7}{7} =$ | $\dfrac{10}{3} \times \dfrac{9}{5} =$ | $\dfrac{0}{8} \times \dfrac{13}{6} =$

Find the volume. All measurements are in inches.

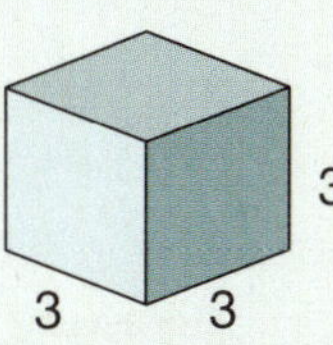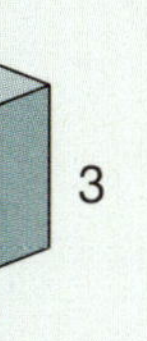

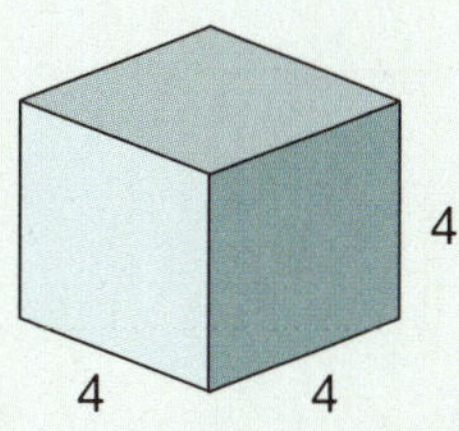

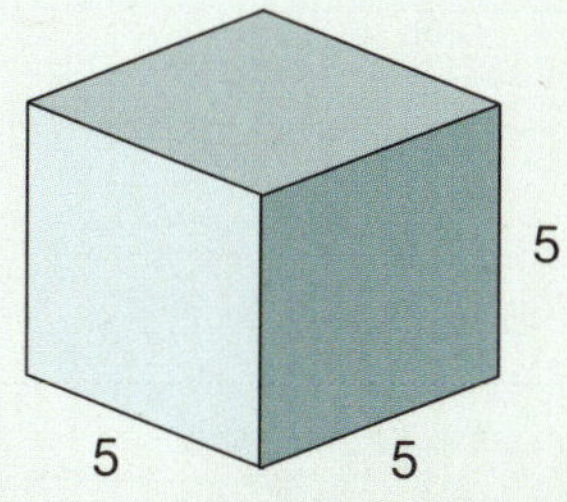

Volume: __________ cu. in. | Volume: __________ | Volume: __________

Complete the ratios. Write each ratio in simplest form.

Each gift basket has 20 star cookies and 15 snowman cookies.

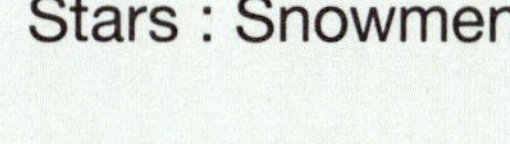

Stars : Snowmen

______ : ______

Snowmen : Stars

______ : ______

Stars : Total cookies

______ : ______

Snowmen : Total cookies

______ : ______

Lesson Activities

7.05 ÷ 5	0.288 ÷ 4	4.340 ÷ 20
Less than 1 / Greater than 1	Less than 1 / Greater than 1	Less than 1 / Greater than 1

Divide Decimals by Whole Numbers with Long Division

1. Divide like usual. Ignore any leading zeros.

2. Place the decimal point in the quotient directly above its place in the dividend. Fill in leading zeros as needed.

Ex. 4 grains of rice weigh 0.116 g. On average, how much does each grain of rice weigh?

$$
\begin{array}{r}
0.029 \text{ g} \\
4\overline{)0.116} \\
-\ 8\downarrow \\
\hline
36 \\
-36 \\
\hline
0
\end{array}
$$

$$5\overline{)7.0\ 5} \qquad 4\overline{)0.2\ 8\ 8} \qquad 2\ 0\overline{)4.3\ 4\ 0}$$

	× 20
1	20
2	40
3	60
4	80
5	100
6	120
7	140
8	160
9	180

Decimal Division Least to Greatest (1-Player Game)

0.095 ÷ 5

0.385 ÷ 5

0.015 ÷ 5

least ___ ___ ___ greatest

Practice

Circle the words that best describe the answer to each division problem.

$0.835 \div 5$	$7.53 \div 3$	$38.28 \div 12$
Less than 1 Greater than 1	Less than 1 Greater than 1	Less than 1 Greater than 1

Use long division to solve. Use the multiplication table to help with the last problem.

$$5 \overline{)0.835} \qquad 3 \overline{)7.53} \qquad 12 \overline{)38.28}$$

	× 12
1	12
2	24
3	36
4	48
5	60
6	72
7	84
8	96
9	108

Solve. Use the completed problems above to find your answers.

The scientist makes 0.835 L of a chemical solution. He divides it equally into 5 test tubes. How many liters are in each test tube?

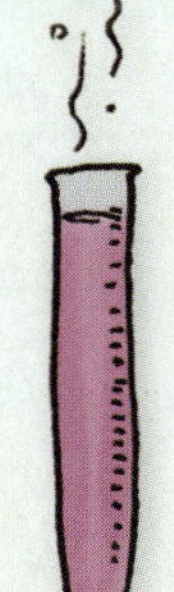

3 bunches of carrots cost $7.53. What is the unit price for 1 bunch of carrots?

12 packs of crackers weigh 38.28 oz. How much does each pack of crackers weigh?

★ The bathroom is 3 m long and has an area of 7.53 sq. m. What is the width of the bathroom?

Review   Match.

5 squared		4^2		64
4 cubed		3^4		1
4 to the power of 1		4^3		25
4 squared		5^2		81
4 to the power of 0		4^1		4
3 to the fourth power		4^0		16

Round to the underlined digit. | Rewrite as a multiplication problem and solve.

7.4810 ≈ _______________

0.057 ≈ _______________

3.156 ≈ _______________

2.098 ≈ _______________

0.97 ≈ _______________

$$4\frac{1}{2} \div \frac{3}{4} =$$

$$9 \div \frac{3}{4} =$$

Find the perimeter and area of the parallelogram.

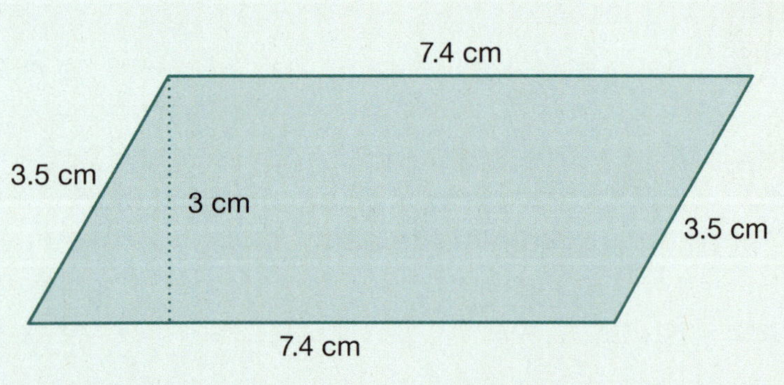

Perimeter: _______________   Area: _______________

Lesson Activities

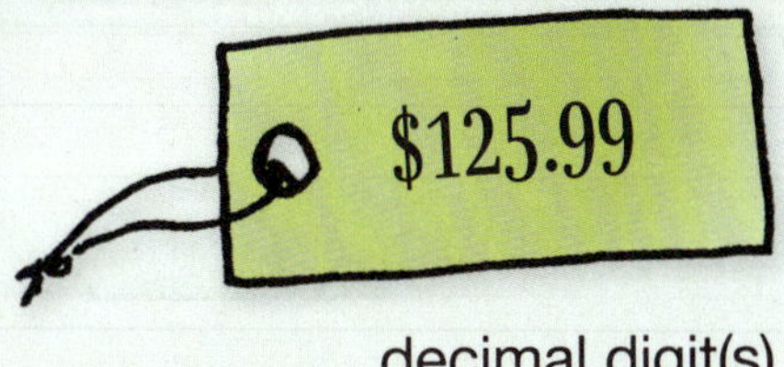

_______ decimal digit(s)

_______ decimal digit(s)

A

U.S. Dollar
Exchange Rate:
0.9574 euros

_______ decimal digit(s)

B

Round Quotients to a Given Number of Decimal Digits

Ex. The baker makes 3.8 kg of bread dough. He wants to split the dough into 6 equal balls. How much should each ball weigh? Write the answer with 2 decimal digits.

1. Set up the long division problem. Tack on trailing zeros in the dividend to match the number of decimal digits you want in the answer.

$$6\overline{)3.80}$$

2 decimal digits

2. Follow the long division steps. Place the decimal point in the quotient directly above its place in the dividend.

```
     0.63
6 ) 3.80
   -3 6↓
      20
    -18
       2
```

3. If there is a remainder, tack on 1 more zero and divide one more time. Round your answer to the correct number of decimal digits.

```
     0.633
6 ) 3.800
   -3 6↓
      20
    -18↓
       20
```

0.633 ≈ **0.63 kg**

The baker wants to split 0.8 kg of dough into 9 equal-sized balls to make dinner rolls. How much should each ball of dough weigh? Write your answer with 2 decimal digits.

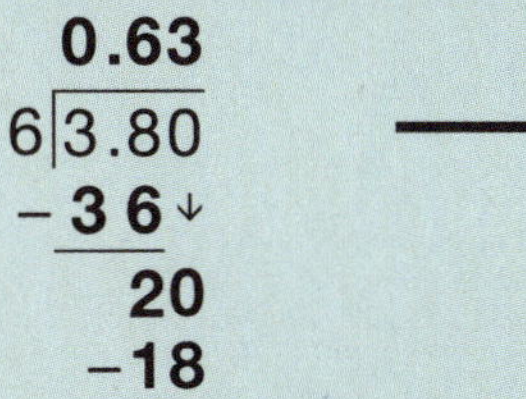

WORK SPACE

The baker wants to split 1.07 kg of dough into 8 equal-sized balls to make scones. How much should each ball weigh? Round your answer to the hundredths-place.

Practice

**Use long division to find the quotients.
Write your answers with the given number of decimal digits.**

2.4 ÷ 7 = _____________
(2 decimal digits)

____

0.43 ÷ 5 = _____________
(3 decimal digits)

____

1 ÷ 7 = _____________
(2 decimal digits)

Solve. Write the equations you use in the work space.

At the farmer's market, 3 baskets of blueberries cost $11.75. What is the unit price for 1 basket of blueberries? Round your answer to the hundredths-place.

____

The jeweler has 0.029 kg of gold. He splits the gold into 6 equal parts to make jewelry. How much does each part weigh? Write your answer with 4 decimal digits.

____

Isabella received the following scores at the archery tournament.

199	218	236
208	167	

What is the sum of her scores?

What is the average of her scores?
Write your answer with 1 decimal digit.

Review 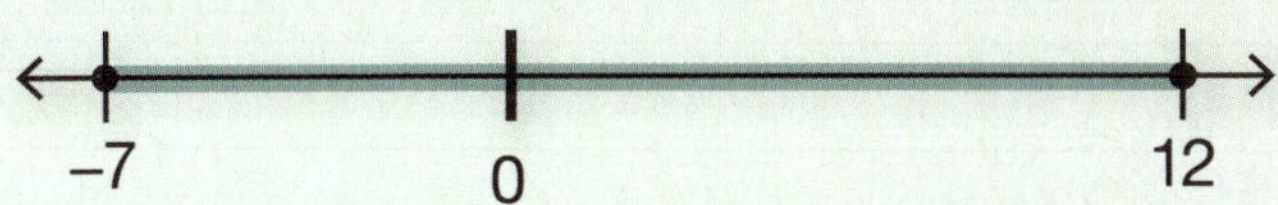

Find the distance between each pair of numbers.

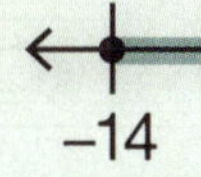
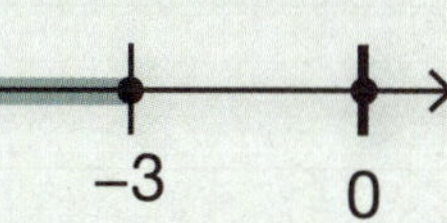

$-7 \qquad 0 \qquad\qquad 12$

$-14 \qquad\qquad -3 \qquad 0$

Distance: _________ units

Distance: _________ units

Use the distributive property to complete the blanks. You do not need to evaluate.

$12 \cdot (13 + 19) =$ _______ $\cdot\, 13 +$ _______ $\cdot\, 19$

$40 \cdot 77 + 40 \cdot 3 = 40 \cdot (77 +$ _______ $)$

$20 \cdot (7 + 65) = 20 \cdot 7 + 20 \cdot$ _______

$52 \cdot 1 + 52 \cdot 49 = 52 \cdot (1 +$ _______ $)$

Match.

the difference between 8 and 4, multiplied by 5	$\dfrac{8 + 4}{5}$
the product of 8 and 4, decreased by 5	$\dfrac{8}{4} + 5$
the sum of 8 and 4, divided by 5	$(8 \times 4) - 5$
the quotient of 8 and 4, increased by 5	$(8 - 4) \times 5$

Use bar models to solve.

At the youth hockey tournament, the concession stand volunteers sold $\frac{3}{4}$ as many cold drinks as hot drinks. If they sold 84 cold drinks, how many hot drinks did they sell?

Cold drinks

Hot drinks

How many drinks did they sell in all?

Unit Wrap-Up

Convert the fractions to decimals. (Use equivalent fractions with a base-ten denominator as needed.) Then, use your answers to complete the comparisons.

$\dfrac{1}{4} =$ ___ $\dfrac{1}{2} =$ ___ $\dfrac{3}{4} =$ ___ $\dfrac{7}{10} =$ ___

$\dfrac{2}{5} =$ ___ $\dfrac{3}{20} =$ ___ $\dfrac{9}{25} =$ ___ $\dfrac{11}{50} =$ ___

$\dfrac{1}{4} \bigcirc \dfrac{3}{20}$ $\dfrac{1}{4} \bigcirc \dfrac{9}{25}$ $\dfrac{1}{4} \bigcirc \dfrac{11}{50}$

$0.2 \bigcirc \dfrac{3}{20}$ $0.3 \bigcirc \dfrac{9}{25}$ $0.2 \bigcirc \dfrac{11}{50}$

Move the decimal point to find the product or quotient.

$4.5 \times 10 =$ ___ $0.801 \times 100 =$ ___ $0.072 \times 1,000 =$ ___

$0.87 \div 100 =$ ___ $179 \div 1,000 =$ ___ $0.4 \div 10 =$ ___

Use the chart to complete the conversions. Think carefully about whether to multiply or divide.

1 cm = 10 mm

1 m = 100 cm

1 km = 1,000 m

3.145 m = ___ cm

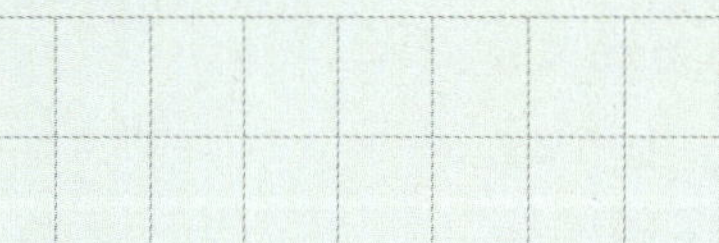

123 mm = ___ cm

0.45 km = ___ m

1,325 m = ___ km

Unit Wrap-Up

At the farmer's market, each stand sets its own prices. Find the unit price for 1 basket of strawberries at each stand. Write your answers with 2 decimal digits. Then, answer the questions.

Stan's Strawberries
3 for $5

Unit price: ____________

Bella's Berries
4 for $6

Unit price: ____________

Frank's Fruit
5 for $8

Unit price: ____________

Which stand has the lowest unit price?

Which stand has the highest unit price?

Solve. Write the equations you use.

The rug is 12 ft. by 13.7 ft. What is its area?

WORK SPACE

On average, each pumpkin weighs 4.8 kg. How much does a crate of 20 pumpkins weigh?

The blue whale's body is 71.6 ft. long. Its body is 4 times as long as its tongue. How long is the blue whale's tongue? Write your answer with 1 decimal digit.

Unit 1 Reference Page

Order of Operations

1. Complete operations in parentheses.
2. Multiply or divide, from left to right.
3. Add or subtract, from left to right.

Ex.

$$15 - (1 + 2) \times 4$$
$$15 - 3 \times 4$$
$$15 - 12$$
$$3$$

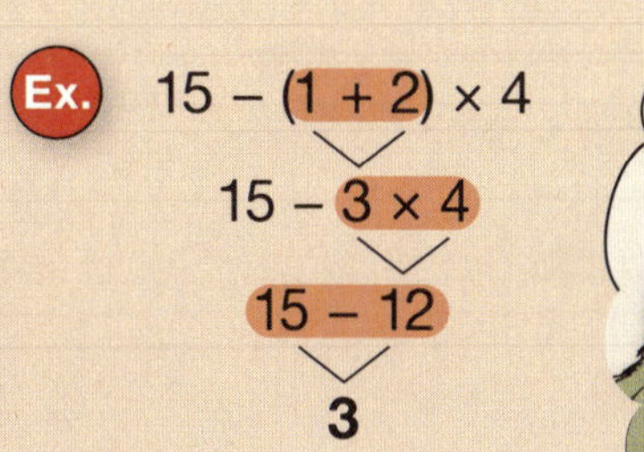

1.1

Exponents

Exponents are a shortcut for writing repeated multiplication. The base is the number you multiply. The exponent tells how many times the base is multiplied.

base   exponent

$$4^3 = 4 \times 4 \times 4 = 64$$

We read 4^3 as "4 to the third power" or "4 to the power of 3."

Ex. $2^5 = 2 \times 2 \times 2 \times 2 \times 2 = \mathbf{32}$

Ex. $7^2 = 7 \times 7 = \mathbf{49}$

Ex. $3^0 = \mathbf{1}$

Any number to the power of 0 is 1.

1.2

Square and Cube Numbers

When we square a number, we raise it to the second power. The result is called a square number.

Ex. What is 5 squared?

$$5^2 = 5 \times 5 = 25$$

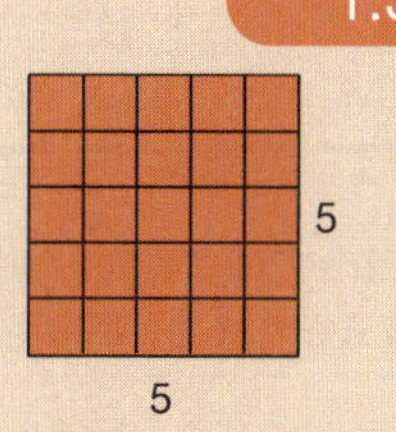

1.3

When we cube a number, we raise it to the third power. The result is called a cube number.

Ex. What is 5 cubed?

$$5^3 = 5 \times 5 \times 5 = 125$$

Order of Operations

1. Complete operations in parentheses.
2. Evaluate exponents.
3. Multiply or divide, from left to right.
4. Add or subtract, from left to right.

Ex.

$$5^2 + (4 - 1)^2$$
$$5^2 + 3^2$$
$$25 + 9$$
$$34$$

1.4

Powers of 10

The powers of 10 are numbers that can be expressed with a base of 10 and an exponent. The exponent tells the number of zeros in the original number.

1.5

Ex. Write 100,000,000 as a power of 10.

100,000,000 has 8 zeros.
So, 8 is the exponent.

$100{,}000{,}000 = \mathbf{10^8}$

To multiply a number by a power of 10, tack on the matching number of zeros. Then, write commas as needed.

Ex. 372×10^5

$372 \times 10^5 = \mathbf{37{,}200{,}000}$

Multiplication Dot

Another symbol for multiplication is a dot.

1.6

Ex. $4^2 \cdot 10^2$
$16 \cdot 100$
$1{,}600$

Associative Property

The associative property of multiplication says that we can group numbers in any order when multiplying. We can use this property to simplify and evaluate long multiplication expressions.

Ex. $5 \cdot 3 \cdot 5 \cdot 3$
$5^2 \cdot 3^2$
$25 \cdot 9$
225

Distributive Property

When we multiply a number by a sum in parentheses, we can evaluate the expression two different ways. Either way, we get the same answer.

Option 1:

Find the sum in parentheses, then multiply.

Option 2:

Multiply in parts, then add. This is called "distributing" the factor.

1.7

Ex. Evaluate $9 \cdot (30 + 8)$ two different ways.

Option 1:
Add, then multiply.

Option 2:
Distribute the factor.

$9 \cdot (30 + 8)$ 
$9 \cdot 38$
342

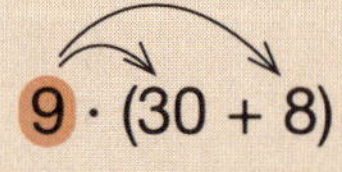
$9 \cdot (30 + 8)$
$9 \cdot 30 + 9 \cdot 8$
$270 + 72$
342

Unit 1 Reference Page

Use a Fraction Bar to Show Division

We can use a fraction bar to show division.

Ex. $\dfrac{20}{5}$

$\dfrac{20}{5} = 4$

$$20 \div 5 = 4$$

The fraction bar is a grouping symbol, just like parentheses. If there are expressions above or below the fraction bar, evaluate the expressions first. Then, follow the order of operations like usual.

Ex. $\dfrac{2 \times 7}{3 + 4}$

$\dfrac{14}{7} = 2$

$$(2 \times 7) \div (3 + 4)$$
$$14 \div 7$$
$$2$$

1.8

Cancel Common Factors

If there are multiplication expressions above and below the division bar, we can simplify the expression before solving. Crossing out (or "cancelling") the common factors is a quick way to divide both expressions by the same number.

1. Look for common factors above and below the division bar.
2. Cross out the common factors in pairs. One factor must be above the bar and one factor must be below the bar.
3. Complete the problem.

1.9

Ex. $\dfrac{6 \cdot 4}{2 \cdot 4}$

$\dfrac{6 \cdot 4}{2 \cdot 4} = \dfrac{6}{2} = 3$

$$\dfrac{6 \cdot 4}{2 \cdot 4} = \dfrac{6}{2}$$

Ex. $\dfrac{9 \cdot 7 \cdot 11}{11 \cdot 7 \cdot 3}$

$\dfrac{9 \cdot 7 \cdot 11}{11 \cdot 7 \cdot 3} = \dfrac{9}{3} = 3$

Ex. $\dfrac{5 \cdot 4 \cdot 5}{5}$

$\dfrac{5 \cdot 4 \cdot 5}{5} = \dfrac{4 \cdot 5}{1} = \dfrac{20}{1} = 20$

Prime and Composite Numbers

Prime numbers have exactly two factors: 1 and the number itself.

Composite numbers have more than two factors.

1 has only one factor. So, it is neither a composite number nor a prime number.

1.10

Ex. Is 18 prime or composite?
Factors of 18: 1, 2, 3, 6, 9, 18
18 has more than two factors, so it is **composite.**

Ex. Is 17 prime or composite?
Factors of 17: 1, 17
17 has exactly two factors, so it is **prime.**

Factor Trees and Prime Factorization

Factor trees help us find all prime factors of a number. To make a factor tree:

1. Write the target number at the top.
2. Draw two branches below the target number. Label the branches with a factor pair for the number above the branches.
3. Continue until each branch ends in a prime number.

Every whole number greater than 1 is prime or can be expressed as the product of prime numbers. This product is called the prime factorization of the number.

1.11

Ex. Draw a factor tree for 28.

There are often many different ways to make a factor tree. Here are two ways to make a factor tree for 28.

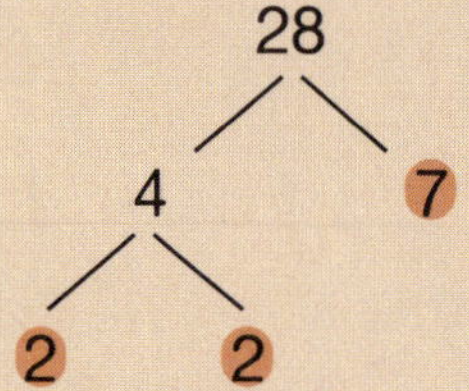
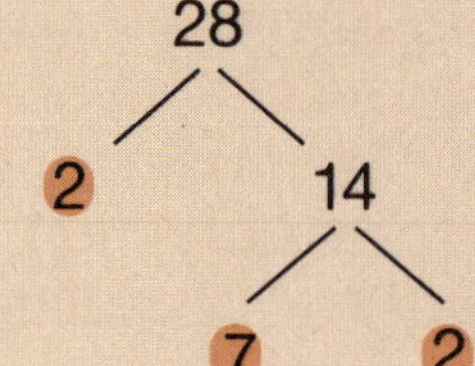

Ex. What is the prime factorization of 28?

$28 = 2 \cdot 2 \cdot 7$

Greatest Common Factor

1.12

The greatest common factor (GCF) of two numbers is the highest factor they have in common.

Ex. Find the greatest common factor of 18 and 30.

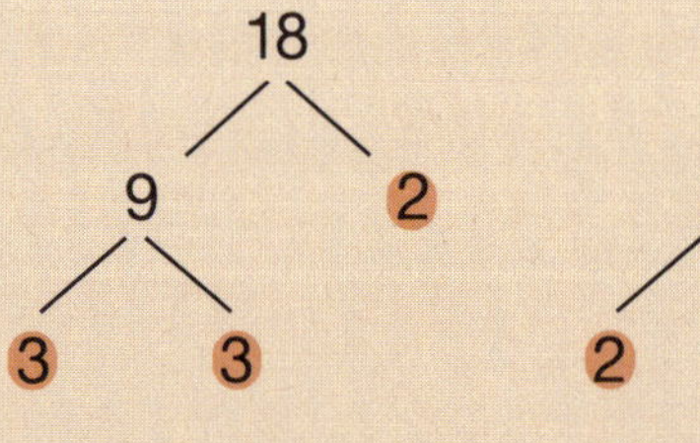
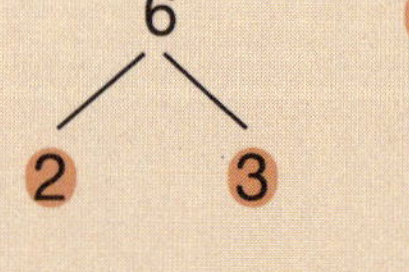

$18 = 2 \cdot 3 \cdot 3$

$30 = 2 \cdot 3 \cdot 5$

The product of the shared prime factors is the greatest common factor.

$$18 = \underbrace{2 \cdot 3}_{6} \cdot 3 \qquad 30 = \underbrace{2 \cdot 3}_{6} \cdot 5$$

$2 \cdot 3 = 6$, so the GCF of 18 and 30 is **6**.

2.1

Fractions

Fractions
- numerator: top number, tells number of parts

- denominator: bottom number, tells how many parts the whole was split into

$$\frac{2}{3}$$ ← numerator ← denominator

Mixed Numbers
- combination of whole number and fraction

- multiply denominator by the whole number and add numerator

$$1\frac{2}{5} = \frac{7}{5}$$

Improper Fractions
- numerator greater than or equal to denominator

- divide numerator by denominator

$$\frac{7}{4} = 1\frac{3}{4}$$

Equivalent Fractions
- different numerator and denominator, but same value

- multiply (or divide) numerator and denominator by the same number

$$\frac{1}{2} \xrightarrow{\times 5} = \frac{5}{10}$$

Simplest Form
- equivalent fraction with the smallest numerator and denominator possible

- divide numerator and denominator by common factors (or GCF) until you can't divide anymore

$$\frac{6}{8} \xrightarrow{\div 2} = \frac{3}{4}$$

Unit 2 Reference Page

Use Cancelling to Simplify Fractions

The simplest form of a fraction is the equivalent fraction with the smallest numerator and denominator possible.

To find the simplest form of a fraction, divide the numerator and denominator by common factors until they have no common factors (other than 1).

Ex. Express $\frac{12}{15}$ in simplest form.

$$\frac{\overset{4}{\cancel{12}}}{\underset{5}{\cancel{15}}} = \frac{4}{5}$$

$$\frac{12}{15} \overset{\div 3}{\underset{\div 3}{=}} \frac{4}{5}$$

Ex. Express $\frac{28}{42}$ in simplest form.

$$\frac{\overset{4}{\cancel{28}}}{\underset{6}{\cancel{42}}} \rightarrow \frac{\overset{\overset{2}{\cancel{4}}}{\cancel{28}}}{\underset{\underset{3}{\cancel{8}}}{\cancel{42}}} = \frac{2}{3}$$

$$\frac{28}{42} \overset{\div 7}{\underset{\div 7}{=}} \frac{4}{6} \overset{\div 2}{\underset{\div 2}{=}} \frac{2}{3}$$

To simplify the fraction in one step, divide both the numerator and the denominator by their greatest common factor (GCF).

Ex. The GCF of 28 and 42 is 14. So, you can divide both by 14 to simplify the fraction in one step.

$$\frac{\overset{2}{\cancel{28}}}{\underset{3}{\cancel{42}}} = \frac{2}{3}$$

$$\frac{28}{42} \overset{\div 14}{=} \frac{2}{3}$$

Find the Least Common Multiple of 3 Numbers

The least common multiple (LCM) of a set of numbers is the lowest multiple they have in common.

Make a list of the first few multiples of each number. Look for the lowest multiple they have in common.

Ex. Find the least common multiple of 4, 5, and 10.

Multiples of 4: 4, 8, 12, 16, 20, 24...

Multiples of 5: 5, 10, 15, 20, 25, 30...

Multiples of 10: 10, 20, 30, 40, 50, 60...

LCM of 4, 5, and 10: **20**

Or, make a list of the first few multiples of the greatest number. Check whether each multiple is also a multiple of the smaller numbers.

Ex. Find the least common multiple of 4, 5, and 10.

Multiples of 10: 10, 20, 30, 40, 50, 60...

20 is also a multiple of 4 and 5, so it's the least common multiple of 4, 5, and 10.

Compare 3 or More Fractions

Use the LCM as the denominator to write equivalent fractions for all the fractions you are comparing. Then, compare the equivalent fractions.

Ex. Write these fractions in order from least to greatest: $\frac{1}{4}$, $\frac{2}{5}$, $\frac{3}{10}$

$$\frac{1}{4} = \frac{5}{20} \qquad \frac{2}{5} = \frac{8}{20} \qquad \frac{3}{10} = \frac{6}{20}$$

$$\frac{5}{20} < \frac{6}{20} < \frac{8}{20} \qquad \frac{1}{4} < \frac{3}{10} < \frac{2}{5}$$

How to Use Common Denominators to Add or Subtract Fractions

1. Find the least common multiple (LCM) of all denominators. You will use this number for the common denominator.
2. Rewrite each fraction as an equivalent fraction with the common denominator.
3. Add or subtract the fractions.

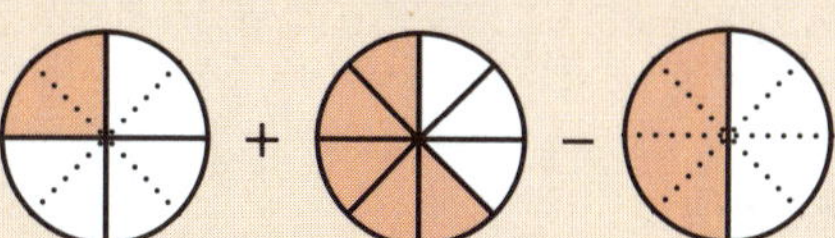

Ex.

$$\frac{1}{4} + \frac{5}{8} - \frac{1}{2}$$

$$\frac{2}{8} + \frac{5}{8} - \frac{4}{8} = \frac{3}{8}$$

2.4

Add Mixed Numbers

1. Rewrite the fractions with common denominators.
2. Add the fractions. Then, add the whole numbers.
3. If you have an improper fraction in the sum, convert the improper fraction to a mixed number. Add it to the whole number.
4. Simplify if needed.

Ex.

$$1\frac{2}{3} = 1\frac{4}{6}$$
$$+ 1\frac{1}{2} = 1\frac{3}{6}$$
$$2\frac{7}{6} = 3\frac{1}{6}$$

$$2\frac{7}{6} = 2 + 1\frac{1}{6} = 3\frac{1}{6}$$

2.5

Subtract Mixed Numbers

1. Rewrite the fractions with common denominators.
2. If the top fraction is less than the bottom fraction, trade 1 whole for fractional parts.
3. Subtract the fractions. Then, subtract the whole numbers.
4. Simplify if needed.

Ex.

$$2\frac{1}{2} = 2\frac{3}{6} = 1\frac{9}{6}$$
$$- 1\frac{5}{6} = 1\frac{5}{6}$$
$$\frac{4}{6} = \frac{2}{3}$$

Two Ways to Solve Fraction Word Problems

2.6

Ex. Aurora has $80. She uses $\frac{3}{4}$ of her money to buy roller skates. How much money does she have left?

Find a Part, Then Subtract

money spent | money left

| 20 | 20 | 20 | 20 |

80

$80 \div 4 = 20$

$3 \times 20 = 60$

$\frac{3}{4}$ of 80 is 60.

The roller skates cost $60.

$80 - 60 = 20$

Aurora has **$20** left.

Subtract, Then Find a Part

money spent | money left

| 20 | 20 | 20 | 20 |

80

$1 - \frac{3}{4} = \frac{1}{4}$

If Aurora spends $\frac{3}{4}$ of her money on roller skates, she has $\frac{1}{4}$ of her money left.

$80 \div 4 = 20$

$\frac{1}{4}$ of 80 is 20.

Aurora has **$20** left.

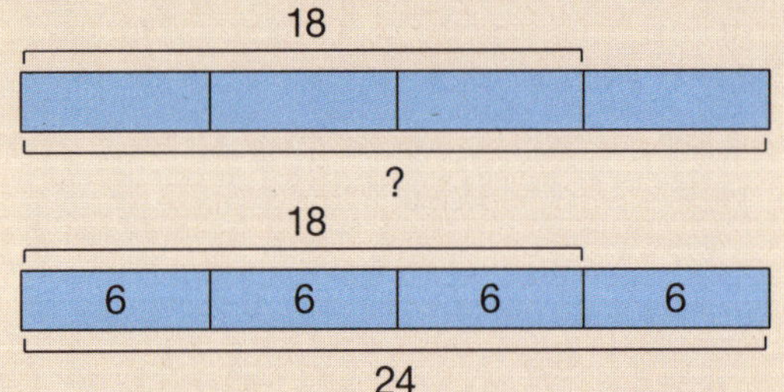

Find the Whole Amount

2.7

Ex. Gideon spends $\frac{3}{4}$ of his money on a bag of marbles. The marbles cost $18. How much money did he start with?

18

| | | | |

?

18

| 6 | 6 | 6 | 6 |

24

$18 \div 3 = 6$

Each unit bar stands for $6.

$4 \times 6 = 24$

Gideon started with **$24**.

2.8

Ex. Austin spends $50 on a hockey jersey. He spends $\frac{2}{5}$ as much on a pack of hockey pucks as he spends on the jersey. How much does he spend in all? How much more does the jersey cost than the hockey pucks?

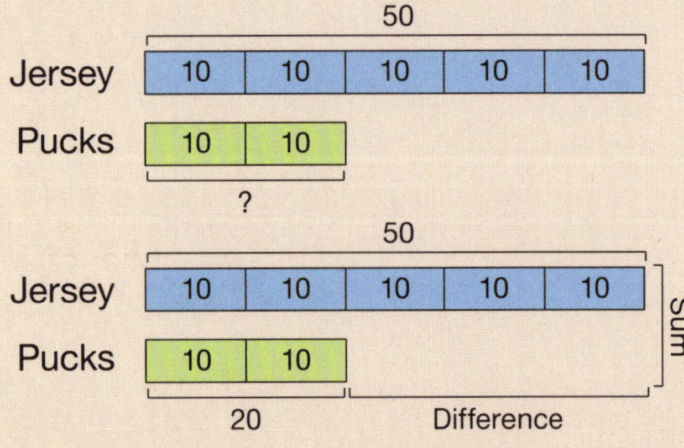

50

Jersey | 10 | 10 | 10 | 10 | 10 |

Pucks | 10 | 10 |

?

50

Jersey | 10 | 10 | 10 | 10 | 10 | Sum

Pucks | 10 | 10 |

20 | Difference

First, find the cost of the hockey pucks.

$50 \div 5 = 10$

$2 \times 10 = 20$

$\frac{2}{5}$ of 50 = 20, so the pucks cost $20.

Add to find the total amount he spends.

$50 + 20 = $ **$70**

Subtract to find the difference between the prices. $50 - 20 = $ **$30**

Formulas for the Perimeter and Area of a Rectangle — 3.1

A formula is an equation that describes a mathematical rule. We can use words or letters to write formulas.

Perimeter = length + width + length + width
$$P = l + w + l + w$$

Area = length · width
$$A = l \cdot w$$

Ex. Find the area and perimeter of the rectangle.

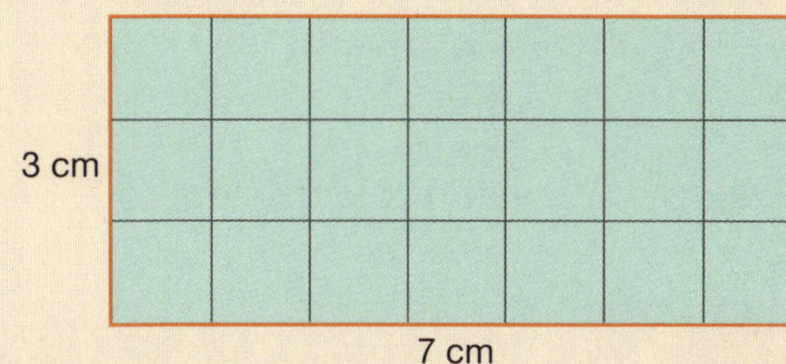

$P = l + w + l + w$
$P = 7$ cm $+ 3$ cm $+ 7$ cm $+ 3$ cm
$P = $ **20 cm**

$A = l \cdot w$
$A = 7$ cm $\cdot 3$ cm
$A = $ **21 sq. cm**

Multiply and Divide Units — 3.2

When we multiply or divide measurements, we multiply or divide the measurement units, too. The units follow the same rules as numbers.

Ex. The garden is 7 ft. by 4 ft. What is the area of the garden?

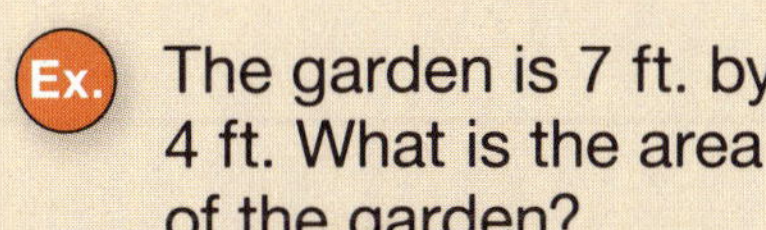

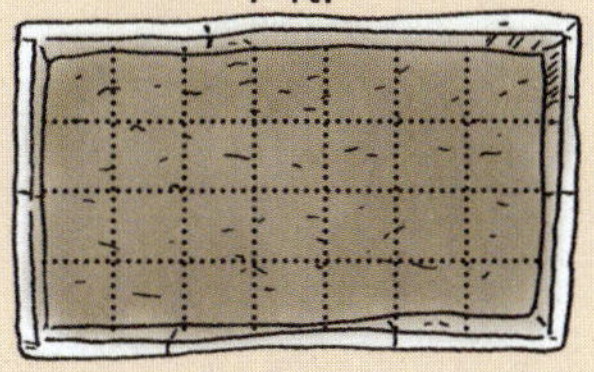

7 ft. × 4 ft. = **28 ft.²**

We can use exponents to show the product of the same unit. An exponent of 2 means square units.

Ex. The photo has an area of 96 cm² and a width of 8 cm. What is the length of the photo?

$$\frac{96 \text{ cm}^2}{8 \text{ cm}} = \frac{96 \text{ cm} \cdot \text{cm}}{8 \text{ cm}} = \textbf{12 cm}$$

If the same unit is above and below the fraction bar, we can cancel.

Ex. Everly has 20 ft. of ribbon. She cuts the ribbon into 4 equal pieces. How long is each piece?

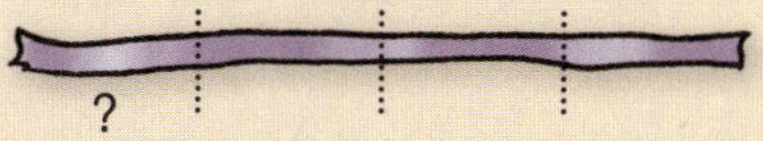

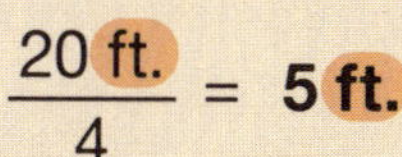

$$\frac{20 \text{ ft.}}{4} = \textbf{5 ft.}$$

Numbers that tell the number of groups or parts do not have a unit.

Area of a Parallelogram

3.3

Any parallelogram can be transformed into a rectangle. Just cut off the right triangle at one end and move it to the other end! You create a rectangle with the same base and height as the parallelogram.

To find the area of a parallelogram, multiply the base by the height.

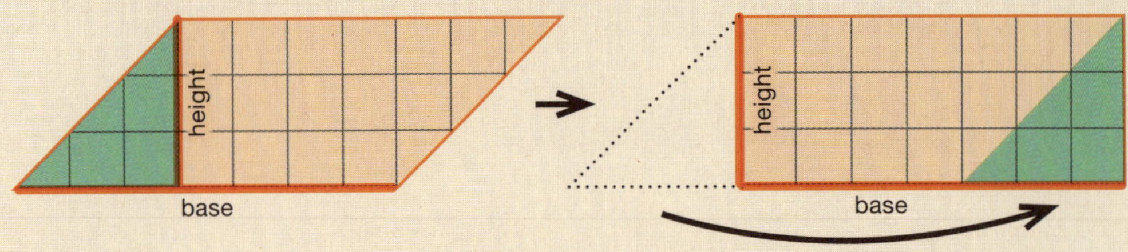

Area = base · height
$A = b \cdot h$

Ex. What is the area of this parallelogram?

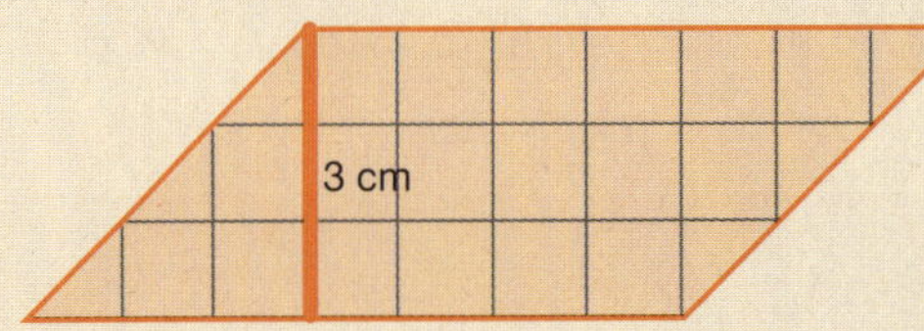

$A = 7 \text{ cm} \cdot 3 \text{ cm}$

$A = \textbf{21 cm}^2$

Area of a Triangle

3.4

Every triangle is half of a matching parallelogram or rectangle.

To find the area of a triangle, multiply the base by the height. Then, divide the product by 2.

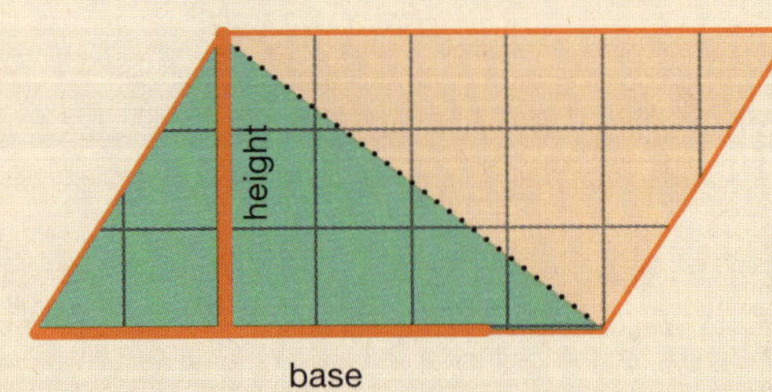

Area $= \dfrac{\text{base} \cdot \text{height}}{2}$ $A = \dfrac{b \cdot h}{2}$

Ex. What is the area of this triangle?

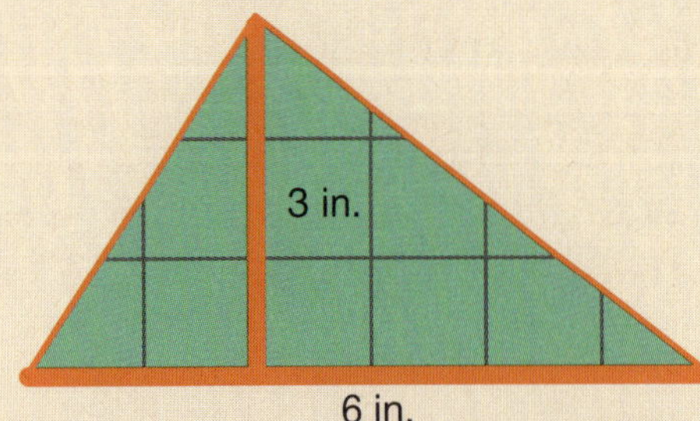

$A = \dfrac{6 \text{ in.} \cdot 3 \text{ in.}}{2}$

$A = \textbf{9 in.}^2$

Area of a Triangle, Part 2

The height of a triangle must always be perpendicular to its base. Sometimes, the line we use to measure height is outside of the triangle.

Obtuse triangles are triangles with one obtuse angle. We often measure their height outside of the triangle.

Ex. What is the area of this triangle?

3.5

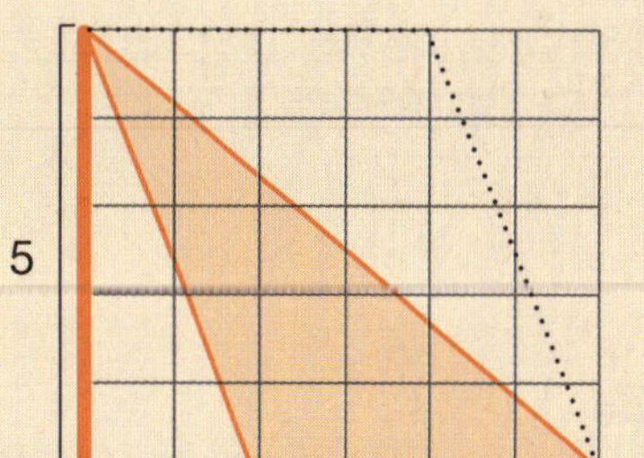

$$A = \frac{b \cdot h}{2}$$

$$A = \frac{4 \cdot 5}{2}$$

$$A = \textbf{10 units}^2$$

Subtract to Find Area

3.6

Ex. What is the area of the grass?

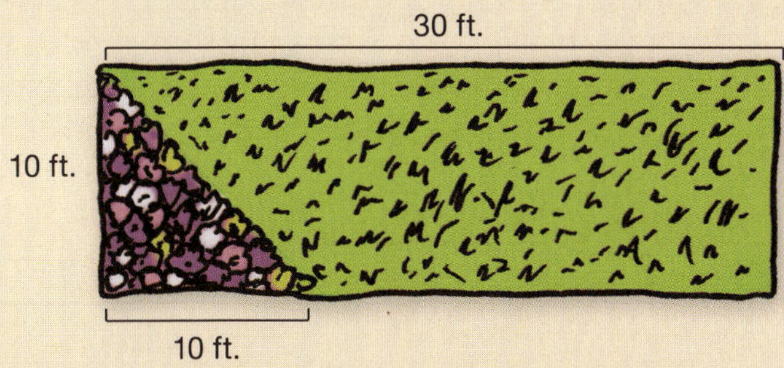

Area of the rectangle:
30 ft. × 10 ft. = **300 ft.²**

Area of the flower bed:
$$\frac{10 \text{ ft.} \times 10 \text{ ft.}}{2} = \textbf{50 ft.}^2$$

Area of the grass:
300 ft.² − 50 ft.² = **250 ft.²**

Add to Find Area

3.7

Ex. What is the area of the wall?

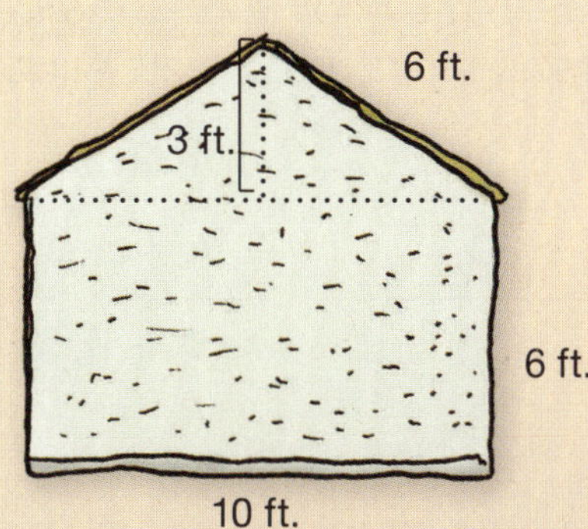

Area of the rectangle:
10 ft. · 6 ft. = **60 ft.²**

Area of the triangle:
$$\frac{10 \text{ ft.} \cdot 3 \text{ ft.}}{2} = \textbf{15 ft.}^2$$

Total area of the wall:
60 ft.² + 15 ft.² = **75 ft.²**

Ratios

4.1

Ratios compare the size of one quantity to the size of another quantity. Some ratios compare two parts of a quantity. Others compare part of a quantity to the total quantity.

To write a ratio, write the size of each quantity in the order you want to compare them. Write a colon between the numbers.

 **Ex.** Abigail mixes 2 bottles of red paint and 3 bottles of white paint to make pink paint.

Part-to-Part Ratios

Red paint : White paint
2:3

White paint : Red paint
3:2

Part-to-Whole Ratios

Red paint : Total paint
2:5

White paint : Total paint
3:5

Simplify Ratios

Finding the simplest form of a ratio is just like finding the simplest form of a fraction. Divide both numbers by common factors until they have no common factor (other than 1).

Ratios that have the same simplest form are equivalent to each other.

 **Ex.** Brandon is making fruit skewers for a party. He puts 3 strawberries and 6 grapes on each skewer. What is the ratio of strawberries to grapes in simplest form?

Strawberries : Grapes

3:6
÷3   ÷3
1:2

There is 1 strawberry for every 2 grapes.

Use Ratio Tables to Find Equivalent Ratios

Ratios that have the same simplest form are equivalent to each other. To check whether two ratios are equivalent to each other, write each ratio in simplest form.

We can use ratio tables to organize the information in ratio problems. Make sure you write each number in the matching row.

Ex. Audrey used 30 mL of vinegar and 120 mL of olive oil. Jonathan used 25 mL of vinegar and 75 mL of olive oil. Who followed the salad dressing recipe (from part A) correctly?

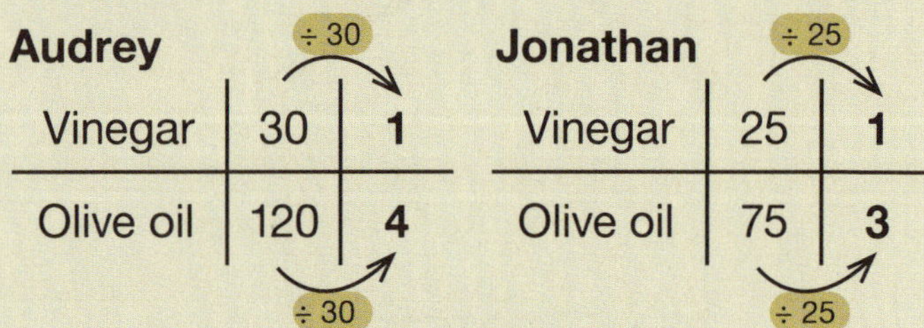

Audrey

	÷30	
Vinegar	30	1
Olive oil	120	4

Jonathan

	÷25	
Vinegar	25	1
Olive oil	75	3

Jonathan's ratio simplifies to 1:3, so he followed the recipe correctly.

Use Ratio Tables to Find One of the Quantities

If you know the ratio between two quantities along with one of the quantities, you can use a ratio table to find the other quantity.

1. Set up the ratio table.
2. Use multiplication or division to describe the relationship between the columns.
3. Use the relationship to complete the missing number.

Ex. Canoe trips at Camp Adventure have a 2:9 ratio of counselors to campers. If 45 campers sign up for a canoe trip, how many counselors do they need?

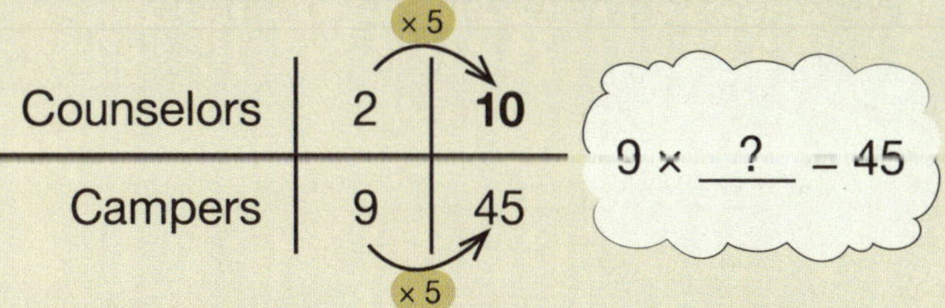

5 groups of 9 campers equal 45 campers. Each group needs 2 counselors, so they need a total of 10 counselors.

(4.4)

Use Ratios to Scale Quantities

When two different combinations have the same ratio, we say that they are proportional to each other.

We use ratio tables with multiple columns to scale quantities up or down so that they are proportional to each other.

1. Set up the ratio table with the original amounts.
2. Simplify the ratio.
3. Use the simplified ratio to find the new amounts.

Ex. Anna mixes 9 fl. oz. of pomegranate juice with 6 fl. oz. of apple juice. She likes the flavor, so she decides to make a bigger batch. If she uses 14 fl. oz. of apple juice in the new batch, how much pomegranate juice should she use?

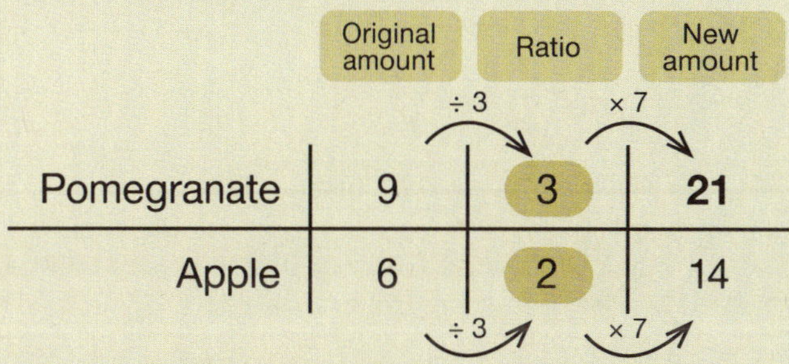

The original batch's ratio of pomegranate juice to apple juice was 3:2. So, the new batch must have the same ratio. She uses 21 fl. oz.

(4.5)

Ratios and Fractions

Ex. In a bag of marbles, the ratio of yellow marbles to green marbles is 1:3. What fraction of the marbles are yellow? What fraction of the marbles are green?

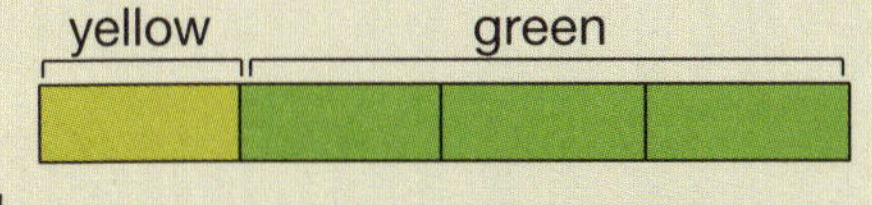

$\frac{1}{4}$ of the marbles are yellow.

$\frac{3}{4}$ of the marbles are green.

Ex. In a different bag of marbles, $\frac{3}{5}$ of the marbles are red. The rest are orange. What is the ratio of red marbles to orange marbles?

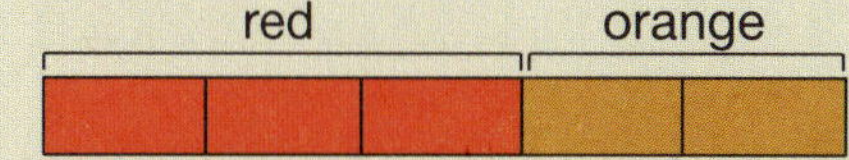

Red marbles : Orange marbles
3:2

(4.6)

Split a Sum According to a Ratio
4.7

If you know the sum of two quantities and the ratio between the quantities, you can find both quantities.

 JJ and Elsie share their lemonade stand earnings in a 3:4 ratio. If the lemonade stand earns $42 in all, how much money does each person earn?

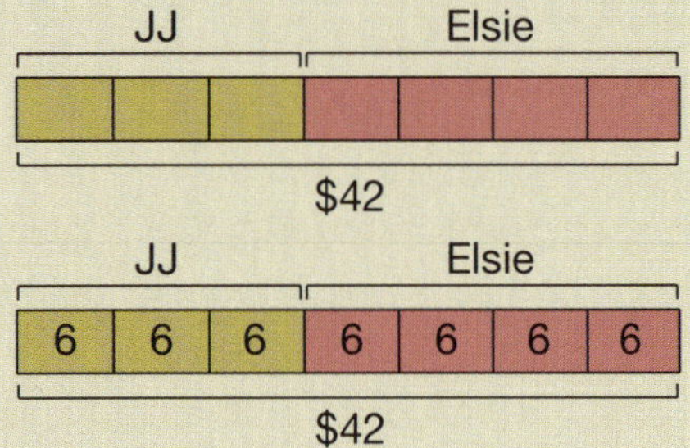

JJ and Elsie split the money into 7 shares.

$42 \div 7 = 6$. Each share is $6.

JJ gets 3 shares. $3 \times 6 =$ **$18**

Elsie gets 4 shares. $4 \times 6 =$ **$24**

Use Ratios and Fractions to Solve Comparison Problems
4.8

 Anja collects dolphin and whale figurines. She has $\frac{2}{3}$ as many dolphins as whales.

What is the ratio of dolphins to the total number of figurines?

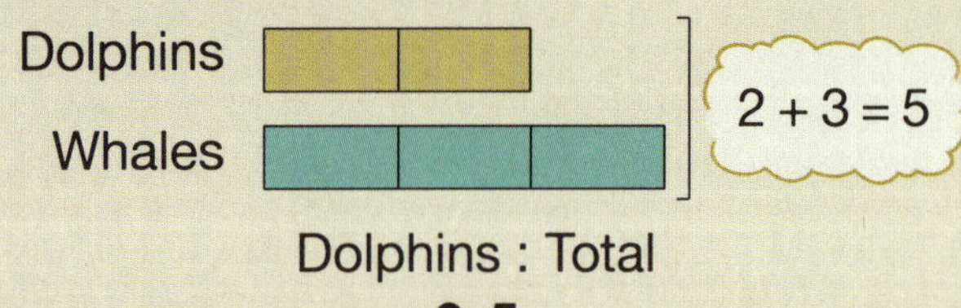

Dolphins : Total
2:5

What fraction of the whole collection is dolphins?

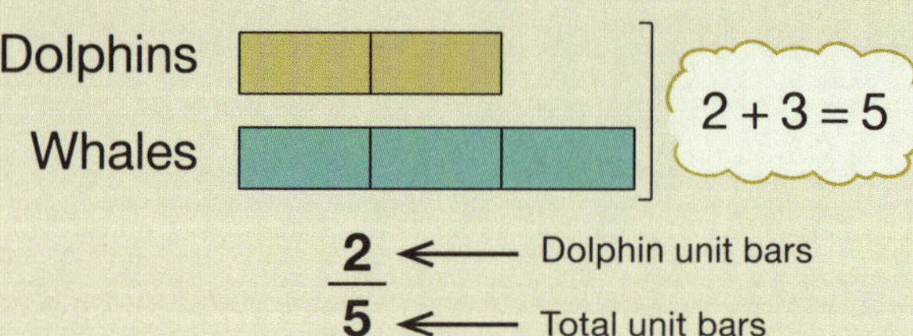

$\dfrac{2}{5}$ ← Dolphin unit bars / Total unit bars

Use the Ratio and Difference to Find Quantities
4.9

If you know the difference between two quantities and the ratio between the quantities, you can find both quantities.

Ex. The ratio of Ellie's age to Brayden's age is 5:3. Ellie is 8 years older than Brayden. How old is Ellie? How old is Brayden?

Ellie's bar is 2 units longer than Brayden's.

$8 \div 2 = 4$. Each unit stands for 4 years.

Ellie: $5 \times 4 =$ **20 years old**

Brayden: $3 \times 4 =$ **12 years old**

Multiply Fractions, Whole Numbers, or Mixed Numbers

Convert mixed numbers to improper fractions before multiplying. Write whole numbers with a denominator of 1.

1. Multiply the numerators.
2. Multiply the denominators.
3. Simplify or convert to a mixed number if needed.

5.1

Ex. The tile is $1\frac{1}{3}$ ft. long and $\frac{1}{2}$ ft. wide. What is the tile's area?

$$1\frac{1}{3} \times \frac{1}{2}$$

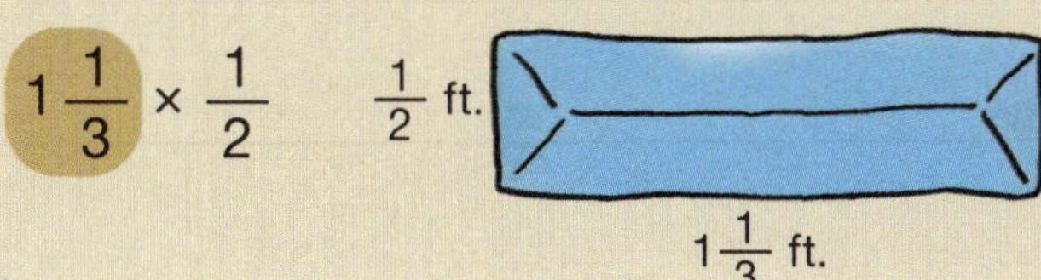

$$\frac{4}{3} \times \frac{1}{2} = \frac{4 \times 1}{3 \times 2} = \frac{4}{6} = \frac{2}{3} \text{ ft.}^2$$

Simplify Before Multiplying

1. Look for a pair of numbers that have a common factor. One number must be above the fraction bar, and one number must be below the fraction bar. They do not have to be in the same fraction!
2. Divide both numbers by the common factor. Use cancelling to show the division.
3. Multiply like usual.

5.2

Ex. $\frac{1}{5} \times \frac{\overset{3}{\cancel{6}}}{\underset{4}{\cancel{8}}} = \frac{3}{20}$

$$\frac{1}{5} \times \frac{6}{8} = \frac{6}{40} \overset{\div 2}{\underset{\div 2}{=}} \frac{3}{20}$$

Ex. $\frac{1}{\underset{2}{14}} \times \frac{\overset{1}{\cancel{7}}}{5} = \frac{1}{10}$

$$\frac{1}{14} \times \frac{7}{5} = \frac{7}{70} \overset{\div 7}{\underset{\div 7}{=}} \frac{1}{10}$$

Ex. $\frac{7}{\underset{1}{\cancel{5}}} \times \frac{\overset{1}{\cancel{5}}}{8} = \frac{7}{8}$

$$\frac{7}{5} \times \frac{5}{8} = \frac{35}{40} \overset{\div 5}{\underset{\div 5}{=}} \frac{7}{8}$$

"Of" Means Multiply

In math, "of" usually means multiply. We multiply to find a fraction of a whole number.

5.3

Ex. Juniper bakes 36 cupcakes. She puts sprinkles on $\frac{3}{4}$ of the cupcakes. How many cupcakes have sprinkles?

$$\frac{3}{4} \text{ of } 36 \rightarrow \frac{3}{4} \times 36$$

$$\frac{3}{4} \times \frac{\overset{9}{36}}{1} = \frac{27}{1} = \textbf{27 cupcakes}$$

Fraction Multiplication
5.4

We multiply to find a fraction of a quantity or equal groups of a quantity.

Ex. The racecourse is $3\frac{2}{3}$ mi. long. So far, Katya has run $\frac{3}{4}$ of the racecourse. How far has she already run?

$$\frac{3}{4} \text{ of } 3\frac{2}{3} \rightarrow \frac{3}{4} \times 3\frac{2}{3}$$

$$\frac{\cancel{3}^{1}}{4} \times \frac{11}{\cancel{3}_{1}} = \frac{11}{4} = 2\frac{3}{4} \text{ mi.}$$

Ex. Abby eats $2\frac{1}{2}$ bags of jellybeans. Each bag weighs $\frac{3}{10}$ lb. How many pounds of jellybeans does she eat?

$$2\frac{1}{2} \text{ of } \frac{3}{10} \rightarrow 2\frac{1}{2} \times \frac{3}{10}$$

$$\frac{\cancel{5}^{1}}{2} \times \frac{3}{\cancel{10}_{2}} = \frac{3}{4} \text{ lb.}$$

Simplify Before Multiplying
5.5

Sometimes, you can cancel more than one pair of numbers before multiplying fractions.

Always simplify the numbers in pairs. Make sure one number in the pair is above the fraction bar and the other number in the pair is below the fraction bar.

Ex. $\dfrac{3}{10} \times \dfrac{5}{6} \rightarrow \dfrac{\cancel{3}^{1}}{\cancel{10}_{2}} \times \dfrac{\cancel{5}^{1}}{\cancel{6}_{2}} = \dfrac{1}{4}$

Ex. $\dfrac{9}{5} \times \dfrac{8}{12} \rightarrow \dfrac{\cancel{9}^{3}}{5} \times \dfrac{\cancel{8}^{2}}{\cancel{12}_{4}^{}} = \dfrac{6}{5} = 1\dfrac{1}{5}$

Multiply 3 or More Fractions

To multiply 3 or more fractions, simplify as much as possible. Then, multiply like usual.

Ex. $\dfrac{5}{8} \times \dfrac{4}{3} \times \dfrac{7}{15} \rightarrow \dfrac{\cancel{5}^{1}}{\cancel{8}_{2}} \times \dfrac{\cancel{4}^{1}}{3} \times \dfrac{7}{\cancel{15}_{3}} = \dfrac{7}{18}$

Area of Parallelograms and Triangles
5.6

We use the usual formulas to find the area of shapes with fractional bases or heights.

Parallelogram
Area = base × height

Ex. What is the area of the parallelogram?

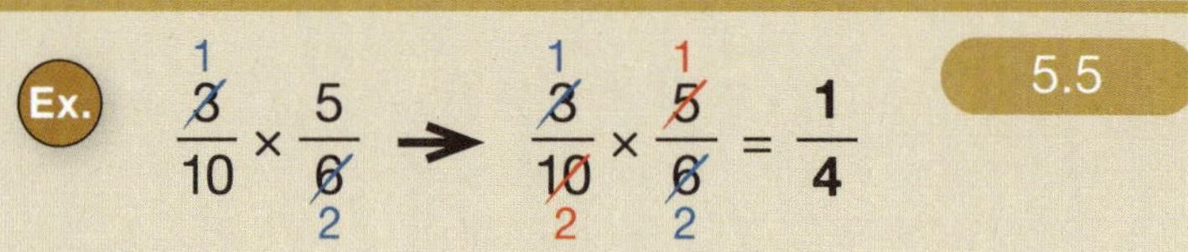

$$2\frac{1}{2} \times 1\frac{1}{4} \rightarrow \frac{5}{2} \times \frac{5}{4} = \frac{25}{8} = 3\frac{1}{8} \text{ in.}^2$$

Dividing a number by 2 is the same as finding half of the number. We can use either of these formulas to find the area of a triangle.

Triangle
$$\text{Area} = \frac{\text{base} \times \text{height}}{2}$$
$$\text{Area} = \frac{1}{2} \times \text{base} \times \text{height}$$

Ex. What is the area of the triangle?

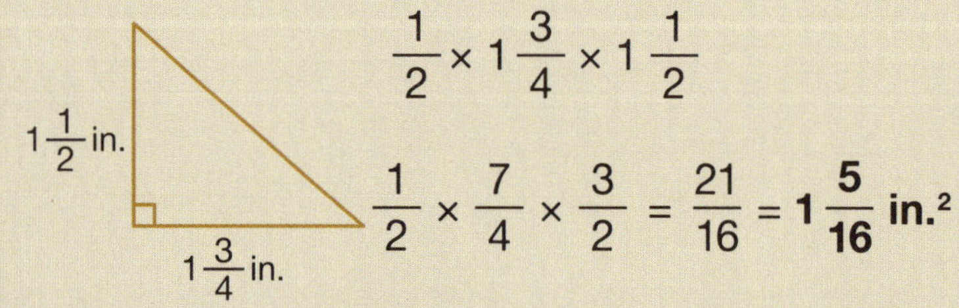

$$\frac{1}{2} \times 1\frac{3}{4} \times 1\frac{1}{2}$$

$$\frac{1}{2} \times \frac{7}{4} \times \frac{3}{2} = \frac{21}{16} = 1\frac{5}{16} \text{ in.}^2$$

Positive and Negative Numbers on the Number Line   6.1

Positive numbers are numbers greater than zero. Negative numbers are numbers less than zero. Zero is neither positive nor negative.

A number's sign tells us whether the number is greater than or less than zero. The numeral itself tells how far the number is from zero.

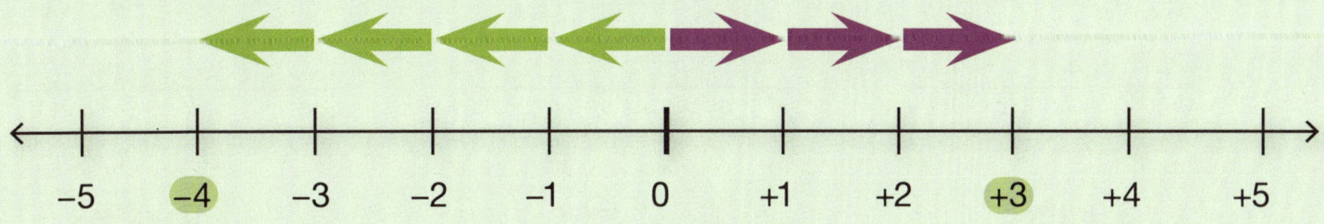

−4 means "4 units less than zero"   +3 means "3 units greater than zero"

We write a minus sign to show that a number is negative. We sometimes write a plus sign in front of a positive number to emphasize that it is positive.

To compare positive and negative numbers, plot them on the number line. Numbers farther to the left are less than numbers farther to the right.

Absolute Value   6.2

The absolute value of a number is the number's distance from zero on the number line. The symbol for absolute value is two parallel vertical lines around the number.

 What is the absolute value of −4?	Ex. What is the absolute value of 0?	Ex. What is the absolute value of +2?
$|-4| = \mathbf{4}$	$|0| = \mathbf{0}$	$|+2| = \mathbf{2}$

Distances on the Number Line

Ex. How far apart are 1 and 4 on the number line?

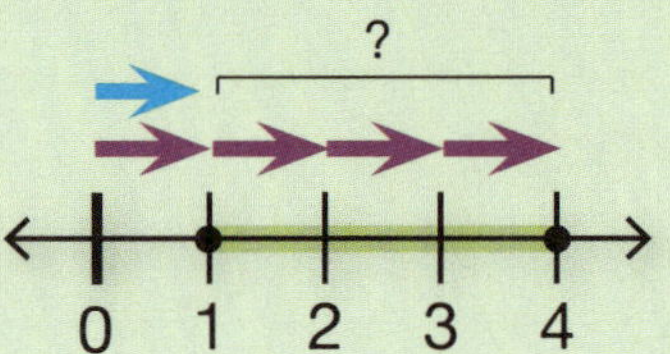

$4 - 1 =$ **3 units**

Ex. How far apart are −3 and −1 on the number line?

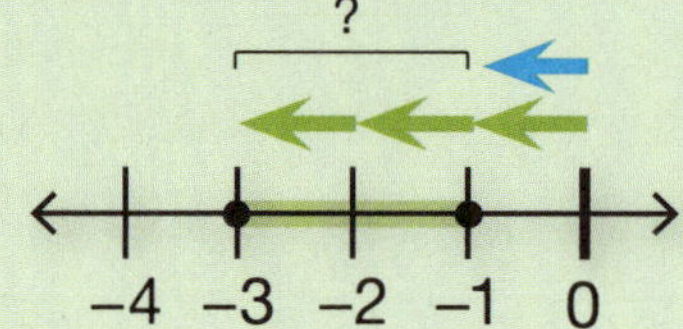

$3 - 1 =$ **2 units**

Ex. How far apart are −3 and 2 on the number line?

$3 + 2 =$ **5 units**

Opposites

The opposite of a number is the number that is the same distance from zero, in the opposite direction. The opposite of a positive number is the matching negative number. The opposite of a negative number is the matching positive number. The opposite of zero is zero.

We use a minus sign and parentheses to show that we want to find the opposite of a number.

Ex. What is the opposite of 3?

$-(3) =$ **−3**

The opposite of 3 is −3.

Ex. What is the opposite of −1?

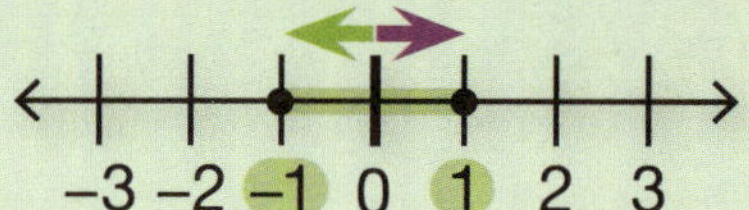

$-(-1) =$ **1**

The opposite of −1 is 1.

Ordered Pairs

An ordered pair tells a location on the coordinate plane.

$$(-3, 2)$$

x-coordinate   y-coordinate

The x-coordinate tells the horizontal distance and direction from the origin. The y-coordinate tells the vertical distance and direction from the origin.

Each section of the coordinate plane is called a quadrant.

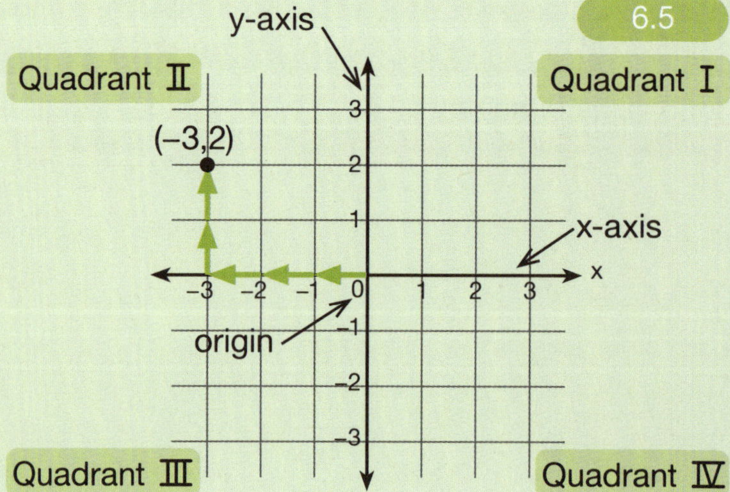

Distance on the Coordinate Plane

6.6

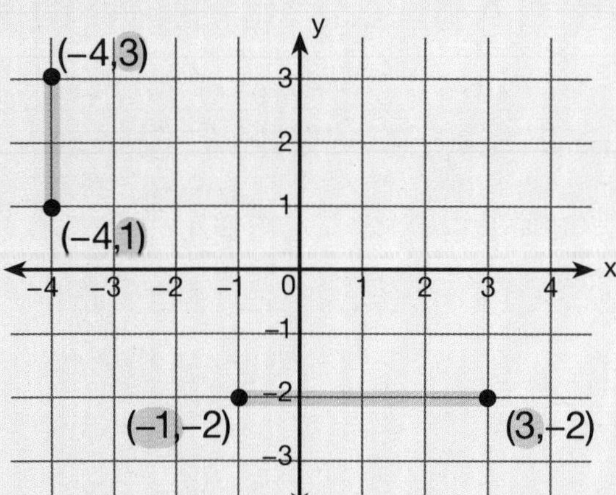

Ex. What is the distance between $(-4,3)$ and $(-4,1)$?

$3 - 1 =$ **2 units**

Ex. What is the distance between $(-1,-2)$ and $(3,-2)$?

$1 + 3 =$ **4 units**

Find Perimeter and Area on the Coordinate Plane

6.7

Ex. What are the perimeter and area of this rectangle?

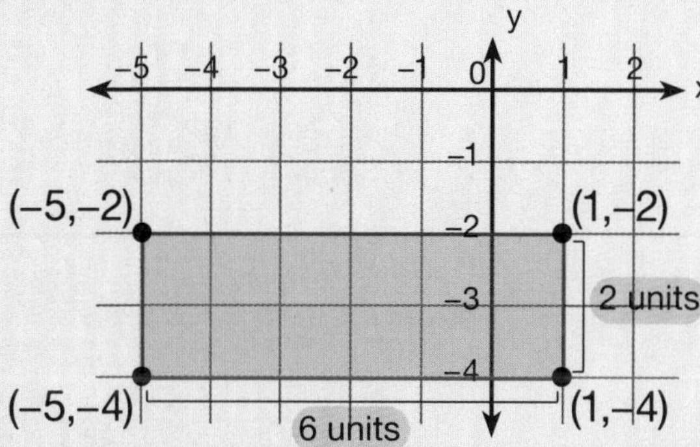

Length: Width:

$5 + 1 = 6$ units $4 - 2 = 2$ units

Perimeter: $6 + 2 + 6 + 2 =$ **16 units**

Area: $6 \times 2 =$ **12 units^2**

Unit 7 Reference Page

Reciprocals

The reciprocal tells how many times the number "goes into" 1.
To find the reciprocal of a fraction, flip the numerator and denominator.

Ex. How many servings are in 1 pie?

Serving size:
$\frac{1}{6}$ of the pie

$\frac{1}{6} \diagdown \diagup \frac{6}{1}$

$\frac{6}{1} = 6$, so 6 is the reciprocal.

1 pie $\div \frac{1}{6}$ = **6 servings**

Ex. How many servings are in 1 pizza?

Serving size:
$\frac{2}{5}$ of the pizza

$\frac{2}{5} \diagdown \diagup \frac{5}{2}$

$\frac{5}{2} = 2\frac{1}{2}$, so $2\frac{1}{2}$ is the reciprocal.

1 pizza $\div \frac{2}{5} = \frac{5}{2} = 2\frac{1}{2}$ **servings**

Divide by a Fraction

To divide a number by a fraction, we multiply the number by the reciprocal of the fraction.

1. Keep the dividend the same.
2. Change the division sign to a multiplication sign.
3. Flip the divisor's numerator and denominator and write its reciprocal.

Keep → Change → Flip

Ex. I have 3 pizzas. If each serving is $\frac{1}{3}$ of a pizza, how many servings are there?

$3 \div \frac{1}{3} = ?$

$3 \times 3 = $ **9 servings**

Ex. I have 3 pizzas. If each serving is $\frac{2}{3}$ of a pizza, how many servings are there?

$3 \div \frac{2}{3} = ?$

$\frac{3}{1} \times \frac{3}{2} = \frac{9}{2} = 4\frac{1}{2}$ **servings**

Divide Mixed Numbers

If the dividend is a mixed number, we first convert the mixed number to an improper fraction. Then, we follow the usual steps.

Ex. After Thanksgiving, Clara's family has $1\frac{1}{2}$ pies left over. If $\frac{1}{8}$ of a pie is one serving, how many servings do they have?

$1\frac{1}{2} \div \frac{1}{8} = ?$

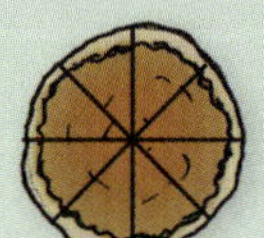

$\frac{3}{2} \div \frac{1}{8} = ? \rightarrow \frac{3}{\cancel{2}_{1}} \times \frac{\cancel{8}^{4}}{1} = \frac{12}{1} = $ **12 servings**

Reciprocals

To find the reciprocal of a whole number or mixed number, write the number as a fraction. Then, flip the numerator and denominator.

The product of a number and its reciprocal is 1.

Ex. What is the reciprocal of $1\frac{1}{2}$? **7.4**

$$1\frac{1}{2} = \frac{3}{2} \quad \frac{2}{3} \text{ is the reciprocal}$$

$$\frac{\cancel{3}^{1}}{\cancel{2}_{1}} \times \frac{\cancel{2}^{1}}{\cancel{3}_{1}} = \frac{1}{1} = 1$$

Divide by Mixed Numbers or Whole Numbers

Ex. Ali has $2\frac{1}{3}$ c. of flour. The cookie recipe calls for $1\frac{3}{4}$ c. of flour for each batch. How many batches can he make?

$$2\frac{1}{3} \div 1\frac{3}{4} = ? \longrightarrow \frac{7}{3} \div \frac{7}{4} = ?$$

$$\frac{\cancel{7}^{1}}{3} \times \frac{4}{\cancel{7}_{1}} = \frac{4}{3} = 1\frac{1}{3} \text{ batches}$$

Ex. Josiah has $2\frac{1}{2}$ kg of clay. He divides the clay into 8 equal lumps to make 8 small bowls. How much does each lump weigh?

$$2\frac{1}{2} \div 8 = ? \longrightarrow \frac{5}{2} \div \frac{8}{1} = ?$$

$$\frac{5}{2} \times \frac{1}{8} = \frac{5}{16} \text{ kg}$$

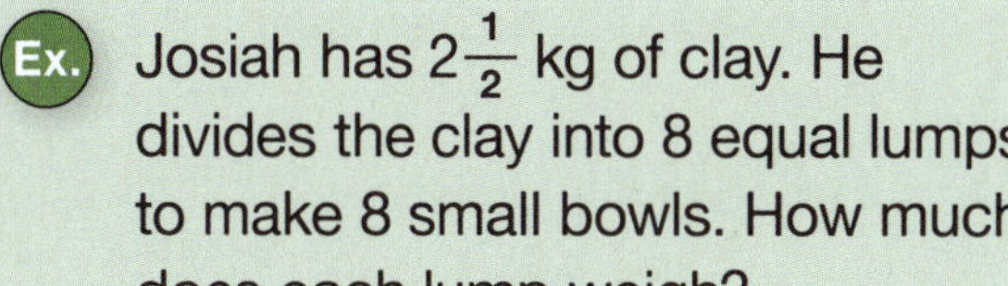

Divide Fractions by Fractions

7.5

Ex. $\frac{3}{8}$ of a pizza equals one serving. If I have $\frac{7}{8}$ of a pizza, how many servings do I have?

$$\frac{7}{8} \div \frac{3}{8} = ?$$

$$\frac{7}{\cancel{8}_{1}} \times \frac{\cancel{8}^{1}}{3} = \frac{7}{3} = 2\frac{1}{3} \text{ servings}$$

Ex. I have $\frac{3}{4}$ c. of molasses. I need $\frac{1}{2}$ c. for each batch of gingerbread cookies. How many batches of cookies can I make?

$$\frac{3}{4} \div \frac{1}{2} = ?$$

$$\frac{3}{\cancel{4}_{2}} \times \frac{\cancel{2}^{1}}{1} = \frac{3}{2} = 1\frac{1}{2} \text{ batches}$$

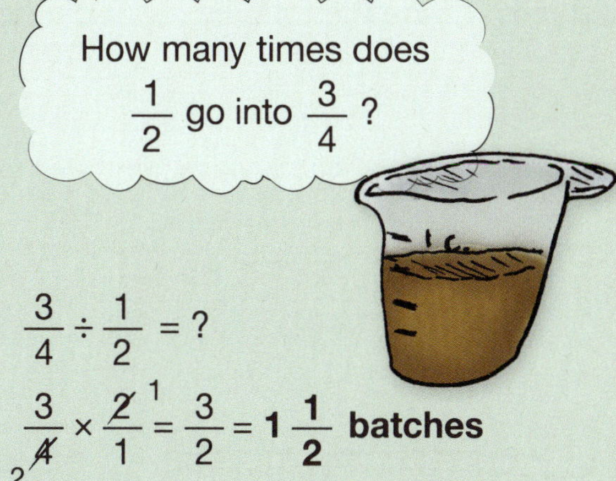

Divide to Find a Fraction of a Quantity **7.6**

To find a fraction of a quantity, we divide the partial amount by the whole amount.

Ex. The track race is 4 km long. Ramona has run 3 km so far. What fraction of the race has she completed?

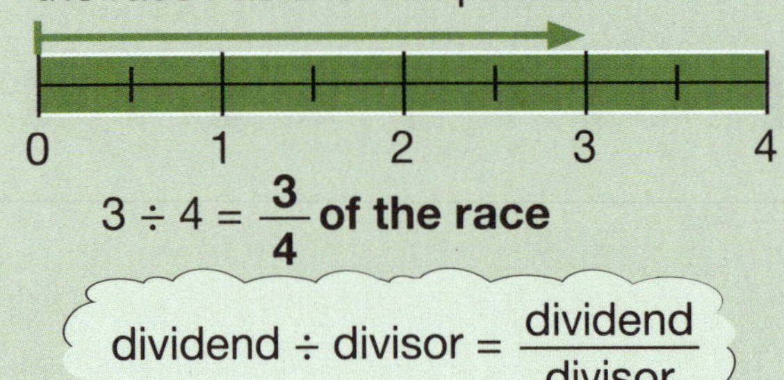

$$3 \div 4 = \frac{3}{4} \text{ of the race}$$

$$\text{dividend} \div \text{divisor} = \frac{\text{dividend}}{\text{divisor}}$$

Ex. The track race is 4 km long. Beatrice has run $2\frac{1}{2}$ km so far. What fraction of the race has she completed?

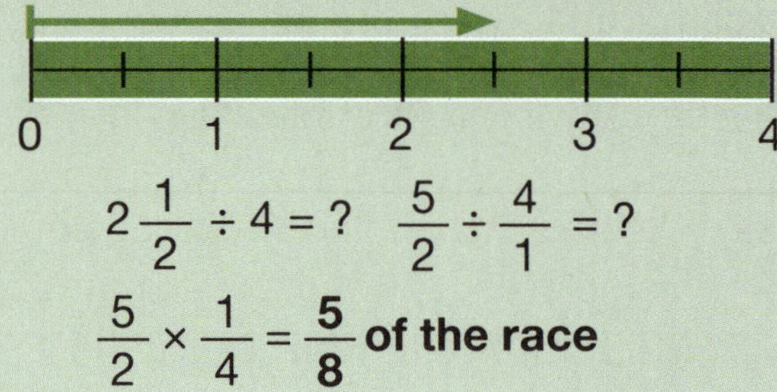

$$2\frac{1}{2} \div 4 = ? \qquad \frac{5}{2} \div \frac{4}{1} = ?$$

$$\frac{5}{2} \times \frac{1}{4} = \frac{5}{8} \text{ of the race}$$

Divide Fractions by Fractions **7.7**

Ex. $\frac{3}{8}$ of a pizza equals one serving. If I have $\frac{1}{8}$ of a pizza, what fraction of a serving do I have?

$\frac{1}{8}$ is what fraction of $\frac{3}{8}$?

$$\frac{1}{8} \div \frac{3}{8} = ? \qquad \frac{1}{\cancel{8}_1} \times \frac{\cancel{8}^1}{3} = \frac{1}{3} \text{ of a serving}$$

Ex. The cookie recipe calls for $\frac{3}{4}$ c. of brown sugar, but I only have $\frac{1}{2}$ c. What fraction of a batch can I make?

$\frac{1}{2}$ is what fraction of $\frac{3}{4}$?

$$\frac{1}{2} \div \frac{3}{4} = ? \qquad \frac{1}{\cancel{2}_1} \times \frac{\cancel{4}^2}{3} = \frac{2}{3} \text{ of a batch}$$

To find the **number** of pieces, divide the total by the size of each piece.

To find the **size** of each piece, divide the total by the number of pieces.

To find a **fractional amount**, divide the partial amount by the total amount. **7.8**

Ex. I have 3 yd. of ribbon. I cut the ribbon into pieces that are each $\frac{3}{4}$ yd. long. How many pieces do I get?

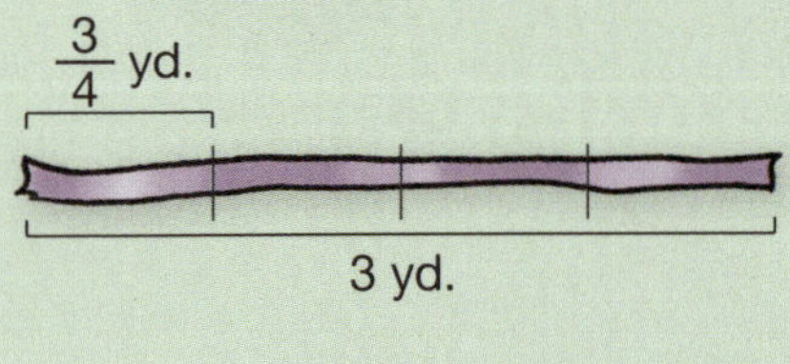

$$3 \div \frac{3}{4} = 4 \text{ pieces}$$

Ex. I have $\frac{3}{4}$ m of rope. I cut the rope into 3 equal pieces. How long is each piece?

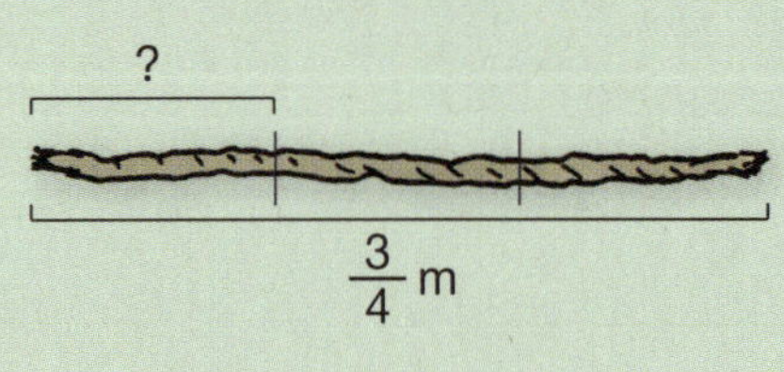

$$\frac{3}{4} \div 3 = \frac{1}{4} \text{ m}$$

Ex. The hiking trail is 3 mi. long. So far, I've hiked $\frac{3}{4}$ mi. What fraction of the trail have I completed?

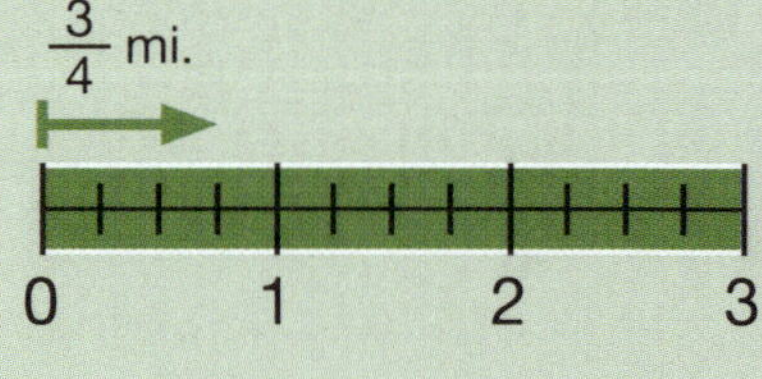

$$\frac{3}{4} \div 3 = \frac{1}{4} \text{ of the trail}$$

8.1

Decimals

| Decimals | • divide by 10 to create places with a smaller value
• expanded form expresses the number as the sum of the value of each digit | $2.4509 = 2 + \dfrac{4}{10} + \dfrac{5}{100} + \dfrac{9}{10,000}$ |

Digit Vocabulary
- decimal digits are digits to the right of the decimal point
- leading zeros come before the first non-zero digit
- trailing zeros come after the final non-zero digit

2.4509
4 decimal digits

0.067
2 leading zeros

1.40
1 trailing zero

Decimal → Fraction
- write decimal digits as the numerator (ignore leading zeros)
- the number of decimal digits equals the number of zeros in the denominator

$2.4509 = 2\dfrac{4,509}{10,000}$

$0.067 = \dfrac{67}{1,000}$

Round Decimals
- round down if the next digit is less than 5
- round up if the next digit is greater than or equal to 5
- drop the digits after the place you round to

$2.4509 \approx 2$
$2.4509 \approx 2.5$
$2.4509 \approx 2.45$
$2.4509 \approx 2.451$

Add and Subtract Decimals
- line up the decimal points
- tack on trailing zeros so both numbers have the same number of decimal digits
- write the decimal point in the answer below the other decimal points

$2.31 + 6.5243 = ?$

```
  2.3100
+ 6.5243
  8.8343
```

Convert Fractions to Decimals

We can use either a fraction or a decimal to represent part of a whole. If the fraction has a base-ten denominator (like 10, 100, or 1,000), the number of zeros in the denominator equals the number of decimal digits.

8.2

Ex. Write $\frac{49}{1,000}$ as a decimal.

$$\frac{49}{1,000} = 0.049$$

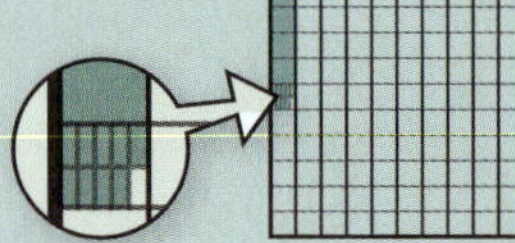

1,000 has 3 zeros, so the matching decimal has 3 decimal places.

For other fractions, try writing an equivalent fraction with a base-ten denominator. Then, use the equivalent fraction to write the matching decimal.

Ex. Write $\frac{1}{20}$ as a decimal.

$$\frac{1}{20} = \frac{5}{100} = 0.05$$

$\times 5$

Use Decimals to Compare

8.3

Ex. Which is greater, $\frac{1}{4}$ or 0.23?

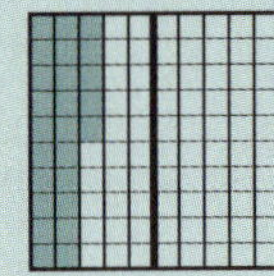

$$\frac{1}{4} = 0.25 \qquad 0.23$$

0.25 is greater than 0.23, so $\frac{1}{4}$ is greater than 0.23.

Ex. Which is greater, $\frac{1}{4}$ or $\frac{3}{10}$?

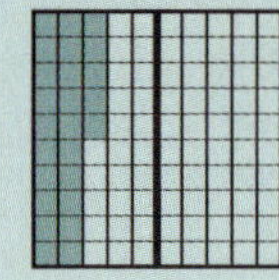 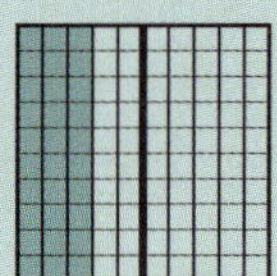

$$\frac{1}{4} = 0.25 \qquad \frac{3}{10} = 0.3$$

0.3 is greater than 0.25, so $\frac{3}{10}$ is greater than $\frac{1}{4}$.

Multiply Decimals by 10, 100, or 1,000

1. Find the number of zeros in 10, 100, or 1,000.
2. Move the decimal point the same number of places to the right.
3. Tack on trailing zeros as needed.

8.4

Ex. Each box of blueberries weighs 0.8 lb. How much do 100 boxes of blueberries weigh?

$$0.8 \times 100 = 80 \text{ lb.}$$

$080.$

Multiply Decimals by Whole Numbers

8.5

Ex. Each screw weighs 0.057 lb. How much do 40 screws weigh?

1. Multiply like usual. Ignore the decimal point and any leading zeros.

$$
\begin{array}{r}
? \\
0.057 \\
\times\ \ 40 \\
\hline
\mathbf{2280}
\end{array}
$$

2. Find the total number of decimal digits in the factors.

$$
\begin{array}{r}
? \\
0.057 \\
\times\ \ 40 \\
\hline
2280
\end{array}
$$

Decimal digits

$$
\begin{array}{r}
3 \\
+0 \\
\hline
3
\end{array}
$$

3. Write a decimal point so the product has the same number of decimal digits as the factors.

$$
\begin{array}{r}
? \\
0.057 \\
\times\ \ 40 \\
\hline
2.280
\end{array}
$$

Decimal digits

$$
\begin{array}{r}
3 \\
+0 \\
\hline
3
\end{array}
$$

Divide Decimals by 10, 100, or 1,000

8.6

1. Find the number of zeros in 10, 100, or 1,000.

2. Move the decimal point the same number of places to the left.

3. Fill in leading zeros as needed.

Ex. A stack of 1,000 sheets of copy paper is 12.7 cm thick. How thick is 1 sheet of copy paper?

$$12.7 \div 1{,}000 = \mathbf{0.0127\ cm}$$

$$0.0127$$

Divide Decimals by Whole Numbers with Long Division

8.7

1. Divide like usual. Ignore any leading zeros.

2. Place the decimal point in the quotient directly above its place in the dividend. Fill in leading zeros as needed.

Ex. 4 grains of rice weigh 0.116 g. On average, how much does each grain of rice weigh?

$$
\begin{array}{r}
\mathbf{0.029\ g} \\
4\,\overline{)0.116} \\
-\ \ 8\downarrow \\
\hline
36 \\
-36 \\
\hline
0
\end{array}
$$

Round Quotients to a Given Number of Decimal Digits

8.8

Ex. The baker makes 3.8 kg of bread dough. He wants to split the dough into 6 equal balls. How much should each ball weigh? Write the answer with 2 decimal digits.

1. Set up the long division problem. Tack on trailing zeros in the dividend to match the number of decimal digits you want in the answer.

$$6\,\overline{)3.80}$$

2 decimal digits

2. Follow the long division steps. Place the decimal point in the quotient directly above its place in the dividend.

$$
\begin{array}{r}
\mathbf{0.63} \\
6\,\overline{)3.80} \\
-\mathbf{36}\downarrow \\
\hline
20 \\
-18 \\
\hline
2
\end{array}
$$

3. If there is a remainder, tack on 1 more zero and divide one more time. Round your answer to the correct number of decimal digits.

$$
\begin{array}{r}
0.63\mathbf{3} \\
6\,\overline{)3.800} \\
-36\downarrow \\
\hline
20 \\
-18\downarrow \\
\hline
20
\end{array}
$$

$$0.633 \approx \mathbf{0.63\ kg}$$

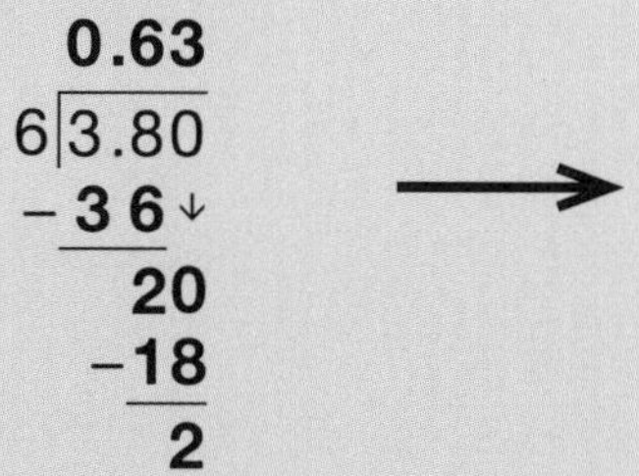